Pooling Talent

Rowman & Littlefield Swimming Series
Series Editor: John Lohn

The Rowman & Littlefield Swimming Series looks at competitive swimming from a number of perspectives, providing readers with the historical context of the events, athletes, and developments that have shaped the sport.

They Ruled the Pool: The 100 Greatest Swimmers in History, by John Lohn, 2013.
Duels in the Pool: Swimming's Greatest Rivalries, by Matthew De George, 2013.
Pooling Talent: Swimming's Greatest Teams, by Matthew De George, 2014.

Pooling Talent

Swimming's Greatest Teams

Matthew De George

ROWMAN & LITTLEFIELD
Lanham • Boulder • New York • Toronto • Plymouth, UK

Published by Rowman & Littlefield
4501 Forbes Boulevard, Suite 200, Lanham, Maryland 20706
www.rowman.com

10 Thornbury Road, Plymouth PL6 7PP, United Kingdom

British Library Cataloguing in Publication Information Available

Library of Congress Cataloging-in-Publication Data

De George, Matthew.
Pooling talent : swimming's greatest teams / Matthew De George.
pages cm. – (Rowman & Littlefield Swimming series)
Includes bibliographical references and index.
ISBN 978-1-4422-3701-8 (cloth : alk. paper) – ISBN 978-1-4422-3702-5 (ebook)
1. Swimming teams–History. 2. Swimmers–Rating of. I. Title.
GV836.4.D47 2014
797.21–dc23
2014007927

∞™ The paper used in this publication meets the minimum requirements of American National Standard for Information Sciences Permanence of Paper for Printed Library Materials, ANSI/NISO Z39.48-1992.

Printed in the United States of America

Contents

Acknowledgments

As always, I am immensely grateful for the opportunity provided to me by John Lohn. Even more so, though, I owe him a massive debt of gratitude for his mentorship and support throughout this endeavor. And perhaps most of all, I'm thankful for this series' ability to reignite in me a passion for a sport I've long since ventured away from. It is my hope that these books provide that service to others.

I would not have been able to complete this project without the constant guidance, consultation, and commiseration of my wonderful partner, Samantha Koch. Her input, assistance, and inspiration have been invaluable throughout the course of this project, and I truly believe this work would not exist were it not for her guiding hand.

I am extremely grateful for the wonderful working relationship with everyone at Rowman & Littlefield, from Christen Karniski on down through all the people on the editorial side who help bring the best out of the work, from cover design on through the smallest placement of commas within the work. Their ability to polish the work into the finished product you see here before you is something I can only try to duplicate.

Finally, in embarking on this project, it was my distinct hope to produce something worthy of standing alongside the enthralling and engaging writing that has animated the sport's past. There are many names you'll encounter in the course of this book, chroniclers of the history of a sport that was never the most lucrative or most popular, without whom this work could not have been brought to life. As time has passed, their words remain the most vivid, most—and sometimes, sadly, the only—tangible records of historic events in the sport. I owe a great deal to the work that has gone before me, and I hope I can repay a portion of that debt by providing a similarly enduring entry in the lexicon of swim writing.

Introduction

To me, this really is what swimming is about. The team is always better than the sum of the individuals. People remember the relays more because they're just more fun.—Michael Phelps[1]

There's a great irony to swimming. At its heart, swimming is an individual endeavor. Hours on end spent in the sensory deprivation wrought by swim caps and the whirring of water can separate teammates by worlds, even if their physical distance is measured in mere feet. The starting block is single occupancy. Sweat and tears are invested on an individual basis, and rewards are doled out by the same measure. The clock is the sole arbiter of success, and it metes out its judgments one by one.

But the individual lens is merely one view of swimming. In many ways, its most profound, most exhilarating, most enduring moments are produced when the paradigm of individualism is briefly interrupted and the concept of a team makes a rare appearance.

The most obvious manifestation of team swimming is its simplest: the relay. Four people swimming the same distances, either in freestyle or one of each stroke for the medley, produce the unique instance in which it's the name of the club, the school, or the county on the scoreboard instead of the individual. The coming together for a collective goal isn't just "fun," as Phelps, unquestionably the greatest athlete ever to dive into a pool, readily attests. It is the epitome of drama. Four swimmers, often from different backgrounds that have brought them into constant competition at various levels with the athletes they will briefly call teammates, uniting for a common goal that goes beyond the self. The results that can be produced are nothing short of temporal alchemy, a magic on the clock that turns ordinary swimmers golden in a way the individual couldn't be on his or her own. It's the only rationale for how Jason Lezak in 2008 could unleash a swim over a second faster than anything he'd ever produced in his storied career to make his 400 free relay team Olympic champions. The weight of the stars and stripes on their suits is the only explanation for how the 1976 American women's 400 free relay, composed of four swimmers whose confidence and hopes for Olympic glory had been emphatically dented by the East Germans throughout the Montreal Games, could come together to manufacture an upset seen as utterly unthinkable. It was about his teammates that Bruce Hayes thought in 1984 as he not only resisted the frantic and historically fast chase of the day's premier swimmer, Michael Gross, but managed to counterpunch in winning the 800 free relay.

Relays have been a variable part of Olympic programs for years, the current Olympic system allowing three each for men and women. A constant through the modern iterations of the Games, though, has been the importance of team delegations, those loose confederations of athletes who've engaged in cutthroat competition against each other for decades, only for the honor of becoming teammates. The glory of representing one's country has a remarkable power to quiet the squabbles that privately play out in the pools of competition and practice. Where Ian Thorpe and Grant Hackett once appeared to be rivals to each other's standing, in the present and for posterity, the sight of them in adjacent lanes representing Australia transformed them into patriotic icons of the resurgence in their nation's most beloved sport. Phelps and Ian Crocker were adversaries first, but when an illness meant the latter seemed fated to leave the 2004 Games without a gold medal, the personal rivalry took a backseat to goodwill and team camaraderie. And for some athletes whose nations had done them few favors in helping them ascend the international stage—like the Americans denied a chance to swim at the 1980 Olympics, or the Unified Team starring in the 1992 Games in the aftermath of the Soviet Union's dissolution—the concept of national pride became a more central aspect of their experience, evolving into a more complex, ineffable phenomenon.

Finally, the globalization of swimming has produced a rich tapestry of individual styles and programs, each forging legendary swimmers with unique and compelling identities. As the pendulum of world power has swung through the decades, various nations and schools of thought have enjoyed periods of ascendency. From the early days of swimming when information traveled at the speed of a steamship, styles peculiar to specific nations arose, from the Japanese crawl's domination in the 1930s to the renaissance of the Australian style in the 1950s. The proliferation of swimming in the United States introduced its own vagaries, from the manner in which talent has tended to aggregate at certain collegiate hubs of dominance to the vertical structures of clubs that govern the development of swimmers from early youth well into adulthood. Each program has developed its own unique ethos, contributing to the many diverse threads that are interwoven in the tapestry that constitutes the identity of American swimming.

In *Pooling Talent*, we explore the impact that each of these three levels of organization—the relay, the squad, and the program—has on the swimmers involved. How does each contribute to the success of individuals in a sport where personal achievement remains the primary metric? How deep is the interplay of identities, the individuals being shaped by the organization and then in turn altering the structure of the larger body? And how profound is the impact of an identity larger than the self on the performances we see in the pool, that inexpressible magic that causes the final product to exceed, often by leaps and bounds, the sum of its parts?

Part I

Relays

Chapter One

1976 U.S. Women's 400 Freestyle

Shirley Babashoff entered the final day of the 1976 Olympics knowing it would be her last at a major swimming event. Already in her second Games, a career that lasted longer than most of her peers', Babashoff should've been looking back on one of the most prolific careers, male or female, in the history of American swimming. The dream of individual gold had already gone by the wayside, one bulky East German winner at a time over Babashoff's four events. What remained for Babashoff and her relay teammates in the 400 freestyle was a last chance at redemption, at revenge, at the gold that time and again eluded them in Montreal.

For a week, the American contingent had seen time after remarkable time what they produced relegated to a lower step of the podium by the performance of an East German team that defied logic. When slighted Americans like Babashoff tried to fill in the blanks, with what some called unsubstantiated theories and others regarded as unassailable fact, they were castigated in the media for being sore losers. In the final relay, another method to prevent that fate emerged, the simplest of all: beating the East Germans.

It was easier said than done, for sure. But when Babashoff anchored the team of Kim Peyton, Jill Sterkel, and Wendy Boglioli to victory in the 400 free relay, finally vanquishing the GDR demon in sensational fashion, the Americans found a ray of light in one of the women's program's darkest hours.

The Montreal Games were indicative of the new world order that had descended upon swimming, a duopoly of dominance across genders. While the American men were busy gobbling up gold in every event save one, the women's competition had become the sole domain of the German Democratic Republic. With times that boggled the mind, most women's events turned

3

into a race for silver, and even that was often won by the next East German in line.

As early as four years prior, the East Germans showed promise of emerging on the world scene. At the 1972 Munich Olympics, the GDR, competing as a separate nation for just the second summer Games, claimed five minor medals, including silver medals in the 400 free and 400 medley relays and a 200 individual medley silver for a promising young swimmer still two months from her 14th birthday named Kornelia Ender. The explosion of the program, beyond what anyone could've reasonably forecast, came at the inaugural FINA World Championships in Belgrade, Yugoslavia, in 1973 when the East Germans won 10 of the 14 golds on offer in the women's competition, including both relays in world-record time. The margin of victory in the 400 free relay over the U.S. exceeded 3 seconds; in the medley relay, the spread from gold to silver covered a staggering 8.96 seconds. The East Germans duplicated the 10-for-14 medal haul at the 1975 Worlds in Cali, Colombia, drawing even with the Americans on the final gold-medal table across both genders. From a nation that less than a decade prior had never competed internationally had sprung a power challenging—and in the women's competition, sensationally usurping—the long-held American dominance. Not until a decade and a half later, with the fall of the Berlin Wall, was the athletic success revealed to be the result of a state-sponsored doping program, where coaches and doctors provided banned anabolic steroids to athletes as young as their early teens, many without their knowledge or consent. The suspicion, harbored by aggrieved nations like the Americans, that such illegal methods were being used was so thick as to become essentially accepted as fact, even absent the proof of failed drug tests.

Within this cloud of suspicion and doubt, Babashoff rose to the elite swimming ranks. She was something of a revelation when at age 15 she set the world record in the 200 free at the 1972 Olympic Trials. In the 1972 Olympics in Munich, she claimed two individual silver medals and gold in both relays. In what was supposed to be the Olympics of Australian freestyler Shane Gould, Babashoff was poised to play the role of spoiler. She got the better of Gould in the 100 free, settling for silver behind fellow American Sandy Neilson. Gould bested her in the 200 free, and Babashoff was fourth in the 400. Her first skirmish with the East Germans came in Munich, with Babashoff anchoring the 400 free relay of Jane Barkman, Jenny Kemp, and Neilson that retook the world record the East Germans had briefly seized in prelims. Babashoff continued to rack up medals in the next Olympic cycle, but few were golden. In Belgrade, she claimed four silvers, all but one (the 200 free, which she lost to countrywoman Keena Rothhammer) behind an East German. The 1974 U.S. Olympic Committee (USOC) Sportswoman of the Year recovered in Cali to claim gold in the 200 free (in a remarkable comeback victory over Ender) and the 400 free (over Australian Jenny Turrall), but settled for silver in the 100 free behind Ender and bronze in the 800, trailing Turrall and American Heather Greenwood. The East Germans made sure Babashoff settled for relay silvers in Cali.

By 1976, it was very clear that the entity standing between Babashoff and her place in swimming immortality was brawny and wearing the colors of the GDR. Babashoff was perfectly in line with the archetype of the ideal female swimmer. Her ability to compete in freestyle events from 100 to 800 meters overlapped the specialties of the likes of Dawn Fraser and Gould, two of the few female swimmers to gain international notoriety after World War II. She was seen as the heir apparent to Debbie Meyer, who did the 200-400-800 gold-medal trifecta in Mexico City in 1968, becoming an instant American hero at the age of 16. The Montreal Games were perfectly positioned for Babashoff to pull off a similar feat. She had the home-continent advantage. In the age of one-Games phenoms, Babashoff would be in her second Olympiad at age 19, a rare chance for an American woman to marry international experience and advanced physical stature. She'd made the move from Huntington Beach Aquatic Club to Mark Schubert's Mission Viejo Nadadores and was flourishing under Schubert's distance-based program. Never one to sit idly by and accept her shortcomings, Babashoff was one of the first American swimmers to embrace the notion of weight training in swimming, one of the only legal and morally acceptable takeaways from the East Germans, in the hopes of closing the gap between the programs. Much like Meyer, the good looks of the homecoming queen Babashoff made her the ideal fulcrum of the quadrennial media circus of the Games and one of the American headliners. In the pool, Babashoff was "virtually a one-girl U.S. team holding back the East German flood."[1] "She bears on her tanned shoulders the full burden of the U.S.'s proud tradition in women's swimming," wrote *Sports Illustrated* in their Olympic Preview issue, one that featured a smiling, blond-haired Babashoff on the cover.[2] After the Olympic Trials in Long Beach, California—where Babashoff set American records en route to victory in the 100, 200, and 400 frees, plus a world record in the 800 free and a win in the 400 IM—Olympic coach Jack Nelson called her "the greatest female swimmer ever for the United States."[3] Her world mark in the 800, upending the 17-day-old standard set by Petra Thumer at the East German Trials, was the only world record held by an American woman entering Montreal. That was thanks to the GDR Trials that featured a staggering 13 world records downed by the *Wundermädchen.*

With Babashoff depicted as the hero in waiting of the Games, it was only natural that a villain had to be posited. Given the Cold War tensions of the day, the East Germans made a perfect foil. The relations in the pool remained particularly frosty, a fact capitalized on in 1974 with one of several dual meets between the nations. Babashoff, without Ender to contend with, set a world record in the 200 free at the meet in Concord, California, while also anchoring the 400 free relay of Kathy Heddy, Ann Marshall, and Peyton to a world record. Even with the 1976 Games—the first Olympic test for the new East German juggernaut since its rise to prominence in 1973—still two years away, accusations of doping had reached a fever pitch. The powers that be in world swimming were reluctant to indict the East Germans, even in the court of public opinion, without physical evidence. To many Americans, though, it was all but accepted that the accomplishments of the East Germans weren't organic. "It was obvious!" recalled Lauri Siering, an American breaststroker at the 1976 Games who won silver in the medley relay. "It was pretty well accepted among the swimmers that, yes, they were using steroids."[4] As early as 1973, which proved to be the very beginning of the program, the case was clearly elucidated by Jean Pierre LaCour in a French newspaper, even if the technical terms had yet to be filled in. "There is talk of a sort of 'vaccine against fatigue,'" he wrote. "It consists of an injection of toxic substances which allows the body to combat fatigue more efficiently. It is believed that male hormones are given to the girls, who, in addition to an increase in vigor, develop a superiority complex with respect to other females from foreign countries. Another device is the use of a doping substance, not currently detectable, which virtually guarantees maximum performance with 98 percent chance of success, as compared to classic training which is about 68 percent successful. These accusations are terrible. The only way for East Germans to answer these accusations is to open their training camps. A simple denial will not be sufficient."[5]

Those accusations were only exacerbated by year after year of frustration and defeat for the Americans, leading to toxic rhetoric between the nations. There was a palpable feeling of disenfranchisement that such illegal activities were allowed to go on, especially with the perpetrators and victims being athletes of such a young age. "I was 16 years old," said 1976 Olympian Linda Jezek. "I thought [the people] running things knew what they were doing, so that if the East Germans were cheating, it would come up." Many American women questioned the joylessness with which the East Germans appeared to conduct their business, under the constant oversight and isolation wrought by legions of taskmaster trainers and coaches. They pondered the cost of athletic success at the expense of the elimination of all signs of femininity, all signs of delight in their craft. Where swimming was a hobby for some Americans, they fell short of allowing it to define their entire existences, wiping out any semblance of a social life—as was the popular, and not wholly ungrounded, perception of the East Germans. "I don't know if we'll ever have a swimming program like East Germany does," Babashoff said in early 1976. "By the looks of it, I don't think they enjoy swimming. When they come here for a warmup, they're told what to do. We get in the water and play games like Diver Dan. You never see them doing that."[6] Between anecdotes of elevated levels of aggression outside the pool, growth of atypical body hair, and deep voices—all consequences of the androgenic hormones the East Germans were being force-fed—the common refrain among the daintier Western swimmers was that "we would have to check the symbol on the door to make sure we had the right bathrooms."[7] To Babashoff's credit, she actively attempted to diffuse notions of rivalry with Ender and the East Germans ahead of Montreal. "I'll be looking for whoever's ahead of me," she said. "I'm not going out to beat her. She's there but so is everybody else. To me it's not a big Babashoff-Ender thing. I came here to win a gold medal. Whoever I have to beat to do it, they're there."[8]

Whatever overtures of goodwill preceded the Games, they quickly dissolved in Montreal. With the East Germans collecting gold medals hand over fist and the clock displaying bafflingly fast times, it's no wonder. The Germans swept out the freestyle events, mostly at the expense of Babashoff. Ender set her 10th world record in the 100 free, defeating countrywoman Petra Priemer by almost a second, with Peyton fourth and Babashoff fifth. Babashoff's 200 free finals time of 2:01.22 was a second and three-quarters faster than her world record from 1974, yet still almost two seconds slower than Ender's world-record swim for gold. Thumer's time in the 400 free shaved almost five seconds off Babashoff's world record from the previous summer. Babashoff, at nearly 1.5 seconds under the world record set by Barbara Krause at the East German Trials, had to settle for silver behind Thumer, whose time would've won silver in the men's race just eight years prior. Babashoff was two seconds faster than her Olympics Trials world mark in the 800 free, but it mattered little. She still found herself trailing Thumer by .45 seconds. Adding fuel to the fire wasn't just the fact that the Americans were getting beaten; it's that the Americans were achieving the time goals they had set for themselves and setting a litany of personal bests that were still getting trounced by East German teams simply too good to be true. For instance, in the 400 IM, an event from which Babashoff withdrew to focus on her freestyle program, Ulrike Tauber won gold with a world record of 4:42.77. That was 9.43 seconds faster than the world record she set a year prior and was 6.02 seconds faster than her teammate Brigit Treiber set at Trials eight weeks prior. It also would've won gold in the men's Olympic final in 1968, a monstrous jump forward for the women's event.

Tensions naturally arose between the wronged Americans and East Germans. Public criticism of the appearance and baritone voices of the East Germans—which was largely decried as the cattiness of sore losers—led to the famous declaration by one GDR official that "we're here to swim, not to sing."[9] There were reports of overt hostilities between the American swimmers, including Babashoff, and their "Bionic Women" counterparts.[10] "They told me that Shirley got on a bus with a few other girls one day and began pointing at (the East Germans) and making fun of them," read one account.[11] So disconsolate was Babashoff after one loss that she refused to acknowledge her East German combatants, leading the American delegation to send roses to the East German swimmers by way of apology.[12] Babashoff wasn't the only one guilty, as Boglioli's public accusation that the East Germans were doped up necessitated her having FBI protection for over a year after the Games.[13]

Whatever the mechanisms used to sustain it, Babashoff at least maintained a high enough level of morale through the meet to believe that an end to the East German medal hegemony was possible. The popular refrain from Babashoff et al. was that the focus was on personal-best times. Anything beyond that was out of their control. Indeed, nine American records were set by the women in Montreal, all nine of which were bested by an East German world record.[14] In retrospect, she told of a conscious effort to avoid the steroid issue in conversation, even if the narrative of "Surly Shirley" the sore loser gained momentum in a self-perpetuating cycle that made Babashoff the convenient "scapegoat."[15] "After the races I don't think I mentioned steroids," she recalled in a rare interview in 1992. "Still, reporters egged me on. One guy asked how I felt getting 'another silver medal.' I said, 'How many silvers do you have?' That got them going, nudging each other—'What can we get her to say now?'"[16] Babashoff also vociferously rebuffed the prevailing notion that she represented her team's best shot at gold.[17] All the while, despite myriad races that seemed to indicate to the contrary, Babashoff maintained a feeling that the East Germans weren't invincible. "The coaches said, 'Yeah, it's obvious they're doing that, but you guys still have a job to do,'" said Siering.[18]

Babashoff's final chance to do that job came in the 400 free relay. The American entered 0-for-12 in the gold-medal category, with 11 of the golds going to the East Germans. (The only other win was earned by Marina Koshevaya in the 200 breast, part of a Soviet medal sweep.) Besides Babashoff's three individual silvers, only Wendy Weinberg (bronze in the 800 free) and Boglioli (bronze in the 100 fly) had managed to claim individual medals. For an entire program, the race was the last shred of hope to salvage an otherwise lost Games.

The relay final shaped up as a three-nation race. The U.S. won the first heat—with Jennifer Hooker subbing in for Babashoff—in 3:50.27, an Olympic record and a spread of 3.13 seconds over the second-place Netherlands. The East Germans lowered that standard the next heat to 3:48.95, less than a second ahead of Canada (3:49.69). With the GDR rolling out its A team for prelims and the U.S. having Babashoff waiting in reserve, a gap of just over a second seemed manageable. The obvious assumption was that the Americans would have to be significantly faster in finals; the target was set at 3:44.7 for their finals time if they wanted a chance at gold. On the strategic front, the decision from Nelson was to match strength for strength with the East Germans. That meant going with Peyton, the best finisher from the individual event, to lead off in hopes that she could remain in contact with Ender. Those hopes, however, took a hit from the start, as Ender's trademark quick start gave her a lead of about a body length by the 15-meter mark. The German wunderkind wasn't far off her world record from the individual event, finishing in 55.79 seconds, just .14 seconds slower than the world standard. Peyton kept it close, though, well ahead of the rest of the field but still over a second in arrears of Ender at 56.95, also .14 seconds off the time that earned her fourth individually.

The middle two legs were where the Americans did their damage. Boglioli, the fourth-place finisher at the U.S. Trials and supposedly the weak link, cut into the lead with her split of 55.81 seconds, .37 seconds faster than an uncharacteristically sluggish Priemer, who had taken silver in the individual event. When Andrea Pollack faltered in the third leg for the East Germans, turning in a split of 56.99 that was slower than Peyton's flat-start leg, Sterkel pounced. With a time over a second and a quarter faster than the one that earned her seventh in the individual 100, she blazed her way to a 55.78-second split, taking the lead off the 250-meter wall for good and handing off a four-tenths advantage to anchor Babashoff. After a relay pickup that was so fast as to be a whisker from illegality, Babashoff resisted the initial surge by Claudia Hempel, never letting the sixth-place finisher in the 100 overtake her. With Hempel's best shot fired, Babashoff's powerful two-beat kick cut through the water in the last 50 as the crescendo rose at the Olympic Pool, the American pulling away as the wall and the most unthinkable of upsets neared. Babashoff brought the team home in a time of 3:44.82, a reduction of 3.98 seconds from the world record set by the SC Dynamo Berlin team of Rose Marie Kother, Pollack, Monika Seltmann, and Krause less than two months prior. Babashoff did more than hold off Hempel; she widened the gap with a split of 56.28 to Hempel's 56.56, giving the Americans a .68-second margin of triumph. In what would go down in history, according to *Swimming World* magazine nearly three decades later, as the greatest relay[19] and greatest Olympic upset ever,[20] Babashoff and company had pulled off the "Miracle of Montreal" to finally claim their gold.

The picture of elation on deck—as the Americans were joined in celebration by several other nations so frequently shunted from the medal picture and so jubilant to have thrown off the yoke of East German domination—stood in stark contrast to the days of futility they had endured in Montreal. For the first time in the week of swimming competition, the Americans had hit their goal—finishing within a tenth of a second of their preliminary objective—and had actually been rewarded with gold. It was a refreshing and hope-restoring change. "We just prayed a lot," Boglioli said. "This was the last night and our last meet, and we really wanted to do it. It's great! I've been swimming for 15 years. This is my first Olympics. I just thought it'd be great to make the team, then to make the finals, then to win a bronze medal, and now a gold!"[21] Donning the colorful suspenders the team had brought to the pool as a morale booster, the Americans showed equal parts ecstasy and relief on the medal stand. "And from their joyous faces at the finish line and on the victory stand," wrote the *New York Times'* Neil Amdur, "you would have thought the United States had never won a gold medal in women's swimming."[22] "I was freaking out," Peyton said. "I thought I'd just bust my suspenders on the award stand. This is definitely the highlight of my life. It's everything I worked for for 13 years."[23]

The deciding factor in vanquishing the East Germans was the ability to come together as a team. Babashoff was the first to admit that all she needed was a little help from her friends to supplement her already fast performances. "I tried my hardest in all of my races, but I guess I had better help in the relay," she said. "There's not too much strategy in the 100 free—you just dive in and sprint your head off . . . that's about it."[24] The medal for Babashoff was her second Olympic gold, joining the Munich relay gold. Over the previous four years, she'd collected 18 medals at Olympics or World Championships, only four of which were gold. Of the other 14 (13 silver), 10 came with an East German on a higher step. What the victory came down to were some outstanding performances by some unexpected faces. No one would've thought before the race that both Boglioli and Sterkel would've outsplit Babashoff, Priemer, Pollack, *and* Hempel. Ultimately, the devotion to pacing her team to victory is what drove Sterkel and Boglioli to both produce the swims of their lives. "You got something extra going for you when you're with a team," Sterkel said.[25]

That something extra made her relay one of the greatest ever.

Chapter Two

1984 U.S. Men's 800 Freestyle

The athletic manifestation of the Cold War took a brief, voluntary, hiatus in the summer of 1984. With the Soviet Union electing to boycott the Los Angeles Olympiad in retaliation for the decision of the Americans and other Western powers to abstain from the 1980 Moscow Games, the medal reckoning in events like swimming were unmistakably altered. At a time when the dominance of the American men's swimming program needed little introduction well into its third decade of unquestioned supremacy, the removal of the Soviet challengers amounted to handing dozens of medals to the Americans.

It seemed there would be no stopping the Americans from unleashing eight years of pent-up Olympic fury in the pool. But there remained an albatross around the neck of the Americans, in a very literal sense. About the only person who could rain on the Red, White, and Blue parade was Michael Gross, a 6-foot-7 West German with a wingspan and ease of movement reminiscent of the stately bird from which his nickname derived. When the 800 freestyle relay arrived, stacking up four rather unheralded Americans against a solid West German team that featured the formidable Gross and his reputation as one of the world's foremost superstars on the anchor leg, the Americans were thrust into a rare underdog role.

What followed was one of the biggest relay upsets in swimming history. The stakes of the moment, the home crowd, and the desire to swim for one another and for their country brought out the best in the team of Mike Heath, David Larson, Jeff Float, and Bruce Hayes. Along with the gold medals earned that day, the team garnered lasting fame as swimming's "Grossbusters."

For a generation of American swimmers, the Olympics had become a complicated symbol. Once seen as the pinnacle of a career in a sport with virtually non-existent professional avenues, it was a shocking and painful ordeal to have the Olympics stripped away in 1980. After the invasion of Afghanistan by the Soviet Union in late 1979, the decree from U.S. president Jimmy Carter was that American athletes would not go to Moscow for the 1980 Summer Games. After months of political machinations and overt intimidation of the U.S. Olympic Committee by Carter, up for a reelection he would lose in a landslide and hamstrung by a storm of political catastrophes occurring under his watch, the Moscow Games became the latest sporting spectacle co-opted for political gains. Among those Western nations opting to boycott was an American delegation that boasted many of the world's best athletes. Events such as swimming—specifically the men's events, with America's unimpeachable prowess—became hollow exercises in second-tier talent. The United States still undertook the selection process in the summer of 1980 with a joyless Trials/Nationals, choosing a swim team that was officially recognized as Olympians, albeit with the largest asterisk in the Games' history. For that group of athletes, many in their late teens or early 20s, a difficult choice loomed: strive for four more years, at a time when few financial accommodations existed to support athletes beyond their college years, for the Olympic glory that was rightly theirs, or swim off into the sunset. Of the 45 Olympic swimmers from 1980, 16 endured to qualify for the joy of an Olympics on home soil, a debut under the intertwined rings for all but one of them.

When the decision came down in May 1984 via a curt memo from the Kremlin that Soviet athletes would not travel to Los Angeles that summer out of concern that the Americans could not guarantee the safety of their athletes, a gold rush befitting California's history was certain to ensue. Standing with the Soviets were a number of Eastern bloc countries plus communist nations around the world, like Cuba, Vietnam, and, most importantly for the swimming community, the East German installation that had dominated women's swimming for the better part of a decade. Without the beefy girls from East Germany, the American women were suddenly thrust back into the role of Olympic favorites. The absence of the Soviet men, specifically their vaunted distance freestyle program, was yet another impediment out of the way for the Americans. The Americans made good on the promise. In 15 events, they brought home 15 medals, including nine golds and victories in all three relays. The American men failed to medal in only three events—the 400 individual medley, 200 butterfly, and 200 breaststroke, taking fourth place in each. (That comes with the sizeable caveat, though, of 200 breaststroker John Moffet being so injured after tearing an adductor muscle in his leg en route to fifth in the 100 that he couldn't participate in the longer event where his time at Trials was mere fractions off the bronze-medal-winning time of Switzerland's Etienne Dagon.)

The heterogeneous mix of ages and backgrounds was nowhere more evident for the Americans than in the men's 200 free field, one that would benefit most from the Soviet absence. Prior to Gross's record onslaught in the summer of 1983, only one other non-American had held the world record in the event: Soviet Sergey Kopliakov from April 1979 to April 1980. The boycott alleviated the threat from three of the finalists from the 1982 World Championships in Guayaquil, Ecuador—bronze medalist Jorg Woithe of East Germany and Soviets Vladimir Shemetov (fifth) and Alexei Filinov (eighth). In a meet where Soviet distance aces Vladimir Salnikov and Sviatoslav Semenov went 1-2 in both the 400 and 1,500 free, the Americans got their stiffest challenge in the 800 free relay from the Soviets, though they still won by three seconds.

The American competitors seeking gold in the 200 free were drawn from a deep and varied field. Larson and Float were holdovers from 1980, both in their final days of competition before retirement. Heath was seen as the favorite, a 20-year-old hotshot who carried on his shoulders the reputation of the middle-distance program. The connections between the relay field, which included alternates Geoff Gaberino and Rich Saeger who swam in prelims, were myriad. Larson, Heath, and Gaberino each hailed from the University of Florida, the latter two part of back-to-back national championship squads in 1983–84. Float and Hayes swam together at Arden Hills Swim Club and attended college in Los Angeles (Float at USC, Hayes at UCLA). Heath and Hayes were even high school teammates at Highland Park High School in Dallas, Texas, the same school that produced 1984 U.S. assistant coach Richard Quick.

The crafting of the 200 free contingent at Olympic Trials entailed one of the most shocking events of the week in Indianapolis. Heath, as many had expected, separated himself, setting American records in prelims and finals (1:47.92) to take the first spot. Gaberino finished second in prelims, followed by Rowdy Gaines, a former world-record holder who had dramatically vacillated in his commitment to pursing the Los Angeles Games over the previous four years. So long a fixture on the American scene, Gaines was a prohibitive favorite entering the finals, and he swam like it for 100-some meters. But Gaines paid dearly for his early speed and faded late in what he called "the stupidest race I ever swam,"[1] finishing an unfathomable seventh, plummeting even from relay consideration. That opened the door for Float, who narrowly beat Hayes and Larson to the wall in one of the fastest 200 free finals ever, with the top four swimmers breaking the cherished 1:50 mark. Gaberino held on for fifth, followed by Saeger, who swam at the 1982 Worlds with Gaines. (Gaines finished second then to Gross by .08 seconds, while Saeger and another swimmer pulled up just after the start of their preliminary heat thinking they'd heard a false start gun and finished well out of the running.) Heath's time, within a half second of Gross's world record from West German Trials in June, signaled him as a legitimate challenger for gold, while the near-two-second difference to his nearest American competitor supported the notion that the 200 free in Los Angeles could quickly become a two-man race. What was absolutely certain, though, is that the Americans faced a formidable challenge from arguably the world's best swimmer.

Few athletes have ever been so aptly named as Gross, whose last name is German for "big." Indeed, the 6-7 Gross cut an imposing figure even larger than his height, thanks to a stunning wingspan of 7 feet, $4^5/_8$ inches, that earned him the poetic nickname of "Albatross" and was striking enough to intimidate even Coleridge. With his close-cropped blond hair, Gross epitomized German athletic efficiency. He was an otherworldly athlete, one who incorporated runs through the forest of up to 15 kilometers a day—at about a none-too-shabby 2:30 marathoner's pace—into his routine. Part of the improvisation was due to necessity, with pool time at his club, First Swim Club of Offenbach (EOSC), severely limited. But Gross's unusual methods also owed to his voracious desire to challenge himself, athletically and psychologically. His brag of never starting a workout before 8 a.m.—a boast that flew in the face of the masochistic mythos of his peers—wasn't borne of laziness or apathy. Instead, the Goethe-studying, wannabe pilot simply didn't believe the mega-yardage techniques espoused throughout the world to be the only way to an elite status. (It made Gross quite the spectacle on his holiday training trips to Mission Viejo Nadadores in California—the club of Mark Schubert, for whom more yardage was the unquestioned gospel—when he'd get out of the pool after a short period of high-intensity, relatively low-yardage work.) In the face of such heresy, yardage evangelist Schubert responded wryly, "Hell, if everybody here had his kind of talent, maybe we wouldn't have to swim so much."[2] Seeking new workouts became an outlet for his meticulous creativity—one account of a Gross practice likened his desire for variation from his coach to the pleas of an aquatic Bach[3]—and whether it was soccer, basketball, or weight lifting, Gross's mind needed to be occupied by novel stimuli beyond the mind-numbing droning of repetitive sets in the pool. Despite being one of the world's foremost butterfliers, only about 10 percent of his usual workouts focused on that stroke. Gross, who twice quit the sport when it ceased to be fun at ages 11 and 13, was an athletic freak who could excel in just about any other "hobby" (for that's all he saw swimming as) and required the sport to engage him.

Part of the appeal of the sport to Gross was his devotion to his team. Not only had he gained a reputation as a stellar relay swimmer, almost single-handedly compensating from the lack of depth in the West German program and vaulting them into the relay reckoning at major events, but his EOSC club was one of a few places where the introverted Gross lowered his guard. He drew the ire of many in 1983 when he was named West German Sportsman of the Year but declined an invitation to the awards dinner to help his team compete in the national club championships the following morning.

The parallel drawn by *Sports Illustrated*'s Craig Neff was of "the Heisman Trophy winner forsaking the Downtown Athletic Club to play for his fraternity in a big intramural basketball game."[4]

The ability of Gross's coaches to pique his interest paid dividends, feeding a cycle of excellence that blossomed in 1982. At that year's World Championships, he claimed five medals, including two individual golds and two relay bronzes. His wins came at the expense of American world-record holders: Gaines in the 200 free and Craig Beardsley in the 200 fly. Gross upped the total to four golds (three individual) and two silvers at the 1983 European Championships in Rome. He claimed world records in the 200 free and 200 fly—becoming the first male swimmer since Mark Spitz in 1972 to simultaneously hold world records in two strokes—plus a European record in the 100 fly. Combined with the emergence of Thomas Fahrner as a world-class 200 freestyler, Gross anchored the 800 free relay to gold in world-record time, all despite suffering a bout of flu in the weeks leading up to Rome.

By the time the Los Angeles Games beckoned, Gross was the unquestioned favorite in the 200 free and 200 fly. The 100 fly would likely be a two-man race between Gross and American Pablo Morales as long as fellow American Matt Gribble continued to battle an injury. The target on Gross's back had managed to outgrow even his sizeable stature, with many Americans hoping the pressure of living up to the world's-greatest moniker would prove to be too much. "All I know is the press is making him out as God and he could go out of here with nothing but silver medals—or less," Float said. "I'm going to be right on his tail and he's going to be sweating."[5] Gross's response, while refuting that he'd think of adapting his in-race tactics to his opponents, was that the "very old" Float was unlikely to improve on his time from Trials.[6]

The major collision promised to be the 800 free relay. Seen as a harbinger of American success, the U.S. had won each non-boycotted installment since 1960, many by gaudy reductions in the world record. American 800 free squads had also triumphed in three of the four Worlds dating back to the meet's inception in 1973, while the fourth was a false start in 1975 where the Americans were well under world-record pace. American coach Randy Reese identified the 800 as a "make or break" competition for Gross, thanks in large part to its central placement in his program.[7] The edge in top-end speed clearly went to Gross's West Germany, and the development of Fahrner and his teammates ensured that the drop-off from Gross had narrowed, reducing the advantage of the Americans' depth. Predicted a prophetic Neff before the LA Games: "In what should be a heart-stopping 4 × 200 free relay, the West Germans will likely lose their world record and the gold medal to the U.S.—but just barely."[8] Few could've guessed how accurate that prognostication would prove to be.

Anyone curious about the mystery of Gross would find out quickly, with three of his event finals coming in the first two days of competition at the McDonald's Olympic Swim Stadium. His reticence to consider his American opposition in the 200 free may have smacked of hubris, but the race convincingly proved his point. He glided to the fastest time in prelims at 1:48.03, nearly two seconds faster than Heath, who was nervous about the occasion and the quality of his taper leading into the meet. Gross turned on the jets in finals, downing his world record in 1:47.44, .11 seconds off his previous mark and his fourth world standard in 14 months. Heath, who admitted to spinning his arms too much, earned silver in a disappointing 1:49.10, well over a second behind his American record at Trials. In the battle for bronze, Fahrner (1:49.69) outtouched Float (1:50.18).

Gross was back in the water the following day, facing the challenge of two American world-record holders in the 100 fly. There was Gribble, the 1982 world champion who set a world mark in 1983 but had dealt with a back injury that limited his training severely in the weeks before the Games. And there was Morales, who trimmed six-hundredths off Gribble's record in winning at Trials. Gross (54.02) and Morales (53.78) exchanged Olympic records in prelims, setting up a two-man race in the final. Morales took the early initiative and turned a half body length ahead of Gross, well under world-record pace. But the Albatross ate into the lead in the final 50, clawing closer with every stroke. Morales hit the wall under the record in 53.23 seconds; Gross, originally believing he'd been beaten, looked up to see a time of 53.08, another gold and another world record. An elated and incredulous Gross, who admitted to not much enjoying the 100 fly, was struck by the graciousness of Morales, even in defeat in his specialty race. "I really pushed myself to the limit," Morales said. "I swam my best time and got beat by a great athlete."[9]

With the 800 free relay later that night, the strategy in the American camp was necessarily centered on neutralizing Gross. He undoubtedly would swim last, so the American design was to front-load the relay with their best, with Heath leading off. Hayes, whose Olympics consisted of nothing more than two relay 200s and whose training was devoted solely to the many vagaries of a relay swim, would anchor. In prelims, the team of Gaberino, Saeger, Larson, and Hayes set a world record in 7:18.87, lopping 1.53 seconds off the mark of the Gross-led West Germans from 1983. The time was almost six seconds faster than the qualifying time of the West German B squad. Hayes's goal for finals, based on their respective flat-start times that summer, was a two-and-a-half-second advantage on the handoff from Float against a guy he joked that he could rarely beat in his pre-swim visualizations.

In the unpredictable, roller-coaster choreography of the pulsating final, Hayes's edge turned out to be barely half that. Heath did his job, opening a gap on Fahrner. Where the spread in the 200 free between the silver- and bronze-medalists was .59 seconds, Heath widened it to 1.16 seconds with his time of 1:48.67. Larson, perhaps too amped up for his only finals swim of the Games, attacked the first 100 meters of his leg to bulge the lead over Dirk Korthals to 2.87 seconds. But the price was steep, and Korthals (1:48.75 split) pegged back Larson (1:49.01) in the second 100, handing off to Alexander Schowtka at the halfway point down just nine-tenths. The same script played out on Float's leg. The Americans' lead ballooned to almost three seconds at 500 meters, but Schowtka slowly reeled in Float in the second 100. Float still outsplit his German counterpart, 1:49.60 to 1:50.26, but he left all the work to be done by Hayes, handing off an advantage of a mere 1.64 seconds. With Hayes's personal-best, flat-start time a 1:49.82, Gross shouldn't have needed all of his world-record speed to track him down.

That appeared alarmingly evident almost from the start of the anchor legs. Hayes popped up from his dive with a lead of about nine feet on Gross. By the time they'd come out of their underwaters from the first turn, they were even. "I thought, 'Oh God, I'm in trouble,'" Hayes said. "I felt like I was turning my arms over three times as fast as he was, but all I could see beside me were these long smooth strokes, keeping him right there."[10] On deck, doubt set in, even among a partisan crowd driven to hysteria. Larson recalled screaming over the din to Heath, "We're going to get silver! That can't happen!"[11] The crescendo that Larson and Heath helped stoke had a special impact on Float, a spiritual and inspirational leader for the entire 1984 squad. In addition to weathering the political storm of the boycott and pinning his hopes on this meet as the culmination to his career, Float had turned to swimming as a refuge for the deafness he suffered as a result of an early childhood bout with meningitis. The sensory deprivation of swim caps and hours on end with a face in the water provided a haven for Float, who had 60 percent hearing loss in his better ear. That didn't make the roar of the crowd any less perceptible. "I've felt the crowd before," Float admitted, "but this is the first time I've ever really heard it."[12]

Gross's initial surge was expected, so Hayes was prepared. "I was really more scared the first 100," Hayes said. "When we turned even at 100, I thought, 'Uh, oh.' But when he didn't pull out on me in the third 50, I said to myself, 'Put your head down and kick.' I thought I could catch him, but I didn't know."[13] Hayes knew there would be a price to pay for that exertion, and that capital would come out of an account already low on funds thanks to Gross's busy program, a tiredness the German readily owned up to afterward. As is often the key, Hayes worked the third 50 of the race. He kept Gross in his sights and didn't let the German pull away. "I think if I would've gotten farther behind than say his waist, then I really would've thought he's going past me for good," Hayes said. "But I was able to stay between his shoulders and his waist pretty much the second half of the race, so I knew if I got home good, I'd have a chance."[14] Gross led by a couple of feet as they turned for home, but Hayes surged to tie him at the midway point of the final 50. They went stroke for stroke down the stretch, making the final result anyone's guess. When the scoreboard revealed its secrets, it set off a paroxysm of joy around the stadium. By .04 seconds, Hayes had gotten to the wall first in 7 minutes, 15.69 seconds.

How fast was that time? To start with, it was over three seconds faster than the morning world record. It represented a cut of almost five seconds from the West Germans' time in 1983. In third place was the team from Great Britain—9.09 seconds back. By the time the Brits finished, Hayes had already gotten his congratulatory high fives from his teammates. Gross's split was the fastest ever, a sizzling time of 1:46.89. Factoring the standard measure of seven-tenths of a second advantage for a relay start over a flat start, it's a fraction slower than his world-record swim in the 200 free final but still worlds ahead of anyone else of his era. That fact tempered any inklings of disappointment. "I only expect to go fast," Gross said. "Sometimes I win. Unfortunately, we finished second in the relay with a time we never expected to get. That's life."[15] Hayes's split of 1:48.41 was no match for Gross's speed, but it got the job done. Considering that the time stood 1.4 seconds faster than his fastest-ever flat-start time, and as the third-fastest split in history, it truly was the swim of his life.[16] "I'm still not sure how I managed to come back," Hayes admitted a week later. "I heard the crowd and I'm sure that made the difference."[17]

For three-quarters of the team, the 800 free relay was the end of their Olympic stays. Float, Larson, and Hayes count it as their only Olympic medal, while Heath returned for the victorious 400 free relay with Gaines, Chris Cavanaugh, and Matt Biondi. The group enjoyed a hit of instant celebrity, riding the wave of their catchy "Grossbusters" moniker to make the rounds of television shows and being whisked away to New York to be photographed for the cover of *Vanity Fair*, hoisting a bathing-suit-clad Raquel Welch.

Gross had a little more work to do in Los Angeles. He nearly brought home the West German 400 free relay for a medal, finishing .29 ticks behind bronze-winning Sweden. For his third individual event, Gross, in typical fashion, eschewed the 400 free since the absence of Salnikov and East German star Sven Lodziewski deprived it the honor of an elite race. Instead, he chose to renew acquaintances with Morales in the 200 fly, dethroning the Olympic record the American had set one prelim heat earlier in 1:58.72. In the final, though, Gross met his match in his complete antithesis, Australian Jon Sieben. Ranked number 25 in the world in the event in 1983, the 5-foot-9 Sieben's first swim under two minutes was his prelim time of 1:59.63. Out of nowhere, Sieben uncorked a world-record 1:57.04 in the finals, robbing Gross (second in 1:57.40) and Morales (an American record 1:57.75 in fourth). Sieben, known somewhat pejoratively as a "scrubber" in Australian swimming, a gutsy if not gifted swimmer, had taken down arguably the world's best swimmer, though he did give Gross another chance to show his graciousness. The certainty with which Gross discussed his future articulated the poise with which he navigated the disappointments. "I will swim as long as it is fun, and when it stops being fun, I will stop, too. Right now, it is a lot of fun," he said. "Perhaps I will swim until 1988. I have not really thought that much about it. One might say that since I have won European, world and Olympic championships, that there is nothing more to prove. That is correct in one sense. However I swim because I enjoy it, not just because I win medals."[18]

After the Games, Gross was chosen by documentarian Bud Greenspan for his "16 Days of Glory" feature, alongside Gaines and the injury struggles of Moffet. Beyond the artistic, slow-motion shots of an albatross riding an updraft were shots of Gross looking decidedly human in the relay replay. That footage came courtesy of a lot of home-nation support and a little teamwork. "The difference between this and all the other relays I've been on is that we were in the States, where everybody loves us and is behind us 100 percent," Larson said. "This is what the Olympics is about. It's for the people of America."[19] Added Float, "As far as Bruce being a Bruin from UCLA and myself a USC Trojan, we're all Americans, unique and extraordinary individuals."[20] For just over seven minutes, they formed a pretty extraordinary team, too.

Chapter Three

2000 Australian Men's Freestyle

The dream scenario was unfolding for Australian swimming. A program so long dormant in a swimming-mad nation, the Land Down Under prepared for the momentous occasion of hosting the first Olympic Games of the new millennium. The hope was that the dawn of the 21st century would represent a new era in Australian swimming, a program that had long toiled through generations of anonymous swimmers and lacked the strength to challenge America's swimming supremacy for almost half a century.

As fate would have it, the Australians weren't just delivered a stage on which to put swimming's best athletes; they were awarded a group of budding superstars to display. At the perfect time, in the perfect place, with even the perfect specialties to suit the Aussie swimming public's sensibilities, the stars appeared to be aligning.

While the cataclysmic and permanent shift in world swimming power that the Australians hoped the Sydney Games would usher in never materialized, the rabid fans Down Under weren't disappointed by what their foremost stars delivered. Nowhere was this more evident than in a pair of dominating performances in the 400 and 800 freestyle relays in 2000. In that area, at least, there would be no question about the power and prestige of the Australian contingent.

Australia had always held an important place in the development of modern competitive swimming, and in turn, the sport held a treasured place in Australian sporting lore. The modern front-crawl stroke utilized in freestyle races owes several key stages of its development to Australian thinkers, so much so that a version known as the "Australian crawl" held sway as the premier style for decades. The Aussies produced legions of Olympic champion swimmers, second in number only to their American counterparts, dating back to before World War I, the overwhelming majority of them specializing in the elegant yet demanding distance events. By the Montreal Games in 1976, however, the program had bottomed out. At that meet, Stephen Holland's bronze medal in the 1,500 free was the only hardware the Aussies claimed. Over the six Olympics spanning the next 20 years, the Australian program claimed a mere seven gold medals across both men's and women's competitions. Only one individual, distance star Kieren Perkins, claimed more than one gold (in the 1,500 at Barcelona and Atlanta), and the only relay gold in that period came from the men's medley at the 1980 Games, an honor that comes with a sizeable asterisk given the boycott by the heavily favored Americans.

The reasons for the hard times were myriad. Some, like Holland's coach Bill Sweetenham, blamed the lack of resources available to the Aussies in terms of facilities and finances prior to 1976. The disparity between the Australians and the state-sponsored programs of nations like East Germany and the Soviet Union was vast. It wasn't a lack of swimming minds, as poignantly illustrated by Australian coach Don Talbot, who had great success in Montreal piloting the Canadian program he helped resurrect with finances devoted to performing at their home Games. "It is not the swimmers and it is not the coaches. It is money," Talbot said. "All the successful swimming nations today—and that includes the United States, East Germany, Russia and even Canada are pouring lots of money into swimming. I am not talking about thousands of dollars—I am talking millions. The day of swimmers performing on a 'shoe-string' financially has gone."[1]

Once the issue of resources was resolved, problems persisted into the 1980s and 1990s. Some thought the scarcity of success was down to individuals, the sights of critics being turned squarely to Dennis Pursley. Many criticized the head of the Australian Institute of Sport in Canberra from 1981 to 1984 for his inflexibility in handling athletes and his failure to take promising young prospects and transform them into polished international stars. After Pursley moved on from Canberra, the tatters of the program he developed were completely shut out of the medals at the 1986 World Championships, a rock bottom part deux for the nation. (Pursley, it should be noted, had plenty of success coaching American swimmers, taking over the national team in 1989.) There were still individuals who managed to make a mark internationally—like undisputed distance king Perkins and Susie O'Neill, long the world's top butterflier—but neither was capable of significantly raising the profile of the nation's program.

From this vacuum of international success, Ian Thorpe emerged in the late 1990s. The story of Thorpe's messianic arrival on the international scene is dotted with legend and lore befitting his superstar status. There was the national reverence for his size-17 feet. There was his flawless six-beat flutter kick, fashioning the power of an outboard motor for the perfect approximation of the freestyle stroke. There were feats of strength like the 10 national age-group records Thorpe set at age 13—in a single meet. The mythology was fed by tales like those of his allergy to chlorine, a swimming superhero weakened by the medium from which he drew his strength. It wasn't just an athletic dream; it was pure bliss for marketers having to sell the stardom of the shy yet poised teenage phenom. At the tender age of 15, Thorpe became the youngest male swimmer to ever represent Australia internationally when he qualified for the 400 free at the 1998 World Championships in Perth. He also became swimming's youngest male world champion in Perth.

For the unique talent that he brought to the pool, though, Thorpe wasn't alone in his meteoric rise to stardom. Just .15 seconds behind him in Perth in that 400 free final and 15 months ahead of him in age was Grant Hackett, a man so accomplished that he would've been the unquestioned face of Australian swimming in just about any other age. Hackett, still five months removed from his 18th birthday at the Perth Worlds, celebrated by adding gold in the 1,500 free to his silver in the 400, his time in the longer event one of the five fastest in history. Eight months after the World Championships, the native of the Gold Coast of Australia issued his claim to the title of greatest distance swimmer of all time when he set the short-course world record in the 1,500 free, downing Perkins's existing mark by almost seven seconds. Where Thorpe was the more versatile of the two, his specialties ranging from 100 to 800 meters with some individual medley thrown in, Hackett epitomized the archetype of the great Australian distance swimmers of the past. Like champions such as Murray Rose, John Konrads, and Boy Charlton, Hackett was most at home over 1,500 meters, the longest competitive swim in a pool. That's where he first made waves, turning heads at the 1996 Olympic Trials when he finished fifth, behind the eventual gold and silver medalists, Perkins and Daniel Kowalski. Hackett had the versatility to successfully come down to 200—he even beat Thorpe to the 200 free world record, setting it at the 1999 Australian Championships before Thorpe took it back five months later at the Pan Pacific Championships—but his wheelhouse was a discipline that few could truly appreciate and didn't make for the best spectator sport.

Nonetheless, the two-headed monster of Thorpe and Hackett began dominating international swimming in short order in the late 1990s. In addition to their show at the 1998 Worlds, Hackett and Thorpe turned the 400 free at the 1999 Short-Course Worlds in Hong Kong into a two-man race, Hackett getting the better of things this time. The narrative of redemption for a nation so long bereft of a reason to get excited about swimming lent itself to romanticism. The triumph was "like cloud-busting spring sunshine," wrote *Swimming World* magazine's Craig Lord, "at first, too bright for the eye to take in, like a new dawn."[2] Thorpe, meanwhile, took home victory in the 200 free, edging out countryman Michael Klim. The dynamic duo added a third formidable face in Klim, who had recovered from a disastrous Atlanta Games—

in which he entered with the top time in the world in the 200 free but failed to even make the finals—to find the form of his life. *Swimming World*'s 1997 World Swimmer of the Year, Klim was golden in the 200 free and 100 fly in Perth, adding silver in the 100 free and bronze in the 50. By the 1999 Pan Pacs—held in the Sydney Olympic Pool a year before the open of the Games—the Australian flag flew all over the freestyle events in the meet that would go down as the fastest in history to that point. Klim won the 100 free, ahead of Chris Fydler in bronze. Thorpe, with a world record of 1:46.00, distanced himself from Klim for gold in the 200, then set a world record of 3:41.83 that was over four seconds faster than Hackett's silver-winning time in the 400 free. Hackett rallied to win the 1,500 in convincing fashion, while Klim claimed the 100 fly.

With the depth provided by Klim and others, it's no surprise that the Australians began a relay revival. The first blow to American hegemony had as much to do with the Americans faltering as it did the Australians advancing. Nonetheless, the 800 free team of Klim, Hackett, Thorpe, and Kowalski took home gold at the Perth Worlds, seven and a half seconds better than the American team (Ugur Taner, Josh Davis, Tom Malchow, and Tom Dolan), which finished a disappointing fifth. The Australian squad of Adam Pine, Richard Upton, Klim, and Fydler came up short in the 400 free relay, though, being touched out by the Americans by a quarter second. Both countries were faster all around by Sydney in 1999. There, Thorpe (with a supremely fast leadoff leg of 1:46.28), Bill Kirby, Hackett (with the fastest non-Thorpe split of 1:46.30), and Klim entered the world-record books, clocking in at 7:08.79 to take gold. The margin to the silver-medal team of Davis, Chad Carvin, Malchow, and Taner was almost three seconds. The Australians, with Klim, Thorpe, Fydler, and Jeff English, duplicated the championship feat in the shorter relay, outdistancing Davis, Bryan Jones, Neil Walker, and Jason Lezak by .73 seconds.

As if that wasn't proof enough of the formidability the Australians had to offer, the nation's Olympic Trials formally signaled the ascendancy of the men's program to the rank of the world's best. Over 100,000 spectators took in the eight-day event, elevating the likes of Thorpe and Hackett to instant national heroes. Thorpe set three world records in as many days, including two in the 200 free. Perhaps more important for the relay reckoning, though, he set a personal-best time of 49.45 seconds in the semifinals of the 100 free, reportedly shaking off a "thumping headache" to do so.[3] Due to its relay ramifications, that was the swim that, in the words of Australian Swimming spokesman Ian Hanson, should've had the Americans "shaking in their boots."[4] Thorpe's 100 was but one reason that Talbot, the head coach of the Australians, had already bestowed upon Thorpe the label of greatest swimmer of the century.[5] Hackett led the way in the 1,500—ahead of Perkins, bound for his third Games—and was second in the 400. Klim finished second in the 200 free but passed on the event for Sydney to focus on the 100 free and 100 fly, allowing third-place finisher Hackett to step into the second individual spot in Sydney.

The Australian freestyle prowess swept into Sydney as one of the Games' top stories, regardless of sport. Within the swimming events, easily the most anticipated of the Games for the home country, the *Sydney Morning Herald* projected that six of the top seven events Australians were looking forward to involved the Australian male freestylers, headlined by the battle of Hackett and Perkins in the 1,500 and Hackett versus Thorpe in the 400. Only the Green and Gold's female butterfliers, Susie O'Neill and Petria Thomas, interrupted the countdown.[6] The freestylers, led by Thorpe's quest for five gold medals, didn't need any extra hype. They got a bit anyway. That transpired when Gary Hall Jr., the brash American sprinter, issued a verbal broadside at the Australians. The winner of two individual silvers and two relay golds in Atlanta in 1996, Hall predicted that the Americans would "smash [the Australians] like guitars." Hall's declaration reverberated through an Australian media devoting the lion's share of its Olympic attention to the drama that would unfold in the pool. To some, Hall's pronouncement was taken as a compliment. "During the late '70s and the '80s, the Australians didn't have a hope in hell of competing as a team against the Americans," said Mark Stockwell, the silver medalist in the 100 free behind American Rowdy Gaines at the 1984 Los Angeles Games. "We had some very good swimmers during that period who would win one-off events, but total team dominance like we're looking at at the moment, I haven't seen in my lifetime. Basically, [Hall] is acknowledging that we're a threat and I think it's a great back-handed compliment paid by the American team because they're actually, for the first time in my lifetime, perhaps going into a competition where they might be beaten."[7] Long had the Australians focused on the Americans as the predominant power in the world; Hall's comments reinforced that desire to supplant the Americans. "We want to build the component of team support that the Americans have," Talbot said, "which others criticize but secretly envy."[8]

At least the world wouldn't have long to wait to see how the splashy drama played out in Sydney. The first day of competition was highlighted by the men's 400 free relay as well as the men's 400 free, much of the world's first look at the phenomenon that was Thorpe. He wasted no time vaulting into the limelight, downing Yevgeny Sadovyi's eight-year-old Olympic record in the prelims, qualifying with the top time by a second over Italian Massimiliano Rosolino. Without Thorpe, the Australian team of Fydler, Todd Pearson, Pine, and Ashley Callus was only second fastest in prelims, its time of 3:17.37 almost two seconds slower than that of the Americans (Scott Tucker, Anthony Ervin, Lezak, and Davis). The Americans looked strong, especially with splits of 48.43 and 48.46 from Ervin and Lezak, respectively, while Davis's anchor leg of 48.74 also would've been the fastest on the Australian team. The Aussies, meanwhile, didn't have anyone dip under 49 seconds. The 49.08-second anchor leg of Callus—the cocksure 21-year-old who announced himself to his potential relay mates at the Australian pre-Olympic camp with the declaration, "I am here to win a gold medal and the rest of you blokes had better pull your finger out"[9]—earned a spot on the finals squad along with the 27-year-old veteran Fydler (49.72 leadoff leg).

That evening's finals would become what Thorpe called "the best day of my life. This was the best hour of my life. These were the best minutes of my life."[10] The evening began with a dominate performance in the 400 free where Thorpe turned in a time of 3:40.59, over four seconds quicker than his prelim swim and a cut of almost three-quarters of a second off his world record from Australian Trials. Almost three seconds back was Rosolino in silver; Klete Keller set an American record of 3:47.00 for bronze that was over six seconds slower than the vapor trail left by the Thorpedo. The gap between Thorpe and the rest of the world was evident, but how it would benefit his teammates remained a question.

The times on paper only tell so much of the tale of what was undoubtedly one of the greatest races in Olympic history, a scene that conjured up images in Thorpe's mind of gladiators doing battle in the Coliseum.[11] Both the Americans and the Australians demolished the surprisingly resilient world record set by the Americans at the 1995 Pan Pacific Championships in Atlanta. The splits show that at each of the three handoffs, the Australians led. But by no means was it a wire-to-wire victory for the Australians in 3:13.67, just .19 seconds ahead of the Americans.

It had the makings of a rout early on thanks to Klim, who set the 100 free world record off the front with a sizzling time of 48.18, a fact Thorpe had to work hard to convince Klim of on deck before stepping up to the blocks himself.[12] Klim took his swim out fast and held on in the second 50, powering home and opening a sizeable gap on the Americans. But Ervin kept them in contention with easily the second-fastest split in the race at 48.89 seconds. A personal-best for the University of California sprinter, it separated the Americans from the rest of the pack in a heat where barely half of the leadoff men broke 50 seconds.

The next three legs followed a similar script. Walker briefly surged ahead of Fydler on the second leg, pulling in front by a hair after the 150-meter wall. But Fydler rallied to preserve the majority of the lead, though he had given back .17 seconds to the Americans. Callus hit the water before Lezak, but the American gobbled up real estate quickly and put himself in the lead by the time the first 50 had been covered. Again, though, Callus survived the threat and finished his leg first, handing off a lead to Thorpe that had been reduced to a quarter second. The pessimists at the Sydney International Aquatics Centre may have closed their eyes briefly when they saw Thorpe, clad from ankles to wrists in his trademark swimsuit, overtaken by Hall on the first 50. As they turned for home, Hall's uncovered torso was the margin between the two. With even 15 meters left, the existing world record long since fated to fall, it appeared that Hall would hold off Thorpe's charge. But the Thorpedo's legs kicked into high gear and he gained ground with every meter, getting to the wall fractions of a second ahead of Hall, the Australian splitting a 48.30 to Hall's 48.24. From the atmosphere of the night, even Thorpe knew how it was destined to finish. "I didn't see the scoreboard, didn't hear the crowd, but I knew to react," Thorpe said. "I would've felt like a fool if I'd been wrong, but I knew to react."[13]

The aftermath maintained a fairly civil air. Amid the pandemonium of the Aquatic Centre, the Australian foursome indulged in a bit of air-guitaring, a less-than-subtle shot at Hall's earlier aspersions. Thorpe's admission that he wasn't at full strength for the relay—common sense for anyone else but shocking in the light of his newly minted demigod status—somehow made his accomplishment in the face of Hall's feverish pursuit even more impressive. "I wasn't feeling all that fresh," Thorpe said, "so I knew I had to work on it to get as far ahead as I could. I wasn't going to let anyone beat me at that stage."[14] Hall, who ended up with a split six-hundredths of a second faster than Thorpe, was deferential, perhaps as impressed by the youthful Australian's performance as anyone. "I doff my swimming cap to Thorpe," Hall said. "He swam a great race. But we swam a great race, too. I've been on a lot of relay teams that have won a lot of races, but this is the best relay team I've ever been on."[15]

The victory in the 400 free relay made the Australians the prohibitive favorites in the 800, reinforcing the regard in which they were held prior to the Games. The intervening three days between relays, though, tossed a couple of curveballs at the Aussies. First, Klim saw his world record in the 100 free go by the wayside courtesy of Dutch sprinter Pieter van den Hoogenband in the semifinals. Then, while van den Hoogenband was busy running away with gold in the final—albeit in a time slower than Klim's world mark from the relay—Klim was beaten to bronze by Hall by a mere hundredth of a second, leaving Klim without a medal. Van den Hoogenband also showed Thorpe to be mortal in the 200 free, taking his world record in the semis and producing an identical time of 1:45.35 in finals to earn gold, .48 ticks ahead of silver-winning Thorpe. Hackett, meanwhile, was as disappointing over 200 meters as 400, again squeaking into the final and taking a disappointing eighth place. The malaise afflicting Hackett—which wouldn't be revealed until after the Games as a virus—was evident in the prelims of the 800 free relay. The Aussie team of Hackett, Kirby, Pearson, and Kowalski qualified first in 7:14.27, a shade under three seconds ahead of the second-place Americans. But much of the over five-second gap to the world record could be attributed to Hackett's labored opening leg of 1:50.31, just the 10th-fastest leadoff leg of 16 prelims squads. The strength of the Aussie squad came in the middle two legs. Kirby and Pearson turned in splits of 1:47.76 and 1:47.68, respectively, to earn surprising berths in the finals. Kirby admitted to turning himself inside out in the prelim swim, becoming physically ill afterward, while Pearson was driven to avoid a repeat of the 400 free relay, which saw him earn a medal for prelims but be relegated to the stands for finals.[16] Kowalski and Hackett, the two men everyone expected to swim in finals alongside Klim and Thorpe, would be spectators. The Americans, meanwhile, were models of consistency, all four splits bunched within .71 seconds. The two fastest were provided by anchor Keller (1:49.19) and Jamie Rauch (1:48.94), leaving Carvin and Nate Dusing out in the cold for finals.

With the U.S.—all due respect to Keller, then an 18-year-old distance swimmer still developing the speed for a 200-meter sprint—still a few years away from boasting a world-class 200 freestyler among its ranks, there was little doubt where the gold would go. Called "the surest of sure things," the only solace *Swimming World* found for the rest of the world in the race was "that Olympic rules do not allow a country to field two relays. Otherwise, there might have been eight Aussies on the victory stand, rather than just four."[17] (To those ends, the flat-start times from Australian Trials for the next four fastest Australians—Hackett, Kowalski, Perkins, and Antony Matkovich—summed to around 7:15; with full health for Hackett, the boost given by relay pickups, and the ability to prepare specifically for the race, it's not inconceivable for those four to have been in the 7:12 range that decided places 2 through 5 in Sydney.)

With those weighty expectations, the Australian coaching staff thought it best to get matters resolved quickly, hence the decision to lead off Thorpe followed by Klim. The plan was executed to perfection. The Thorpedo didn't recover his world record, but his time of 1:46.03 staked the Green and Gold to a 3.5-second lead over Great Britain (thanks to Edward Sinclair's great leg) and the United States' Scott Goldblatt. By the time Klim finished his leg in 1:46.40, the fourth-fastest in the race, the Australians were over three seconds under world-record pace. The only moment of suspense remaining in the last eight victory laps was the pickup between Pearson and Kirby. Pearson wasn't resting on his laurels, turning in a swim of 1:47.36, while Kirby's 1:47.26 anchor leg was also an improvement on his prelims time. By the time Keller brought home the Americans for silver, holding off the charge of van den Hoogenband by a scant .06 seconds, the Aussies had already completed their handshakes, winning gold by 5.59 seconds in a world record of 7.07.05, lopping 1.74 seconds off the mark set a year prior in the same pool. The post-race comments were about as succinct as the victory. "We were going in tonight ranked No.1 and expected to win," said Klim, who placed the win right up there with the 400 free in terms of sentimental value, "and we did the job."[18] The energy of the arena and the enormity of the moment wasn't lost on the swimmers. "Last night, I was probably in more pain during that third lap," Kirby said. "But as soon as I turned and came off the wall, I didn't feel anything but just joy. There was no pain at all. I touched the wall, and it was joy, joy, joy all the way home."[19] Added Pearson, who allowed that a gold-winning relay was a lot more fun to watch from the water than the stands,[20] "You could feel it through your body, and all they wanted to see was you perform at your best."[21]

Half of the Olympic program remained after the 800 free, but few moments surpassed the excitement the host nation had produced. There was still "the big one," the 1,500 on the Games' final day.[22] In a race that elicited mixed emotions, Hackett managed to upset Perkins's quest for three straight golds, ushering in a changing of the guard in 14 minutes, 48.33 seconds, decisively faster than Perkins (silver in 14:53.59) and American Chris Thompson (bronze in an American record 14:56.81). While Hackett was a popular figure, Perkins had been the sentimental favorite, the nation backing him to close his storied career with gold. The American hegemony in the medley relay continued despite an Australian team that included 100 backstroke silver medalist Matt Welsh, 100 fly bronze winner Geoff Huegill, and Klim on the anchor leg, having to settle for silver.

The medley relay silver was a minor damper on the excitement created by the Aussies in Sydney. Considering that the relay results in Atlanta four years prior left the Australians nothing more than bronze in the medley, a silver on the heels of two golds more than sufficed. To end a losing streak in the 800 free relay that dated to 1956 and claim two golds from an American program that had entered the Games having swept up 25 golds in the 26 Olympic men's relays in which it had participated was quite the accomplishment.

The reactions of the men involved, though, indicated that there was something more. World-class talents had long graced the Australian swimming roster; many more would follow in the next decade, few of whom lived up to their promise as did those in 2000. What the Australians had done in Sydney was fulfill the goals set by Talbot before the Games: to create the kind of cohesion that so often typified American delegations and allowed individuals to assemble into a whole that exceeded the sum of its parts. That's precisely what happened in the longer relay, with Pearson and Kirby pushing a budding superstar in Hackett and a three-time individual medalist in Kowalski to the grandstands. Ultimately, that ability to rise to the occasion as a unit defined the legacy of the Australian class of 2000. "I've got two gold medals, and I've shared them both with my great mates on the Australian team," Klim said after the 800 triumph. "This has been an incredible meet."[23] Thorpe echoed those sentiments. "I've got three gold medals and two of them I have shared the experience with my great mates from the Australian team," he said. "It's been an incredible meet for me. Tonight I went out and I wanted to be able to enjoy that race in front of this home crowd because it's the Olympic Games and I'm never going to have this opportunity again, and it was something really special."[24]

Chapter Four

2000 U.S. Women's Medley

The dawning of the new millennium brought new optimism in the ranks of American women's swimming. The past three decades of international competition had been an uphill battle against the specter of illegal drug use the world over. For generations of promising American swimmers, the road to Olympic gold and glory was blocked by one chemically-aided athlete after another.

For over two decades, the culprits were the systematically doped East German contingent, fueled by the fervent desire of the communist state to devote endless resources and research toward the accumulation of international prestige in the athletic arena. When it seemed in the early 1990s that the path to the podium's top step had been cleared by the fall of the Berlin Wall, the reunification of Germany, and the slow revelation of secrets hidden for decades, another power swiftly and dubiously swept to the forefront of women's swimming. With the alacrity and totality of domination shown by the East Germans two decades earlier, the 1994 World Championships in Rome threatened to herald another era of swimming: that of the pharmacologically-enhanced Chinese. Their utter stranglehold on gold in Rome—12 in 16 women's events—had one analogue in swimming history and drew observers to only one inescapable conclusion.

Where it took nearly 20 years to peer behind the convoluted veil of state-sponsored secrecy in the German Democratic Republic, the Chinese reign was far shorter. Between increased scientific screening, a willingness to learn from the past, and decades of American disillusion, the truth behind China's precipitous rise was soon revealed. When the Sydney Olympic Games, perhaps the most anticipated swimming competition ever, began, all that was left were a few symbolic and decisive swipes of the eraser on the world-record board. The Americans were more than happy to oblige. They bookended the competition in Sydney with a pair of gold-worthy, world-record-breaking performances in the 400 free relay and 400 medley relay. The latter squad—composed of B. J. Bedford, Megan Quann, Dara Torres, and Jenny Thompson—saved the best for last, delivering a swim that authoritatively closed the book on the forgettable era of Chinese dominance.

The story of triumph in Sydney traces its roots all the way back to 1993, to a time when Thompson was compiling one of the greatest swim careers ever seen in the NCAA ranks, Torres was relishing in retirement number 2, and Quann was an anonymous elementary school student. Entering that year, the Chinese weren't exactly strangers to the international swimming scene. The four-gold, nine-medal haul from the 1992 Olympics was a notable sidebar in Barcelona. Few would've thought of it as merely the appetizer for the following year's explosion of talent. From 1989 to 1992, a total of 28 Chinese swimmers finished a calendar year ranked in the top 10 worldwide in an event, 10 of them in 1992. In 1993 alone, 28 Chinese swimmers earned that accolade, including a mind-boggling eight of the top 10 times in the 50 free. [1] The poster child for this eruption of talent was Dai Guohong. She finished 1992 ranked 34th in the long-course 200 breaststroke course, the only event in which she cracked the top 150 in the world. By the end of 1994, she owned five medals, four gold, from the 1993 World Short-Course Championships, plus two golds and a silver from the 1994 Long-Course Worlds in Rome, including the coveted 400 individual medley title. The ascent of the Chinese was simply unprecedented. "No other nation has come to dominate a sport so quickly and so totally as the Chinese have come to dominate women's swimming," wrote *Swimming World* magazine's Phillip Whitten, with the ultimately damming caveat, "not even the late, unlamented East Germany." [2]

The defense proffered by the Chinese reiterated many hallmarks of the East German's rise to power in the early 1970s. They pinpointed seven factors supposedly responsible for the rapid proliferation of elite athletes, trumpeting the nation's centralized system, state-sponsored incentivization of athletic success, and superior process of early talent identification. Methods like altitude training and the use of mystical herbal concoctions, like worms and fungi from China's many remote regions, were credited with supplementing the superior work ethic of Chinese women. Accusations of performance enhancement, absent concrete evidence, were seen as xenophobic slants at a culture outsiders misunderstood. "You ask questions about doping because of misunderstanding and jealousy," was the response of assistant coach Zhou Ming in 1994. "It's a sort of political thing. The sports world has always been the domain of Western people. They just can't tolerate Asian people being good at sport." [3]

The facts told a different story though, the similarities to the East Germans too striking to discount. The burgeoning musculature and deep voices of the Chinese girls were merely the tip of the iceberg. The Chinese bluntly denied the obvious physical growth of Chinese competitors—see world champion Le Jingyi being listed at 5-9 and 122 pounds by the team in Rome when she stood at over 6-foot and around 140 pounds.[4] The confinement of the shocking improvement in times to the women's side—with all nine of the medals from the 1992 Barcelona Games and a staggering 19 from Rome on the women's side of the ledger—also roused suspicion. Were androgenic steroids in play, that's precisely the result expected. Much like the East Germans, the problem was gender, rather than sport, specific, with the international medal boon extending to female distance runners in 1993. The success in the pool came primarily in the sprint events, where drugs would be most likely to yield significant results. Experts even noted striking similarities in the techniques of Chinese and East German athletes, both of which sacrificed technical acuity to accommodate off-the-charts speed and power.[5] There was even a physical trail of scientists from East Germany finding refuge in China after the reunification of Germany and the brief intermission between the fall of the German sport system and the rise of the Chinese.

The Western responses to the Chinese surge covered the entire spectrum. Some, like renowned coach and swimming author Forbes Carlile, chose to remain diplomatic, terming it "very strong circumstantial evidence"[6] of drug use, though in his typically wry humor, Carlile also equated claims of China's herbal miracle substances to "believing in fairies."[7] To elite swimmers like Janet Evans, whose prime bridged the late East German days and early advances of China's rise, the parallels were too much to overlook. For many, especially among the American delegation so long relegated to lower steps of podiums, the emergence of a threat like China spurred a call for greater testing and sanctions. Swimming powers like the U.S. and Australia voted not to invite the Chinese to the 1995 Pan Pacific Championships. Longtime American coach Richard Quick, who professed to having "no doubt whatsoever in my mind that the Chinese are using illegal drugs,"[8] threatened a boycott of the 1998 Worlds if measures weren't taken to eradicate a repeat of the sham of 1994.[9] As early as 1994, when Chinese world champion Yang Aihua became the fifth Chinese swimmer to test positive for banned substances in 20 months, Quick was eager to decry China's systematic circumvention of the rules. "I think this is orchestrated, institutionalized cheating," he said. "These are the same coaches who said [they] are not doing any steroids at all."[10]

Perhaps taking after her coach, Thompson, Quick's prized pupil at Stanford, was among the most vocal critics of Chinese malfeasance. "It's inconceivable that the depth could come in one year," Thompson said in 1994. "All of a sudden they've developed incredible depth. It's just ridiculous. I'm not going to hide my feelings any more. It's obvious there's something more going on than normal elite competitive swimming. They're definitely using steroids."[11] Few felt the sting of Chinese transgressions as acutely as Thompson. The native of Dover, New Hampshire, penned a reputation as the world's foremost relay swimmer over four Olympics, leading the Stars and Stripes to eight relay golds from 1992 to 2004. But the glaring omission on the résumé of the most decorated American female Olympian of all time is individual gold. The closest she got was silver in the 100 free in Barcelona . . . two-tenths behind Zhuang Yong in an event Thompson entered with a world record. To add insult to injury, a crestfallen and livid Thompson was screened for a random drug test afterward, not Zhuang.[12] As a fixture on the national team for almost two decades, the Chinese drug-aided heyday overshadowed much of Thompson's prime. In 1994, Thompson anchored three American relays to minor medals, including the medley relay of Lea Loveless, Kristine Quance, and Amy Van Dyken that finished almost five seconds back in the wash of Le Jingyi and the world-record-setting Chinese. To the popular image of her as the archetypal, Red, White, and Blue American swimming hero, Thompson added the role of international anti-drug crusader. "They've proved themselves guilty," Thompson said in 1994. "I can say that with confidence after their National Games last September. . . . Things like that don't happen in one year. I want the play in my pool to be fair."[13]

Where others had been skewered for their criticism, history ultimately vindicated Thompson. Seven positive tests for the steroid dihydrotestosterone in 1994 and 1995, including world champions Lu Bin and Yang, defended the stance of Western powers.[14] Chinese swimmer Yuan Yuan was apprehended at Sydney Airport in 1998 en route to the World Championships in Perth with 13 vials labeled "HGH," though the human growth hormone was claimed to belong to assistant coach Zhou Zhewen. In all, 27 Chinese swimmers tested positive for drugs in the 1990s.[15] Given her history, it's no surprise that Thompson called the Yuan incident "the happiest day of my life."[16]

Though the systems of oversight were functioning properly, tensions on deck were hardly diffused. For some swimmers, like Van Dyken, the absence of China at meets like the 1995 Pan Pacs meant the deprivation of an outlet for pent-up frustration. "I would rather have the Chinese here," she said. "It's good that we are making a stand, that we're saying we're not going to put up with this because so many of their swimmers have been caught. . . . Being ranked first in the world right now, I'm upset they're not here. I'm thinking what if the Chinese would be here. I could get up and race them. They're not going to go away."[17] Van Dyken, never one to ignore the mental aspect of racing, notoriously stared down Le before beating her for gold in the 50 free in the 1996 Olympics, and with Thompson she refused to acknowledge the mere presence of Shan Ying, coached by Zhou, at the 1998 Worlds. "She's not a part of this," was Van Dyken's explanation of a meet where the Chinese medal haul crashed to three female golds and six total medals. "Everyone else—the Japanese, Sandra Völker from Germany, everyone—is a part. She is not a part."[18] Asked about Shan's bronze in the event, Van Dyken unapologetically quipped, "I don't know. Maybe she was just more in touch with her feminine side today."[19] To Van Dyken, the precipitous plummet in the standings for the Chinese from their top times in 1997 to their modest placing in Perth months later was joyfully more than coincidence. "It's kind of interesting when 13 vials of human growth hormone are taken from them, all of a sudden they don't swim so well," Van Dyken didn't mind pointing out. "Seems funny to me."[20] While the feisty Van Dyken, who courted controversy from time to time by spitting in the lane of competitors before races, took a more aggressive line, Thompson was more compassionate, even if just as unequivocal about the measures necessary. "I don't feel angry with the swimmers," she said in Perth. "More than anything, I think I feel sorry for them. They're just doing what their coaches tell them. I think they're like the East Germans that way."[21]

Against that backdrop, the world descended upon the swimming oasis of Sydney in 2000, seeking the light at the end of a three-decade-long, drug-blighted tunnel. Try as they might, though, the issue of illicit substances still pervaded Sydney, and in more than just the buttons worn by Thompson displaying a slash through a cartoon needle.

For Bedford, the 2000 Games were a fourth and final chance at Olympic glory. A five-time national champion in the 100 backstroke, she had a disastrous time at the 1996 Olympic Trials, entering as the favorite in the 100 and 200 back. The native of Etna, New Hampshire, finished an agonizing third in the 100, then 12th in prelims of the 200—so demoralizing a result that she scratched out of the semifinals and promptly retired. A veteran of two world championships, three Pan Pacs, and about every major meet the U.S. could enter, the issue of drugs at the 1994 Worlds had a unique impact on her. After earning bronze in the 100 back, Bedford, then a senior at the University of Texas, was drug tested. The process took so long that she missed dinner and, seeking the calories every swimmer needs, she headed to an ice cream parlor nearby in Rome. The trip made her 20 minutes late for the team's 10:30 p.m. curfew, raising the ire of head coach Dennis Pursley, who threatened to send her home from the meet. While the intervention of Quick and assistant coach Jon Urbanchek allowed her to compete in the 200 back (she finished fourth), she was denied a place on the medley relay team that won silver.[22] At age 27, the trip to Sydney was the culmination of Bedford's swimming career and included a sixth-place finish in the 100 back.

The story of the 33-year-old Torres was one of the few that could challenge Thompson for top billing in Sydney, a fitting competition given their collisions on the road to the Games. Torres emerged on the American swimming scene in the early 1980s and made three Olympic trips, netting four relay medals, two gold. For a variety of reasons, though, the Olympic experiences left Torres with a sense of emptiness. Somewhere between modeling gigs and television spots in the late 1990s, the competition bug bit Torres, who decided to make her second comeback, eight years after a return to the pool netted her gold on the 400 free relay in Barcelona. Already ancient for a swimmer, Torres contacted Stanford coach Quick, who made arrangements for her to relocate to California and train with Stanford. Tensions between Torres and Thompson, though, soon boiled over. Each practice in Palo Alto resembled the intensity of an Olympic final with the two competing for spots on the Olympic team in three of the same events—the 50 free, 100 free, and 100 fly. The age of each swimmer (Thompson at 27 was widely thought to be in her final Olympic cycle) ratcheted up the desperation of each workout. The two had to be placed in separate training groups, Thompson training with a Cardinal squad from which she'd graduated five years earlier and Torres working under Quick's watchful eye at Santa Clara Swim Club.

But even apart, one thread linked them: suspicions of drug use. Many questioned how Torres, at an unprecedented age, was swimming faster than she did as a teen in the mid-1980s. The workout freak explained it away with her exercising diligence and a health zeal that transcended her status as an athlete. But coupled with the many supplements and specialists, therapists and experts swelling her entourage, the whispers were amplified to a dull roar by Sydney. If it appeared too good to be true for a female swimmer, history dictated that it generally was. The juxtaposition was obvious: There was Thompson, the consummate crusader for free and fair competition, swimming alongside a teammate—with whom she maintained at least "overtly friendly"[23] relations despite their earlier spats—whose performances many were convinced had to be chemically aided. Complicating matters was the presence of Glen Luepnitz, the nutritionist employed by both Thompson and Torres whose methods and products were a lightning rod for controversy, while both subscribed to similar regimens of nutrition and recovery at the behest of Quick. To Thompson's credit, she remained openminded to the possibility that some performances, like the show-stealing swims of Dutchwoman Inge de Bruijn in Sydney, were on the up-and-up. De Bruijn, who was setting world records at 27 after seeing her career bottom out so badly that she didn't pursue a spot in Atlanta in 1996, found her way into the sights of skeptics thanks to a three-gold-medal haul after a long career devoid of major hardware. Through it all, Thompson maintained a stance of conscientious questioning. "It's a sad state of events when everyone who does well gets questioned," Thompson said. "But at the same time, there's reason to question. There's cheating in the sport. I'm not going to say that Inge is cheating. At the same time, it's good to question."[24]

About the only one above—or perhaps below the age limit for—the crossfire of drug talk was Quann. The spritely, hyper-determined native of Puyallup, Washington, possessed the star quality that drives the quadrennial media circus of the Olympics. Like Bedford and Thompson, the 16-year-old arrived at the apex of the sport from well off the beaten path. She burst onto the scene as the latest breaststroke prodigy when at age 14 in 1994 she went from the 20th seed to the national champion in the 100. From there, the precocious teen set a string of American records in the event, culminating with a win at the 2000 Olympic Trials over a field that included 1996 breast-stroke wunderkind Amanda Beard and NCAA champ Kristy Kowal. At Trials, she set the American record twice more, all without any semblance of a taper. Her age placed her as a rare exception on the oldest American Olympic swimming squad to date and the first instance in which the American women were older than the men. While Torres, at over twice her age, was bogged down with questions over the legality of her training, Quann was more than willing to divulge stories of her gold-painted fingernails, her self-imposed moratorium on dating, and her nightly visualization ritual. She also had no temerity about talking trash to 1996 double-gold medalist and world-record holder Penny Heyns, boasting with the confidence of youth, "I think she's going down."[25]

The concern over drugs, "splashy sitcoms,"[26] and youthful declarations of exuberance took a backseat once the action started in Sydney. Those looking for a broadside at the past needn't look any further than opening night. The opening salvo was made by Ukrainian star Yana Klochkova, who set a world record in the 400 individual medley in a doping double takeout, erasing the world record set by Chen Yan at the ludicrously fast Chinese National Games in October 1997 and the Olympic mark set two decades prior by East Germany's Petra Schneider. Two finals later, another Chinese record bit the dust thanks to the American 400 free relay team. The squad of Van Dyken, Torres, Courtney Shealy, and Thompson proved themselves to be, as *Swimming World* elatedly put it, "the best women's relay team this old planet has ever seen."[27] Van Dyken stayed close to Australia's Susie O'Neill, and Torres gave the Americans the lead for good with the second-fastest relay split in history at 53.51 seconds. Shealy and Thompson, swimming her custo-mary anchor leg, brought home the win, holding off a surge by the Nether-lands—led by the fastest relay split ever, de Bruijn's 53.41—to claim gold in a 3:36.61, 3.22 seconds faster than the Dutch. Gone was the Chinese standard from 1994, by 1.3 seconds. The podium that night showed what remained for the athletes involved. Van Dyken, who overcame a shoulder injury that threatened to derail her career, sobbed uncontrollably while Torres welled up with tears. Stoic, though, was Thompson, her eyes set firmly on the prize of individual gold.

By the arrival of the medley relay on the final day of competition, Thompson had faced the paradox of her career: She was the most decorated American female Olympian of all time, but not among those 10 medals was an individual gold. On the second night of competition, she looked in prime position to clinch the 100 fly. But Thompson readily admitted that she tightened up with the wall in sight and faded to a shocking fifth, passed by de Bruijn, Slovakia's Martina Moravcova, and Torres, who snuck into bronze. The event for Torres had been designated at Olympic Trials as merely a warm-up to stretch her legs and shake out the jitters; Thompson, however, owned the holy grail of world records, the prior year winning the race to unseat Mary T. Meagher's 18-year-old world record in the event. De Bruijn would break that mark three times, culminating in the Olympic final swim. The disappointment for Thompson was clear, requiring a mid-Games re-grouping.

Faltering late struck Bedford the next night, as she led the 100 back until the final 25 meters in a bid to upstage the favorites, Romanian Diana Mocanu and Japan's Mai Nakamura. The pace caught up to the red, white, and blue–haired Bedford, who slipped to sixth as Mocanu got to the wall first. The ending was reversed for Quann, who outkicked Heyns and Australian Leisel Jones to claim gold in the 100 breast. When the time came for Thompson to get back in the pool, she went to her wheelhouse, delivering a stellar anchor swim in the 800 free relay to chase down Australia's Petria Thomas and earn gold for the team of Diana Munz, Samantha Arsenault, and Lindsay Benko. Day 6 delivered one of the Games' tightest races, and certainly the most taut medal ceremony, when Torres and Thompson improbably tied for the bronze medal in the 100 free—again behind the unstoppable de Bruijn—to crowd onto the narrow third step of the podium.

The medley relay wasn't the only thing on the mind of Torres as the Sydney Games approached their final two days. There was qualification for the 50 free, in which Torres advanced to the finals with the third-fastest time, .85 seconds behind yet another de Bruijn world standard. That swim excused Torres from prelims of the medley relay, though Van Dyken survived that test for the U.S. while qualifying fourth for finals in the 50. Van Dyken brought home the prelim squad of Shealy, Staciana Stitts, and Ashley Tappin a comfortable fourth, within 1.5 seconds of the top-seeded Australians. On the final night, Torres and Van Dyken had the unenviable task of trying to solve that riddle that was de Bruijn. They couldn't, with the Dutchwoman taking her third gold, but Torres outtouched Van Dyken for an American record in 24.63 seconds and another bronze medal.

That just left the medley relay, a squad composed of three swimming senior citizens and one teen. Their triumph provided a fitting conclusion to a stellar meet for the Americans, setting a world record of 3:58.30. The gold was special on so many fronts. The medley almost perfectly matched the margin of victory from the 400 free relay (.07 seconds wider a margin at 3.29 over the Aussies). It erased the tainted world record of the Chinese by a stunning 3.37 seconds while going down in history as the first medley relay in history to break the hallowed four-minute mark, doing so by almost two full seconds. And as if they needed any more flourish on the crowning achievement of the Games, the Americans led a wire-to-wire win in comprehensive fashion, recording the fastest split times for each leg. Bedford gained a modicum of personal revenge by turning in a time of 1:01.39 on the leadoff leg, distancing herself from Nakamura and Australian Dyana Calub. Quann routed 15-year-old Jones, outsplitting her by over a second and a quarter to put the race out of reach before the midway point. Thompson still blistered her first 50 en route to a fly split of 57.25 to hand off to Torres, who turned in a 53.37-second freestyle leg, .04 faster than de Bruijn's split seven days prior and the fastest 100 free ever swum from a relay start.

Just as their paths to the Land Down Under had been so varied, so too were their reactions to the final gold. There was no bridling the joy for Bedford at what proved to be the only Olympic medal of her career. "We were going to show them what we could do," she beamed. "I don't have the words, and that's a rarity."[28] The portrayal of Thompson's Games slanted toward the negative, with the assumption that this marked the end of her competitive career. (She'd prove that wrong in Athens, going back for two relay silvers, though she failed to medal in two individual events, running her career medal total to 12.) While the pictures showed a happy Thompson parading on deck with her teammates, she felt the need to state that she was "at peace"[29] with how the Games had transpired while striving to "stop looking at what I don't have, and to look at what I have."[30] Torres made no effort to hide her plans to ride off into the sunset, a path she'd well worn by then. Ending on such a high note emphasized just how much she'd miss it. "I'm bummed it's over," a tearful Torres admitted. "It's just kind of hit me that it's over."[31] At least it ended with the highest of highs.

Chapter Five

2004 U.S. Men's Medley

Rare are the occasions that a U.S. Olympic delegation, especially on the men's side of the draw, is left looking to salvage its Games in the final relay. With a stranglehold on the title of the world's foremost swimming power largely unchallenged in the last half century, the final days of Olympic competition have generally become victory laps for conquering American heroes.

In 2004, though, the customary script hadn't exactly transpired. They'd had success, for sure, including the introduction of the world to the dominant force that Michael Phelps would soon become. But entering the culminating event of the Games, the 400 medley relay, the Americans were in the unusual position of needing a gold medal to earn a modicum of redemption for many of the names featured in the pre-meet hype who'd failed to deliver on the promise of major medals.

In a race more notable for which American wasn't there than for those who were, the team of Aaron Peirsol, Brendan Hansen, Ian Crocker, and Jason Lezak continued the American dominance of the event in world-record time. Considering the adversity each had faced to that point in Athens, their relay swim was nothing short of unbelievable, a remarkable coming together of four individuals to collectively banish the demons of a disappointing meet.

The buzz gripping swimming as it turned its eyes to Athens surrounded Phelps, who'd positioned himself for a feat no human had ever managed at an Olympic Games: winning eight gold medals. Everyone, from his rivals in the pool to Mark Spitz, the only man to win seven golds in an Olympiad, weighed in on his chances leading up to the Games. The consensus was that it couldn't be done. By the second night of competition, with gold in the 400 individual medley already in hand, the quest officially ended in the 400 freestyle relay with the Americans settling for bronze. Phelps added another bronze the following night, relegated to the podium's third step by Ian

Thorpe and Pieter van den Hoogenband in the 200 free. He still rallied to take home six golds, including the completion of the IM sweep by winning the 200 and wins in the 100 and 200 butterfly events. In the shorter butterfly race, he faced his stiffest individual test of the six golds, courtesy of a familiar face.

Four years prior at the Sydney Games, the American men's team was one of the youngest in decades and, in a rare occurrence, featured more youth than the women's squad. The figurehead for that youth was Phelps, who qualified in the 200 fly to become the youngest American male Olympic swimmer in 68 years. But while he was finishing fifth in his only event of the Sydney Games, other teens were making waves for the Americans. Some, like 18-year-old Klete Keller, a bronze medalist in the 400 free, and 19-year-old Eric Vendt, a silver medalist in the 400 IM, would become mainstays on the national team for the better part of the next decade. Also among that group were 17-year-old backstroke phenom Peirsol, who earned silver in the 200 back in Sydney, and 18-year-old butterflier Crocker, just outside the medals in the 100. Because of their overlapping specialties, Crocker and Phelps would find themselves in constant competition over the next two Olympic cycles.

The irony in the matchup was that they represented near polar opposites in their approach to the sport. Both were extremely driven and magnificently talented racers. But Phelps, under the tutelage of club coach Bob Bowman, had a meticulously scripted choreography, day to day, year to year, of goals they sought to accomplish. The image of Crocker that was lodged in the minds of most before Athens was the *Swimming World* magazine cover of Crocker, strumming a guitar while leaning up against his prized possession, a 1971 Buick Riviera. Crocker's personality, his penchant for the music of Bob Dylan, and his out-of-the-way upbringing in Portland, Maine, were distinctly different from the path taken by most swimmers. Nonetheless, he was positioned as the most likely individual to upset the quest of Phelps. His *Swimming World* cover story, complete with a double-truck image of Crocker in mid-stroke with the headline "Super Flyer," put him squarely in the sights of Phelps, who hung the poster on his wall as a constant reminder of the competition pushing him toward Athens.

Whatever the methods, the results before Athens were world class, positioning Crocker for what some thought to be a haul of as many as four gold medals. At the 2003 World Championships in Barcelona, he upstaged Phelps in the 100 fly, taking the title and the world record that Phelps had set a day prior. His time of 50.98 seconds was .83 seconds faster than the world record entering the event, which was lowered three times in a space of two days. Crocker hacked more time off that at the 2004 Olympic Trials in Long Beach, California, setting the mark at 50.76 seconds entering the Games. In his senior season at the University of Texas, he also had one of the most memorable NCAA Championships ever in the spring of 2004, knocking almost a second off the short-course world record in the 100 fly and claiming a world record in the 100 free over the short-course discipline. Branching out into the 100 free at Olympic Trials, Crocker rode that wave of momentum into second and an individual berth in the event, in addition to winning the 100 fly, setting himself up for two individual events in Athens and the possibility of two relays, almost assuredly medal winners for the deep American program.

Once in Greece, though, Crocker's Olympic hopes came to a grinding halt. His first swim of the Games came under the bright lights of the finals in the 400 free relay. As the second-place finisher at Trials, Crocker had earned the right to step into the finals squad without having to audition in prelims. He joined Lezak, the winner at Trials, and Neil Walker, the fastest swimmer from prelims, on the team. The fourth selection was a controversial one, with Phelps, who swam a flat-start time of 49.05 in a meet in February, getting the nod over three-time Olympian Gary Hall Jr., whose relay-start split in prelims was 48.73. A jilted Hall started a media firestorm over favoritism toward American darling Phelps. Crocker made sure to render it moot in the finals, though not in the way anyone would've wanted. Suffering from an illness, Crocker's leadoff swim put the Americans dead last in the eight-team field, his time of 50.05 seconds almost a full second slower than his time from Trials and the slowest of the race. Phelps, Walker, and Lezak rallied to salvage a bronze for the Americans, but that hardly mitigated the shock of the Americans' second straight loss in that event. "Well, if somebody had told me Ian Crocker was going to go that slow, there's no way I would have believed it," U.S. coach Eddie Reese, who also coached Crocker at Texas, said of the swim. "He just can't go that slow. Not in my mind, not in his mind."[1] Crocker had the support of his teammates, but it only went so far. "The only thing I said to Ian was 'Good job' and 'Keep your head up,'" Lezak said. "There's nothing really you can say."[2]

There was little else to say after the 100 free, for either Lezak or Crocker. Lezak, who'd emerged as the face of the American sprint program with his decisive win at Trials, was billed as being on the precipice of a major breakthrough. He was in his second Olympic Games, a late bloomer at age 28 and one of the leaders on the American team. His Trials-winning time of 48.17 was a personal best, an American record that stood as the top time in the world in 2004 entering the Games. (Appropriately enough, it would also be the exact time with which van den Hoogenband took home gold in the event.) He showed himself to be in decent form in the 400 free relay, taking the Americans from fourth to second before being overtaken by the irrepressible van den Hoogenband for silver. But the 100 free proved to be an unmitigated disaster for both Crocker and Lezak. Crocker finished the third-to-last preliminary heat an improbable sixth in a time of 49.73 seconds, tying him with

Ukraine's Yuriy Yegoshin for 17th place, .01 seconds off the time of Algerian Salim Iles that earned the 16th and final spot in the semifinals. Lezak, swimming in the fourth lane of the final heat reserved for the top seed, finished an incomprehensible fifth, his time of 49.87 seconds 1.7 ticks behind his personal best, consigning him to 21st and a role as a spectator for the rest of the event. For a nation that had taken 27 medals in the event from the 20 previous Olympics, had 13 times won gold in swimming's signature event, and had never had its best-placed swimmer claim worse than sixth, it was an unqualified disaster. Crocker had the illness to fall back on as an excuse, expressing hope that he'd be better in time for the 100 fly. Lezak individually, and Reese at large, were left more puzzled. "I felt fine," Lezak said. "I just didn't take care of the race part of it and I paid for it."[3] "I don't think any of us know what happened," Reese assessed. "That's not like [Lezak] at all. The 100 free is one of the best events of the meet. We just won't be a part of it."[4]

By the time the sixth day of competition in Athens rolled around, the illness Crocker suffered had finally abated. He was the fastest qualifier in the prelims of the 100 fly and third-fastest from semifinals, just .18 seconds behind Phelps's Olympic record. Victory in the final appeared to be his, as Crocker followed his usual race plan by charging to the lead and trying to hold on for the finish. But he was passed in the final few strokes by Phelps, who touched him out by four-hundredths of a second. Crocker settled for silver, .07 ahead of Ukrainian Andriy Serdinov. A gold medal, it seemed, was not to be for Crocker.

Lezak and Crocker had company in the non-gold-winning ranks on the medley relay foursome, and few had as woe-begotten a story as Hansen. There were elements of similarity to the others, though. Hansen, who had missed out on the 2000 Games by finishing third in both the 100 and 200 breaststroke events at Trials, spent the ensuing four years on a personal mission to ensure that no such disappointment would befall him again. He had been relegated to silver and bronze at the 2003 World Championships, both behind world records of Japan's Kosuke Kitajima. But he'd spent 2004 erasing those marks from the record books, setting world standards in the 100 and 200 at Olympic Trials to become the first American man since John Hencken in the 1970s to simultaneously hold both. But the coronation many expected for Hansen in Athens fell flat on the second night of competition, and controversially so.

Hansen and Kitajima had the Olympic-record pinball between them in prelims and semis, Hansen taking it to the final at 1:00.01. The two went stroke for stroke in the final, Kitajima getting to the wall first in 1:00.08, .17 ahead of Hansen, though well behind the Texas grad's world mark. But something appeared amiss in Kitajima's stroke, a fact evident in real time on the deck in Athens. Replays clearly showed Kitajima utilizing an illegal butterfly kick as part of the pullout from his turn at the 50-meter wall. The infraction was blatant to everyone but the officials, precipitating a firestorm of criticism and finger-pointing from the Americans, led most vociferously by Hansen's teammates. "He knew what he was doing. It's cheating," said Peirsol, Hansen's usually laidback college teammate. "Something needs to be done about that. It's just ridiculous. You take a huge dolphin kick and that gives you that extra momentum, but he knows that you can't see that from underwater. He's got a history of that, and pay attention to it."[5] "He definitely did a dolphin kick," added Lezak. "I just remember the whole crowd doing a little 'aah' when they saw it and then they took it off the camera real quick once they knew that what he did was wrong. This time, they didn't show the replay, but in live time, it was just real obvious."[6] About the only one not up in arms was Hansen, the normally fiery competitor who was dealing with a mix of disappointment in failing to duplicate his best time and the pragmatism of knowing that the 200 breast, arguably his better event, lay ahead. The protests of his teammates, specifically his good friend Peirsol, put him in the awkward position of having to go on the defensive on two fronts. "I don't agree with [Peirsol's] actions because the U.S. is very diplomatic on these sorts of things," Hansen said, while also expressing an appreciation for the gesture, if not the methods, of his fellow Longhorn. "He was a little fired up and he was protecting his teammate, that's all."[7] The ramifications of the "Kitajima kick," as it became known, were so profound as to necessitate a fundamental change in the rules governing breaststroke after the Games.

Hansen at least had the power to change the fate of his Games four days later in the 200 breaststroke. Though there were no improprieties this time, the result was no less disappointing. The cracks were evident starting with prelims, from which Hansen qualified with only the fifth-fastest time. He was faster in the semis, swimming .05 seconds faster than Kitajima, though the Japanese swimmer wasn't pushed en route to an easy win in his heat. In the final, Hansen faded late and couldn't keep pace with Kitajima. Hansen's world record survived Kitajima's assault in a final that he won by over a second, but Hansen had to settle for bronze behind Hungary's Daniel Gyurta. It left Hansen in an all-too-familiar American position: looking to the medley relay as the last chance at gold.

The only participant in the medley relay finals squad for whom that wasn't true was Peirsol. It wasn't all smooth sailing for the backstroker in Athens, though, and about the only thing that separated his admittedly "roller-coaster"[8] ride of a week from the others was that his actually hit the highest of heights. Like his relay mates, Peirsol was riding high as Athens approached. He was something of a backstroke prodigy from a swimming family—his younger sister, Hayley, was a distance freestyle star on the international scene—who surprised many not just by making the 2000 Olympic team but by claiming silver in the 200 back behind countryman Lenny Krayzelburg, the winner of both backstroke golds in Sydney. He embarked on a winning streak after Sydney that brought him into Athens as the unquestioned favorite in both the 100 and 200 back. He'd set his first world record in the latter event in 2002, the first of his 13 individual world marks, and bettered it at Olympic Trials to 1:54.74. He qualified first for the Athens finals in the 100 back and managed to separate himself from a crowded field in the finals to claim gold in 54.06 seconds, fractions off Krayzelburg's world record from the previous Games and three-tenths of a second ahead of Austria's Markus Rogan.

In the 200 back final two days later, Peirsol stamped his authority on the event, setting an Olympic record of 1:54.95 that was just off his world mark en route to winning the final by 2.4 seconds over Rogan. But there was a hiccup in the results, which originally showed Peirsol as disqualified. The ruling by one judge on deck was that Peirsol had inserted an illegal kick while flipping over onto his stomach for a turn, something that Reese identified on the tape as a miniscule flaw. "It's almost something you can't see," Reese told reporters. "To call Aaron on that, you would've had to disqualify the other seven guys in backstroke for the same thing."[9] After deliberation on deck, the disqualification was overturned due to what officials termed an "inadequate" explanation by the official that was "not in the working language of (swimming's governing body) FINA," either French or English.[10] The ruling, which was offered before the Americans could lodge a formal protest, survived challenges by the Austrian federation on behalf of Rogan and the British, who sought to have James Goddard reinstated as the bronze medalist. Rogan, who'd trained in the Washington, D.C., area with the Curl-Burke Swim Club and competed against Peirsol in his college days at Stanford, was under no illusion that he'd been wronged. "I feel like the second-best backstroke swimmer in the world; the best is Peirsol," he said. "I never felt like an Olympic champion; I never accepted it in my heart."[11] Rogan was the one who raised the possibility that retribution for Peirsol's scathing criticism of officials could have played a part in the temporary disqualification. Peirsol, though, thought it better not to be drawn on the question, instead thanking Rogan and the others for their grace and patience in the matter. "Aaron is a very honest person," Rogan said. "I am sure he swam fairly. For a moment, I thought about gold and the idea was just beautiful but, after all, it's fair like this."[12] Rogan added the he was "glad friendship prevailed over politics."[13] Peirsol called it "a weird one, but it happens, even at this level. . . . It turned out the way it probably should have, and I know the guys understand that."[14]

By the time each of the favorites had meandered their way through Athens to the medley relay, there were plenty of question marks. But the redemption narrative hit a potential speed bump in prelims. The American B team of Krayzelburg (fourth in the 100 back), Mark Gangloff (fourth in the 100 breast), Phelps, and Walker qualified with the fastest time by over a second and a half. But the composition of the group was out of the ordinary. Krayzelburg and Gangloff, as the runners-up at Trials and in Athens in the respective 100-meter strokes, were entitled to spots on the prelims team, which would get the same medals as the finals squad. But Crocker's presence presented a conundrum. He was entitled to swim the free leg in prelims as the second-place finisher at Trials and could earn a chance to swim the fly leg in the finals depending on his placement relative to Phelps in Athens. Due to Crocker's illness and the fact that the prelims of the medley relay fell on the same day as the 100 fly final, the decision was made to have Crocker save his strength and eschew the morning relay swim. Walker was drafted in as the fastest 100 free swimmer of the remaining candidates after his performance in the 400 free relay. When Phelps inched ahead of Crocker in the 100 fly final in a reversal of their Trials finish order, the math shifted. Peirsol and Hansen would undoubtedly swim the first two legs, and Lezak retained a claim to the anchor leg. But Phelps, as the gold medalist in the 100 fly, was entitled to swim that leg. That arrangement would mean that Crocker faced the prospect of leaving Athens without a gold medal.

To Phelps, already guaranteed whatever medal his peers got in an event where something catastrophic would need to occur for them to be denied gold, Crocker's predicament was unthinkable. "I felt an odd kinship with the guy behind the poster on my wall," Phelps wrote in his autobiography. "He pushed me. If he hadn't been that good, he couldn't have pushed me that hard. If I didn't respect him as much, I might not have trained that hard in the butterfly."[15] Phelps no doubt drew a parallel in Crocker's struggles with illness in Athens to the debilitating back injury suffered by Phelps's sister, Whitney, which derailed a promising swim career that seemed destined to end in Olympic glory. There was an inherent risk involved, Phelps relinquishing control of his gold-medal fate, especially given Crocker's struggles. For Phelps, though, deferring to his teammate was a no-brainer and turned out to be the moment that defined his Olympics.[16] "It wasn't right," Phelps wrote about Crocker's prospect of leaving without gold. "It just didn't seem fair for a guy who, for as many times as I had looked at his photo, was someone for whom I had developed abundant and profound respect. He was rival and competitor, yes. But also my teammate and my friend."[17] Phelps approached Bowman, an assistant on the U.S. staff, to lobby for the change and give Crocker "another chance."[18] Bowman took the plan to Reese, who called it a "hell of a gesture,"[19] and to U.S. head coach Mark Schubert. Once approved by the hierarchy, Reese told Crocker, who was initially reluctant to make the switch but eventually relented. "I'm kind of speechless," Crocker recounted. "I feel like it's a huge gift that is difficult to accept but it makes me want to just go out and tear up the pool."[20]

Drawing from the eternal spring of optimism that the Games can engender, Hansen recalled after the relay finals, "I had a feeling we were going to do something special."[21] That became evident from the starting gun. Peirsol rectified the one noteworthy omission from his Olympic résumé by opening the race with a world record in the 100 back, clocking in at 53.45 seconds and giving the Americans a cushion of .8 seconds on the field. Hansen was again bested by Kitajima, the Japanese swimmer turning in the fastest split in history at 59.35 seconds. But Hansen was just .02 seconds back with the second-fastest ever, keeping the Americans in the lead by a comfortable margin. Given the edge, Crocker made good on the faith bestowed on him by Phelps, who cheered poolside, waving an American flag. After a start on the precipice of illegality, Crocker uncorked a leg of 50.28 seconds, the fastest split in history, opening up the gap to 2.37 seconds over Japan. Lezak's free split (47.58) was only the second fastest of the heat, .12 seconds behind German anchor Lars Conrad. All that signified was that the American margin of victory in the race for redemption failed to climb over three seconds, the clock stopping at a world record of 3:30.68. The spread back to silver-winning Germany, in a European record of 3:33.62, was 2.94 seconds. The American time amounted to a reduction of almost a second from the world record set by the same squad in Barcelona and a chop of over three seconds from the time used by the Americans to win gold in Sydney four years prior. Along with the first gold medals for the meet, and the first of Hansen's career, the win brought, as *New York Times* correspondent Lynn Zinser put it, "a matched set of relieved smiles."[22]

The celebration needed little explanation between Crocker and Phelps. "He said, 'Congratulations,' and I said, 'Thank you,'" Crocker said of the post-race hug between the teammates and rivals. "He gave me a great opportunity, and I wanted to take advantage of it."[23] For the 11th time in 11 non-boycotted Games, the medley relay gold belonged to the Americans, a string of wins that made the triumph in Athens almost predetermined. In an Olympiad that hadn't gone according to plan for any of the Americans in the race, though, that sense of destiny was understandably muted, no matter the historical component. For the first time in the meet, the pieces came together in the water in the precise manner they were expected to, and the relief for all involved was palpable. "Everything just kind of fell into place tonight," Peirsol said. "It was just a great way to end our meet."[24]

Chapter Six

2004 South African Men's 400 Freestyle

As the sport of swimming hurtled into the 21st century, surprises at major meets no longer became, well, so much of a surprise. The globalization of the sport in the new millennium drastically widened the scope of talent introduced to and developed to elite status in the sport. They weren't regarded as world powers, but suddenly countries from Austria to Zimbabwe had managed to carve out a share of the haul of precious medals.

Where the surprises often stopped, though, was in the relays. A one-off prodigy, an expat who learned swimming in the United States and then wanted to represent his or her country of birth, that was one thing. But to cultivate a foursome of swimmers in the proper specialty or specialties strong enough to dethrone the established powers, the odds were still stacked against upstart programs. In a climate where the U.S. men's teams had claimed 27 of the 31 relay golds contested from World War II to 2000 in non-boycotted Games, sneaking up to snatch an occasional bronze rated a program-defining triumph for most. Having a country's first male gold medal in Olympic history come in a relay, ripped from the wheelhouse of the Americans and the Australians, was almost incomprehensible.

That's exactly what happened in Athens, thanks to a special group of South African sprinters. Their meteoric rise on the international scene made the victory hardly shocking. But the accomplishments of the "Awesome Foursome" of Roland Schoeman, Lyndon Ferns, Darian Townsend, and Ryk Neethling in the 400 freestyle relay in 2004 was nonetheless representative of the global reach of swimming.

To say that South Africa wasn't a traditional swimming nation requires a hefty qualifier: South Africa had its history of swimming success, just never on the international level. The apartheid reign of state-sponsored racial segregation that lasted until the early 1990s made South Africa nation non grata in international diplomatic circles. Among the pressures heaped upon the South African government to encourage it to change its exclusionary ways was a near-total elimination of its sporting prospects by 1977. The International Olympic Committee [IOC] withdrew an invitation for the 1964 Games in Tokyo. When the parties embarked on a path toward readmission for 1968, a boycott threat constructed by a bloc of African nations scuppered plans. By 1970, the South Africans were formally expelled from the IOC, not that that inoculated the Olympic movement from their virulent influence. The boycott du jour in 1976 was fueled by South Africa's sporting affiliation with New Zealand. A similar African bloc as in 1968 petitioned the IOC to expel the Kiwis for agreeing to play South Africa (a non-Olympic member) in a rugby tour (a non-Olympic sport). The movement failed to gain steam thanks to the hesitance of either Cold War power to jump on board, a decision that hampered wide-ranging support on the African continent for the American boycott of the Moscow Games four years later. Seldom has a team that fielded no athletes in the Games so profoundly impacted them as did the South Africans.

Just because the program remained so insular and self-contained, that didn't dent interest in swimming in South Africa. The growth compared to nations able to strive for international medals may have been stunted, but the first swimming stars to emerge from the African continent were South Africans, even if they often had to travel abroad to make an impact. The distinction of being the youngest athlete—not just swimmer—to set a recognized world record belongs to Kimberley native Karen Muir, who posted history's fastest time in the 100-yard backstroke a month and five days before her 13th birthday on August 10, 1965. Muir, an International Swimming Hall of Fame inductee, set 15 world records in a career blighted only by the lack of Olympic hardware. In the 1970s, just 20 days after the Olympics in Montreal, Jonty Skinner set the world record in the 100 free at the U.S. National Championships, a time .55 seconds faster that the gold-winning time of American Jim Montgomery. Skinner went on to the University of Alabama, where he won the 1975 NCAA championship in the 100 free, the first Alabama swimmer to claim an NCAA crown. A 19-time All-American in Tuscaloosa and five-time champ at Nationals, Skinner became a coach with the U.S. National Team, serving in several capacities for 14 years. The South Africans also earned some hardware in the Olympics when eligible to compete from 1904 to 1960. The women's 400 free relay won bronze in 1928 and 1956, Jenny Maakal was third in the 400 free in 1932, while the only gold was Joan Harrison's from the 100 breaststroke in Helsinki in 1952.

What persevered the Olympic ban and made possible the continued growth of swimming were extensive structures for competition in South Africa. That reality was obvious to Cecil Colwin, a native of Port Elizabeth who became one of the world's foremost writers and researchers on competitive swimming. As a coach, Colwin was responsible for stocking the pre-ban South African Olympic teams with talent. Afterward, he had coaching success in Australia and as the national team director for Canada in the 1970s. What Colwin appreciated about his native country was the importance of high school swimming. The South African government placed a premium on fitness, requiring school-age children to participate in athletic activities, and the combination of a favorable climate and ample resources created an environment amenable to the growth of swimming. Government funding of high schools meant that many were equipped with 50-meter pools, and long-established rivalries between schools fed the excitement around the programs. In the absence of the possibility of international meets, the national high school championships represented the pinnacle of competition. The entire system was unfortunately suffused with racial undertones—swimming was seen as a white sport, while the resources thrown at it were alarmingly disproportionate to those devoted to the nation's black Africans—but such was the system of white privilege at the time.

Those developmental avenues allowed the South Africans to keep a baseline level of talent before an agreement was forged in 1991 to readmit them to the Olympic movement for the 1992 Barcelona Games, their first participation in 32 years. There wasn't much to write home about from the Piscines Bernat Picornell, though. Peter Williams, the elder statesman at age 24 for a very young squad, tied for fourth in the 50 free, the only South African to make a final. The two relays fielded by the men, the 400 free and 400 medley, finished 11th and 14th, respectively, and no other South African man made an individual semifinal. The women's draw was only marginally better, with Marianne Kriel advancing to the semis of the 50 free and 100 back before finishing 13th and 10th, respectively. The first post-ban medals came four years later in Atlanta when 21-year-old breaststroke sensation Penny Heyns claimed double gold in the 100 and 200. Kriel added bronze in the 100 back, but the South African men came up empty again. The first South African male Olympic medal was Terence Parkin's silver in the 200 back in Sydney in 2000, where Heyns was forced to settle for bronze in the 100 breast. The medals may not have been there yet, but the progress was clear. The 2000 South African Trials featured 13 national records. Neethling qualified for the 2000 Games in every distance from 100 to 1,500, including a continental record in the 100. He chose to compete in the two longest distances in Sydney, taking fifth for the second straight Games in the 1,500 and finishing eighth over 400 meters. The 400 free relay, sans Neethling, finished 11th, fueled by Schoeman (11th in the 50, 15th in the 100) and Brendon Dedekind (ninth in the 50). Parkin was fifth in the 400 individual medley, while Brett Petersen was seventh in the 100 back.

What really put the South African team over the top, what really brought the program out of a long dormancy, was the ability of an unlikely developmental partner thousands of miles away to achieve that same feat. The University of Arizona had never exactly been a swimming oasis in the desert. There had been glimmers of gold in the past, the Wildcats program incubating American Olympians like George DiCarlo, Peter Evans, Rick DeMont, and Doug Northway. That modesty changed in 1989 when Arizona appointed former Cincinnati coach Frank Busch to the same position. In his 22 years at the helm before becoming the technical director for USA Swimming in 2011, Busch built on the humble success of the past by turning Arizona into a national power. He won two NCAA Championships, finished in the top three at NCAAs four times, and piloted the Wildcats' club team, Tucson Ford Aquatics, to three national titles. Along the way, Busch earned places on the American coaching staffs of the 2004 and 2008 Games. Busch, seen as a long shot to get the job among a pool of applicants that included legendary University of California coach Nort Thornton, guided 63 swimmers to NCAA titles and made Arizona a prime destination for swimming's elite, from America and abroad, looking to advance their craft.

Busch mentored Olympians from a variety of countries, seven at the 2008 Beijing Games alone. One of the richest veins of talent he tapped, though, was from South Africa. Over a stretch of 13 NCAA Championships from 1997 to 2009, a quintet of South Africans led the Wildcats to new heights in a self-perpetuating cycle. Neethling, who represented Arizona from 1996 to 2000, won nine NCAA titles, including sweeps of the 200, 800, and 1,650 frees in his sophomore and junior seasons. The anonymity he enjoyed in Tucson was a welcome departure from the star status he'd attained in South Africa, being named the nation's sexiest man in 2005 and achieving the kind of star status reserved for the likes of Ian Thorpe in Australia.[1] Schoeman, who arrived in 1998, proved to be a late bloomer and didn't win an NCAA title until the 50 free in his senior season in 2002. A gifted athlete who originally was drawn more to athletic endeavors like cricket and rugby, Schoeman only began swimming at age 16 to impress a girl he liked at a local swim club and didn't see his best days until after his college years. Ferns's senior season in 2006 saw him win the 100 fly and take part in a trio of victorious relays. The following year, Florida transfer Townsend won the 200 free, then took the 200 IM crown as a senior as well as taking part in three relays. The last of the group, Jean Basson, won the 500 free as a senior while taking part in the last two editions of a three-year winning streak by the Wildcats in the 800 free relay.

For the team of Neethling, Schoeman, Ferns, and Townsend, the familiarity on two continents helped forge the bonds that would ultimately translate to gold in Athens. They had a blend of veteran talent with Schoeman, who at age 24 was just hitting his peak, and Neethling, who refocused his energies to shorter distances after Sydney and at age 26 was entered in only the 100 free. Complementing that was 20-year-old Ferns and 19-year-old Townsend, who had also qualified for the 200 IM. Their cohesiveness paid dividends from the start in Athens. Where other teams shuttled in members, seeking to use the prelims as tryouts or rest the big guns for a final they were assured of making, the South African relay team was four members and four only.

The biggest leap forward heading into Athens came from Schoeman. Neethling was a known commodity, shifting his area of expertise to extend his career. But Schoeman arrived in Athens with a bitter taste from the 2000 Games. He entered as a medal favorite in both the 50 and 100, the marquee matchup in the former being a reignition of a budding rivalry with American and University of California sprinter Anthony Ervin, who bested him by .01 seconds in the 2000 NCAA Championships. Given the pressure heaped on his shoulders at home and at his home away from home, his 10th- and 15th-place finishes in Sydney precipitated an overhaul of his approach for Athens. Schoeman initially suspected that the lack of power in Sydney might have been the result of overtraining, but he discovered after the Games that he had been competing with a case of mononucleosis. The pressure of the Games, as the face of arguably his nation's most popular team, left him starstruck. Four years later, though, he was much better prepared, physically and mentally. With Busch and DeMont, as an assistant at Arizona, the physical preparation had been optimized, leading to Schoeman turning in two of the top times in the world in the 50 in early 2004. Having Olympic experience lessened the nerves that adversely affected him before, and the comfort with his team-mates helped diffuse some of the pressure. Schoeman had also come to peace with his failures four years prior. His mantra, that "everything happens for a reason," helped shift the perspective of what once were demoralizing short-comings to his advantage. "He's grown up so much as a person," Busch said. "That's the whole difference. Sometimes as an athlete you get caught up in the spectacle of it all. You get caught up in what was behind you and not what is in front."[2]

When the 400 free relay arrived on the Athens Olympics' second day, there was no posturing or gamesmanship from the South Africans in prelims, just fast swimming. They found a gear that no other team had, creating an unusual situation. The South Africans qualified first by winning the first heat in 3:13.84, just .17 seconds off the world record set by the Australian team in Sydney four years prior. Their early speed created a bit of panic for other teams, and the result was the first of two semifinals producing the four fastest times in qualifying, with the United States, Italy, and the Netherlands well back. When Australia finished second in the second heat behind the Russians, the more leisurely pace meant they were 3.8 seconds behind the South Africans. Much of the chaos was wrought by Schoeman, who blistered the leadoff leg with a time of 48.38 seconds. It was the fastest leadoff leg of prelims, the next closest being Rolandas Gimbutis of Lithuania (49.11). Schoeman put himself over a second and a half ahead of American leadoff man Gabe Woodward (49.93), a lead that propelled the squad to the wall 1.99 ticks faster. Of the 64 legs swum by the 16 prelims squads, Schoeman's time was the sixth fastest, a remarkable feat given that the typical head start for a relay pickup compared to Schoeman's flat start is around three-quarters of a second. Two of the five faster splits were turned in by teammates: Ferns in 48.34 and Neethling's anchor of 47.99, the only sub-48 swim. The South Africans had announced themselves as serious medal contenders. A little distraction for their nearest competition put them in prime position to steal gold.

Going into finals, U.S. coach Eddie Reese knew a few things. He knew that the spots of Ian Crocker and Jason Lezak, the Americans who qualified for the individual 100 free, were set in stone. He knew, from pre-Olympics meets, what Michael Phelps was capable of providing to the team. So the decision was made that the prelims of the relay would be a competition for two spots at the most. The cutoff, based on Phelps's personal best, was set at around 48.3 seconds. If two Americans could get under that, Phelps would be displaced from finals. Neil Walker managed the feat, his third leg of 48.16 seconds earning a second swim. But missing that standard were Nate Dusing (49.01 on the second leg) and anchor Gary Hall Jr. (48.73). For the brash Hall, a three-time Olympic relay gold medalist and reigning gold medalist in the 50 who sought to atone for losing the race in Sydney four years prior, the exclusion amounted to a slap in the face. Hall had emphatically celebrated his third-place finish in the event at the Olympic Trials in Long Beach, overcoming a sluggish start to presumably book a relay spot and running into the stands to celebrate with his father, former Olympian Gary Sr.[3] In Athens, though, that swim seemed to be of no consequence. A miffed Hall initially didn't speak to the media but vented his frustrations via agent David Arluck. "Gary is one of the best Olympians of all time," Arluck said. "I can't believe they kept him off the relay for some 19-year-old guy (Phelps) who is going after something that he's not going to accomplish anyway" (referencing Phelps's quest for eight gold medals).[4] When Hall eventually spoke out, after having gained a measure of vindication by winning the 50 free, the bitter disappointment still pervaded. "I felt like I had egg on my face," Hall said. "I very much wanted to be part of the relay that reclaimed that medal."[5] The emphasis for Hall, who could've made many an American relay based on reputation alone, was in the failures of the selection process. He proved himself to be among the top four fastest at Olympic Trials, while Phelps didn't compete in the 100 free in Long Beach, apparently having already staked a weighty claim to a relay spot. "There were no exceptions for anyone else," Hall argued. "No one qualified for the Olympic team in February except Michael Phelps."[6]

Despite Hall's ire, the Phelps choice wasn't the riskiest. Though he'd yet to be tested over 100 meters of freestyle at a major event, Phelps had silenced doubters who thought he'd never become an elite freestyler. Earlier in the night of August 15, Phelps took home bronze in the 200 free, his American record of 1:45.32 just behind Thorpe's Olympic record of 1:44.71 and Pieter van den Hoogenband of the Netherlands in what was widely billed as the race of the century. Instead, the biggest gamble was on 21-year-old Crocker, better known as a butterflier who rode a wave of good form into sudden freestyle prowess. Among his many accomplishments in 2004 was a world short-course record in the 100 free at NCAAs, the capstone accomplishment of his senior season at the University of Texas.

It was clear in the 400 free relay finals that something wasn't right with Crocker. Later termed an illness by Reese, also his coach at Texas, Crocker was the last swimmer to finish the first leg of the relay, his split of 50.05 the only one of the final over 50 seconds. At the other end of the race, Schoeman had thrown down the gauntlet, splitting a lightning-fast 48.17 that opened a gap of .99 seconds on the next-fastest swimmer, Italy's Lorenzo Vismara, and almost two seconds on the Americans in an adjacent lane. The race, it seemed, was over before it could even begin. The rest of the "Sprintboks"—a play on the nickname of the South African rugby team, the Springboks—weren't content to merely defend the margin fostered by Schoeman. Ferns turned in the second-fastest second leg in 48.13, taking another .17 seconds out of the second-place Italians with Filippo Magnini in the water. Phelps split a respectable 48.74, just .01 slower than Hall's morning swim, to spring the Americans up to sixth, though the margin to the high-flying South Africans ballooned to an insurmountable 2.49 seconds. When Townsend hit the water, the other nations finally had a chance to gain. His split of 48.96 seconds was the slowest of the four, though still faster than Italy's Michele Scarica (49.21) to stake Neethling to a 1.43-second bulge after 300 meters. The back-loaded relays of the U.S. and the Netherlands intensified their medal charges. Knowing that the in-form rocket that was van den Hoogenband was primed to launch on the anchor, Klaas-Erik Zwering (48.51) advanced the Dutch from eighth to fourth. The Americans, riding Walker's outstanding leg of 47.97, climbed into third, less than a tenth of a second behind the Italians with Lezak mounting the block.

Gold, which had long since been decided, was finalized by Neethling, who split 47.91 to bring home the South Africans in a world record of 3:13.17. Van den Hoogenband, facing a deficit of .81 seconds to Lezak, churned up water to reverse that, and then some. His sterling time of 46.79, the fastest split in history, took the Dutch past the Americans by .26 seconds and into silver. Lezak, with a 47.86, managed to get by the flagging Christian Galenda (49.08) before being overtaken by "Hoogie" to salvage a medal for the Americans. Galenda, meanwhile, was nearly overtaken by Russian anchor Alexander Popov (48.06) as the Italians and Russians split fourth, 2.68 seconds back of the South Africans, who celebrated the first male gold medal in their country's Olympic history. "This was our day," Schoeman said. "As the movie says, 'Any Given Sunday.' For the relay, I told the guys, this is our Sunday."[7]

The win set off celebrations all over the nation, an unforgettable moment in its swimming history. The elation was compounded three days later when Schoeman came within .06 seconds of doubling his gold count. Instead, his time of 48.23 seconds earned him silver, just behind van den Hoogenband but .23 seconds ahead of Thorpe, who had snuck into the finals with the eighth-fastest time. A mere .07 seconds but seven lanes from Thorpe in the final was Neethling, who nearly stole a medal from Lane 1 but settled for fourth, not that he was terribly disappointed with the time of 48.63. "I've said all along that I've got to be satisfied with my best time," Neethling said. "I learned that lesson in Sydney. I'm going to have to be satisfied with the gold I already have."[8] With Schoeman the only 100 free medalist also contesting the 50, he inherited the mantle of favorite in swimming's hectic splash and dash. For Schoeman, the consummate underdog, the change in narrative caused an adjustment. "I never consider myself to be the favorite in any event," he said. "I always consider myself the underdog."[9] He qualified fastest from semis in 21.99 seconds but was a hair off that time in finals, settling for bronze in 22.02 seconds, behind Hall (21.93) and Cal-educated Croat Duje Draganja (21.94).

The Athens triumph reverberated throughout the country and had a profound impact on the trajectory of South Africa's swimming program. Schoeman, a fixture on the World Cup circuit, parlayed his success into golds in the 50 free and 50 fly at the 2005 World Championships in Montreal, as well as silver in the 100 free, a spot ahead of Neethling, who also took bronze in the 200 free. Though the South African contingent was shut out of the medals in Beijing in 2008, the system spit out Olympic champions for the 2012 London Games, including 100 breaststroke world-record holder Cameron van der Burgh and 200 fly gold medalist and 100 fly silver winner Chad Le Clos. Competing alongside them in London was 32-year-old Schoeman, who cited national pride in shaking off big-money overtures to compete for Qatar in the latter stages of his career. Schoeman had finaled in both Beijing and London in the 50 as well as piloting South African 400 free relay squads to finals in each meet. The gold won in 2004 remains among the greatest sporting accomplishments in South Africa's history. "It's been unbelievable," Neethling recalled in 2006. "I think anything I tell you, you really have to be here and have to see it to understand the impact that it has had on the country. Even now, when I go around the country, people still talk about it, together with the World Cup rugby (title won in 1995), as being one of the greatest sporting moments in South African history since we were allowed back into international competition. When we were swimming we had no idea that it was going to have that kind of impact."[10]

The 400 free relay stood as the crowning achievement of the sterling legacy left by the South Africans in Athens, such a stirring performance as to render the other circumstances of the final secondary. The Phelps-Hall debate, for one, had become moot. Replacing Phelps's relay swim with Hall's fastest Olympic split—a leg of 47.45 from the Atlanta Games eight years prior, a degree of speed it's highly doubtful the 29-year-old still possessed—wouldn't have changed the outcome. Likewise, replacing Crocker's terrible swim with his time from Trials, 49.06, wouldn't have swayed the fate of gold, though it could've made the difference between bronze and silver. (Crocker, in 49.73, and Lezak, in 49.87, were 17th and 21st in the 100 free, failing to qualify for the semifinals, a historic failure in an event that was long a hallmark for the Americans.) Also washed away by the South African achievement was the dazzling fiasco of an Australian team that returned half of the 2000 gold-winning squad—including Thorpe and former 100 free world-record holder Michael Klim—and finished a puzzling sixth.

What shone most vividly from the Olympic Aquatic Centre was how impressively the South Africans had won the gold, not how others had lost it. In a testament to their fortitude, as individuals and as a team, all four members of the Sprintboks significantly improved their times from prelims. Schoeman and Ferns each went .21 seconds faster in the evening than in prelims, while the margins for Townsend (.17) and Neethling (.08) were more slight. Taken together, though, it amounted to a drop of .67 seconds, getting them under the Aussies' world record by precisely a half second. The only squad that went unchanged from prelims to finals, they managed to extract a little extra speed from each member, not relying on a big gun like van den Hoogenband or Popov to tip the balance with just one leg. Lezak, in assessing his squad's shortcomings, illustrated just how vital a point that was. "We didn't overlook them at all," he said. "If you put all of our best swims together, we have a world record. It's all about coming together as a group of four and putting it all together."[11] Lezak didn't come out and say it, but then he didn't have to: Beyond a doubt, no squad at the 2004 Olympics put together the pieces like the South Africans.

Chapter Seven

2008 U.S. Men's 400 Freestyle

The summer of 2008 was undoubtedly the summer of Michael Phelps. On the back of Phelps's quest for 8 in '08, swimming vaulted into the media spotlight at the Beijing Games, and the drama in the Water Cube exceeded the imaginations of even the most optimistic media executives. What once was reserved for pool decks and the insular, specialized world of swimming folks was suddenly must-see television, watercooler talk, and a source of national pride.

So monumental was Phelps's quest that it's impossible to separate a single moment from the Games as the defining instant of the defining week of swimming's new—and arguably finest—era. But one stands out for a simple fact: for just a hair over 46 seconds on August 11, 2008, Phelps stood powerless on deck, his race swum, a spectator like the rest of us as his spot in history was decided. By eight-hundredths of a second—a margin Phelps would later make look gargantuan—Phelps's quest for eight gold medals survived, on the back of a world record authored by the team of Garrett Weber-Gale, Cullen Jones, and the irrepressible Jason Lezak. How that team got to overcome the challenge of France is a tale of controversy, near misses, and plenty of drama. How it ended, though, was courtesy of a team performance far superior to what seemed possible from the sum of its parts.

The biggest obstacle in describing the accomplishments of Phelps is often brevity. The youngest American male Olympic swimmer in 68 years when he qualified for the 200 butterfly in Sydney in 2000, the Beijing Games represented his third Olympics. He's the youngest man ever to break a world record, one of his record-setting 39, including 29 individual. He ventured into a brief hiatus from his storied career after the 2012 Olympics as the most decorated Olympian, regardless of gender or sport, in history, with 22 medals, 18 gold, not to mention 26 world championships. After finishing fifth in the 200 fly in Sydney, he left Athens with six gold medals and two bronze, seen by some as a disappointment. The bronze in the 400 freestyle relay, behind South Africa and the Netherlands, proved to be a blessing in disguise, prematurely cutting short Phelps's quest to better Mark Spitz's tally of seven gold medals from the 1972 Olympics and alleviating that pressure.

When he sought a feat of Spitzian proportions in 2008, the 400 free relay again presented itself as a potential stumbling point. By that time, it had become pretty clear that Phelps was in a class by himself. That didn't make him a swimming snob, though, hesitant to have his fate tied to inferior swimmers—a good thing, since peers of his caliber were scarce. Part of it owed to the fact that there existed such a gulf between Phelps's specialties, like the 200 butterfly and individual medleys, and the legs swum by most relay swimmers. Phelps's ability to excel at both testified to his range, but it also meant that the instances where he competed directly against his eventual relay teammates were few and far between. The other part, though, was Phelps's innate magnetism to team sports. From an early age, he'd developed a spectator's interest in team sports like football and basketball, while some of his first forays into competitive sports, like many a Maryland kid, came on the lacrosse field. In many ways, Phelps regarded the relays, the events that fell outside his meticulous control, as "the funnest events."[1] On occasions like the 400 free relay in Beijing, Phelps had a habit of viewing the team not as four individuals, but as one cohesive unit.

A unified front is exactly what the American relay needed. The program found itself in the unusual position of an Olympic drought, having not owned the 400 free relay title since 1996. In 2000, home-pool advantage helped the Australians lay claim to the title in Sydney, behind the world-record speed of Michael Klim, the churning kick of Ian Thorpe, and the desire to silence the trash-talking of Gary Hall Jr. and the Americans. Four years later, some American disharmony, with Phelps and Hall at the epicenter, opened the door for a historic triumph by the South Africans. No American had held the world record in the 100 free since Alexander Popov took Matt Biondi's mark in 1994. The shortest Olympic relay seemed the most accessible, the easiest to gain proficiency in for a passel of nations queuing up to colonize the fringes of the contracting American swimming empire. Going into 2008, the Australians continued to churn out top-flight freestyle talent, though tending more toward the shorter distances than in the past. The South African team that reigned in 2004 remained a fixture on the World Cup circuit. The two-time reigning World Champion in the 100 free, Filippo Magnini, turned Italy into an instant contender. And any Dutch squad that featured Peter van den Hoogenband couldn't be easily discounted.

Then there were the French. Hardly a traditional swimming power, the French had enjoyed limited success in the Olympics. Their only men's relay medal of the modern era was a bronze from back in 1948. The 400 free team in 2004 finished seventh, just behind a supremely disappointing Australian effort that featured Thorpe, Klim, and eventual 100 free world-record holder Eamon Sullivan. The lone French male medal of those Games was bronze in the 100 breaststroke for Hugues Duboscq. Save for a Duboscq bronze in the 100 breast, the French men were shut out of the 2005 World Championships, too. They yielded the same total from the 2007 Worlds, a bronze in the 400 free relay thanks to the team of Fabien Gilot, Frederick Bousquet, Julien Sicot, and Alain Bernard. Bousquet, a standout at the University of Auburn, was at the forefront of the program's development, making waves when in 2005 he became the first swimmer to cover 50 yards in under 19 seconds. At the 2008 European Championships in Eindhoven, though, the program truly emerged from the dark ages, and seemingly from out of nowhere. Bernard won the 50 and 100 frees, the latter in world-record time, while Amaury Leveaux finished second to Germany's Paul Biedermann in the 200 free. In June of that year, the team of Leveaux, Bernard, Gilot, and Bousquet set a European record in the 400 free relay and came within .08 seconds of the world record set by the Americans at the 2006 Pan Pacific Championships. It didn't instantly make France the new world power on the block, but combined with Laure Manaudou's three medals in the women's draw in Athens, it sufficed to get a buzz going about the French program.

On the other side of the Atlantic, there were plenty of reasons to worry about the Americans' prospects in Beijing. Phelps would be there for sure. But the composition of the remainder of the team was a quandary. The 33-year-old Hall, so long a fixture of the Americans' supreme relay depth, chose to focus on qualification for the 50 free. Ian Crocker, whose poor leg in 2004 due to illness plus a false start in the medley relay at the 2007 Worlds gave him at best a checkered relay past, passed on the 100 free to focus on the 100 butterfly and his rivalry with Phelps. Veterans like Lezak, Neil Walker, and Gabe Woodward brought name recognition and international experience, but that wouldn't get the Americans to the wall any faster. A changing of the guard was imminent, and the outlook entering Olympic Trials in Omaha was guarded, bordering on bleak.

Some rays of hope shone through in Omaha. Phelps, swimming prelims as essentially a time trial to book his place, clocked in with the second-fastest time at 47.92 seconds before scratching from the semifinals. Despite an iffy semis swim, Weber-Gale turned in two sub-48-second swims, the fastest his prelim time, an American record of 47.78, before winning the final in 47.92 seconds. The second spot in the individual event went to Lezak, who trailed Weber-Gale by .13 in the finals. But the talk of the event, if not the Trials at large, was the American-record time of 47.58 he posted in the semis, just eight-hundredths off Bernard's world record. With Jones, Nathan Adrian, and Ben Wildman-Tobriner also clocking in under 48.6, there was a ready arsenal of young guns to shoot for the fourth spot.

The Americans' newfound optimism did little to quell the surge of confidence from the French. That soon boiled over into a stream of bulletin-board quotes in the media. Echoing the braggadocio of Hall in Sydney that the Americans would "smash [the Australians] like guitars," Bernard issued the same promise to the Americans. "The Americans? We're going to smash them," Bernard sniped. "That's what we came here for."[2] That bluster represented the latest in a line of big talk from Bernard, who installed himself as the favorite for the 100 free as well. The hubris of the French wasn't completely incongruous with the country's swimming accomplishments, both for the group in Beijing and the program as a whole. But it made Bernard's declaration that he would skip prelims and unquestionably start his Olympics in the final of the relay somewhat absurd, especially from a program not far removed from needing its big guns just to qualify for an Olympic final. Bousquet later recalled the covert plan in great detail, hoping that the Americans would better the world record in prelims, making a finals triumph by the French all the more monumental.[3] With the results of Olympic Trials cementing Phelps's quest for eight golds and swimming immortality, the relay was made more pivotal as an early stumbling block, predicted by many as the most daunting of the eight to win.[4]

Even before the events in Beijing began, the three Americans assured to be part of the final—Lezak, Weber-Gale, and Phelps—began preparing. Much of the group's growth was fostered by Lezak. At age 32, no one had to tell him that this was potentially his last shot at Olympic hardware. His trophy case was hardly empty, including the obligatory medley relay golds from Sydney and Athens that come with being among the top eight swimmers in America. But missing from the group was any individual Olympic accolade, while silver and bronze reminders of the stinging failures in the 400 free relays of the last two Games also served to fuel his competitive fire. Beyond the quest for revenge, there was something different in Lezak as he readied to Beijing, something his teammates easily picked up on. "He was more relaxed and more social this year than I had ever seen him before," Phelps wrote in his autobiography. "It was obvious that he was appreciating what we had this time, and unbelievable sense of team and of camaraderie."[5] Lezak was certainly relishing the role as a leader and as the elder American male statesman. But something else was also at play, according to longtime coach Dave Salo. There was no doubting Lezak's determination, as he essentially coached himself to Beijing, swimming 90 minutes a day after electing not to follow Salo's move from the Irvine Novaquatics club to the University of Southern California. But the enigmatic and soft-spoken Lezak was finally renowned as the cornerstone of the American sprint program, freed from the long shadow of Hall, with whom he'd had a less than amiable past. So long "his cross to bear,"[6] in Salo's words, the absence of Hall in Beijing had a liberating effect on Lezak. Where others, among them medley relay prelims participant Matt Grevers and 800 free relay contender Ricky Berens, admitted to being nervous about playing such a major role in Phelps's search for history, Lezak had the veteran know-how to be immune from such concerns.[7] Just before the Olympics opened, Phelps and Lezak convened a swimmers-only meeting, sharing memories of past failures and triumphs and putting forth goals for Beijing. Unsurprisingly, at the forefront of that list was returning the Stars and Stripes to the 400 free relay throne.[8] For all the hype surrounding him at the Games, that type of swimming solidarity was what most impacted Phelps in Beijing. "The sense of togetherness on this 2008 U.S. men's Olympic swim team will forever be one of my great memories from Beijing," Phelps said. "In the pool, we had to compete. Outside of it, we were not just teammates but brothers. Every single one of us."[9]

That Red, White, and Blue resolve would be tested early and often in Beijing, as Phelps began the meet with a decisive win in the 400 IM, distancing himself from the challenge of countryman Ryan Lochte on the first night of competition to mine gold number 1. The following session, it was made clear just how heated the relay promised to be. The American "B" team of Adrian, Jones, Wildman-Tobriner, and Grevers laid claim to a world record in 3:12.23, Jones's split of 47.61 seconds earning him the fourth spot on the finals squad. Within two-tenths of that time, also under the deposed world record, were the French squad of Leveaux, Gregory Mallet, Boris Steimetz, and Bousquet and the Australian foursome of Andrew Lauterstein, Leith Brodie, Patrick Murphy, and Matt Targett. (The top six teams in prelims were all under the winning time from the 2004 finals, and only a second and a half separated teams 1 and 8). There would be substantial changes for each team entering finals, but the Olympic record of 47.76 by Leveaux off the front of the French team and Bousquet's 46.63-second anchor leg, the fastest in history, made the prospect of adding Bernard to that group terrifying. A winner seemed almost impossible to choose. "How many times have I broken this down in the two weeks? Every time I do it, it comes out France," NBC commentator Rowdy Gaines said on the broadcast. "The Americans are certainly capable of doing it. . . . [The Americans and Australians] each have to have the perfect race to be able to beat the French."[10] In the quest for any advantage, there was trash talk on the bus over to the Water Cube before the final, and the French unsurprisingly believed that they owned the psychological advantage. "They didn't look at us, although they usually do," Bousquet recounted. "We could sense that they were a little bit afraid."[11]

What unfolded August 11 in Beijing was arguably the greatest race in swimming history on certainly its biggest stage, a race that Phelps, on the first page of the prologue to his autobiography, glowingly described as "the most amazing, thrilling, exciting, supercharged swimming race ever, an instant classic if ever there was one."[12] There was no doubt, after the reserves threw down the gauntlet in prelims, that it would take a world record to win (and that anyone harboring aspirations of a medal of any color should be near the existing world mark). What wasn't necessarily expected was that an additional world record would come via Sullivan, who turned in a 47.24-second leadoff leg to authoritatively chase Bernard's record. Phelps was just .01 off Bernard's mark, setting an American record in 47.51. Leveaux, meanwhile, put the French fourth after 100 meters, thanks to his time of 47.91 and a surprisingly fast Canadian record swim from Brent Hayden (47.56). The French were back into second place at the halfway point, with Gilot (47.05) and Weber-Gale (47.02) producing almost identical splits and capitalizing on Lauterstein's comparatively pedestrian 47.87. The fate of gold appeared to turn when Bousquet improbably matched his prelim performance to the hundredth of a second, another 46.63. The anticipated American weak link Jones turned in a 47.65, more than respectable, but it still saddled Lezak with a deficit of .59 seconds going up against a newly displaced world-record holder in Bernard. However fleetingly, the enormity of the task entered Lezak's mind. "I saw how far ahead [Bernard] was, and it crossed my mind for a split second: There's no way," Lezak said. "[But] this is the Olympic Games. I'm representing the United States of America." [13]

That representation of his country turned out to be one for the ages. Bernard did his bit, with what would go down as the third-fastest split in history at 46.73 seconds. If the 25-year-old made one mistake, though, it was that he hugged the lane line separating the U.S. in lane four and France in five. That allowed the veteran Lezak to ride his draft and stalk him through the first 50. Just after surfacing off the turn, Lezak made his move, gobbling up the deficit between the two with his trademark, big-hitched stroke as Bernard noticeably tightened up. The two hit the wall just about simultaneously, Bernard gliding longer to the wall while Lezak thrust his hand forward at full speed, absolutely nailing the finish. When the scoreboard blinked to life, it read in favor of the Americans, a world record 3:08.24, a scant eight-hundredths ahead of the French. "I had no words. I had only screams," said Phelps, posing for his first of many iconic images of that Games with a Stars-and-Stripes-clad Weber-Gale, each straining every sinew of their bodies in exultation with the delirious Water Cub. "Because this was not about me. It was epic. Of course I had won a gold medal, and that was the goal. But this was about something way bigger than any personal accomplishment. We swam together, competed together, four as one, together, as a team and as Americans." [14] When the clamor died down and the math was done, the realization dawned that Lezak split a 46.06, the fastest ever authored, and by a mind-boggling margin of over a half second. The swim was easily over a second faster than the world record from a flat start (a gargantuan margin when you consider the standard measure of the relay start advantage is only around seven-tenths). Compared to Lezak's personal-best flat-start time, the rocketed relay leg was over a second and a half faster. "I was going to have to swim out of my mind," a disbelieving Lezak said. "I had more adrenaline going than I've ever had in my life."[15] The swim did much more than merely reinforce Lezak's long-standing reputation as one of the sport's best relay anchors; it turned a richly deserved spotlight on a swimmer so long respected by his peers but lacking recognition from the general sporting public. "I just happened to have the swim of my life at the right time," said Lezak.[16]

The rest of Phelps's search for eight gold medals is well-documented history. He had little trouble setting world records in the 200 fly, the 200 IM, and the 400 IM. The 800 free relay with Berens, Lochte, and Peter Vander-kaay turned into another world-record romp. The only thing that could possibly upstage Lezak's swim came when Phelps outtouched Milorad Cavic by .01 seconds, the smallest recognized margin at the international level, in the 100 fly to keep the pursuit of history alive. His dominance in Beijing was capped by another relay, a surprisingly tight medley relay victory over Australia keyed by Phelps's fly leg and brought home by none other than Lezak, this time in a more mortal 46.76. When Lezak struck out on his own, he garnered a bronze medal from lane 7 in the 100 free, tying Brazilian Cesar Cielo in 47.67 seconds. He was well behind Bernard's golden time of 47.21, one-hundredth off the world record the Frenchman had set in the semis, and slower than Sullivan's silver-worthy 47.32. Bernard added bronze in the 50 free, where Leveaux claimed silver behind Cielo.

The enduring legacy from Beijing was Phelps's unprecedented medal haul, but the popular caveat was that it only came to fruition thanks to Lezak's heroics. Therein lay the central paradox to Phelps's Games—that what was regarded as arguably the single greatest individual achievement in the history of sports was only salvaged by a team. "Swimming is so often an individual sport, with swimmers going straight ahead, but the relays and the elaborate machinations for choosing teams for preliminaries and finals, are a team sport," wrote the *New York Times'* George Vecsey. "On Monday morning, Michael Phelps swam a 47.51 first leg, but he was part of a team. The team helped to pull him through, to keep him in contention for the medal chase he will not, cannot, acknowledge, but which is the biggest thing in these first few days of the Summer games."[17]

Phelps's dependence on Lezak and company led to the faulty reasoning of reciprocity, that somehow the thought spurring Lezak to so impressively exceed expectations in the relay was of Phelps's fate. The ability to brag about a front-row seat to history wasn't what swimmers strove for decades to achieve, and it certainly wasn't worth surrendering a chance at the glory they sought. No one on the American team required Phelps to provide a boost to drive them toward their best; the weight of the Olympic stage, as it had always been, provided plenty of impetus. "Michael knows we didn't do it for him," Lezak said. "He was just a part of it, and we were part of it. Whether he wins eight gold medals or not, it wasn't going to be our responsibility for that to happen."[18] Aaron Peirsol, who led off the medley relay victory and spent a decade as a national-team fixture alongside Phelps, with whom he roomed in Sydney in 2000 when both were mere teenage upstarts, perhaps summarized it best. "We absolutely respect and admire Michael's goals, but the feeling on the team is that by no means does one man come first," he said. "No one here is racing for second place, even the guys racing Mike. The feeling on our team is, we're all racing to win. He's doing exceptionally well; we're all rooting for him. But by no means is he the only one we're rooting for."[19] The chance to be part of something special was independent of Phelps's presence (though it certainly didn't hurt), and that was enough for the world-class swimmers assembled. "I've never been a part of something that is so historic," Weber-Gale said. "You represent the hopes and dreams of Americans all over the place. What we did, people get really excited about."[20] The unbridled joy that Lezak felt with gold around his neck proved just how special the moment was, no matter who else was standing next to him on the top step of the podium. "I can't even explain it, it was unreal," he said. "I've been a part of the two teams at the last two Olympics that came out behind, and I think I wanted it more than anybody, not just for myself, but to show that we are the nation to be beat in that relay."[21]

The misapprehensions about the mind-set of the relay, however, don't discredit the simple fact that the squad was one of the greatest ever assembled. That distinction far exceeds the simple calculus of being the fastest ever; each Games seems to have plenty of those, a yardstick of the last four years in swimming progress. What made the U.S. squad special was the ability to rise to a challenge, a gauntlet that, thanks to Phelps's presence and the recent stumbles by the program, had been thrown down for all of them. To weather the storm of scrutiny and strenuous pressure around them, they would have to come together in a way few relays ever had. Phelps recalled Weber-Gale's role in facilitating that just before they went on deck at the Water Cube: "This, he said, is not a 4 × 100 relay, four guys each swimming a 100. There's nothing here about swimming a leg individually. This is a 400 relay; we're all together. We're all going to be one. He said we have to prepare ourselves to go out there and kick it."[22] That's how they swam, and that's how they entered the pantheon of swimming immortality.

Chapter Eight

2012 French Men's 400 Freestyle

When Michael Phelps turned pro in 2001, hot on the heels of becoming the youngest world-record holder in male swimming history, he set out a simple mission statement: To transform the way the sport was seen across the world. With three Olympics and over a decade remaining in his career, there was no way that Phelps could know at age 16 that his success in spreading the gospel of swimming could impinge on his ability to collect medals in the pool.

Indeed, the climate of swimming had changed markedly by the time Phelps prepared for his supposed swan-song Olympics in London in 2012. The duopoly of the U.S. and Australia had weakened thanks to the diffusion of swimming power to nations like China, South Africa, and Brazil. Not only had the resources and attention devoted to swimming greatly increased, but they had also become less concentrated in just a select handful of nations. Where the U.S. still retained its unquestioned grasp on the top spot, thanks to depth cultivated by decades of meticulous development of the age-group system and collegiate competition, the deficit to the next group of would-be powers had not only been narrowed, but it seemed there were more pursuers than ever.

By the time Phelps briefly stepped away from the sport in 2012, he'd traveled to four Olympic Games, each featuring a men's 400 freestyle relay champion from a different continent. From the neutral perspective, then, there was something oddly symbolic about Phelps and the long-dominant Americans not winning the first relay of what was anticipated as the final meet of his career, instead being displaced by the first relay gold in French swimming history. Dubbing them the face of a new era of swimming may be too much to put on the shoulders of Amaury Leveaux, Fabien Gilot, Clement Lefert, and Yannick Agnel. But there's a convincing case that they may be at the forefront of one of the most wide-open, democratized ages the sport has ever seen.

France's Olympic swimming history makes for light reading. Prior to 2008, the French program had yielded a total of 26 medals from 25 swimming competitions, 17 garnered by male participants. The vast majority of those came prior to World War II, in events like underwater swimming and in pools that were generally roped off portions of oceans or tidal basins, archaic conditions by modern standards. In the modern era, French men accounted for just 12 medals, seven in freestyle events. The only Frenchman to win Olympic gold between the Second World War and 2008 was 400 freestyler Jean Boiteux in 1952. Not until Laure Manaudou's three-medal haul in 2004 did a French woman win gold. There were brief glimmers of international notoriety for the French—Jean Taris was among the world's best distance freestylers between the two World Wars, and Stephan Caron won bronze medals in the 100 free in back-to-back games in 1988 and 1992. There were some pockets of stroke talent, like 1992 Olympic bronze medalist in the 200 butterfly Franck Esposito, backstroker Simon Dufour, and Hughes Duboscq in the breaststroke. But droughts were more the rule than the exception. Alain Mosconi's bronze in the 400 free in 1968 was the only male medal for France from 1956 to 1980. Shutouts in 1996 and 2000 were only assuaged by Duboscq's bronze in the 100 breast in 2004. The four biennial FINA World Championships held from 2001 to 2007 produced just four French male medals, though two were bronzes in the 400 free relay in 2003 and 2007. When Alain Bernard burst onto the scene at the 2008 European Championships in Eindhoven by claiming the sprint double, including a world record in the 100 free, his pair of gold medals doubled the total won by French men at the previous four continental championships combined. The results didn't exactly indicate that a swimming renaissance was brewing.

What was bubbling beneath the surface, though, was a concentrated growth of one program, sprint freestyle. There was nine-time All-American Romain Barnier, who starred at Auburn University in the United States. He was followed there by Frederick Bousquet, whose 21 All-American selections included the honor of being the first man to break 19 seconds over 50 yards of free, an honor that highlighted the 2005 NCAA Championships. Despite the attraction of some to the American system, the real lightning rod for change was a name few outside the world of swimming knew: Claude Fauquet. After the massive disappointment of a complete medal blanking over both genders in Atlanta, Fauquet was brought in as the national team's technical director. His approach, known as the "Fauquet Method," involved a comprehensive overhaul of the systems that had so long underserved the program. Gone was the tendency to coddle athletes in their development. By streamlining the coaching hierarchies and club structures, Fauquet's maneuverings made it easier for coaches to focus attention on transforming the talented into world elites. His lack of sentimentality for anything less than the best was evident in his desire to replace old with new.

The centerpiece of the system was nine "Poles Frances," state-of-the-art training centers dotting the country aimed at providing French swimmers similar training and equipment with which to fulfill their potential as afforded their counterparts around the world. To feed the system, which relied on a combination of public funds, private contributions, and government subsidies, Fauquet also established 29 centers for young swimmers to identify promising prospects at a young age. The results weren't immediate, but many of the French swimmers who eventually populated major event podiums had the fingerprints of Fauquet's method on them. Manaudou, for example, trained at a center in Melun, on the outskirts of Paris. Bernard's star arose from a club in Marseille, while the Olympic Nice Natation club developed 2012 London standouts Camille Muffat and Agnel. The changes, even over a relatively short period, were obvious to those involved. "An entire new generation of French swimmers is doing well," Agnel said in 2013, with a hint of irony as he moved his training base to Phelps's old club, North Baltimore Aquatic. "We train really hard by putting in lots of kilometers in our practice sessions. I hope the French are proud of what we are doing. . . . I see a lot of children getting attracted to competitive swimming. I hope more people discover that though there's a lot of hard work involved, it is a really fun sport."[1] The sentiment was echoed by a jubilant Bernard after setting two world records in as many days at the 2008 Euros. "I believe in my group, I believe in my coach," he said. "The French team is getting stronger and stronger. I'm happy to be one of the leaders."[2]

The rise to prominence by the French freestyle program was anything but smooth, and the bumps in the road were hardly subtle. Before the French ascended to the standing of champions in 2012, they had to first fulfill the role of the jilted, naively overconfident upstart four years prior. The French felt assured they would be the ones to tear asunder Phelps's quest for eight gold medals in 2008. After the team of Leveaux, Gilot, Bousquet, and Bernard (with a 47.27-second anchor leg) set a European record and buzzed within .08 seconds of the world mark in the summer of 2008, the French contingent was deservedly buoyant about their medal chances in Beijing. Hostilities broke out, however, when Bernard—in homage to the ill-fated guarantee by American sprinter Gary Hall Jr. that his squad would "smash" the Australian team in Sydney "like guitars"—promised that his French squad would "smash" the Americans.[3] Instead of triumphing, the French played the foil in one of swimming's greatest dramas. A tense prelims heat saw the American B team, from which only Cullen Jones was held over for finals, set a world record, followed closely by the French (.13 seconds back in a European record) and the Australians (.18 back), all three squads getting under the existing world mark. The finals started with Eamon Sullivan of

Australia setting a world record in the 100 free, and they looked destined to end with the French triumphing. Despite Phelps setting an American record off the front, a time just .01 away from Bernard's displaced world mark, an insane split of 46.63 by Bousquet gave the French a seemingly insurmountable lead of .59 seconds, with Bernard, the ace in the hole, waiting to dive in. Instead, American Jason Lezak ruined the party, storming back with the fastest relay split in history at 46.06, to claim gold ahead of Bernard (with the third-fastest split at 46.73). By eight-hundredths of a second, the French were denied.

It quickly became evident that the French program wasn't a one-and-done, lightning-in-a-bottle generation. There were very notable positives to build from in Beijing. For one, the total of six swimming medals for the French men equaled the total of the previous 10 Olympiads combined. Bernard charged back to reclaim his 100 free world record from Sullivan, though the Aussie took it back one semifinal heat later. Ultimately, Bernard got to the wall first in the final for gold, and he added a bronze in the 50 free, a spot behind Leveaux. Those medals helped mitigate what could've been a devastating loss. "Alain is wounded," Fauquet said after the relay silver. "When you are the last swimmer in a relay and that you have the opportunity to bring a title of this importance to your country, you don't get out of this unhurt. But I don't think that Alain lost the race. It's Lezak who won it."[4] The Lezak loss forced the French to confront a new step in their development, the ability to cope with the pressure of the world stage. The lower rungs of the ladder had proven easy to climb, but individually and collectively, the final steps would require much more effort and dedication. "Bernard is a champion, but he has to learn how to deal with defeat and, when he has learned that, to spring back," Fauquet said. "That is the sign of a champion."[5]

A relay that arrived in Beijing with controversy understandably left with plenty of questioning in its wake. In May 2009, Bousquet revealed that not everything had gone according to plan in Beijing. With a brashness borne of a decade training in the United States, the tattooed sprinter refused to mince words when it came time to assigning blame: "I'm holding my federation responsible for the loss."[6] Bousquet disclosed that the French swimmers had devised an order for the relay only to see it abruptly changed. The plan was to use Leveaux to lead off given his outstanding starts, followed by Bernard, partially to get the French into clean water as the leaders and to shield Bernard from knowing if Sullivan, who would undoubtedly lead off for the Australians, was successful in downing his 100 free record. That plan positioned Bousquet, then age 27 and by far the most internationally experienced of the squad, as the anchor. "My teammates said 'We trust you. You have the experience and you know how to race the U.S. guys,'" explained Bousquet.[7] The French coaches, though, intervened and altered the order, putting Bernard on the anchor. To Bousquet, who had spent the majority of his international career training with American programs and non-French coaches like Australian Auburn alum Brett Hawke, the implication was clear. "I know I'm going to get in a lot of trouble for saying it, but I don't care. What I believe is, whoever anchored the relay gets all the credit, all the cameras go onto him," Bousquet reasoned. "Our federation was so confident of us winning no matter the order, and the picture of French swimming they wanted all the cameras to be put on was Alain's face. I don't think they did it against me. I think they did it for Alain, who was their guy."[8] Bousquet, who allowed that overconfidence may have played into the loss, was correct in several regards. First, he'd been in tremendous form, his split of 46.63 in the preliminary heat the fastest ever at the time. Bernard also had made several obvious errors. He took the first 50 out too fast, a sign of nerves that permitted Lezak to make up significant ground in the final 50, outsplitting him by nearly a second. Bernard also swam too near the lane line separating the Americans and the French, allowing Lezak to ride his draft over the first 50 and conserve energy. And finally, Bernard turned to look for Lezak in the final 25 meters, one of a litany of miniscule factors that could've summed to the microscopic margin between them.

Whatever lessons were to be gleaned from Beijing's shortcomings needed to be internalized quickly. Given the understanding of how difficult it would be for Phelps to try—or even desire to try—to top Beijing and the lack of depth in programs like the Australians, the French were installed as the favorites in the freestyle relays. Instead, the French crossed the English Channel in 2012 with a track record largely composed of underwhelming performances. They failed to deliver in their first major test at the 2009 Worlds in Rome. As a testament to the speed in Beijing, the American win in Rome was in the minority of non-world records set at a meet where the techsuit craze led to 43 world marks. The team of Phelps, Ryan Lochte, Matt Grevers, and Nathan Adrian settled for a time .97 seconds behind their Beijing counterparts, but still .31 seconds faster than the runners-up from Russia. Earning bronze, .78 ticks back, was the French team of Gilot, Bernard, Gregory Mallet, and Bousquet. Bernard delivered the fastest split of the event with his second leg of 46.46 seconds, joining Adrian's 46.79 anchor leg as the only sub-47 splits of finals. The only split over 48 seconds among the 12 medal-winning swimmers was Mallet's 48.28. The French set the fastest qualifying time at the 2011 Worlds in Shanghai by almost a second and a half over the Americans. When the Americans faltered in the final with Garrett Weber-Gale and Lezak each failing to get under the 48-second mark, the door seemed wide open for the French. But Bernard was sluggish off the front in the final, posting a time of 48.75 that was 1.26 seconds behind Australian James Magnussen's lead-off leg, a world's best swim in textile suits. Though Jeremy Stravius, William Meynard, and Gilot fought gallantly, Gilot outsplitting Sullivan by a half second on the anchor leg, the Australians prevailed by .14 seconds, consigning the French to silver. Even in continental competition, the French squad of Gilot, Agnel, Meynard, and Bernard was relegated to silver by the Russians at the 2010 Euros. The breakthrough finally came at the 2012 Euros, where the team of Leveaux, Bernard, Bousquet, and Stravius finally earned major hardware, outdistancing the Italian runners-up by 1.16 seconds.

Much like in 2008, the French rode a wave of momentum from the summer into the Games. And as had been the case in the past, there were serious reservations about the other nations involved. The question marks for the Americans were obvious. Once again, they'd lean on Phelps and Lochte, both overstretched in their quests for multiple medals. The hope was that Olympic Trials would produce at least one medal contender in the 100 free. Instead, the pacesetter was Adrian in 48.10 seconds. Jones, regarded as a solid finals—if not medal—contender who would take part in the relay unless someone stepped up to dethrone him, was second at Trials at 48.46. Sixth in the finals was Lezak at 48.88, his undisputed reputation as a stellar relay swimmer arguably his most valuable asset. Only three swimmers—including the 48.38 of Jimmy Feigen in semis before he finished fifth in finals—got under the 48.5-second mark. The Australians, meanwhile, were building a stable of sprinters so deep that former world-record holder Sullivan was only fourth-fastest at Trials in 48.53, missing out on a chance to compete individually in London. Ahead of him was Magnussen, nicknamed "the Missile"; James Roberts; and Matt Targett. While the Americans scuffled in vain for a sub-48 guy, Magnussen had ripped off a textile-best 47.10. Then there was the Russian team, which lacked a bona fide medal contender but boasted a group of swimmers capable of the high-47, low-48 range. For the first time in Olympic history, not only was an Olympic gold medal looking downright unlikely, but there was a very real concern that a few bad breaks could leave the Americans without a medal in the London final.[9]

The Australians did little to dispel their portrayal as favorites in prelims. With something between their A and B teams, the squad of Cameron McEvoy, Roberts, Tommaso D'Orsogna, and Magnussen set the fastest time, brought home by Magnussen's split of 47.35. Second were the Americans, three-tenths back courtesy of Feigen, Grevers, Ricky Berens, and Lezak. Fastest of the group was Grevers's 47.54. The French squad of Leveaux, Bernard, Lefert, and Stravius finished fourth, just over a second in arrears of the Aussies and six-tenths behind the Russians. When it came time to make changes for the finals, the Australians' were obvious. In came Targett and Sullivan to go with Roberts and Magnussen, a team that appeared rock solid on paper. Grevers's split was impressive, but it couldn't budge the American lineup, with the top two from Trials in Jones and Adrian, plus Phelps and Lochte. The choice from the French, which had held Agnel and Gilot in reserve, was to take the two fastest from prelims: Leveaux (48.61 flat start, which equates to around 47.9 with a relay pickup factored in) and Lefert (48.14), leaving former world-record holder Bernard (48.31) on the sidelines. As he failed to qualify for the Games in either of his individual events, the former shining star of the French program was limited to a lone 100 meters in London.

The choices worked out for the French, backfired for the Americans, and simply melted down for the Australians. True to form, the Aussies followed the usual script of putting their fastest swimmer first, moving Magnussen to the leadoff leg. To counter, the Americans front-loaded their squad, starting with Adrian and Phelps and leaving Lochte to cling to a (hopefully) sizeable lead on the anchor. Despite his lack of experience, with the distance and the anchor role, Lochte was seen as the hot hand, a day after a landslide win in the 400 individual medley, his time of 4:05.19 nearly four seconds faster than silver medalist Thiago Pereira of Brazil. With Phelps having opened London with a fourth-place finish in the 400 IM—his first Olympic final without a medal since his fifth place in the 100 fly in Sydney as a fresh-faced 15-year-old—the second leg afforded a less pressure-packed haven. The French, meanwhile, readied Agnel for the anchor, countered Phelps's second-leg speed with Gilot, and utilized the starts of Leveaux to open.

What ensued was a back-and-forth battle among the top four. The American plan worked with regard to the Aussies, Adrian's time of 47.89 opening a slight gap on Magnussen (48.03) and Leveaux (48.13). Slipping to fifth were the Russians after a 48.57 from Andrey Grechin. Hidden in the numbers was the fact that Leveaux swam a half second faster than his prelim time, the first of four occasions in which the French rose to the occasion while others stumbled. Phelps responded superbly with a leg of 47.15, opening the gap on Gilot (47.67) and Targett (47.83), while Nikita Lobintsev's 47.39 brought Russia back into the medal picture. The next Frenchman up, Lefert, delivered a swim .75 seconds faster than prelims, but Jones's 47.60 leg neutralized his ability to gain ground. The momentum, though, was building for the French: Lefert, who had trailed by .78 seconds at the 250-meter wall, cut the deficit to .55 at the handoff to Agnel. Sullivan's inability to gain ground on the Americans with 47.68 left the Aussies to battle for bronze, while the race at the front was between the Americans and the French as Lochte and Agnel entered the fray. The 20-year-old Agnel delivered a swim that, ironically enough, could only be described as his Lezak moment. He covered the first 50 with poise and control, eroding .25 seconds of Lochte's advantage. But where the underwater prowess of Lochte allowed him to bury most competitors off the wall, Agnel hung tight, perhaps sensing that Lochte, who had swum the semis of the 200 free 82 minutes earlier, was about to crack.[10] Stroke by stroke, Agnel used his 6-foot-7 frame to reel in Lochte. With 25 meters left, it looked like a photo finish would decide gold; by the time the distance to the wall was halved, there was no doubt who was surging to the front. The final margin between the teams was surprisingly decisive, with the French clocking in at 3:09.93, .45 ahead of the Americans. The more emphatic statement came via the splits: Agnel had outpaced Lochte by a full second, clocking in at 46.74 to Lochte's 47.74.

The symmetry between what the French had endured four years prior and what they doled out in London was striking. In describing Agnel's feat, the only term that seemed to capture the full magnitude was an apropos neologism: "Lezak-esqe."[11] In his post-swim appraisal, Lochte echoed many of the criticisms voiced by Bernard in 2008. "I was just really excited and I think I overswam the first 50 and it hurt me for the last 50," Lochte said.[12] American coach Gregg Troy, who was also Lochte's mentor at the University of Florida, admitted that it may have been "a bit of a coaching error"[13] to put Lochte on the anchor leg, but that was about the extent of the controversy. There were brief grumblings about the U.S. staff having erred by excluding Grevers, no doubt exacerbated by Troy's prized pupil being the one run down by Agnel's comeback. But at the start of the relay, Grevers would've been just 29 minutes removed from the semis of the 100 back, an event he proceeded to win. Grevers's prelim time was almost four-tenths slower than Phelps's split and only two-tenths quicker than Lochte's, not enough to sway the destination of the gold medal. Grevers quickly defused any hints of discord, and the American delegation wanted no part in vilifying Lochte. Lochte had pieced together a great swim. What was required by the French, however, was excellence. "I don't think Ryan let anybody down, and neither does anybody else on this team," Jones said. "He put forth the effort and swam an extremely fast 100-meter freestyle. I know he's beating himself up."[14]

The events at the Aquatic Center spawned plenty of conclusions. For the Australians, the defeat was yet another log fueling the fire of fatalism about the national team's hopes, a stirring condemnation of a long-held hubris that seemed sillier and sillier with each passing defeat. The Americans took the loss as a reminder of the closing ranks of the swimming world, the obvious message that more work was needed to prevent the success of the Phelps era from walking off the deck with the lanky Maryland native. (The tide was at least briefly stemmed when the American team of Lochte, Conor Dwyer, Berens, and Phelps coasted by the French 800 free relay team by 3.07 seconds for gold, Phelps withstanding the push of Agnel's superb anchor-leg split of 1:43.24.) The French triumph also brought into focus how impressive Round 1 between the squads in Beijing had been. Lochte didn't lose the race in London; Agnel wrested the medal from the Americans' hands by delivering a once-in-a-lifetime swim. "You can't predict a 46. You just can't," Jones said. "That's an out-of-his-mind swim. . . . Yeah, I'd say 46.6 is a superman-level race, and Lezak had that Superman race in 2008."[15] The usual script played out, only this time was a rare occurrence that wasn't in Phelps's favor.

"I've thought back to a lot of those memories recently," said Phelps, who at least found solace in the first silver in his collection of nearly two dozen Olympic medals. "I mean, things have to fall into the perfect place at the right time."[16]

The win signified plenty for the French. The prominence of 20-year-old Agnel—reinforced by an extraordinary win in the 200 free where he dusted China's Sun Yang, South Korea's Park Tae-Hwan, and Lochte by nearly two seconds—signaled a changing of generations. The relay success transcended just one or two swimmers, a comprehensive effort that showed the program to be more than just a Bernard here or a Bousquet there. Coupled with the 50 free win by 21-year-old Florent Manaudou, the next wave in French swimming had arrived with authority. For 2008 veterans Gilot and Leveaux, there was a revenge factor at play. But more so, it was the recognition of a new, unique identity to the burgeoning French program. "What happened four years ago, that was really tough," Gilot said. "This is an extraordinary revenge. . . . We have been rewarded for all the years when we missed out and were given nothing. Today we have won one of the finest medals and it is one which can never be removed."[17] "It was a change from four years ago," Leveaux added. "Now we're in front and it's incredible. We were under pressure because we wanted to win for each other. It was a form of revenge."[18]

Part II

Squads

Chapter Nine

1924 U.S. Olympians

The 1920s hold an enduring and alluring romanticism for many Americans. Out of the doldrums of World War I emerged a prosperous nation that literally and figurative roared into a new era of modernity. As the United States distanced itself from its rural past and toward sprawling, bustling cities, the notion of entertainment as an industry first came to prominence.

From the rise of Hollywood to the growth of professional sports leagues as bona fide American pastimes, Americans possessed newfound time, access, and means to enjoy forms of entertainment growing at a prodigious pace. That atmosphere gave rise to new icons of Americana, from vaudeville stars to professional athletes to the lure of the wealthy socialite.

From a sporting perspective, the hagiography of the 1920s is unmatched in any other era of American history. Those were the days of Babe Ruth, Ty Cobb, and myriad other stars of the baseball diamond; gridiron glitterati like Red Grange; and Olympic heroes like Paavo Nurmi. Around each new sport or league venturing into the national consciousness, there was a mythology constructed for its biggest stars, from the Babe calling his shot to the Galloping Ghost that was Grange.

To the constellation of sports stars, swimming added its fair share of contributions. Perhaps nowhere was this more clearly on display than the 1924 Paris Olympics, a spectacle so thoroughly dominated by the Americans that their exploits were lapped up on the other side of the Atlantic, instantly vaulting names like Johnny Weissmuller, Duke Kahanamoku, and Gertrude Ederle into the realm of superstardom. The fact that those figures became household names and embodied the face of the sport for years only constituted part of the picture. Far beyond legend, their success changed the way in which the sport was approached by millions of Americans, redefining who could compete and why swimming was important in America.

The fact that the Americans were comprehensively, almost exclusively dominant in Paris in 1924 wasn't necessarily the groundbreaking aspect of their performance there. The Olympics, which represented the only regularly scheduled international swimming meet of any widespread significance, were just over a quarter century old. Evolved from events like underwater and obstacle swimming, modern swimming had only really arrived at the Games in 1904, and the first women's participation in the pool wasn't until 1912. With the cancellation of the 1916 Games while the world went to war, the 1924 Olympiad was only the fifth of consequence for swimming, making it difficult to discern the balance of the scales of international power. The Americans had certainly done well at the 1920 Games in Antwerp, winning eight of 10 gold medals, including all six of the individual women's medals. But 1924 would be the first chance for the women to swim an event other than freestyle, with backstroke and breaststroke also on the program.

Paris certainly solidified America's claim to the international swimming throne, with the Stars and Stripes claiming 9 of the 11 gold medals on offer and 19 of the 33 totals medals handed out, including 17 of the 27 individual medals. Put in terms of the day's point system for international events, the final margin (including diving) was a blowout for the Americans, who won 217–58 over the nearest challenger, Sweden. So lopsided was the margin that the Americans had clinched the title by the fifth day of the eight-day competition.

The domination commenced with a clean sweep in the 400-meter free with Martha Norelius, Helen Wainwright, and Ederle, the latter a surprising third after struggling with illness and training irregularities since her arrival in Europe. All three were club teammates in the New York City area at the Women's Swimming Association (WSA), a pioneering club for women's swimming and women's sports in the nation. Ederle had set an Olympic record of 6:12.2 in the heats, 11 seconds faster than Norelius and 34 quicker than Wainwright. The five-swimmer final soon resembled a WSA training session, with Norelius surging ahead late to win in 6:02.2; second was Wainwright in 6:03.8, and another second back was Ederle. The fourth-place finisher, Great Britain's Doris Molesworth, was over 20 seconds back in the wash of "America's peerless mermaids."[1] On the men's side, world-record holder Warren Kealoha earned gold in the 100 back, well ahead of countryman Paul Wyatt. The men's 200 breast final went down as "a magnificent duel" between American Bob Skelton and Belgian Joseph De Combe, gold unsurprisingly going to the American.[2] The only American qualifier for the women's 200 breast final, Agnes Geraghty, took home silver, sandwiched between Great Britain's Lucy Morton and Gladys Carson.

The records continued to fall for the Americans, and even when they didn't, the races still scintillated those in attendance. Sybil Bauer set a world record in the 100 back in the heats, then bettered it to 1:23.8 in finals en route to gold. Hawaiian Mariechen Wehselau set the world record in the 100 free in the prelims, mere fractions ahead of Ethel Lackie and Ederle, both of whom were also under the existing world standard. In the final, Lackie didn't quite down Wehselau's world mark, but she topped her for gold by four-tenths, using a furious charge in the back half of the race and forcing Ederle to again settle for bronze. Weissmuller and Arne Borg didn't come anywhere near the world record, owned by the latter and awaiting international ratification after being set several months earlier, in the 400 free. But the team-mates—and often when traveling to meets, roommates—at the Illinois Athletic Club (IAC) produced the "most thrilling race seen in a week replete with sensations and broken records."[3] Never separated by more than five feet, the lead yo-yoed between the two titans of distance swimming, Weiss-muller constantly falling behind thanks to his sub-par turns and charging back to overtake Borg before the next wall. When the same script played out over the final 50 meters, Weissmuller got his hand to the wall first in 5 minutes, 4.2 seconds, an Olympic record 1.4 seconds faster than Borg and 2.4 ticks quicker than Australian distance star Boy Charlton. With a more favorable ratio of swimming to turning in the 100 free, Weissmuller had no intention of duplicating the spectacle of the longer race. Instead, he proved himself to be "in a class by himself,"[4] clocking an Olympic-record time of 59.0 seconds, 1.6 seconds behind his world record but 1.4 seconds ahead of the brothers Kahanamoku, Duke in silver and Samuel in bronze, fractions ahead of Borg.

The two relays contested also, predictably, went the way of the Americans. In the women's 400 freestyle relay, the squad of Euphrasia Donnelly, Ederle, Lackie, and Wehselau became the first to ever go under five minutes with its time of 4:58.8, an improvement of nearly 13 seconds on the world record from Antwerp four years prior. A margin of 18.2 seconds separated the Americans from the silver-winning Great Britain squad. There was some intrigue to the men's 800 free relay, but Weissmuller saw to it that an upset wasn't in the script. Ralph Breyer led off and furnished a lead of seven meters for Harry Glancy, but Charlton quickly cut into the advantage. The Americans had stabilized the gap by the time Wally O'Connor handed off to Weissmuller for the anchor. That was all the "Human Hydroplane" needed, outdistancing Australian anchor Ernest Henry "like a frightened porpoise" and bringing home gold for the Americans in 9:53.4, the first team ever under 10 minutes.[5] The Americans stopped the clock 11 seconds faster than the world record and nearly nine seconds ahead of the Aussies. The praise showered upon the American domination in the pool was unprecedented for the program. "Never since the renewal of the Olympic Games has a team outclassed the others in any branch of sport as the Americans did the representatives of the twenty-five other nations competing," wrote the *New York Times*.[6] While the statement was accurate, it only encapsulated a portion of what made the showing in 1924 so pivotal for the nascent American swimming establishment.

The swimmers who returned from Paris weren't just national heroes. They weren't just anomalous in the sense that they had become sports stars at a time when many children had yet to dream of that as a possible career path. Those swimmers came to define an era of swimming royalty, changing the perceptions of how the sport of swimming was done at its elite levels.

Foremost among those trailblazers was Weissmuller, who until the emergence of Mark Spitz almost a half century later remained the gold standard for American men's swimming. The man best known as Tarzan in many a Hollywood film was to swimming fitness what Adonis was to beauty. "It seemed as though Johnny had been deliberately invented and carpentered for the sport," was how author Paul Gallico described Weissmuller in profiling the leading lights of the 1920s.[7] The epitome of the ideal swimming body, the 6-3 Weissmuller revolutionized freestyle with his high line in the water and arched back, ushering in a new era of technique. Many people tried to emulate Weissmuller's style of almost hydroplaning on the water's surface, but the propulsion required to overcome the resistance generated by that position was something few could replicate.

The legend surrounding Weissmuller was grand, though it wasn't fully laid low until after his death. The consummate American hero, a rags-to-riches story from the working class of Chicago who learned to swim in Lake Michigan, was in fact born in Romania. It was even well known in the Banat region of Romania, part of Hungary at the time of Weissmuller's birth in 1904, that Weissmuller was one of their own. Though he was born in Freidorf, which would later be incorporated as a district in the Romanian capital Timisoara, he and his family moved to Windber, Pennsylvania, before his first birthday. Weissmuller's birth certificate listed his birth name as "Peter John," the name of his brother, whose records may have been used to obtain Weissmuller's citizenship. Suspicion of that fact surfaced just before the Paris Games when Illinois representative Henry Riggs Rathbone pushed Weissmuller to provide proof of his citizenship. The combination of adequate documentation and his excellence at the Games apparently satiated anyone interested in digging deeper from thinking of Weissmuller as anything other than the absolute American boy. The secret was safe in his homeland, where many felt connected to his success and even, according to legend, covered for Weissmuller when the Freidorf authorities came looking for him for compulsory military service when he turned 18. In Chicago, Weissmuller's family was part of a vibrant community of Banaters, many of them rising to prominence as local businessmen and community figures. The shared yoke of the immigrants' struggle and the mutual understanding of the stigma Weissmuller's German heritage placed on him in the days after World War I made how he'd found his way to America unimportant. The association with a small town like Windber only enhanced his heroic credentials. When Windber, in 1950, declared a "Johnny Weissmuller Day," there was no doubt to the swimmer where home was. "I have always wanted a hometown, and now I have one," Weissmuller said. "This is the biggest thrill I ever had in my life and this includes the events when I won the Olympic titles in 1924 and 1928 and was presented medals by the queen of the Netherlands."[8]

In the pool, few deigned to challenge Weissmuller's supremacy. After learning to swim in Lake Michigan, the creation myth of Weissmuller the swimmer entailed his recommendation to the Illinois Athletic Club in his teens as a sickly eighth-grade dropout to bolster his health with physical fitness—and perhaps also to fill the void left by the death of his father from tuberculosis. (For what it's worth, the health narrative is one that Weissmuller, living high off the Hollywood hog for decades, distanced himself from later in life, though clubs like IAC did play an important role as the only organized athletic outlets for children of the working class.) However he landed at IAC, there's no doubt that it changed his life, linking him with coach Bill Bachrach. The coach of the 1924 Olympic team, Bachrach saw the raw, unpolished talent in an often frustrating young Weissmuller and allowed it to flourish. Whatever circumstances led him to Bachrach's door, Weissmuller was persistent once within the club, positioning himself to work with the coach. At first, he was a middling backstroker, but Bachrach saw the potential in his freestyle. In Weissmuller's physique, Bachrach saw the power required to combine the upper-body strength of Norman Ross, the triple-gold winner in the 1920 Antwerp Olympics, and the kick of Kahanamoku. They set about isolating muscle groups, an innovative approach for the time, with Weissmuller working out his arms with an inner tube lashing together his legs, or kicking for laps on end with a primitive kickboard buoying his arms. Bachrach also advocated having Weissmuller perfect his stroke in front of a mirror, helping to foster an acute sense of body awareness.

Weissmuller's ascent at IAC wasn't instantaneous, and he took his lumps as a youth. But by 1921, he had burst onto the national team. In the eight months from August 1921 to March 1922, he set 17 world records, including taking part in four IAC world relay marks. It didn't take long for him to be christened the "greatest swimmer of the present age, undoubtedly the greatest swimmer of all time," as the *New York Times* opined in April 1922.[9] Much of that success sprung from his relationship with Bachrach, equal parts coach and handler, promoter, and midway barker. Bachrach organized barnstorming tours throughout the nation with Weissmuller; by often guaranteeing spectators a world record in his vaudeville-type show, Weissmuller learned to mete out his effort, incrementally downing standards rather than lopping off time as his abilities hinted he could have. When time drops were the objective, though, Weissmuller could deliver, chopping two seconds off the 50 free world record just 10 days before setting sail for Paris in 1924.

Whatever Bachrach's methods, the results were paradigm altering. In his career, Weissmuller set 51 world records. He won 56 national titles, including a title in the modern pentathlon. Weissmuller also set records in backstroke and won Olympic bronze in 1924 as a forward on the American water polo squad. His unique style advanced the discipline of the crawl stroke as few individuals ever had. In the early 1910s, American Charlie Daniels had set the latest unbreakable record with his new stroke. A decade later, Weissmuller had cut 14 seconds off that time, a record that would endure well into the next decade. The time drops by Weissmuller provided the most "conclusive evidence of the striking manner in which the American crawl has revolutionized the art of swimming."[10] Soon after winning two golds in the 1928 Amsterdam Games, Weissmuller officially turned professional, though his ability may have persisted to pursue Olympics into the 1930s. He instead turned to Hollywood, following other swimmers like Eleanor Holm and Esther Williams to the movies.

Part of Weissmuller's rise to prominence on the American swimming scene meant vanquishing the former king of the program, Duke Kahanamoku. The presence of both swimmers in Paris, a monumental torch passing of swimming power, was a sight to behold. The majority of the records broken by Weissmuller belonged, at one time or another, to the "Bronze Duke of Waikiki," who went to Paris for this third Olympics to conclude a storied career. Kahanamoku had won gold in the 100 free in Stockholm an eternity ago in 1912, also taking silver in the 800 free relay. He doubled up on gold in Antwerp in 1920, and a month shy of his 34th birthday, he decided on one more go at Paris. Along the way, he also became one of the founding fathers of the sport of modern surfing. "With the possible exception of Johnny Weissmuller," wrote renowned swimming coach and author Cecil Colwin in 1999, "Kahanamoku did more than anyone else to popularize swimming around the world."[11] The importance of Kahanamoku to his homeland was made abundantly clear in 1990 when Hawaii declared a monthlong celebration to commemorate the centenary of his birth. Wrote the *Honolulu Advertiser*'s Red McQueen, Kahanamoku "has been to both (surfing and swimming) exactly what Babe Ruth was to baseball, Joe Louis to boxing, Bill Tilden to tennis, Red Grange to football, and Bobby Jones to golf. He has been Mister Surfer and Mister Swimming rolled into one incredible giant of a man."[12]

If there was a mysterious lore surrounding Weissmuller's gravitation toward the pool, it was nothing compared to Kahanamoku's. Thanks to the isolation of his upbringing in Hawaii and the mythos surrounding the island paradise—which at the time of his 1890 birth was still an independent kingdom, to the royal line of which Kahanamoku can trace descent—Kahanamoku's tale is a central legend in Hawaiian history. Kahanamoku learned to swim out of impulse in a Hawaiian culture built around the sea, developing a technique distinct from anything taught in the United States, Australia, or Europe at the time. Drawing elements from the styles used since time immemorial by Pacific islanders, the wholly self-taught (or was it instinctual?) Kahanamoku developed a kind of "surfer-swimmer" stroke used by Hawaiians to navigate the rough tide, one that relied on a powerful kick that would become known as the "Kahanamoku kick."[13] He dropped out of high school to make a living off the sea, crafting surfboards and canoes as well as working as a fisherman. Kahanamoku rose to international prominence in 1911 when he downed Daniels's world record in the 100 free, though it was disputed by authorities as being aided by the saltwater and ocean tides of Honolulu's Mamala Bay. Nonetheless, the Amateur Athletic Union (AAU) invited a Hawaiian delegation to their championships in Pittsburgh, Pennsylvania, the following year for Kahanamoku to prove it, which he did. His speed was evident, but there was no recognizable form to his stroke and he lacked endurance, not to mention familiarity swimming in a tanked pool. He nonetheless downed Daniels's record and earned a trip to the 1912 Games in the process. After a crash course with Olympic coach Otto Wahle, which included teaching him turns, Kahanamoku was readied for Stockholm, bringing home gold in the 100 free. The story goes that Kahanamoku was nowhere to be found before the final of that 100 free. "They found him asleep under a bridge, snoring," Kahanamoku's brother, Sargent, recounted in 1990. "He got up, said sorry, got in the water to loosen up, and then won the race. His mind was clear."[14] Kahanamoku cashed in on his stardom to travel the world, giving surfing demonstrations and instructions on carving longboards out of koa wood. He was regarded "like a prophet" in Australia when he visited in 1915, and the pioneering board he brought remains a treasured relic almost a century later.[15]

By 1924, there was no doubt of Kahanamoku's Olympic swimming credentials. But even he saw the writing on the wall as early as 1922 in the form of Weissmuller. After a trip by Weissmuller to Hawaii, Kahanamoku promptly announced his retirement. "All talk about a meeting between Johnny Weissmuller and myself to settle the matter of supremacy is foolish," he said. "He is the greatest swimmer the world has ever seen."[16] Part of the motivation for the trip was to debunk the notion that Weissmuller's supremacy over Kahanamoku owed solely to the turns required in tanked pools. When Weissmuller beat Kahanamoku over a 100-meter straightaway in the ocean, that argument became moot. Kahanamoku nonetheless returned to the pool to train with the Los Angeles Athletic Club, earning a spot at the 1924 Trials. Illness prevented Kahanamoku from participating in the 1928 Olympic Trials, but his times in 1932 were faster than two decades prior, though his only Olympic participation was as an alternate on the water polo team. He never stopped being a celebrity, though, enlisted by Hawaii as the official greeter whenever visitors of consequence came to the islands. Kahanamoku also followed the well-worn path from the pool to the movies. In 1925, Kahanamoku made mainland headlines by leaping into the waters off California, using his surfboard to save eight of the 17 passengers of the ship *Thelma* that capsized in rough seas. He went on to become a sheriff in Honolulu, participating in local competitions for swimming, surfing, and canoeing well into his 50s. A bronze statue of Kahanamoku graces Waikiki Beach in Honolulu.

While generations of men's swimming collided in Paris via Weissmuller and Kahanamoku, one of the first great eras of women's swimming was emphatically dawning. Ederle, Wainwright, and Bauer represented the first crop of female swimmers who specifically trained for Olympic glory, using methods and facilities that had previously been reserved only for males. Bauer came through Bachrach's IAC, one of the first women to be admitted in 1918. She set backstroke records so fast that they threatened the men's marks in those events.

Ederle, meanwhile, grew up in a working-class section of the Bronx, the daughter of a German immigrant who worked as a butcher. She and her two sisters learned to swim in the ocean surf off the coast of Highlands, New Jersey, and Ederle used swimming as a retreat from a hearing deficiency stemming from a bout of measles in her youth. That disability forced Ederle into a social shell, and her mother pushed her and her sisters toward the newly formed Women's Swimming Association as a means of socialization. The egalitarian nature of the club, stripped of the ubiquitous anti-German sentiment the family was constantly on guard against, was part of the appeal of coach Louis Handley's team. The formation of WSA came at a complicated time, when swimming was being encouraged for young people as a lifesaving technique but when women were still forbidden to get in the water in anything less than full stockings. On one hand, there were the efforts of Charlotte Epstein's Women's Life-Saving League to prevent needless deaths; on the other were the vaudeville shows of Annette Kellerman, an Australian swimmer who toured the world giving swimming demonstrations in a giant glass tank that were equal parts impressive and scandalous. In 1917, Epstein formed the WSA in New York City as an instrument of "self-protection . . . healthy, physical improvement and recreation."[17]

What the 19th Amendment did for women's political power, WSA did for their swimming prospects. One of the big coups was Handley, who arrived as a volunteer and stayed for 40 years. He'd been one of the early innovators of the trudgen stroke for men and had been a world-class water polo player, winning gold in the 1904 Olympics while playing and coaching at prestigious New York–area clubs like Knickerbocker Athletic Club and New York Athletic Club. A prolific stroke innovator and author, Handley experimented with a variety of kick sequences with swimmers but was unflinching in seeing the importance of a strong kick, not yet a widely accepted perspective.

The son of a prominent American-born sculptor who served in the court of two popes, the pool was Handley's cathedral, and he approached the study of swimming with a voracity that bordered on religious fanaticism. Despite that fervor, though, Handley was the ideal man to lead a group of women. He supported Epstein's motto that "good sportsmanship is greater than victory"[18] and exhibited no remnants of the era's inherent sexism, giving him no qualms about working exclusively with women. From the dank basement of a Brooklyn Heights apartment building, Handley set about coaching a stable of talented female swimmers like none the world had ever seen. There was 1920 Olympian Ethelda Bleibtrey, who came to the WSA to cope with a curvature of her spine caused by polio and turned into one of the first female superstars. There was Aileen Riggin, who recovered from a bout of Spanish flu to win gold as a diver in 1920, then silver on the board and bronze in the pool in 1924. The others names highlighting the women's swimming landscape of the early 1920s like Holm, Wainwright, and Geraghty were all Handley's handiwork. Over the years, they set 51 world records and dominated the AAU's early efforts at exerting dominion over women's swimming, claiming some 200 titles.

Then there was Ederle, who became the most accomplished, most famous, and most inspirational of all. She adapted as well as anyone to the motivational techniques of Handley. Her coming-out party was the 1922 Day Cup race, a 3.5-mile event in choppy seas at Manhattan Beach set up by Epstein as a spectacle to showcase her talented girls. Through iffy weather, the winner was Ederle in a shocking result, even to Handley, who hadn't expected her to even enter the race and regarded her as a "rank outsider."[19] She beat Wainwright, then seen as WSA's darling; Riggin; and Hilda James, the British champion brought across the Atlantic for the race, by a whopping 45 seconds. Where others rigorously trained through the winter, Ederle's work was sporadic. But when summer arrived, Ederle was unfailingly in the water in the idyllic settings of the Jersey shore while also participating in numerous other athletic activities. The Day Cup win launched a two-year streak when Ederle was beaten just twice, both times by Wainwright. In one match race at Brighton Beach in August 1922, Ederley lapped Wainwright and James, beating them by 20 and 40 yards, respectively, while setting a series of world marks over 400 yards, 400 meters, and 440 yards. The feat of setting seven world records in 1923 was voted by famed columnist Grantland Rice as the year's most outstanding sporting achievement. She was quickly becoming a celebrity, the modest, ideal American girl who still tended to household chores in between breaking world records.

The newfound celebrity didn't stop the 1924 Games from representing the height of agony for Ederle, though. She handled her affairs succinctly at the Olympic Trials, defeating the increasingly frustrated Wainwright to earn a berth in the 400 free, while her spot on the relay was virtually guaranteed with Handley, the Olympic coach, handpicking the squad. But the nine-day trip across the Atlantic via steamer created problems. The only area in which to practice was a makeshift canvas tank full of seawater on deck where swimmers were allotted 30 minutes a day to work out, swimming in place restrained by a leather harness that altered Ederle's stroke patterns. That left Ederle with little to do but eat, and diminished activity led to severe cramping and increased anxiousness. In Paris, the accommodations of the women's team miles away from the pool further limited training and meant that Ederle spent more time on cramped car rides than in the pool. Her inability to mount her usual finishing kick en route to bronze in the 400 free caused her to break down in tears. Then her hearing issue caused her to get a late start in the 100 free, relegating her to bronze in a close finish between the three Americans. In between, she led off the 400 free relay, staking the team to a lead of five meters in a race that was never in doubt. While Ederle was consoled by the success of her team, she nonetheless regarded the 1924 Games as the "greatest disappointment of my life."[20] The inconvenient lodging and transportation conditions with which the cash-strapped American Olympic delegation was saddled developed into a subject of much consternation, and a list of complaints drawn up by Handley after the Games listed Ederle as among the most adversely affected.

Ederle's success as a swimmer came largely outside the pool. In 1926, she drew upon her open-water prowess to become the first woman and just the sixth person to swim the English Channel. In a suit designed by her sister, Meg, and goggles fastened to be watertight with candle wax, Ederle's time of 14 hours, 31 minutes, on August 6 was the fastest in history. It helped erase the memory of her Olympic shortcomings and a failed attempt the previous summer where Ederle—a last-minute stand-in for a trip already funded for an injured Wainwright—made it 23 miles over almost nine hours before being pulled out of the water. Ederle returned to New York to a hero's welcome equated with that of Charles Lindberg's, getting a ticker-tape parade through the streets of Manhattan that drew an estimated two million people. She was whisked away to the White House to meet President Calvin Coolidge, who dubbed her "America's best girl,"[21] and to Hollywood for a short film on her life and to serve as the inspiration for the song "Trudy." Her accomplishments made her a symbol for what could be accomplished by women and, through her work with the Lexington School for the Deaf, the hearing impaired. Her career in the water was cut short in 1933 when she fell down a flight of stairs and fractured her spine, an injury doctors predicted would prevent her from walking or swimming again. Though she was in persistent pain for the remainder of her 98-year life and confined to a cast for over four years, she recovered to perform in Billy Rose's Aquacade show at the New York World's Fair in 1939 before withdrawing from the public eye, the pressure of which had led to a nervous breakdown in the late 1920s.

As Ederle could attest, the 1924 Games may not have been what some in the American camp expected them to be. But there is one enduring image that demonstrates the gaiety surrounding those Olympics. To the dismay of the stodgy swimming officials, Weissmuller and American diver Harold "Stubby" Kruger entertained the Paris crowd with an intermission entertainment show. Weissmuller would play the straight man, executing dives at the Olympic pool, only to be followed by Kruger's slapstick versions of the same maneuvers. The performance served as an advance for a tour the duo embarked on through Europe and America, a trip which included Weissmuller paying a visit to Coolidge's White House. While the performance in the water got rave reviews, the shows put on by Weissmuller and Kruger underscored the joy of what Weissmuller called "a great experience, which I will always recall with pleasure."[22] In the days when the line between athletics and entertainment were so faint, Weissmuller and his fellow American starred on both accounts. Without the show they put on in Paris, the course of swimming history might have been drastically different.

Chapter Ten

1950s Hungarian Women's Olympians

The sporting achievements of Hungary in the early 1950s are the stuff of legends. On the soccer pitch, on the track, and in the water, the small Eastern European nation went from a peripheral participant in the Olympic movement to one of the major challengers to the United States–Soviet Union duopoly in the Games immediately after World War II. Some of the most memorable sporting events of that era—the Magical Magyars soccer team that authored the soccer match of the century in 1953, the 1956 "Blood in the Water" water polo match against the USSR—involved Hungarian teams that were among the most formidable of their age.

A prominent facet of that dominance was the ability of Hungarian swimmers to collect Olympic medals. While Hungary had in the past entered a select few names to the pantheon of swimming greats, the 1952 Olympics in Helsinki took that to a new level. Instead of a smattering of champions through the years, Hungary tied the United States for the most gold medals with four and finished second on the overall medal table with seven pieces of hardware to the Stars and Stripes' nine. The most impressive part of the medal haul was that it came exclusively from the women's competition, where the Hungarians had temporarily usurped the United States and Australia as the world's foremost power.

With expectations raised four years later, glimmers of the Hungarian swimming prowess shown in Melbourne. But the delegation sent to those Games was a conflicted one, the athletes' homeland being torn apart by conflict with the Soviet Union, leaving many participants at the Games unsure of the fates of their loved ones and devoting their mental energy to plotting a way to escape the strife at home from the safe haven Down Under. The lore of Hungarian swimming's golden generation lies as much in what was accomplished in 1952 as in what could've been achieved with less acute doses of adversity in 1956. Nonetheless, Hungary stands as one of the few nations able to mount a serious challenge to the established order of swimming powers after World War II.

Some of the earliest success in Olympic swimming was provided by competitors flying the flag of Hungary. The first swimming medal at the inaugural Olympiad in Athens in 1896 was won by Hungarian Alfred Hajos. (In those days, it should be noted, winners received silver and runners-up bronze; after standardizing the medal hierarchy at the 1904 Games, the International Olympic Committee retroactively amended those medals.) On the same day, Hajos won the 100-meter and 1,200-meter freestyle events held in the chilly waters of the Bay of Zea. Hajos, who devoted himself to swimming competency after seeing his father drown in the Danube River, won the longer race by sheer "will to live" after he and eight other competitors were ferried into the bay and told to swim back to shore.[1] Hajos's athletic gifts extended beyond the water, as he was also a national champion on the track in the 100 meters, 400-meter hurdles, and discus, as well as taking part on three national champion soccer teams. Swimming was always foremost among Hajos's loves, though, as he became an architect and designed many of the country's sporting facilities, winning an Olympic silver medal for architecture in an arts competition attached to the 1924 Paris Olympics.

Hajos wasn't alone among the early Hungarian innovators. The honor of "the first great swimmer from continental Europe" was bestowed upon Zoltan Halmay, who won seven swimming medals, two gold, over three Olympics.[2] His range was impressive, claiming victories at distances from 50 to 4,000 meters. He won three medals, including silver in the 200 and 4,000 free at the 1900 Games. In 1904, he won double gold by sweeping the 50 and 100 frees and added two silvers in the 1908 Games. (Halmay also won silver in the 100-meter free and gold in the 4 × 250-meter free relay at the 1906 Intercalated Games in Athens, no longer recognized as an official Olympiad.) Despite being shut out in the 1912 and 1920 Games, the former of which was the first participation for female swimmers in the Olympics, Hungarians medaled in swimming in each of the next four Games prior to World War II, punctuated by Ferenc Csik's surprise gold in the premier event of the 1936 Berlin Games, the 100 free. Along the way, Hungary spawned the first European swimmer to break the hallowed minute mark in the 100 free, Istvan Barany, though it was only good for silver at the 1928 Games behind American Johnny Weissmuller.[3]

After World War II, the balance of Hungarian medals began to shift. Where winning Olympic medals had once exclusively been the purview of men, the women got in on the party starting with the 1948 London Games. The beginnings were humble, with Eva Novak claiming bronze in the 200 breaststroke, three seconds behind champion Nel van Vliet of the Netherlands and just fractions ahead of countrywoman Eva Szekely. But it was a start. Novak's sister, Ilona, was also near a medal, settling for fourth in the 100 backstroke. Those accomplishments were overshadowed by another solid performance by the men, who claimed three minor medals. Geza Kadas couldn't break the American blockade of Wally Ris and Alan Ford in the 100 free in garnering bronze. In the 1,500 free, Gyorgy Mitro finished a distant third behind American Jimmy McLane. Kedas and Mitro teamed with Imre Nyeki and Elemer Szatmari for the 800 free relay and put a scare into the Americans, but the Hungarian squad settled for silver behind Team USA's world record.

Despite the unmistakable strides taken in London, there was little hint that the Hungarian women would enjoy the medal explosion that occurred four years later. The field in 1952 was among the deepest ever assembled, with the Soviets and their satellite republics competing for the first time and Japan returning after being absent from the 1948 Games. But that meant little to a Hungarian squad that took 6 of the 12 individual medals on offer in Helsinki and won four of the five events contested in the women's draw. The only individual event from which Hungary came away without a medal was the 100 backstroke, won by South African Joan Harrison ahead of pre-meet favorite Geertje Wielema. Hungary's only contestant in the event, 15-year-old Magdolna Hunyadfy, bowed out in the semifinals.

Perhaps the biggest highlight came in the 100 free, which got off to a record-setting start from an unlikely source. In Round 1, Judit Temes clocked in at 1:05.5, unseating the 16-year-old world record of Rie Mastenbroek from the Berlin Games. The semifinals set up a stirring finale, with all eight finalists clustered within eight-tenths of a second. Temes snuck into the final's eighth and final spot with a time of 1:07.4, just barely edging Denmark's Ragnhild Hveger, the former world-record holder who at age 31 was 10 years Temes's senior and making a last-ditch effort at rectifying the glaring omission of an Olympic gold on her otherwise stellar résumé. American Jody Alderson set the pace in the semis at 1:06.6, while the second semifinal featured a three-way tie for first at 1:07.2 between Harrison, Hungary's Katalin Szoke, and Great Britain's Angela Barnwell. The final was a predictably wild affair, with the top six finishers clocking in within a half second. Temes took the early initiative and led most of the way. Harrison surged down the homestretch and appeared to take the lead for good with 10 meters to go. But up came fellow 16-year-old Szoke and Dutchwoman Hannie Termeulen. After some deliberations between the finish judges, Szoke was ruled to have gotten to the wall first in 1:06.8 for gold. Termeulen was second in 1:07.1, and Temes found enough in the tank to slip into bronze, awarded the same time as Harrison and Alderson but adjudged to have gotten her hand to the wall first.

On paper, the 200 breaststroke shaped up as another battle for the Hungarians to dominate. With reigning Olympic champion van Vliet not competing, 1948 holdovers Szekely and Eva Novak looked like solid medal chances, even if Szekely was 25 and one of the oldest competitors in the field. It also provided an interesting contrast of styles. In the days before butterfly splintered off as a separate stroke, the double-overarm recovery that now characterizes the stroke was an acceptable way to swim breaststroke, which was primarily defined by the presence of a frog kick instead of the flutter kick popularized by freestyle. Szekely utilized the butterfly technique while Novak was a devotee of the classical underwater stroke. No matter how they covered the distance, they did so with record-setting alacrity. In the first heat of the first round, Novak set an Olympic record of 2 minutes, 54.0 seconds, trouncing the mark set by van Vliet (2:57.2) in the 1948 final. Three heats later, Szekely also comfortably got under van Vliet's mark in 2:55.1. Szkeley, equaling her time of 2:54.0, and Novak won their respective semifinals, Novak followed closely by Klara Bartos, whose time of 2:56.5 gave the Hungarians the three fastest times entering the final. Falling by the wayside in the semis were 1948 Olympic silver medalist Nancy Lyons of Australia, who finished 13th, and reigning European champ Raymonda Vergauwen of Belgium, who settled for 11th. Though Novak entered the event as the favorite, Szekely made that prognostication look silly in the final, flying away with gold in 2:51.7, an improvement of 2.3 seconds on her Olympic record and 5.5 seconds faster than van Vliet four years prior. Novak wasn't challenged for silver, clocking in at 2:54.4. A Hungarian sweep was only prevented by Great Britain's Elenor Gordon, who recorded an identical 2:57.6 as Bartos but was awarded bronze.

The 400 free appeared poised to provide another classic tilt. Included in the field was Hveger, with her dubious reputation as the greatest swimmer never to win Olympic gold, and fellow Dane Greta Andersen, the reigning European champion who won gold in the 100 free in London four years earlier. Coupled with the sudden strength of the Hungarians plus the presence of Harrison and the always formidable Americans, spots in the finals would be at a premium. While Hveger set the early pace in Round 1 with her time of 5:19.6, 1.3 seconds ahead of Szekely, the Olympic record went down two heats later in a tie. American Evelyn Kawamoto and Great Britain's Daphne Wilkinson both clocked in at 5:16.6 to share the mark, though Kawamoto won the heat. The effort clearly took a lot out of Wilkinson, who faded to 11th in the semis in 5:27.2. Kawamoto won her semifinal heat in 5:21.2, edging Novak by a tenth. All four swimmers in the second heat were faster than Kawamoto, led by Hungary's Valeria Gyenge, a surprise inclusion who made a charge at the Olympic mark but settled for a time of 5:16.9, over five seconds quicker than her prelims time. Hveger finished fourth in the second semi but easily made the finals, while Andersen scraped into the eighth and final spot of the championship heat, a second faster than Harrison. Szekely entered the final seeded third, and Eva Novak was sixth. The final appeared to be the storybook ending Hveger had long sought, with the Dane leading most of the way. But the 31-year-old faltered late, opening the door for the two Hungarians, Novak and Gyenge, to charge. The younger and less heralded of the two, the 19-year-old Gyenge, produced the most convincing final push, edging out Novak, 5:12.1 to 5:13.7, for gold and the Olympic standard. Kawamoto cleaned up bronze in 5:14.6, Hveger plummeted to fifth in 5:16.9, and Szekely missed a second individual medal by settling for sixth.

The form of the Hungarians made the 400 freestyle relay a virtual certainty. In April of that year, the team of Eva Novak, Szekely, Szoke, and Maria Littomericzky had set a world record that was pending ratification, downing the 14-year-old standard set by Hveger-anchored Denmark way back in 1938. The Olympic record went in a different direction in the first round, though, with the Americans winning their heat in 4:28.1, 1.5 seconds ahead of the Netherlands. The third-fastest time of the preliminary round belonged to Hungary (4:32.5), with Littomericzky swimming in place of Temes. The order was shuffled for the final, with Ilona Novak going from third in prelims to leading off the final squad, while Eva Novak slid from second to third to accommodate Temes in the second leg with Szoke anchoring. The result was a decisive win by four and a half seconds over the Dutch and a world record of 4:24.4, almost three seconds faster than the time Hungary had posted earlier in the year. Ilona Novak got the Hungarians out to an early lead, clocking in at 1:07.8 to edge out the Dutch's Marie-Louise Linseen-Vaessen and Team USA's Jackie LaVine (both 1:08.1). Ilona Novak, who finished ninth in the 100 free with a time identical to her relay split, would be the only Hungarian not to split sub-1:06. Temes followed with a 1:05.8, a 1.3-second improvement on her bronze-worthy time and enough to balloon Hungary's lead to over two seconds. Eva Novak followed with the fastest split of the bunch, a 1:05.1 that increased the margin to 3.4 seconds and put the fate of gold beyond doubt. Szoke brought it home with a flourish, splitting a 1:05.7 that was 1.1 ticks faster than the time that won individual gold. While the Americans and Dutch battled it out for silver—the latter getting there first in 4:29.0—Hungary had yet another piece of hardware to celebrate, while the Novaks earned the distinction of being the only sister tandem to win Olympic swimming gold.

The triumph of the Hungarian female swimmers was one of many for the nation at that time. That year coincided with the height of the Magical Magyars era of the Hungarian men's national soccer team, led by Real Madrid icon Ferenc Puskas. That team starred in some of the most memorable games in soccer history, including a victory in the final of the 1952 Olympic Games over Yugoslavia; the 6–3 triumph over England at Wembley Stadium in 1953, dubbed the "Match of the Century"; and the "Miracle of Berne" loss to West Germany in the final of the 1954 World Cup. At the 1952 Games, the Hungarian delegation finished third in the medal table in golds and overall medals, with 16 and 42, respectively, trailing the much larger powers of the United States (40, 76) and Soviet Union (22, 71). In addition to soccer gold, Hungarian teams took the title in men's water polo, a sport in which they'd emerged as a world power, and men's sabre. They also won silver and bronze in team gymnastics and bronze in the prestigious 4×100-meter relay on the track. About the only down note of the Games was a lackluster showing from the men's swimming team, with the best the Hungarian guys could muster being a fifth-place finish from Kadas in the 100 free and fifth in the only relay, the 800 free.

For all the laudable accomplishments of the 1952 Games, though, there were whispers of politicization suffusing the swimming squad. That was unavoidable, to a degree, for athletes of a nation so often jockeying between independence and possession, either outright or by irresistible influence, by the many empires that rose up in Eastern Europe through the 20th century. In the latter stages of World War II, Hungary was occupied by the Soviet Union, which stripped it of its territorial acquisitions made from 1938 to 1941 and, after a failed experiment with puppet democracy, installed a harsher regime orchestrated by the Soviets. A flurry of regime changes, some espousing brutal crackdowns on dissidents and others offering more moderate reforms, ensued in the early 1950s.

The influence invariably trickled down to the athletes carrying the Hungarian standard into international competition. Szoke, for instance, changed her name just before the Helsinki Games to distance herself from the legacy of her father, Marton Hommonai, an Olympic gold-winning water polo player in the 1930s who became a radical right-winger and fled to Argentina in the late 1940s to escape prosecution for war crimes.[4] Szekely's athletic trajectory was altered by politics, with the swimmer being expelled from her local club team in 1944, being labeled a "religious undesirable" because of her Jewish heritage and forced to live for two years in a safe house in Budapest.[5] Gyenge and others recall the inherent prestige associated with their roles as athletic stars, affording them privileges—from an unprecedented freedom to travel domestically and abroad to access to scant supplies of delicacies like chocolate and oranges—far out of reach for the destitute masses of the country struggling under the yoke of a stagnant command economy. Try as they might—Gyenge always maintained that "she wasn't interested in the politics. All I was interested in was swimming. The Olympics was my dream"[6]—the athletic success striven for by individuals was always apt to be spun as being for the nation and the party. When the Hungarian athletes returned home from Helsinki on a train with a gold "16" painted on the side, they became political capital for a flagging regime. Such heroes were "a healing balm for a country caught under the thumb of a brutal despot, Matyas Rakosi, who governed using the tools of terror, secret police, kangaroo courts and concentration camps."[7] The marriages of Gyenge,

Szekely, and Szoke to star water polo players Janos Garay, Dezso Gyarmati, and Arpad Domyan, respectively, assumed tinges of political convenience, creating celebrities of the Communist Party and, in the most cynical of views, an avenue of selective breeding for the next generation of athletes. (The fact that the daughter of Szekely and Gyarmati, Andrea Gyarmati, won two swimming medals at the 1972 Olympics reinforces that notion.) The Hungarian Olympic heroes walked a fine line between embodying a symbol of intense pride for a nation of people desperately looking for hope and having their accomplishments co-opted for the good of the Soviet-supported regime. "Those were the darkest days in human terms in Hungary," Gyenge said of the predicament in 1952. "It was terror. But the masses and the people were so touched by the results that they just loved us dearly."[8]

Those politics came to a boiling point in 1956, leaving the looming Olympics in the crosshairs. The timing was poor in a number of ways for the Hungarians. The 1956 Games in Melbourne were slated to be the first Southern Hemisphere Olympics, and the climatological timeline meant the "summer" Games wouldn't open until November 22. In late October, a student-led uprising in Budapest was put down by Soviet troops and led to a coup by Imre Nagy, a moderate reformer who'd run afoul of the Soviets in the past but was allowed to briefly take power in a bid to restore order. His reign lasted about a week, as his intended modifications to the government—which included a coalition incorporating non-communists, relaxing government control of the economy, and a withdrawal from the Warsaw Pact to seek total independence—led the Soviets to retake control of the nation in early November, installing a new regime that executed bloody reprisals against adversaries of the state.

While their nation was under siege, the Hungarian Olympic hopefuls had to somehow still prepare for the Games as if all was normal. After all, the prospect of Olympic glory wouldn't wait for the travails of a small nation tucked away in Europe's interior. From the hotels near their countryside training bases, Gyenge and other members of the Hungarian team could see the fires of an overrun Budapest burning in the distance. The Soviet troops that mobilized to quell the student rebellion pulled back on October 30, allowing Nagy's government a brief window to establish itself. That relaxation in tensions provided the Olympic delegation its opportunity to leave the country, somewhat furtively, through the safer haven of Czechoslovakia. With the favor of the Soviet mechanisms unavailable or too risky to try, the Hungarians followed a circuitous route through Istanbul, Karachi, and Singapore that took weeks to get to Melbourne. When they arrived in Australia, they were hit with the news that the rebellion had failed, Nagy's government had been toppled, and the Soviets had reasserted harsh control via a puppet regime loyal to Moscow and looking to punish the perpetrators of the revolt to assure that such an insurgency never propagated again.

Under this pall, the Hungarians prepared to compete in Melbourne. Instead of training for the pinnacle of their athletic lives, many were feverishly exploring diplomatic channels for information about loved ones, many of whom were in jeopardy of imprisonment, deportation, or worse. Gyenge received word in Melbourne that Garay had defected to Vienna. With Garay having made Gyenge promise that she would bolt for the safety of the West if her athletic travels provided an opening, Gyenge joined a multitude of athletes who turned their attention to defection plans. Some of the athletes faced uncertain futures themselves. Gyarmati, who was the captain of the Hungarian water polo team in his third Olympics and well on the way to becoming "the most decorated Olympic water polo personality of all time," was a known sympathizer of the student revolution that had been violently squelched.[9] Gyarmati's intervention, personally meeting with Nagy in late October, had helped facilitate passage of the athletes to Melbourne, ostensibly to represent what many hoped to be a newly freed Hungary.[10] With Nagy and the revolution that swept him ever so briefly into power displaced, many of the young athletes loyal to the cause were left representing a nation they didn't recognize, one that at best was contrary to their values and at worst sought to persecute them and their families.

In the face of such crippling adversity, athletic considerations became secondary. The starting gun or bell of Olympic events served as a jolt from a world of preoccupation to the athletic tasks that had lost much of their luster. "During that time, there was no possibility to train," Gyenge recalled almost a half century later. "There was strange food, plus the emotional strain. And we'd left everyone behind. The further we got from Europe, the less we knew."[11] Szekely and Gyarmati, both competing in Melbourne, had to consider the fate of their two-year-old daughter at home. Under such stress, Szekely reported barely sleeping in Melbourne and losing 12 pounds before competition.[12] The only power the Hungarians retained so far from home lay in the subtle acts of defiance within the Olympic ceremony. Instead of the national flag, the Hungarians displayed pre–communist era standards with a black mourning stripe memorializing the dead and incarcerated. As the Soviets entered during the procession of nations, the Hungarians turned their backs in unison.[13]

Facing such strife, it's no surprise that the Hungarian effort fell short of the lofty heights of Helsinki. They dropped a spot in the medal table to fourth, supplanted by the host Australians, with 9 gold and 26 total medals, well short of the halcyon days of Helsinki. The tally was propped up by gymnast Agnes Keleti, the most decorated athlete of the Games with four golds and two silvers, including team gold in the portable apparatus competition and silver in the overall team standings. The men's sabre team, light middleweight boxer Laszlo Papp, and the men's water polo team all repeated as gold winners. The latter sport proved to be a flashpoint for the tensions between Hungary and the Soviet Union. Already with a rich recent history of controversial encounters, Hungary met the Soviet Union in the semifinals in Melbourne. The match was taut from the beginning, with physicality on both sides and verbal barbs being lobbed from all directions, including from a capacity crowd. With Hungary up 4–0 late, Soviet standout Valentin Prokopov delivered a vicious punch to the face of Hungary's Ervin Zador after the whistle, setting off a melee between the players in the water and on the bench. As Zador, blood gushing from the right side of his face, walked off the deck to seek medical attention, the match was halted, awarding the win to Hungary as missiles and chants of "Hajra Magyarok!" ("Go Hungary!") rained down on the Soviets from the partisan crowd. The iconic Olympic moment was immortalized as the "Blood in the Water" game, which Hungary parlayed into a 2–1 win over Yugoslavia in the final for gold.[14]

Though the Hungarian swimmers reaped just two medals, one per gender, from Melbourne, the performance was remarkable given the circumstances. On the men's side, Gyorgy Tumpek won bronze in the 200 butterfly, the first Games in which the nascent stroke was contested, falling just one-tenth of a second behind silver medalist Takashi Ishimoto of Japan. Of the nine swims by Hungarian men, Tumpek was the only one to qualify for a final, including the 10th-place 800 free relay.

In the women's draw, the questions of "what if" were palpable: so often the Hungarians were so close to medals that the inevitable curiosity of what they could've done under ideal conditions beckons. In the 100 free, Szoke was the 17th-fastest finisher in prelims, one spot and one-tenth of a second away from the semifinals in 1:08.0. The time was 1.2 seconds slower than the time she used to win gold four years prior. Gyenge (1:06.6) and Zsuzsa Ordog (1:06.5) made semis, but neither could advance, finishing 11th and 14th overall, respectively. Gyenge's battle to defend her 400 free title almost hit a premature end. She set the fastest time in the first of four Round 1 heats with a 5:14.2, then saw successive Olympic records set by American Marley Shriver and Australians Dawn Fraser and Lorraine Crapp. Gyenge's time stood as the seventh-fastest of prelims, and she and Ripszima Szekely each qualified for the final. The pace in the final, though, quickly left both behind. Crapp ran away with the win in 4:54.6, a stunning improvement of 17.5 seconds over Gyenge's victorious time in Helsinki. Ripszima Szekely was well off the lead in the final, taking fifth in 5:14.2, seven seconds out of the medals, while a spent Gyenge faded to eighth in 5:21.0. To hear her discuss the ordeal, though, that time seems like a massive achievement. "I don't even remember how I got to the blocks," she said. "And then I heard the starter gun, and so I jumped in the pool and tried to pull myself together."[15]

The theme of close calls carried through the meet. Only one other event final, the 100 backstroke, occurred without a Hungarian after Eva Pajor and three-time Olympian Temes bowed out in prelims. In the 100 butterfly, the

29-year-old Littomeritzky qualified from preliminaries with the fifth-fastest time and improved one spot in the final, taking fourth, a half-second slower than bronze medalist Mary Sears. A very deep 400 freestyle relay comprised of Littomeritzky, Szoke, Temes, and Gyenge was relegated from fifth-fastest in Round 1 to seventh in the final in 4:31.1, three seconds back of the prelim time and nearly seven slower than in Helsinki. The only consolation from Melbourne for the Hungarian swimmers came via Eva Szekely, then an ancient 29, in the 200 breast. She won the second of two Round 1 heats in 2:55.8 to be the fourth-fastest finals seed, two spots behind Bartos. In the final, Germany's Ursula Happe pulled away late in an affair where the top five finishers hailed from Eastern Europe. Szekely rallied to beat a crowd of swimmers to silver, posting a time of 2:54.8. Fifth was Bartos in 2:56.1, a spot behind her finish in Helsinki. For a 10-time world-record holder and 68-time national champion, it may have seemed like a dour ending to her career, but that's not how Szekely saw it. "Even though it was one of the few times that I have been beaten in competition," she said, "considering everything, I am very proud of the silver medal."[16]

The winding down of competition meant the attention of the Hungarians turned to the future and how they would cope with the upheaval of a homeland that bore little resemblance to the hopeful, resurgent nation they left. Many athletes turned to the media for aid. The *Toronto Star* procured passage for Gyenge to Canada for exclusive rights to her story. Time Inc., with its new sports periodical, *Sports Illustrated*, also engaged in a bit of intrigue to furnish the defection of 34 Hungarian and four Romanian athletes to the United States, setting up promotional tours and aiding their assimilation to the new nation.[17] Gyenge and Garay married in Vancouver at a reception thrown by Canadian swimmers, and Gyenge remained in Canada where she became an accomplished photographer and novelist. She returned to her homeland in 1964 when amnesty was declared for defectors, and in 2008, she was honored by the Hungarian government for her sporting and artistic achievements. Among her most prized possessions, as she recounted in a 2009 interview, was a photograph with her 1952 teammates on their heroes' welcome to Budapest.[18] Szoke and Domyan found a home in California, where he became a prosperous real estate developer. Gyarmati returned to Hungary before he and Szekely spent time in the United States, eventually returning to their homeland upon the amnesty decree.

Whatever the fates of the individual athletes, the sporting power of Hungary would never again be the same. Through the years, many elite swimmers—Andras Hargitay, Zoltan Verraszto, Krisztina Egerszegi, Tamas Darnyi, and Laszlo Cseh, to name a few—have called Hungary home. But the days of Hungary as a comprehensive sporting power were never to return, what once was an empire lying "forever shattered" by the revolution and the unrest the followed.[19] "Helsinki was the pinnacle of Hungarian sports," recalled Gyarmati in 2012, 60 years on from the nation's athletic high-water mark.[20] For its swimmers at the heart of that excellence, no performance in the years before or since has matched it.

Chapter Eleven

1968 U.S. Olympians

There was no sugarcoating the expectations heaped upon the 1968 U.S. Olympic swim team ahead of the Mexico City Games. The team was expected not just to be the best in the pool in Mexico City—and overwhelmingly so. The group assembled at Olympic Trials was saddled with the imperative to be the greatest collection ever sent to an Olympic Games. How that would be measured, in spite of changing Olympic programs, wasn't quite certain. But whatever the metric, the Class of 1968 was pushed to measure up.

The most telling aspect of the 1968 team is how lofty the goals they inspired were, goals so high that no team, before or after, has achieved. While the team story from the Games was one of American triumph, the most compelling individual tale focused on an American who fell short of the goals that he—and the swarm of publicity he invited—had fueled.

Through the adversity in Mexico City, the American team persevered and prospered. Where one member of the team stumbled, others stepped up in heroic proportions. Where some found their pre-meet expectations to be an anchor weighing them down, others transformed them into a pivot to launch into swimming history. The composite was the most prolific Olympic swimming performance ever produced.

The promises in the media in the summer of 1968 tended toward unequivocal terms. You could put "virtual certainties"[1] like Don Schollander down for assured medals, or you could bet on the likes of Debbie Meyer or Mark Spitz. The early predictions put the number of medals to be claimed by the Americans at an astronomical 57 from 29 total events, 24 individual.[2] Long before the Games commenced, they had already been ordained as the "dream team."[3] "This is the greatest women's team ever assembled. Our second string could win at Mexico City," boasted Sherm Chavoor, coach of the women's team. "I think my wife could coach this bunch to victory in the Olympics."[4] "This certainly is the best team of girls we've sent to the Olympics," added George Haines, head coach of the American delegation, after Olympic Trials. "We've never had so much depth before. I've never seen a meet like this one."[5] Informing the forecasts of success was the expansion of the Olympic program from 18 events to 29, a nuance sure to accentuate the superior depth of the Americans. There was little wiggle room in those evaluations, and even less chance of another nation knocking the U.S. off its perch in a home-continent Olympiad.

The optimism was borne out of a variety of factors. The Americans were coming off their latest greatest-team-in-history performance in the 1964 Games, a title unequivocally bestowed upon the squad by men's coach Doc Counsilman after his team returned from Tokyo with 13 golds from 18 events and 29 total medals.[6] The performance at the 1968 Trials hinted that the times of the 1964 stars would go the way of the dinosaur quickly. At Trials, world records dropped like flies, 16 in all going by the wayside. Schollander, counting down the final meets of his stellar career, set a pair of world marks in the 200 free despite sputtering to fifth in the 100 and missing his chance to defend his title from Tokyo. Spitz thrust himself into the limelight with a world mark in the 100 butterfly, while the 400 individual medley standards fell to Charlie Hickcox and Claudia Kolb, who also captured the 200 IM mark. Meyer positioned herself to be the darling of the Games with an amazing 200-400-800 free triple world-record swoop, the shorter world mark taken the same day that Linda Gustavson had displaced the standard and marking the fourth American woman (along with Sue Pedersen and Edith Wetzel) to undercut the record in eight weeks. Combined with Catie Ball's mark in the 100 breast, the American women set seven world marks at Trials, plus Sue Pedersen was off a 100 free mark by one-tenth of a second.

The two headliners of the 1968 Games—Meyer and Spitz—followed similar pathways to Mexico City but ended with drastically divergent results. Meyer moved to California from Haddonfield, New Jersey, to train with Chavoor's Arden Hills Swim Club. She faced a major adjustment from her former training habits, at about 2,000 yards a week, to Chavoor's ultra-distance methods that had her logging as much as 14,000 a day, six days a week. Despite her early struggles—like only enduring four laps of her 20-lap warm-up on her first day at Arden Hills—she had a championship mentality that Chavoor instantly recognized, no matter how much her physical state lagged. Chavoor recalled a Junior Olympics race in which he promised Meyer a spot on a relay if she could post a sub-30-second time, then a career best by a long way, in the 50 free. Meyer went 27.8.

By the summer of 1966, Meyer was seeing massive time drops. At the Outdoor AAU Nationals, she was under the world record in the 1,500 free, though she finished second by three seconds to teammate Patty Caretto. Later that year, she bested Caretto's American record in the 1,650 free by 15 seconds. In about a year, she had cut over a minute off her personal best in the 1,650. Whatever criticism Chavoor took for his methods of "new style pain-barrier experimentation"[7] that some people thought bordered on cruelty, Meyer was a sterling example of their efficacy. She also displayed the stamina and savvy in the water to utilize Chavoor's preferred method of distance swimming, the "go-out-hard-and-hold-it" technique the coach adapted from the successful Japanese swimmers of the 1930s.[8] Meyer was one of six Arden Hills swimmers on the American team, plus Spitz, whom Chavoor had coached in the past and would coach again after 1968.

Meyer had seemed to find her counterpoint on the men's side in Spitz, a swimmer who prospered at an early age under Chavoor's tutelage and earned a handful of world records in free and fly before his junior year of high school was up. He had burst onto the scene at age 15 when he was named the outstanding swimmer of the Maccabiah Games, benefitting from a change of scenery to Santa Clara Swim Club under Haines. With the 1968 Games scheduled for the summer before he went off to college, Spitz was tabbed as one of its stars. Despite the times, not everything was rosy for Spitz. Santa Clara wasn't the best fit for him for a variety of reasons, including his Jewish heritage, which earned him teasing and taunts. Taking a cue from his authoritarian father, Arnold, Spitz developed a tendency of setting extremely high goals and clearly articulating them, a habit that informed his success. When those goals were invariably accomplished, he had no problem celebrating the achievement. In certain contexts, those good-natured expressions of triumph were viewed as brash pomposity. At Olympic Trials, for instance, Spitz celebrated his third-place finish in the 100 free by exclaiming, "I'm in five events now!" presuming he had earned the right to swim the butterfly leg in the medley relay after winning the event at Trials.[9] His public proclamation that his goal stood at five or six gold medals in Mexico City smacked of overconfidence to some. Innocently ebullient on the face of it, such cocksure statements rubbed some, including 100 fly rival Doug Russell, the wrong way.

Spitz and Meyer weren't alone in facing difficulties leading to the Mexico City Games, which acquired the dubious moniker of "the Problem Olympics."[10] The choice of venue was a calculated risk for the International Olympic Committee, based on the length of travel for much of its constituency, Mexico's sketchy reputation on the world stage, and the pioneering status as the first Games in Latin America. From a competition perspective, staging the Games at altitude introduced all sorts of problems for athletes and worries about the safety of competitors, especially for endurance athletes dreading the prospect of sub-optimal levels of atmospheric oxygen. For American distance swimmer Mike Burton, that fear—fueled by a 1966 meet in Mexico City in which he swam 79 seconds slower than his world record in the 1,500 free—was so palpable that he withdrew from UCLA to train for three months at the U.S. Air Force Academy at 7,000 feet. Then there were concerns over drinking the water in Mexico and the resulting bouts of turista in many athletes. The combination of low oxygen and undrinkable water fueled what was termed "the Altitude Monkey" that many athletes struggled with. "After each event, we would have to go and lie down on a cot in some little back room while a Mexican medical guy sprinkled sugar into our open mouths," Hickcox recounted. "It was supposed to make you bounce back quickly or something. But mostly he sprinkled sugar into our eyes."[11] The qualms weren't about whether an athlete would get sick; that was a virtual certainty. The challenge was managing the illness, retaining the most strength possible, and rebounding with the least amount of downtime.

All those looked like minor inconveniences, though, when the Games were put in jeopardy just 10 days before the Opening Ceremonies when the Mexican army forcibly suppressed a long-brewing student protest occupying the Plaza de las Tres Culturas in the city. What became known as the Tlatelolco massacre, after the neighborhood in which it took place, resulted in dozens of deaths, the true extent of which was concealed as a matter of state policy, and hundreds of arrests. Once there, swimmers faced the challenge of what they saw as sub-par facilities, certainly for an event of the Olympics' magnitude. Not only was the pool slow, but there was also a lack of warm-up and cool-down space. "It's murder in there. You make the turn and suddenly you're going bump, bump, bump over the waves," Ken Walsh said of the turbulence in the pool during the 400 free relay. "Almost enough to make you seasick."[12] About the only recourse for swimmers was a public display of discontent, like the simultaneous false start in the finals of the 200 fly. There was also a fair amount of scandal peppered into the proceedings in Mexico City, from a Dutch cycling masseuse sent home for possession of illegal vitamins to the unlawful presence of alcohol in the Olympic village to the open solicitation of track athletes by shoe companies, an uncouth invasion of commercialism into the hallowed halls of pure sport.

The problems for Spitz, though, started much sooner. In an effort to prepare for Mexico City's altitude, the national team convened at the Air Force Academy for a pre-meet training camp. It was hardly the harmonious retreat some hoped it would be. In the words of Gary Hall Sr., who would go on to compete in the 1972 and 1976 Games, the pre–Mexico City summit was the "most divisive" he had ever been part of.[13] Fueling the fire, quite inadvertently, was Spitz. He missed the bulk of the first two weeks of training—the heavy-yardage, aerobic-base-forming foundation—with a case of tonsillitis, exacerbated by his discomfort with the altitude. For a group of teammates hoping to knock Spitz down a peg and exhausted by the nonstop, glowing attention lavishly showered on him, the illness wreaked of a prima donna's aversion to hard work. The dynamic within the team was growing toxic, with roommates Russell and Walsh—aged 22 and 23, respectively, and seeing Spitz as a sincere threat to their final shot at Olympic glory—leading the anti-Spitz bloc. Spitz, meanwhile, roomed with backstroker Ronnie Mills, a 17-year-old from Texas who wasn't much liked either, not helping Spitz's social status. Spitz was joined on the Olympic team by six teammates from Santa Clara, which would've been a positive had he not already had to endure tense times there. There were aspects of Spitz's performance at Trials—his edging out Russell in the 100 fly; his disputed third ahead of Schollander in the 100 free; and his qualification for the 800 free relay in a special, USA Swimming–sanctioned swim-off instead of the actual event, seen as a concession to his busy program—that didn't ingratiate him to his new teammates. Even without Spitz, the camp's ambience was being dragged down by the presence of essentially two teams: the swimmers who qualified for individual events, and a faction of seven relay alternates with almost no chance of swimming in the Games unless someone, like Spitz, was too ill or injured to travel. With their training, limited to a focus on 100 or 200 meters, having a remote possibility of coming to fruition, they had plenty of time to contemplate what it would take to ascend to the Olympic stage.

Out of the pool, Russell and Walsh sought to provoke Spitz with various stunts, like preying on Spitz's hypochondria by faking negative reactions to a routine injection given at camp.[14] In the water, Russell pleaded to train with the middle-distance contingent to boost his endurance and get a chance to go to work on Spitz psychologically, racing him each chance he got. The fact that he and Spitz's rivalry would come to a head became a foregone conclusion once Russell eschewed the 100 back and 200 IM to focus on fly. Spitz unintentionally invited some of the ridicule, like when he begged for a 100 fly time trial after practice one day; his hubris, swimming when still far from full strength from his illness, led to him posting a time slower than some of Russell's practice reps, further dashing his confidence. Despite his youthful follies and social missteps, Spitz didn't deserve much of the abuse thrown his way, especially given that much of it was suffused by anti-Semitic feelings. Haines and Chavoor experienced as much firsthand when they kept tabs on Spitz when he and fellow swimmer Sue Shields went on a golf outing during camp, able to hear the taunts and verbal jeers he was on the receiving end of. Spitz had the coaches on his side—he had worked with both Haines and Chavoor in the past and had committed to swim under the men's assistant coach Don Gambril at Long Beach State. But that didn't help his case much with his peers.

From what was generally a highly successful meet, Spitz turned in some of the highest and lowest moments of the 1968 Games, courting controversy at most turns, but attention at each. His program began with a leg in the final of the 400 free relay. The Americans qualified first, 2.4 seconds faster than the Soviet Union, secure in the knowledge that three of the four Soviet swimmers would contest the finals while only Stephen Rerych was a hold-over for the U.S. The final, on the first day of competition, was put to bed quickly. Zac Zorn's split of 53.4 seconds put the Americans up 1.3 ticks on the Soviets, and the lead only grew from there. The rest of the squad followed with remarkable consistency, with Rerych (52.8), Spitz (52.7), and Walsh (52.8) lengthening the lead to a world record of 3:31.7. The Soviets were second at 2.5 seconds back, a gap Haines admitted he thought the American B team easily could've slotted into.[15] Spitz's first individual event, the 100 free, was something of a long shot for him to win, and some didn't favor him to even medal. He'd finished third at Trials in the 100, after Zorn tied Walsh's world record. Despite that history, Australian Michael Wenden was the person riding highest into the final, setting an Olympic record in the semis with a time of 52.9, three-tenths off Zorn's world mark. Walsh entered the finals in seventh, one-tenth behind Spitz. The final appeared to be a race to see who would get least washed away by Zorn's wake. But Zorn took his first 50 out far too fast and had nothing left in the tank at the end, allowing the other seven swimmers to overtake him. First to the wall was Wenden in 52.2 seconds, a world record. Walsh was just two-tenths off his former world mark from the 1967 Pan Am Games in taking silver in 52.8, while Spitz snuck into third, a half second clear of fourth-place finisher Bobby McGregor of Great Britain. It wasn't gold, but the 18-year-old Spitz was satisfied by the piece of hardware. "I'm pretty happy with the way it came out," Spitz said. "I tried my hardest, and it's my best time. I was going to go as hard as I could tonight and I had a feeling I would be either the first or second American."[16]

Spitz's next test two days later would be his most daunting: the 100 fly. Not only did he carry the world record into the event, sizeable target that that is, but he did so against the likes of Russell and Ross Wales. Where Spitz was stretched in many directions, over various distances in free and fly, Russell and Wales had the benefit of pinpointing every moment of pre-Olympic training solely on the 100 fly and stalking Spitz. The fact that Spitz had a perfect nine-for-nine record against Russell in major competition certainly wasn't missed in Russell's psychological preparation. Russell took the early initiative from the first heat of Round 1, turning in an Olympic-record 57.3 seconds that was the fastest of the preliminary round by nearly a second. When Spitz broached that kind of speed in semis, winning the first of three heats in 57.4, Russell consolidated his Olympic record with a 55.9 in the final heat, easily outpacing Wales (58.2). The final would come down to Spitz and Russell, two swimmers with diametrically opposed styles. Spitz, the butterfly purist and 200 specialist, would bide his time and give the sprinters free rein to tire themselves out, then charge late. Russell was the epitome of the sprinter, of the go-hard-and-hope-to-hang-on ilk. Russell, though, flipped the script in finals. Instead of trying to take the early lead, Russell held back, allowing Spitz to cover the first 50 first, with Wales and several others still in touch. With the power in his legs held in reserve, Russell took the sting out of Spitz's anticipated charge down the homestretch, matching him stroke for stroke and getting to the wall first in 55.9 seconds, a half second quicker than Spitz. Bringing up the bronze was Wales by a comfortable margin. The ever-analytical Wales was far enough behind to assess the situation. "[Russell] really tore it up in Colorado Springs," Wales said. "He was working so hard, and Mark was in and out of the infirmary so much that I knew he'd win. I swam my race just about as expected. I wanted to be out with them and try and get ahead before the end. The outcome was just about what I'd expected."[17]

From there, things went downhill in a hurry for Spitz. He faced a quick turnaround for the final of the 800 free relay, his eighth swim in five days. Exacerbating the pressure was their second seed in finals, the Australians qualifying first from prelims by a third of a second. With Wenden clearly in form and waiting on the anchor leg, the usually infallible Americans had reason to be concerned. Those apprehensions were quieted when John Nelson and Rerych split matching 1:58.6s in the first two legs, opening up a 2.5-second gap on Australia and over six seconds on everyone else. But where Spitz was expected to put the race out of reach on the third leg, the Aussies mysteriously remained in contact. Bob Windle split a 1:59.7, carving almost a second out of the lead of a fatigued Spitz, who turned in a sluggish 2:00.5 split. Dreams of a comeback never materialized, with the veteran Schollander bailing out the hotshot kid, covering the final 200 meters in 1:54.6 to prevent Wenden (1:54.3) playing spoiler. Gold was the Americans' in 7:52.3. The Olympic and world records, though, survived. Spitz's ego wasn't so lucky, as he took criticism for not ceding his spot to a fresher swimmer, not putting the team good above his own. The connection between him losing his spot on the medley relay to Russell and staying on the 800 free squad was obvious. Even Schollander, without naming him specifically, cited the accumulation of races as the reason for the lack of a record in the event.[18]

With the relay team at his side, a down day for Spitz still yielded gold. Going it alone in the 200 fly didn't work out so well. Spitz didn't look much worse for wear, posting the joint-fastest time in prelims with teammate John Ferris. The final was positioned as Spitz's to lose. Following the theme of the week, the stiffest challenges were to be provided by his countrymen. Among them was Ferris, a former Arden Hills teammate whom Spitz hadn't lost to in butterfly since they were children. The other was Carl Robie, at age 23 one of the elder statesmen on the team. He had a long history with the event, four times setting the world record. The last of those marks, though, came in 1963, a year before he traveled to the Tokyo Olympics as a favorite for three golds and left with just a solitary silver from the 200 fly. Having been at the top so long, Robie had developed into a "mechanical superstar" who flat-out "choked" on the Olympic stage.[19] After graduating from the University of Michigan, where he'd led the Wolverines to two NCAA titles, the "Philadelphia Flyer" decided that "he wasn't ready to die as a swimmer" yet, despite taking classes at Dickinson College Law School in his home state of Pennsylvania.[20] Given his past success at altitude, Robie elected to give it one more go, coaching himself at a YMCA in rural Pennsylvania between his studies. The work paid off in the final, with Robie filling the gaping hole in his résumé by getting to the wall first in 2:08.7. Second was Great Britain's Martyn Woodroffe (2:09.3), followed by Ferris, who recovered late to capture bronze. Spitz was never a factor. He hung back as usual, biding his time and waiting to pounce on a tiring field. But when he reached deep for his trademark burst, there was nothing there beyond the ability to bring up the rear, a distant eighth in 2:13.5.

It was a low point for Spitz, already feeling isolated among his teammates. (An incident with team manager William Lippman, who upbraided Spitz for using the tub in his private suite to shave down before a swim, didn't help Spitz's fragile psyche either.) Among the chorus of detractors was Ferris, who crafted his race around Spitz, hoping to ride his wave up the field; luckily for him, when it became obvious Spitz was faltering, he shifted tactics and pulled himself back into the medal picture. Spitz and Russell's simmering conflict also boiled over when Russell got wind of Spitz, somewhat dryly, remarking to the press that he hoped Russell failed a drug test. That led to an altercation back at the dorm, with Russell throwing his medal at Spitz, daring him to take it from him. Overall, his first Olympic foray was an ordeal that, though it netted Spitz four medals, two of which were relay gold, left him to reevaluate his swimming future. His rise to prominence four years later occurred largely because of the decisions taken in the immediate aftermath of Mexico City, such as relocating from Haines's Santa Clara and opting for the nurturing atmosphere of Counsilman's Indiana University instead of Long Beach State.

Though Spitz struggled to come to terms with the challenges of Mexico City, many others with loaded programs succeeded. Meyer's week started out swimmingly with the 400 free, a race in which she led by two body lengths after 100 meters and was never seriously threatened. She won in an Olympic record of 4:31.8, almost four seconds quicker than Gustavson. But as the week wore on, Meyer began feeling weaker, developing a sore throat and intestinal troubles that sapped her strength. Even slightly limited, she still managed a decisive victory in the 200 free. Meyer set an Olympic mark in preliminaries of 2:13.1, then held off a stiff challenge from countrywomen Jan Henne and Jane Barkman in the final to win in 2:10.5, well off her world record but still an Olympic mark. The final test was the 800 just a day later. Again, Meyer set the pace with an Olympic record in prelims, but this one lasted just a few minutes, taken the very next heat by 14-year-old Australian phenom Karen Moras by 4.5 seconds. In the final, though, Meyer stamped her authority on the field. She took the swim out fast and didn't stop, winning in an Olympic mark of 9:24.0. Though it was well short of her world record (9:10.4), she took gold by a massive margin over American Pam Kruse (9:35.7) "as easy as water running off a duck's back."[21] With that, Meyer became the only American woman—through the 2012 London Olympics—to capture three freestyle gold medals in the same Games.

Seeing the evidence around him, Burton was plenty justified in a bit of nerve jangling. Already concerned about the effect of the altitude, Burton was buying into reports from endurance runners and rowers of struggles over the longest-distance races. Seeing runners collapse during the 10,000 meters—and teammate Ferris swoon on the medal stand after he clinched bronze in the 200 IM—didn't do much for his mental state. Nor did a bout of illness, the standard-issue welcome packet from the Mexico City bureau of tourism, that greeted him on his arrival. A win in the 400 free provided only so much comfort. It was a significant accomplishment, especially given that Burton's malaise almost forced him to miss the preliminaries. When he got to the pool, he false started on his first attempt. Nonetheless, he qualified comfortably with the fourth-fastest time. In the final, the "Pocket Battleship" found a second gear, running away with gold in 4:09.0, decidedly quicker than Canadian runner-up Ralph Hutton (4:11.7) and bronze medalist Alain Mosconi of France (4:13.3). "I was really lucky. I've been sick, I passed out, thrown up, but for the last two days I've been getting stronger," Burton said after the win. "I took it out like I wanted to, at a minute, I could have gone out faster but I didn't dare. I always go out to win, and I felt I had it from the last lap going home."[22]

The shorter triumph didn't assuage Burton's feeling that victory in the 1,500 was "the impossible dream."[23] Complicating matters was the presence of the home crowd's darling, Guillermo Echevarria. The two had a history. In July, Echevarria swiped Burton's world record in the 1,500, doing so close to home at the Santa Clara Invitational. Burton replied by shaving almost 20 seconds off Echevarria's best at the Olympic Trials, reinstalling himself as the favorite at the Games. Burton had the honor of the opening salvo in Mexico City, winning the first Round 1 heat comfortably in 17 minutes, 27.2 seconds. Three heats later, that proved to be only the fifth-fastest time, trailing countryman John Kinsella, Australians Greg Brough and Graham White (the pacesetter at 7:10.1), and Echevarria (17:11.0). The final proved just how much Burton had kept in reserve. He separated himself from the field early and stayed away. His time was nowhere near the 16:08 world record, with the clock finally stopping at 16:38.9, an Olympic mark, but the margin to Kinsella's silver-winning time was still over 18 seconds. Echevarria, meanwhile, labored home, taking a distant sixth in 17:36.4. In one of the most challenging doubles of the competition, Burton had emphatically proved his might.

Those successes were among many crowning achievements in Mexico City. The Americans got a surprising gold in the men's 100 breast when Don McKenzie's "take-charge race" snuck him ahead of the Soviet favorites.[24] It made up for Brian Job only getting bronze in the 200 breast behind Mexican hero Felipe Muñoz. The breaststroke events, given the Eastern European proficiency in that stroke, proved the only stumbling block to medal-podium hegemony.

The women's events could've gone much differently had not Ball suffered one of the most severe bouts of illness among the squad. She was out fastest in the 100 breast but faded terribly to finish fifth, 2.5 seconds behind her world record. Ball, who had recovered from a battle with mononucleosis six months before the Games, had a post-race exam that revealed swollen glands and a high fever, leading the coaches to withdraw her from the 200 breast and send her home. Sharon Wichman picked up the slack in the 100, earning a bronze medal. In the 200, she earned a measure of revenge on the two swimmers who beat her over the shorter distance, Yugoslavia's Durdica Bjedov and the Soviet Union's Galina Prozumenshchikova, by winning comfortably in on Olympic-record 2:44.4.

The early-meet effort included almost complete dominance of certain nights, like when on October 20 the Americans won eight of nine medals. Kolb was first in the women's 200 IM, leading Pedersen and Henne to the wall. (Later in the meet, Kolb also dominated the 400 IM, outdistancing American runner-up Lynn Vidali by a staggering 13.7 seconds.) Hickcox made sure the 200 IM wasn't much of a race, winning ahead of Greg Buckingham and Ferris the same night as Meyer's 400 free triumph. Henne and Pedersen also played into the medal picture in the 100 free, with the former earning the win in another medal sweep, Gustavson claiming bronze. In the longer IM, Hickcox ruled the day, albeit in a tight race with Hall. The women's backstroke race involved a slight surprise, with Kaye Hall turning in the only world record on the women's side when she got the better of Canadian Elaine Tanner in 1:06.2. Not only was the two-tenths cut off Karen Muir's world mark "unexpected," but so was getting the better of Tanner, a native of Vancouver whom Hall, hailing from Tacoma, Washington, raced regularly but hadn't beaten in 10 years.[25] "I just took it out as hard as I could and then just tried to stay ahead of her because she really bombs it home," Hall said. "I was hoping to win, but I didn't know if my plan would work."[26] Jane Swaggerty garnered bronze. Tanner avenged the loss in the 200 back by tipping Hall, but it was good only for silver, over two seconds behind American Lillian "Pokey" Watson, a converted freestyler who unabashedly called her victory "an accident."[27]

There were impediments along the way for the Americans. The women's butterfly golds, for instance, were taken by surprising Australian Lyn McClements in the 100 and Dutchwoman Ada Kok in the 200. But American Ellie Daniel pushed into silver behind McClements and ahead of Shields, then took bronze in the 200. The men's backstroke was the dominion of East Germany's Roland Matthes, who doubled up on gold. The U.S., led by Hickcox and Mills in the 100 and Mitch Ivey and Jack Horsley in the 200, cleaned up the minor medals. The 200 free was supposed to be Schollander's grand farewell, but Wenden spoiled the celebration for the nine-time world-record holder in the event. Using his choppy, rapid stroke cadence that was in stark contrast to the languid, graceful movements of Schollander, the Aussie managed to hold off the Yale grad, 1:55.2 to 1:55.8, with Nelson slotting into bronze.

There was no stopping the Americans in the relays. In addition to the two men's freestyle triumphs, the men's medley relay of Hickcox, McKenzie, Russell, and Walsh resisted the early charge of Matthes, who staked the East Germans to a three-second lead off the front. By the time Russell handed off to Walsh, the Americans were over a second clear of the field, a lead they solidified to win in 3:54.9, a world record. The East Germans put a scare into the American women's 400 free relay, with Barkman leading by just three-tenths after the first leg. The three medalists in the 100—Henne, Gustavson, and Pedersen—opened up the lead quickly, though, to win by 3.5 seconds in an Olympic record. The women's medley relay of Hall, Ball, Daniel, and Pedersen looked vulnerable when Aussie Lynne Watson closed the gap on a weakened Ball to within three-tenths. But Daniel held serve against McClements, and Pedersen delivered the anchor-leg hammer to take the lead to 1.7 ticks and an Olympic record of 4:28.3.

The final count for the Americans was 52 medals from 29 events, six times more than the nearest country (the Aussies and Soviets had eight each). The Americans captured 21 of 29 golds, a share of 72.4 percent, slightly higher than four years prior. But the 1968 squad significantly improved on 1964's percentage of total medals, capturing 52 out of the 87 on offer (59.7 percent). In terms of the individual medals, the Americans claimed 47 of 72 available, a staggering 65 percent. The reviews of the American performance raved. In the pool, wrote the *New York Times*' Steve Cady in praising an "American Monopoly," "the competition has been as one-sided as a bull-fight."[28] The American success included victories in 7 of the 11 new events, a fact that wasn't missed by opponents of the expansion. "If there is one decision the international amateur fathers may ultimately regret as they survey the changing scope of their Olympic structure," wrote the *Times*' Neil Amdur, "it is the decision to expand the swimming."[29] Whatever the future had in store, the present was obviously illustrious for the Americans. "We are up to here in heroes and heroines," Chavoor beamed. "I mean, look at Debbie

Meyer. Look at Mike Burton. Kids like this make America great."[30] In the pool in Mexico City, that certainly held true.

Chapter Twelve

1973 East German Women's World Championships

The hope entering 1973 was that a new era of swimming openness would dawn. The year would play host to the inaugural FINA World Championships, envisioned as an Olympics between the Olympics to bring together the world's best talent and put aquatics in the athletic limelight. Worlds also gave swimmers and developmental programs another carrot to aim for, another chance for athletes to represent their countries and an opportunity for swimmers from smaller countries to take another shot at breaking the medal embargo held by the sport's traditional powers.

The events that transpired in early September in Belgrade, Yugoslavia, entered a relatively new name onto the medal table. But the arrival of the German Democratic Republic onto the women's swimming scene was so comprehensively dominant that it altered the sport's landscape for decades to come. The East German women didn't just win 10 of 14 events at the Tasmajdan Sports Center and 18 total medals. They instantly installed themselves as the preeminent women's swimming program in the world.

History hasn't looked favorably on the accomplishments of the East Germans, a two-decade reign of success fueled by illicit performance-enhancing steroids force-fed to athletes without their consent by a ruthless state-sponsored program. Proof of that wide-ranging system of doping wasn't available in the 1970s, no matter how pervasive the suspicion was. But certain facts were abundantly clear: the East Germans were the best, and the methods that could be discerned from a distance were ones to be emulated. The 1973 Worlds weren't just the launching pad for two decades of East German dominance. They also signaled a paradigm shift, with the East German model—of training, of talent identification and inclusiveness, of state backing of athletics—becoming the prevailing ideology in the world of swimming.

The East Germans weren't entirely arrivistes on the swimming scene in 1973. They'd won medals in continental competition dating back to Jutta Langenau's win in the 100 butterfly at the 1954 European Championships. Medals came in fits and starts through the years, but nothing like what would happen in 1973. The program proved adept at churning out elite sprinters, with East Germany laying claim to the 100 freestyle European champ in successive competitions in 1962 (Heidi Pechstein), 1966 (Martina Grunert), and 1970 (Gabriele Wetzko). While the 1962 meet featured a medley relay win for the East Germans, there was only a smattering of minor medals in 1962 and 1966. The only East German triumphs of the 1968 Olympics came on the men's side, where Roland Matthes established himself as the premier backstroker of his age. The East German women managed just three pieces of hardware at the Mexico City Games, two silvers (Helga Lindner in the 200 fly and the 400 free relay) and one bronze (Sabine Steinbach in the 400 individual medley). The 1970 European Championships indicated that brighter days lay ahead, with the East Germans garnering 9 gold and 16 total medals in the women's draw. That included a clean sweep of the freestyle events—Wetzko in the 100 and 200, Elke Sehmisch in the 400, and Karin Neugebauer in the 800—plus decisive wins in the 400 free and medley relays. Expectations for the 1972 Olympics near home soil in Munich were understandably lofty, but the East Germans fell well short of hopes. The depth was sufficient to nab a pair of relay silvers, both behind the Americans, but individual medals were few and far between. Kornelia Ender took silver in the 200 IM, Roswitha Beier was second in the 100 bronze, and Gudrun Wegner took bronze in the 400 free, but that was it for the East Germans. With two individual golds plus relay silver and bronze, Matthes nearly matched the output of the East German women single-handedly.

The East Germans arrived in Belgrade with a spotty track record in international competition. But the times the GDR contingent had posted in the summer leading up to the inaugural Worlds seemed unimpeachably fast. At the East German Trials, four world records were set, three by Ender (100 free, 100 fly, 200 IM), who at age 15 had made a convincing case as the best swimmer in the world. The East Germans were already tacitly approved by the Americans as a formidable opponent, garnering sufficient interest to schedule a dual meet in Leipzig in 1971 that was hailed as a landmark athletic event bridging the Iron Curtain. What was yet to be determined was whether the East German women would follow the model of the men, a group of middling international swimmers surrounding a star like Matthes, who brought the entire program acclaim. In Belgrade, it would soon become evident that the East Germans were much, much more than just Ender's backup singers.

Ender, though, certainly led the chorus of medal winners. Her victorious performance in the 100 free underscored just how monstrous the leaps in speed made by the East Germans were. It had taken eight years for the world record in the 100 free to drop from the time of 58.9 posted by Dawn Fraser in 1964 to the 58.5 turned in by Shane Gould in 1972. That's eight years and a scant .4 seconds separating two swimmers unquestionably recognized as among the greatest in history. Just 19 months after Gould's last record and about year after her abrupt retirement at age 17, Ender had chopped the record by almost a second all by her lonesome. Ender's world record of 58.25 seconds at the GDR Trials was undercut at a tune-up meet for Worlds in August, and even that record's days were clearly numbered in Belgrade. She started by leading off the 400 free relay with a time of 57.61, then won the individual event comfortably in 57.54, easily separating herself from American Shirley Babashoff (58.87). Ender was also first in the 100 fly in what became a two-woman race between her and countrywoman Rosemarie Kother. Ender just edged out Kother, 1:02.53 to 1:02.68, with the closest American contestant being Deena Deardruff in fourth. Ender was shown to be mortal in the 200 IM, settling for silver, though still a startling statement on her versatility. It took a world record, from her better-rested teammate Andrea Hubner, though, to unseat Ender's quest for a third gold by .7 seconds.

Despite Ender's sprint prowess, the American freestyle program managed to hold off the advances of the East Germans in Belgrade. Keena Rothhammer and former world-record holder Babashoff went 1-2 in the 200 free, the former pulling the upset over her more heralded teammate in a time of 2:04.99 that was well off Gould's world record (and nowhere near the 2:03.22 that Ender would log as the world mark the following summer). Rothhammer wasn't able to double her gold in the 400, with Heather Greenwood springing a surprise and swimming away to victory in 4:20.28 to Rothhammer's 4:21.50. Novella Calligaris made sure Ender's wasn't the only freestyle world record to fall, with the Italian claiming the 800 free gold to go with bronze in the 400. Calligaris's time of 8:52.97 easily outdistanced American silver medalist Jo Harshbarger (8:55.56), etching Calligaris's name in the record book as the only female gold medalist not from the U.S. or GDR. The East Germans' medal haul in freestyle was surprisingly meager, garnering just 3 of 12 available, with Andrea Eife's 200 bronze and Wegner's 800 bronze joining Ender's gold. The 400 free went down as one of only two events whose medal podium didn't include an East German (the Americans, meanwhile, missed three podiums).

The Flying Frauleins more than made up for it in the stroke program, though. Aside from the 200 back—a race dominated by world-record holder Melissa Belote of the United States, who easily beat Edith Brigitha of the Netherlands and Hungarian rival Andrea Gyarmati—the East Germans made a clean sweep of the non-freestyle events. Even with the presence of 1972 Olympic champ Belote, the 100 back was almost a foregone conclusion to be a "battle for second" behind East Germany's Ulrike Richter.[1] Richter's world record of 1:04.99 off the front of the medley relay—a time almost three-quarters of a second less than Belote's winning time from Munich—prior to the individual event solidified the notion that it was her race to lose. She didn't quite duplicate the relay speed, clocking in at 1:05.42, but it was still well ahead of Belote's 1:06.11 that earned silver. Breaststroke was almost an exclusively Eastern show, thanks in large part to Renate Vogel, the only woman to join Ender among the ranks of the double winners. Vogel benefited from the absence of Cathy Carr, the world-record holder and 1972 Olympic champ who opted—perhaps in deference to the eye-catching times Vogel had posted in 1973—to compete in the World University Games staged simultaneously in Moscow. Without Carr, Vogel faced little resistance in swimming away with gold in 1:13.74, well ahead of the USSR's Lyubov Rusanova (1:15.42) and East Germany's Brigitte Schuchardt (1:15.82). In the longer breaststroke event, Vogel again reigned supreme, but this time she got a scare from teammate Hannelore Anke. By the halfway point of the race, Anke and Vogel were over two seconds clear of the field, the former ahead by a half second to set up a decisive final 100 meters. Vogel had the stronger second half, getting to the wall in 2:40.01 to Anke's 2:40.49. American Lynn Colella, who finished fifth in the 100 breast, rallied to slip into bronze.

Colella added bronze in the 200 fly, but that was so far behind the pace that she never challenged Kother. In a testament to the groundbreaking speed of the East Germans, Kother cut .12 seconds off Karen Moe's world records in prelims, then dashed nearly two seconds off that in finals to win in an absurdly fast 2:13.76. Her time was 3.01 ticks ahead of Beier and almost six seconds faster than Colella. But that still doesn't quite capture how impressive her swim was. It was, in the words used by *Swimming World* magazine, "one of the most recklessly paced races ever," Kother's first 100 split being almost three seconds faster than Moe's when she bested the world record the previous summer.[2] The ferocity with which she attacked the race "completely intimidated the rest of the field," including Colella, who admitted afterward that Kother's early lead disrupted her from her race plan.[3] In the 200 IM, Kathy Heddy scared the American record of Claudia Kolb, coming within .34 seconds of the mark. That was good only for bronze without hope of contending for gold. Ender took the race out fast, seizing on her butterfly specialty and backstroke prowess. But Hubner rallied on the breaststroke leg, and while Ender challenged her in freestyle, Hubner had enough to clock a 2:20.51 and hold off Ender (2:21.21). Both swims were well under Ender's world record of 2:23.01. The sorting out in the 400 IM occurred at a similarly early juncture, with two East Germans joining Calligaris at the front of the pack. While Calligaris eventually fell off the pace, both Angela Franke, the world-record holder, and Wegner were under world-record pace. Wegner took a modest lead after 300 meters and ballooned it to almost 3.5 seconds at the wall, becoming the first woman to ever break the five-minute barrier, and emphatically so. She checked in with a time of 4:57.51, well ahead of Franke's 5:00.37. Both got under Franke's world standard of 5:01.1. Calligaris claimed bronze in 5:02.02, while the nearest American challenger was Terry Potts in fifth, 12.5 seconds behind Wegner.

It came as no surprise that the relays were just as lopsided as the individual events. The medley relay assembled by the East Germans was the stuff of poetry. "If such a thing as perfection in swimming is possible," praised the glowing recap by *Swimming World*, "it was in this event that it happened."[4] As the concluding event of the meet's first day, it proved to be a fitting harbinger of the relative fates of the gold-winning East Germans and runner-up American team. The race started with Richter's world record in backstroke. Vogel followed with a 1:12.93, over three seconds faster than the split by American Marcia Morey. Kother's fly leg of 1:01.71 trounced Deardruff's 1:03.25. And even with the race and a world record clearly decided, Ender added a 57.23 anchor leg, 2.7 seconds quicker than Babashoff. The collective result was a 4:16.84, just short of four seconds faster than the world record the U.S. had used to win the final in Munich a year prior. At those Games, the East German relay went 4:24.91 to earn silver. In a year's time, they had cut an unprecedented eight seconds. The Americans in Belgrade, meanwhile, limped home for silver in 4:25.80, a massive margin of 9.04 seconds back. "Their margin of victory was so great (20 meters) that not even a wide angle lens could register the winning margin," illustrated *Swimming World*. "It was the worst defeat ever by an American relay team."[5] The destination of gold in the 400 free relay, consequently, wasn't in much doubt. "The only questions," opined *Swimming World*, "was by how much would they better the existing [world] record."[6] The answer was, by a lot. The prelim swim of 3:56.55 was a second off the world record from the Americans in Munich. When it came time for cuts, Franke's 58.9 split wasn't good enough to make the top half. Joining Hubner and Sylvia Eichner from prelims was Eife and of course Ender. The latter led off for her world record of 57.61 seconds, carving out a 1.45-second lead over Kim Peyton and almost two seconds over anyone else. The American team of Peyton, Heddy, Greenwood, and Babashoff didn't go quietly, clocking in at 3:55.52, .33 off the pace that won gold in Munich. But they never challenged for gold thanks to the East Germans. Eife (a stellar 57.4) and Hubner followed Ender, each expanding the lead by subtle margins, and Eichner finished it off by outsplitting Babashoff to seal the win and the world record in 3:52.45, a cut of close to three seconds off the world standard.

The effect of the East Germans' sudden and spectacular emergence can't be understated. Al Schoenfield, the editor of *Swimming World* and the prevailing voice in swimming media at the time, dubbed it "a new era in swimming" in an editorial accompanying the magazine's coverage of the events.[7]

The jarring arrival of that new era was only peripherally related to the formation of the World Championships as an Olympic-caliber meet. Instead, it was
all about the East Germans. The popular view at the time was that the East
Germans had been preparing for this meet for four years, a plan put in place
soon after the 1968 Olympics in Mexico City. The Munich Games were too
early to see the completion of that ideal, but it came to stunning fruition in
Belgrade. With it came a shift in the global swimming power balance. "The
East Germans are now developing a program comparable to what the United
States has had the past couple of years," said American coach Gus Stager
after witnessing just two days of domination in Belgrade. "What with their
girls taking build-up vitamins—they're awfully big girls—they're doing
something right."[8]

Reasons for the sudden rise of the East Germans were proffered from
every corner of the sports world. Part of the relative success compared to
their American adversaries was due to the shortcomings of the Stars and
Stripes. Where the East Germans saw Belgrade as a long-term objective, the
Americans saw it as just another international meet. The American squad
was split between Worlds and the World University Games, which also
yielded somewhat dour results. The majority of swimmers in the American
delegation swam faster at AAU Nationals in Louisville, Kentucky, which
served as Trials for both events and was for most swimmers the main event
of the season.

Part of the revolution ushered in by the East Germans was relatively
benign: their swimsuits were an innovative break with the past. The swimsuits, which were also worn in Munich, were much more hydrodynamic, the
skintight outfits making the East Germans "resemble sleek wet seals."[9] So
profound was the impact of those suits on the consciousness of swimmers in
1973 that the designer, West German Dr. Conrad Dottinger, began marketing
them as the "Belgrad." Among the observers of the success of swimmers in
the suits, *Sports Illustrated*'s Jule Campbell opined that "one wonders if the
fabric has been injected with a miracle drug that gives the swimmers added
strength."[10] Vague allusion to doping aside, the suits, made of an ultra-
lightweight Nylon-Lycra blend that weighed as little as four ounces, constituted a major adjustment in terms of modesty. They represented the first
major change in suits in over a decade, with most swimmers clinging to the
White Stag Speedo models that debuted in 1958. Where old suits required
glue or other fastening at the neck, arm, and leg openings, the Belgrad featured rubber bands for watertightness. For many American swimmers, the
immodesty of the suits and their overly revealing nature bordered on the
scandalous, a price too high for winning. (That refrain—that the devotion to
winning by the East Germans, whether in terms of provocative suits, joyless
and draconian training regimens, or drastic alterations in body size and
shape, was too unwomanly to take root among the American girls—would

become increasingly popular as the East German sporting machine gathered steam.) But they were soon adopted universally, led by Americans like Rothhammer and Babashoff. One of Babashoff's first experiences in the suit came at the AAU Indoor Short-Course Nationals, where she shaved four seconds off the American record in the 500 free and took aim at concerns of indecency about the suits.

The suits, though, were but one possible source of the East Germans' speed. One popular explanation for the East German women's international success centered on one of the chief tenets of the sporting system, one that even in the light of later proof about doping had its merits. What the East Germans did better than anyone else was select talented individuals at the youth level and provide them the opportunities, in terms of training resources and financial backing, to reach their full athletic potential. At a time before college opportunities for female athletes in the United States enjoyed any kind of standardization or legal imperative, the East German system provided promising athletes everything they could possibly need, from lodging to state-of-the-art facilities and access to coaches and doctors using the latest technologies. Former Olympic swimmer Donna De Varona, who would go on to play a major role in the fight for equal athletic standing for women through statutes such as the 1978 passage of Title IX, was one of the loudest voices trumpeting those virtues of the East German system. Putting aside the issues of skinsuits, which she reasoned could only account for so much of the East Germans' speed, she was able to tour the East German swimming establishment in 1974, meeting many top officials. The visit came on the heels of another stirring performance by the East Germans, winning 15 gold medals and setting 10 world records at the 1974 European Championships. Writing for the *New York Times*, De Varona shared her observations. "East Germany is the only nation in which the individual's right to physical recreation is included in the constitution," she noted, adding that one in eight East German children takes part in some kind of sport.[11] Where funding in the United States has been consistently cut for physical education from the earliest years of elementary school, the East German system and the underlying Teutonic mythos emphasizing physical fitness required participation in athletic endeavors from a very young age. That hastened the process of identifying talented individuals, allowing them to be paired with specialized coaches and methods at an earlier age, as young as eight, to speed up their development.

In the swimming ranks, the East Germans mimicked the age-group system from the United States, but instead of a diffuse network of privately held clubs, the East Germans used state-sponsored clubs over which the national organizations had central influence and direct input. The East Germans provided logistical support, like busing from schools directly to sports centers and special training camps that were among the most advanced in the world, all underwritten by a government whose aims weren't necessarily wholesome but who used sporting achievement to prop up a flagging sense of national pride. What De Varona specifically gleaned from her experience was the equality of the program: while the best athletic opportunities in the United States, including virtually all the money for athletics at the college level, were reserved for men, the East Germans made a more equitable split. With the devotion of millions of dollars and boundless reserves of attention to the development and implementation of androgenic hormones for women, drugs that would produce male characteristics in women and give them a marked advantage in terms of size and strength over their global counterparts, it could even be argued that the East German women received a disproportionately large share of the program's resources. On the international fields of play, they certainly earned an outsized return of medals and accolades. So divergent were the directions of the programs that De Varona termed the pending dual meet in 1974 between the GDR and the USA as a "test of the efficiency of diametrically opposed national development programs and social systems."[12]

Even in the early 1970s, though, there were suspicions that the prolific accomplishments of the East Germans were fueled by more than skimpy suits and institutional inclusiveness. Proof was in short supply, deterring most from openly discussing their misgivings about the East Germans' methods and limiting the doubters to a whisper that wouldn't reach a crescendo until the late 1970s. After a week of being soundly beaten by the East German women, the increasingly jilted cynicism of the Americans led to them casually referring to their eastern aggressors as "those guys."[13] Shrouded by a veil of secrecy—East German athletes were seldom allowed to speak to the media, and in the rare instances they did, it was under the close watch of a handler or official—suspicions ran rampant. After Belgrade, *Swimming World* charted the rapid increase in height and weight for the East German medal winners, some putting on as many as 15 kilograms from 1972 to 1973. "There is talk of a sort of 'vaccine against fatigue,'" wrote Pierre LaCour. "It consists of an injection of toxic substances which allows the body to combat fatigue more efficiently. It is believed that male hormones are given to the girls, who, in addition to an increase in vigor, develop a superiority complex with respect to other females from foreign countries."[14] The mysterious, almost mythical substances couldn't be identified, with all variety of potions and concoctions, both the suspected steroids and other chemical enhancements, being invoked. At that early juncture, any accusations were couched with the disclaimer of a lack of proof. Schoenfield gives prime placement in his editorial to the fact that FINA's medical commission did random drug tests, a facet of international competition receiving greater attention after American Rick DeMont tested positive at the 1972 Games, without a positive in Belgrade.[15] Lacour's article comes with an editorial disclaimer that "one must realize that many of the same accusations have been offered before when other swimmers have shown a superiority over their competition. . . . The comparison of heights and weights over one year shows the girls to be bigger and stronger, however, the reasons for the increase remain unconfirmed."[16] Even De Varona alluded to the "open conjecture" of anabolic steroid use, citing the notes of the French Swimming Federation physician Michel Leglise on the East German women's "muscle and fatty development that is unusual in girls their age . . . a special skin quality, a bit of hairiness unusual in girls of this age, rather curious voices and certain signs in their step."[17] In the same breath, though, De Varona was careful to point out that proof of indiscretions had yet to emerge.

It would take another quarter of a century, through the fall of the Berlin Wall, the reunification of Germany, and the process of reconciliation of the German people with the repression and surreptitiousness of the former regime, for the secrets to finally come out. The East German state, under State Planning Theme 14.25, orchestrated a system whereby elite athletes were identified for use as agents of the state, separating them from their families to train with coaches and doctors financed and overseen by the state sports committee. The GDR devoted millions of dollars in research to developing new drugs, such as the 1965 introduction of anabolic steroid Oral Turniabol. Working the other side of the street, the East German labs placed themselves at the forefront of detection techniques that they then availed to international sporting bodies, all the while devising ways for their own athletes to avoid them. These drugs were incorporated into athletes' training regimens, allowing them to practice longer and harder and gain body mass in unheard of proportions. Often the steroids were disguised as vitamins and given to athletes without their consent, without any notification of the well-known side effects and without the athletes having any idea what was being put into their systems. There was no option for athletes: those who refused drugs would be expelled from the system and effectively barred from the possibility of athletic achievement. Also in place was a hierarchical structure of coaches and trainers who compiled meticulous records of drug use and training logs that were disseminated to their superiors. The entire bureaucratic system was girded by a culture of secrecy within the nation, with legions of citizens working as informants for the East German secret police, the Stasi, to report on any activities that could potentially be counter to the nation's objectives.

The thumping received by the U.S. in Belgrade had immediate ramifications for the American women's program. Inklings harbored before the event that American supremacy was dwindling were verified; suddenly the Americans were left to be the pursuers in the race for international domination. The confidence of many swimmers of that era was decisively dented, a pall that carried over into the next summer's dual meet with the East Germans in California and endured through most of the 1970s and 1980s. Combined with the mounting evidence of illicit activities by the East Germans, the United States entered many meets with dim hopes of success. "Belgrade hurt us for a lot of years," Babashoff recalled in 1991. "Morale was down. Some of our girls were going in . . . already beaten."[18] Babashoff was emblematic of the injustice of East German cheating. Over two Olympic Games and two world championships, Babashoff won 18 medals, four of them gold, but none in individual Olympic events. Among her hardware are 13 silver medals, 10 of which came behind doped East Germans.

In the immediate aftermath of Belgrade, the Americans tried to emulate the aspects of the East German approach that were recognizable and legal. Babashoff, with coach Mark Schubert at the Mission Viejo Nadadores club, was at the fore of a novel emphasis on weight training and work outside the pool to build strength and speed. Western swimmers, under the assumption that the East German training efforts, at the minimum, involved some form of monitoring how the body is fueled and relied on regimens of vitamins, refocused attention on diet and nutrition. The adoption of lighter racing suits was spurred by the East Germans' supreme utilization of them.

But the greatest impact on swimming and other sports came from what, all drug tests aside, was unquestionably underpinning the East German system: state sponsorship of athletics. Command economies like the Soviet Union began appropriating large sums of money and resources toward developing athletes. The Western response was a push not to have governments directly fund athletes but to make it easier for qualified athletes of all genders and economic backgrounds to get access to resources that would help them achieve the most they could. Government earmarks and tax breaks headed to organizations like USA Swimming, which presented the first unified and organized front for that sport and doled out grants to make it more financially feasible for athletes to compete without fear for their financial security. They were all lessons learned the hard way in Belgrade.

Chapter Thirteen

1976 U.S. Men's Olympians

There was no way the U.S. men's team could've known in 1976 just how unprecedented a performance they were compiling. The numbers compared to the past were startling, for sure, but as the American men in Montreal were blazing a well-worn path to the top step of the podium, few could've imagined such a dominant performance as the end of an era.

The U.S. men were nearly infallible in Montreal, winning 12 of 13 gold medals and 25 of the 33 possible individual medals on the men's side. It was a fitting capstone to the reign over the world swimming scene that the American men had enjoyed almost unchallenged for some two decades, a rule that reached its height in 1976. Little did the Americans know that its days of dominating the world were so numbered.

Retrospect heightens the accomplishments of the American men in Montreal. Cold War tensions and the use of athletes as geo-political pawns would rob the world of a true display of the world's best swimming talent for the next 12 years, with the Americans boycotting the 1980 Games in Moscow and the Eastern bloc retaliating at the 1984 Los Angeles Olympiad. By the time the swimming community reconvened in Seoul in 1988, a litany of nations had entered swimmers in the medal picture, the wealth of hardware being shared more widely than ever. The ruling prior to the 1984 Games which limited each nation to just two individual entrants per event—directly aimed at preventing the gaudy medal totals of powers like the American men and East German women, especially as the program of events expanded— negated the superior depth that was the calling card of America's halcyon days.

Before those sea changes in the swimming landscape, though, there was one last display of power for the glory days of American swimming, one that had no equal and was so comprehensive as to precipitate some of the changes that would prevent it from ever occurring again.

What the 1960s were to political change in the United States, the 1970s were to change in swimming, an escalating arms race in technique and speed yielding some of the most precipitous time drops in history. Much was in response to what the American women endured in the early 1970s at the hands of the East German women, who burst onto the scene at the inaugural FINA World Championships in 1973 and set times that boggled the mind. It soon became evident to most involved—though, crucially, not beyond a reasonable doubt—that the East Germans were being fueled by clandestine and illicit drugs, the genesis of the masculine characteristics (and times) in their female swimmers. With the world's governing bodies unable or unwilling to ban the East Germans, the challenge to the rest of the world was to keep pace. From that quest sprung all manner of innovation—in training, in the use of weights and various other devices, in attire, and even in reevaluating entire nations' systems of talent identification, development, and funding. With the official explanation emanating from behind the Iron Curtain that the pills being fed to teenage girls were vitamins and nutritional supplements, Western coaches took a renewed (and often first) look at nutrition in athletes. A concerted effort to understand the body's response to the stress of training and how to optimize results while minimizing and focusing effort was widely undertaken. This was also an era of rapid development in swimsuits, also hastened by the sleek, skintight suits debuted by the East Germans that quickly supplanted the bulky, cumbersome suits the Americans had utilized. While the crux of these queries involved improving the plight of women's swimming, there was an inevitable carryover effect on the men's side, with energy and resources at previously unheard of levels devoted to find and train Olympic contenders.

That escalation in swimming excellence arguably reached its pinnacle in 1976. Of the 26 events on the Olympic program, only one world record from prior to 1976 survived the record-setting onslaught. (That was Mark Spitz's time from the 1972 Olympics in the 100 butterfly, a testament to his timeless dominance.) A total of 60 world records were set in 1976. In Montreal that summer, only four events lacked a world record, and the only event where the winner was faster in Munich four years prior was Spitz's 100 fly. There were 26 golds on offer in Montreal: 13 went to the United States, and 11 were captured by the GDR women. Between them, the twin powers of the swimming world seized 67.9 percent of the total medals in Montreal (53 of 78) and 71.2 percent of the individual medals (47 of 66).

While the East German dominance was vilified, the prowess of the American men's developmental machine was a matter of intense pride. The process of culling the foremost talents in the world to a mere three contestants per event, though, was an uncomfortable task, as was discovered at the

1976 Olympic Trials. It's often said that the American Trials are the fastest meet in the world; never was that more true than in 1976. The consensus among swimmers was that making the team was more important than setting a world record. Nonetheless, two world standards and three American marks were downed at Trials, but the truest depiction of the meet's speed involved those who didn't make the cut rather than those who did. Take for instance Andy Coan, who won gold in the 100 free at the 1975 World Championships. His time in the prelims at the Olympic Trials in Long Beach, California, was 51.85 seconds, a time that only two non-Americans had topped in 1976. Coan finished ninth among his countrymen, not even making finals. In 1974, Mike Bottom turned in the second-fastest time in history in the 100 fly; on an off day in Long Beach, he didn't even survive prelims, despite his personal best being one-tenth of a second faster than his brother, Joe's, winning time. In the 1,500 free, Casey Converse's time of 15 minutes, 15.76 seconds, was the fifth fastest in the history of the event. But three of the faster times were in the pool alongside him, consigning him to fourth and spectator status in Montreal.

Compared to the dogfight in Long Beach, Montreal had to be easy, and the Americans made it look that way, even if they shouldered the weight of plenty of advance pressure. "This will be one of the strongest international teams we've ever assembled," was the early appraisal of head coach Doc Counsilman. "We're competitive in every single event. Of course, the rest of the world will respond with other goals. But I think we can win over half of the events. Naturally, we'd like to win every one, but we have to be reasonable and look at it objectively."[1] The team Counsilman ventured to Montreal with included seven world-record holders, including the owner of both marks in breaststroke (John Hencken) and the distance events (Brian Goodell). The event program in Montreal had been scaled back slightly, with the 200 individual medley and 400 free relay omitted. (American Bruce Furniss, who also held the 400 IM world mark, owned the world record in the former event before Montreal, and the Americans were heavy favorites for gold in the latter.) Fewer events brought the total on the men's side to 13, 11 individual, lessening the chances of anyone duplicating Spitz's haul of seven golds in 1972. But where the Americans in 1976 lacked an all-rounder to match the versatility of Spitz, they boasted a squad replete with some of the greatest specialists each discipline has ever seen. Look no further than the reaction of distance swimmer Doug Northway, who finished seventh in the 1,500 and eighth in the 400 at Trials, but snuck into sixth in the 200 free to earn a spot on the 800 free relay in Montreal. All Northway got was a chance to swim prelims, an open audition for one, possibly two, finals spots, yet he was ecstatic to be a part of it. "It's an honor just to be on this team," Northway said in Montreal. "Just think. I'm the last man on the team and I've got a world record."[2]

Northway's exuberance was indicative of the team spirit that permeated the American squad. Though competition to qualify at Trials was fierce, those former competitors quickly meshed into a cohesive unit that supported each other on the Olympic stage, a mood that was anything but guaranteed (as the 1968 Americans can attest). The fact that most were virtually assured medals simply for being American undoubtedly contributed, as did an appreciation that the Olympic Trials they had withstood represented the sternest test imaginable. But there was also a coaching component. Counsilman, a master molder of personalities, had what could've been a volatile mix. Of the 51 swimmers representing the United States in Montreal, 27 hailed from clubs based in California, a mixture of familiarity that could've bred contempt. The other major bloc within camp was Counsilman's Indiana University swimmers, a core that he had coached to six consecutive NCAA titles from 1968 to 1973. Four of those titles came ahead of runner-up University of Southern California, which had won the last three titles, two of them a place ahead of Indiana. It was a vibrant rivalry that could've spilled over into the Olympic pool. But Counsilman was able to quell those fears, making individuals check their previous allegiances at the door. "Doc's ability to bring the team together as one team was probably the biggest factor in getting everybody to swim so well," said Rick Colella, a University of Washington breaststroker who hailed from outside the swimming establishment.[3] The reconciliation of various factions before any trouble sparked was aided by the two older statesman of the team, Long Beach State alum Tim Shaw and Indiana grad Gary Hall Sr., bridging the gap. (Hall's stature as a leader was solidified when he was chosen by the United States Olympic Committee to be the nation's flag bearer at the Opening Ceremonies, the first time that honor had ever been bestowed upon an American swimmer.) Also helping the cause for Counsilman, whose reputation was beyond question, were veteran assistants, former Santa Clara Swim Club and then UCLA coach George Haines and Long Beach State turned Alabama coach Don Gambril. "This team is a working entity that draws strength from one another," said backstroker John Naber, one of the USC stars.[4] As if their inimitable talent wasn't enough, the Americans also possessed an unmistakable edge in the intangibles category.

Perhaps the best example of that camaraderie in Montreal was the 100 fly, contested on the fourth day of competition and representing a seventh gold in seven events for the Americans. The three swimmers representing the Stars and Stripes exemplified the team's differing backgrounds. The winner at Trials was Joe Bottom, a 21-year-old native of Ohio who was part of Peter Daland's USC dynasty. Hall, who as a 24-year-old, third-year med student was attempting a comeback after two lackluster Games, was second at Trials. And the third-place finisher in Long Beach and Montreal dark horse was Matt Vogel, a native of Fort Wayne, Indiana, powering a swimming renaissance at the University of Tennessee. That field was unique not just in composition, but in the stiffness of the test received in Montreal. The pace in the prelims and semifinals wasn't set by an American, but rather by East German Roger Pyttel, who entered with an impressive international pedigree that included two fly silvers at the previous summer's Worlds. Pyttel won the second semifinal heat in 54.75 seconds, well faster than Bottom's 55.26 in the first semi and only a hair faster than Vogel, who nearly chased Pyttel down in 54.80. Pyttel seemed poised to rain on the American parade, certain to grab a medal and perhaps even garner gold. The final didn't play out that way, though. The task of dislodging Pyttel fell to Hall—in his one and only Olympic swim, his last last chance—who went out fastest, a ploy uncharacteristic of the former world-record holder in the 200 fly and 400 IM. Hall hit the halfway wall first, just one-hundredth of a second behind Spitz's world-record pace, with Vogel in second, Pyttel fourth, and Bottom sixth. With Pyttel unable to match the early speed, the sorting out came at 75 meters, morphing into a three-man—make that three-American—race. While Bottom uncorked the fastest back half in the race, splitting 28.49 over the final 50 meters, four-tenths faster than Spitz's record swim, Vogel and his shaved head got to the wall a hair quicker, 54.35 to 54.50. A further .15 seconds back was Hall, who easily outswam Pyttel for bronze. With his last chance for individual gold and a spot on the next evening's medley relay gone, Hall could've been disappointed. He was anything but. "When we took 1-2-3, it was just the greatest thrill in the world for me," Hall said. "It was worth it a million times to be out there competing. It was a great honor just to be in my third Olympics. But when I saw the sweep, I think emotionally I almost came to tears. I never saw a race where three guys were pulling for each other as much as in this one."[5]

Vogel's triumph in the 100 fly was just one entry in the golden guestbook for the Americans, whose precious metal mining operation began from the first night. Over seven days of competition, the United States entered 33 individual swims in the men's draw; 31 of those swimmers made finals, and 25 walked away with medals. The American swimming haul of 13 golds and 34 total medals (12 and 27 from the men) accounted for around a third of the American delegation's total medal accumulation, the United States' 34 golds a surprising third behind the Soviet Union and the East Germans. As a testament to their depth, not only did the American men claim all but one of the golds on offer; they also attained all but one individual silver medal. Once the success began, the team's confidence snowballed, producing a nearly invincible juggernaut. "You watch all the American men do so well and you realize that you're on the same program and the same taper," IMer Rod Strachan said, "and it gives you more and more confidence that you're going to do well."[6]

The men's events in Montreal commenced with a daunting challenge to the Americans via the 200 fly, an event in which Pyttel owned the world mark, having been the first man under two minutes. Pyttel cruised to victory in his preliminary heat, but fastest from prelims was American Steve Gregg, whose time of 2:00.24 set an Olympic record that was .04 quicker than his East German counterpart. In the final, an American was out fastest, though it wasn't Gregg. Instead, Bill Forrester covered the first 100 meters a half second quicker than Mike Bruner, trailed by Pyttel and Gregg. Bruner made his move on the third 50, surging to a slight lead over Pyttel, with Forrester and Gregg in hot pursuit. The 1-2 punch eventually got to be too much for Pyttel, who faded to 2:00.02, just under four-tenths slower than his world record. With the East German scuffling, up surged Bruner, who got to the wall first in 1:59.23, a world record that was 1.5 seconds faster than Spitz in Munich. Bruner narrowly outkicked Gregg to the wall, while Forrester nipped Pyttel into bronze as the Americans occupied all three steps of the podium. For Bruner, the slick-headed UCLA student who suspended his studies for the Games, the excitement of winning was mostly due to who finished just behind him. "As soon as I saw that it was a sweep, I freaked out," said Bruner, who along with Vogel was nicknamed a "Kojak kid" for his shaved dome. "That's the best thing that could have happened to us— sweeping the first race for the U.S.A."[7]

The second evening became the John Naber Show, in which the lanky native of Illinois whose nickname was "snake" became the first swimmer to win two individual Olympic medals in the same day. (Three days later, East Germany's Kornelia Ender duplicated the feat.) The performance allusion is appropriate for Naber, one of the few swimmers possessing the showmanship to play to the crowd, encouraging applause and recognizing the spectators for their support. The spectacle in the pool was certainly one to behold. First up was Naber's weaker event, the 200 free, in which he only scraped into the championship heat's eighth and final spot. His qualifying time of 1:52.78 was almost two seconds slower than the Olympic-record time of countryman and top qualifier Bruce Furniss (1:50.93), Naber likely feeling the effects of the prelims and semis of the 100 back the previous day. He didn't hold back in the final, taking the lead after the first wall and leading until just after the 150-meter mark. But there was no denying Furniss, his USC teammate and the world-record holder for whom the desire of a gold medal had been burning bright since his brother Steve returned from Munich with a bronze. Bruce surged late, his smooth, assured strokes getting the better of Naber and trimming three-hundredths of a second off his world record to win in 1:50.29. Naber claimed silver in 1:50.50, barely holding off the late charge of Jim Montgomery by a scant .08 seconds. Though he didn't win, Naber was upbeat at the silver, giving him plenty of confidence for his second swim. "I swam my best time. I couldn't have swum a better race," Naber said. "I wasn't concerned about the two races so close together. I was not quite as scared of it as I should have been."[8]

In the back half of his doubleheader, Naber again revealed his prelim time of 56.19 to be the product of prudent preliminary restraint. That proved a fortunate decision, since he was facing the intimidating prospect of East German world-record holder Roland Matthes. The three-time world champion and winner of every backstroke gold over the last two Games, Matthes's interest in his career waxed and waned until he struck up a relationship with Ender, eight years his junior, and resolved to have another Olympic go. A relentlessly focused man, Matthes felt he owed the 1976 Games as much to his country and its men's swimming program, so drastically dwarfed by the success of the women, as he did to himself, to prove that he could go out on a high and still perform at a third Olympiad. Naber, though, didn't exactly hang the streamers for Matthes's going-away party. The American's idea of hospitality was taking Matthes's world record in semis with a time of 56.19 seconds, 1.29 ticks faster than the time in which Matthes had won the first semifinal. In the final, Naber found still another gear, hacking seven-tenths off his day-old world record to win in 55.49. Silver went to American Peter Rocca, who at 56.34 was a hair off the world mark Matthes brought into the Games. In the face of Naber's unprecedented speed, silver suited Rocca fine. "It's a thrill to get second," Rocca said. "It's a thrill just to swim with Roland Matthes. He's been the best in the world since I was a little kid. I think I swam my smartest race tonight but John just overpowered me. Still, I'm really happy with what I did."[9] Matthes, meanwhile, quickly realized that his chances of topping Naber were slim. "I swam my own race," Matthes said in his typically matter-of-fact yet deferential way. "If I had concentrated only on Naber, I would have stopped my race after 50 meters and applauded."[10] The bronze turned out to be Matthes's parting gift from swimming. He finished fifth in the 100 fly, never seriously in the medal picture, then scratched the 200 back to call time on his distinguished career.

Day 3 was another tour de force, courtesy of Hencken and the distance contingent. Hencken joined rare company by setting three world records in as many swims, tying his world record of 1:03.88 in prelims, lowering it to 1:03.62 in semis, and winning the final in 1:03.11. The ever-stoic engineering student at Stanford won the first battle against British rival David Wilkie, who was second in 1:03.43. While Hencken's effort was impressive, it couldn't match the historic collision in the 1,500 between Goodell, countryman Bobby Hackett, and Australian Stephen Holland. A cagey preliminary heat revealed little, with Hackett and Holland clocking in the 15:25 range while Goodell coasted in at 15:34. The pace was set by American Paul Hartloff, who set an Olympic record in 15:20.74. In the finals, Hackett, often accustomed to going out fast and trying to hang on, played the rabbit. Goodell, a notoriously strong finisher, stayed in contact, as did Holland, after falling behind in the first 300 and surging in the middle of the race as was his trademark. But there was a twist: where Hackett usually went out fast in absolute terms—like when at Trials he set the world record in the 800 free off the front of his 1,500—his effort was more judiciously meted out this time, doling out enough to lead while reserving some for the kick home. Not until about the 900-meter mark did Holland recognize Hackett's slower pace and move to the front. All the while, Goodell bided his time, building up to the final few hundred meters. He finally made his move at 1,350, overtaking Hackett, then Holland about 50 meters later, and soloing to the wall in 15:02.40, a world record and a gob-smacking 50 seconds quicker than Mike Burton's winning time in 1972. Hackett's strategy also worked in what he called the first negative-split 1,500 of his life, overtaking Holland over the last 50 to slip into silver in 15:03.91. Holland, who afterward admitted that he "should have really swum my own race,"[11] settled for bronze in 15:04.66. Goodell's finish was so fast that he came home almost four seconds faster than Hackett's 800 free world mark, a staggering 7:57.35, without the aid of a start and despite being weighed down by 700 meters of effort. "During the race the negative side of me was saying, 'You're too far behind; you can't catch them,'" Goodell said. "But the positive side was saying, 'Get out, get going . . . let go of the cookie,' which means to get your head together and just get going."[12]

In addition to the 100 fly sweep on Day 4, the Americans also had the secure gold of the 800 free relay. The roster was so deep that the B team of Northway, Shaw, Bruner, and Bruce Furniss set a world record in prelims of 7:30.33, a cut of two-tenths off the previous standard. With Montgomery and Naber due to be subbed in, the final shaped up as a laugher to be authored by the three American medalists. Counsilman was so confident in success that he let the swimmers set their order, sending the ostensible weak link, Bruner, out first. West Germany's Klaus Steinbach, who finished fifth in the 200, beat Bruner by .17 seconds. But Furniss curtailed any suspicions of an upset, ripping off a leg of 1:49.56 to stake the Americans to a lead of almost a second and a half. Though Naber was admittedly sluggish with his 1:51.20, Montgomery cleaned up the mess in 1:50.11, bringing the team home in 7:23.22, a victory by 10 meters over the Soviet Union and a reduction of over seven seconds from the hours-old world mark.

There were hopes that the American hegemony would end on July 22, Day 5 of the meet. Like just about every other international hope in Montreal, they were dashed. The 400 free turned into the anticipated "Brian Goodell–Tim Shaw heavyweight fight."[13] Though Goodell had won the 1,500, the junior at Mission Viejo High School ceded the sentimental advantage to Shaw, who had won the 1975 Sullivan Award as the nation's top amateur athlete but had endured a tumultuous Bicentennial year fighting a nagging shoulder injury and a case of energy-sapping anemia. They traded

Olympic records in prelims, Shaw going 3:56.40 a heat before Goodell's 3:55.24. In the final, it quickly became clear that the gold would be decided between the Americans. Shaw took the early initiative and was fastest at 200 meters. But Goodell stayed within striking distance and stalked Shaw's pace, finally charging with just over 100 meters to go. Shaw, and the rest of the world for that matter, couldn't match Goodell's final surge, and Goodell got to the wall first in a world record of 3:51.93, over a second under his time from Trials. Shaw also got under the existing world mark in 3:52.54, but it only meant silver, though Shaw wasn't too downtrodden. "When I got out of the pool, I felt I had given it my best effort," Shaw said. "That's all anybody can ask. I'm very happy for Brian. Right now he's the best swimmer in the world—he has proven it to everybody. And I'm almost as happy as him because I did the best I could."[14]

With the distance corps not wavering, there was almost no chance of the American medley relay faltering . . . especially not after another prelims world record from a B team. This standard, compiled by the team of Rocca, Chris Woo, Bottom, and Jack Babashoff, trimmed nine-tenths off the world mark, stopping the clock in 3:47.28. With the world-record holders in the 100 back, breast, and free and the winner of the 100 fly waiting in the wings, it would take a massive blunder from the Americans to come away with anything but gold. That didn't happen. Naber staked the team to a two-second lead—despite national records from Steinbach, Aussie Mark Kerry, and Great Britain's James Carter in the 100 back—and the margin never got any closer. The host country seized a surprise silver, but that didn't scare the American time of 3:42.22, five seconds faster than prelims, even with the squad of Naber, Hencken, Vogel, and Montgomery, as the latter admitted afterward, playing it safe on their relay pickups.

As the Olympic program wound into its sixth day, observers wondered if anyone could break the American gold blockade. The 200 back wouldn't be the occasion, thanks to Naber's form. Going for his fourth gold and fifth medal, he was not going to be denied, no matter how much the exertion hurt at the end of a long program. Naber made good, becoming the first swimmer ever under two minutes and almost bypassing 1:59 altogether with his time of 1:59.19. Second was Rocca again, while Dan Harrigan, who won gold in the 1975 Pan Am Games but waged a harrowing battle with hepatitis contracted in Mexico City that led to a lengthy recovery and nearly threatened his chances for Montreal, took bronze in the highlight of a lifetime. The fourth sweep of the Games, it made the U.S. 10-for-10 in the gold department.

That was the pressure lumped on Wilkie as the 200 breast neared that night. Wilkie and Hencken had been a two-man wrecking crew in the event since before the last Olympics, with Hencken setting five world records and Wilkie one. Hencken usurped what was supposed to be the Brit's specialty in the final in Munich, and the two had waged epic battles at the college level, Wilkie representing the University of Miami. As if the Scotsman didn't have enough pressure with the British pining for him to end a 68-year Olympic gold drought, he was suddenly imbued with the pressure of single-handedly stopping the torrent of American domination. "At first, I don't think the other swimmers could believe that the American men were swimming so well," Wilkie said. "I think it really had a bad effect on many teams because they went into every race thinking that the Americans would win it."[15] Wilkie, though, seemed unfazed. His preliminary time of 2:18.29 set an Olympic record that was almost three seconds faster than Hencken's time. Wilkie's swim, though, was experimental, with the Scot testing how fast he could go out before shutting down the pace halfway though. That confidence allowed Wilkie a little bit of fun at the Americans' expense. "After the heats, [Coach] David Haller and I walked past the American coach, Don Gambril, and David shouted in a voice that couldn't fail to be heard: 'Well, David, a 2min 15sec tonight, then,'" Wilkie recalled. "It was a laugh but we weren't joking, we were serious. I was very confident. John was three seconds behind me in qualifying and I knew for him to beat me that night he would have to drop six seconds on his time because I fully intended to swim another three seconds quicker. Logically I knew, after the heats, that there was no way he or anybody else could win."[16] Wilkie's self-belief, as much as his unparalleled kick and smooth technique, guided him in the final. His confidence only increased when he and Hencken were shoulder to shoulder at the halfway point of the final. Hencken, the shorter-distance specialist, could only hope to build a lead and force Wilkie to panic. But Wilkie didn't, sure that the power in his legs would propel him through the second half of the race. The final transpired as planned, Wilkie gliding home in 2:15.11, a world record over three seconds faster than Hencken's world mark that Wilkie admitted "felt like 10 seconds" between him and Hencken.[17] The Stanford grad was the comfortable winner of silver in 2:17.26, also under world-record pace, and bronze went to Colella in 2:19.20. For all the pressure applied from external sources, Wilkie made sure the only nation he was swimming for was his own, even if he did relish in the role of spoiler. "I wanted to win very badly and I wasn't worried at all about the run of American successes," he said. "I just swam for myself and for Britain. A great deal of effort and hard work went into the achievement. I'll always cherish the moment."[18]

While dreams of American perfection were sunk, there still remained two more golds to decide on the final day of competition. The 100 free, it seemed, wouldn't be much of a competition. That was made apparent once Montgomery won his semifinal heat by almost a second, setting a world record of 50.39 seconds and installing himself as the prohibitive favorite. That wide margin got Counsilman and Montgomery, his college pupil, thinking strategy, and the pair decided on a risky course of action. "After the prelims we figured we had the race pretty much won," said Counsilman. "So we risked it. We swam the race to break the record by going out harder. We figured that even if he died a little coming home, he'd still have enough to win."[19] Montgomery went out fast, taking a six-tenths lead on Babashoff after 50 meters. The adrenaline of the moment, the confidence in his taper, and the triumphal ethos of the Americans brought him home just as strong. The clock read 49.99, making Montgomery the first man to break the vaunted 50-second barrier. Second was Babashoff in 50.81, while West Germany's Peter Nocke prevented an American sweep by earning bronze.

The 400 IM was a sterling opportunity for redemption for Tim McKee, who was wrongfully denied a share of gold in the event in Munich because he finished a mere two-thousandths of a second behind Swede Gunnar Larsson. The McKee-Larsson controversy caused FINA, swimming's international governing body, to reevaluate how time is measured, and it weighed on McKee, who took a brief retirement before deciding to challenge for Montreal. The only thing standing in McKee's way was, well, another two Americans, in Strachan and Steve Furniss, who traded the Olympic record in prelims in the 4:27 range while McKee clocked a 4:29. The final played into McKee's plans. While Strachan went out fast to compensate for his weaker breaststroke leg, McKee lay in wait. Once the race hit the third 100, McKee moved in breaststroke, hoping to fashion a large enough cushion to hold off Strachan's freestyle surge. Strachan managed to stay in contact and reeled in McKee in the final 100, getting to the wall first in 4:23.68, a cut of over two seconds off the world record of Hungary's Zoltan Verraszto. McKee was also under the world mark, but he had to settle for silver, again, in 4:24.62. If there was any disappointment, he didn't show it. "I just thought, 'second again.' That seems to be my lucky number," McKee quipped. "When I came out of retirement I thought it would take a 4:24 to win it. I told myself that if I went 24 and didn't win it, I couldn't complain. That's as fast as I thought I could go."[20]

McKee's sentiment was applicable for a number of Americans in Montreal. Where there was only one gold available per event, there was no limit to the number of personal-best times that could be achieved. Unlike the American women, who often found their personal bests relegated to a step on the podium by the East German women with whom they harbored such an adversarial relationship, the American men were consoled by the fact that their best was only kept from the top step of the podium by the more illustrious accomplishments of their teammates. Coupled with the togetherness the American team was built around and the abundance of individual medals, the celebrations struck a collective chord. "The thrill comes from doing as well as you're capable of," was Naber's reaction to the medley relay win.[21] While it may have been easy for Naber, with his suitcases heaving with hardware, to say, the statement still rang true. The conclusions drawn from the

American performance in Montreal were unavoidable. "The U.S. male swimmers must be accorded the title of the greatest Olympic team ever assembled," wrote *Swimming World* magazine editor Al Schoenfield.[22] Even the calculated Counsilman was effusive in describing his squad. "I think now I can say we have the greatest international team we've ever had," he declared.[23] It's a statement that has stood the test of time.

Chapter Fourteen

1980 U.S. Olympians

Some teams earned gold medals by the bushel. Some set records not to be touched for years. Some received fond farewells and ticker-tape receptions reserved only for conquering heroes.

The 1980 American Olympic team got none of those. All they received for their efforts, for years of toil spent striving for the zenith of their sports, was to play a pawn in international dead-end politics and receive an asterisk next to their names that no amount of congressional decrees could dim.

The American Olympic swimmers who were denied a chance to compete in Moscow in 1980 due to the U.S. Olympic Committee's boycott were denied their proper place in history. They had earned the right to inherit the mantle of American swimming dominance on the sport's largest stage, the only available avenue to stardom and tangible financial gain from their sport. While their Olympic accomplishments can only be explained in the hypothetical, the Americans who didn't compete in Moscow constitute one of the most unique squads in swimming history. Their accomplishments shouldn't just be preserved for posterity but celebrated, not just for the lament of what they could have been but what they were in real, concrete terms.

Long before the 1980 Olympics were even on the horizon, politics infringed upon the purity of sport that the Olympic movement sought to showcase. Seeking to solidify power in Afghanistan after a series of regime changes and ineffectual governments, the Soviet Union marched troops into the Middle Eastern nation in late December 1979 to stem the tide of unrest and rebellion. The mobilization of troops, one of the largest in the Cold War era, drew harsh condemnation from the international community, including an official vote of rebuke from the United Nations. One of the loudest voices in the chorus, unsurprisingly, came from the United States. Led by President Jimmy Carter—in an election year with a second term in the White House looking increasingly unlikely—the U.S. measured responses against what it saw as untoward Soviet aggression aimed at a key piece in the balance of East–West power. With diplomatic options few and far between—given the frostiness of the relationship between the superpowers, and Carter's credibility, domestically and internationally, being severely hampered by a number of high-profile missteps—the commander-in-chief sought to extract political capital from the pair of Olympics slated for 1980. The fact that each Cold War power had the honor of hosting one—the Winter Games were in Lake Placid, New York, with the Summer Games to follow in Moscow—perfectly positioned them as one-aside bargaining chips. For fear of jeopardizing the legitimacy of the Lake Placid Games by angering the Soviets and their Warsaw Pact allies to the point of boycott, the Carter administration bided its time. But as winter turned to spring, it became painfully obvious that a boycott of Moscow remained the only recourse.

Boycotts had become a popular—though not wholly effective—political maneuver within the Olympic movement. The most notable such attempt came in 1976 when outrage over the sporting ties between New Zealand and South Africa's (already banned) apartheid regime in the non-Olympic sport of rugby in the early 1970s precipitated a push by African nations to boycott if New Zealand was not barred from the Games. That movement, which failed to garner support from either of the major powerbrokers in the U.S.-USSR standoff, fizzled, yielding few long-term results . . . beyond 28 African nations missing a Games in which New Zealand freely participated.

Despite the checkered past of usefulness, Carter hinted at the possibility of a boycott of Moscow within a week of the Soviet incursion. When economic sanctions like embargoes on the trade of high-tech electronic and oil-drilling equipment, a reduction of grain sales, and revocation of international fishing rights predictably failed to deter the Soviet military action, Carter turned his threats inward toward the U.S. Olympic Committee. On January 20, 1980, Carter issued a public ultimatum to the Soviets to withdraw troops or face the prospect of an American boycott, one he hoped would gain backing from Western nations to sufficiently diminish the spectacle of the Games (not to mention send tourism, television rights, and sponsorship revenues plummeting). The deadline for Soviet withdrawal was strategically set at February 20, conveniently in the middle of the Lake Placid Games so as to assuage the American sporting establishment's apprehension that the Soviets would retaliate with a preemptive boycott. Non-binding boycott proposals citing concerns over national security were sent to both houses of Congress and passed by overwhelming margins. Carter issued envoys to the International Olympic Committee and outgoing chairman Lord Killanin rather sternly exhorting them to strip Moscow of its hosting privileges or to cancel the Games altogether given their belligerence. (It was perhaps at this time that Carter was reminded by the IOC and Killanin, who had a comically low opinion of him and his political aptitude, that no less than three times had the United States been involved in active military campaigns when staging or winning the rights to host Games.) The brusqueness of Carter's overtures and the clumsiness of his methods—including positioning Secretary of State Cyrus Vance to deliver a railing diatribe against the Soviets in what was supposed to be a celebratory atmosphere to open the Lake Placid Games just before the IOC's vote on the matter—led the vote on cancellation or relocation to be 73–0 against. Despite approaches to various voting blocs like the African nations—the very same body whose cause the United States showed no interest in championing four years prior—and much of Europe, widespread support for a boycott was muted.

When the IOC shrugged off Carter's toothless posturing, he turned his sights toward the USOC, despite admonitions from the IOC over governmental intervention in sporting bodies' affairs. None too subtle insinuations were made by Carter's White House that funding cuts and the revocation of privileged tax status would befall the USOC if its membership's vote on the boycott ran counter to Carter's position. He'd also put the American Olympic body in an awkward position within the international community, making patriotic appeals to USOC head Robert Kane and other key figures to exert pressure on the IOC over Moscow, grandiosely emphasizing the "security of our nation and the peace of the world."[1] By that time, with the Lake Placid Games in the rearview mirror and the "Miracle on Ice" hockey triumph perhaps emboldening the anti-Soviet feelings, the rhetoric was intensified. Carter's plan had public support, with opinion polls showing as much as 75 percent of the population having bought into the national security argument proffered by Carter. The spiel of making the world safe from communism provided catchy campaign stumping as Carter warded off the threat of Massachusetts senator Ted Kennedy for the Democratic nomination for president in the 1980 election. The Soviets, though, weren't taking the threats sitting down. They launched their own public-relations strategy, offering free transportation, lodging, and any number of additional perks at the General Assembly of National Olympic Committees in February in Mexico City, hoping to pull the purse strings to entice nations to Moscow. The IOC also availed some of its funding reserves to nations on the fence, hoping to safeguard its investment in and the prestige of the Moscow Games.

Carter's efforts were successful in swaying the opinions of many governments. But what Carter failed to grasp was that in principle, governments didn't control their national Olympic committees, which tended to be staunchly anti-boycott, for reasons both idealistic and self-interested. The push-and-pull experienced in the United States was replicated in a multitude of Western nations, all with varying degrees of vitriol. Despite Carter's opposite number in Great Britain, Margaret Thatcher, roundly supporting his boycott proposal, the British Olympic Association asserted its independence by voting decisively to participate, the idea of a boycott going down as "an absolute non-starter from the beginning,"[2] in the words of BOA chairman Sir Denis Fellows. Australian prime minister Malcolm Fraser was a proponent of the Carter propaganda machine and tried to flex his executive muscle to keep his delegation home, but the Australian committee narrowly approved participation. West Germany was perhaps the most telling illustration of the opposing forces at play. Their legislative branch, the Bundestag, voted 446–8 in favor of a boycott. The West German Olympic Committee's vote, however, was much closer, at 59–40 for the boycott, a vote complicated by the candidacy of West German sports executive Willi Daume to replace Killanin as the IOC president and the fact that the vote was televised at the last minute, a surprise to voters and an unwelcomed trace of added scrutiny.

In the United States, the vote was put off until April. But the official policy of Carter's administration was to view it as a mere formality. After all, the president had infamously declared on March 21, "Ours will not go." He did so with the assuredness that nothing would sway that decision. "I say that not with any equivocation; the decision has been made," Carter decreed, addressing an assembly of athletic hopefuls for Moscow at the White House. "The American people are convinced that we should not go to the Summer Olympics. The Congress has voted overwhelmingly, almost unanimously, which is a very rare thing, that we will not go. And I can tell you that many of our major allies, particularly those democratic countries who believe in freedom, will not go."[3] The speech, repeatedly appealing to the sensibilities of peace and patriotism among the athletes, stressed in almost equal parts a thinly veiled desire to punish Russia in the only way the Americans could at the time while also advocating the role athletes could play in preserving international harmony. When the USOC finally convened to vote on the matter, the threats levied by Carter proved to be too much. While 797 voters opted to participate, 1,604 supported the plan for boycott. Just like that, there would be no Olympics for the Americans in 1980. Carter ultimately fulfilled his promise, succeeding in keeping a handful of nations from Moscow. A total of 62 boycotted the Games, the most sparsely attended since Melbourne in 1956. Some, like Israel and Japan, abstained to preserve their military- and financial-aid pipelines from the United States. Others, like China, had separate conflicts with the Soviets, and still others in the Middle East boycotted in solidarity with the Afghan cause, not the United States'. The total number of nations taking part in Moscow was 81; of those, 16 took the decision to march under the Olympic flag, a subtle protest against the ugly, nationalistic subplot the Games sometimes entailed.

The news that the Olympics, the carrot occupying the hopes and dreams of athletes for years, were off the table had devastating effects to the psyches of athletes across the nation. The timing of the news seemed particularly harsh for swimmers, with many of America's best assembled in Austin,

Texas, for the 1980 Indoor Nationals when the decision was handed down. For Rowdy Gaines, one of the brightest hopes for the Americans in Moscow, the boycott announcement came on the heels of him setting a world record in the 200 freestyle, a mark he reclaimed from Soviet Sergey Kopliakov, no less. (American Mary T. Meagher also set a world record in the 100 butterfly in Austin.) The detail seemed to be poetic overkill for what was already a monumental disappointment for the Americans. The atmosphere in Austin tended toward the positive and borderline defiant, not of the decision but of its supposed ramifications. "You ask a swimmer what 'get the Russians' means and they'll tell you that it means beating them in the pool at the Olympics or in dual meets or whatever," USA Swimming president Ross Wales said.[4] Some swimmers struck an equally hopeful chord, even if it was merely a put-on brave face. "I don't care where I swim. You give me a pool and I'll try to swim my best time; I don't care if it's in Moscow or Timbuk-tu," said Mike Bruner, who won two golds in the 1976 Montreal Games and would end up as *Swimming World* magazine's American Swimmer of the Year in 1980. "I just love the sport. I just want to swim."[5]

The boycott came at a pivotal time for the U.S. swimming establishment. The men's team in 1976 had been almost infallible, taking 11 golds from 12 events, 10 of them in world-record time. There was little question that the Americans would again be the prohibitive favorites in Moscow simply by showing up. The women, however, were in an altogether different predica-ment. It took a minor miracle from the 400 free relay team of Shirley Babash-off, Jill Sterkel, Kim Peyton, and Wendy Boglioli for the Americans to upset the East German juggernaut and salvage any gold from Montreal. With swimming in the past for three-quarters of that squad and the vast majority of the star-crossed 1976 delegation, the American women's program was undergoing a monumental generational change. The main players in that resurgence were hoping to finally be tested on the Olympic stage. Tracy Caulkins, who at age 15 set five American records at the 1978 AAU Cham-pionships, was at the vanguard of the new generation after claiming six medals, five gold, at the 1978 FINA World Championships. Sippy Wood-head, who had pulled an impressive 500-1,650 double at the 1978 AAUs at just 14, was quickly emerging as one of the world's best distance swimmers, one of the only areas of vulnerability for the East German squad. And there was Meagher, who had set three world records in the 200 fly in 1979 and figured to provide a stiff challenge to the East German stroke prowess. A chance to compete in the 1980 Games, which for swimmers like Caulkins and Woodhead could conceivably have been their first of two Olympic cy-cles at a time when that was a rare occurrence, could have paid major bene-fits for an American program that had rebounded from the thumping at the 1976 Olympics but still sought Olympic validation for its progress. With the Olympic payoff delayed for the 1980 hopefuls, many swimmers elected to continue until the 1984 Games, competing until ages at which they normally would've hung up their suits. That collision of generations crowded out some younger swimmers angling for Los Angeles in 1984. There was also the positive effect, though, of showing that swimmers could maintain world-class fitness well into their 20s, banishing the long-held notion that swimmers peaked during their college years and had no justification for pursuing athletic opportunities beyond the cessation of their studies.

There were many in Eastern swimming circles who were also disheartened at the prospect of an American-less Olympics. Swimmers had been at the forefront of the athletic attempt to bridge the East–West rift dating back to dual meets with the East Germans and Soviets in the early 1970s. Mark Schubert's Mission Viejo club, one of the premier factories for American talent, had taken training trips into the Soviet Union for showcase meets while also hosting Soviet delegations in sunny California, providing a rosy image of Americans to some behind the Iron Curtain. "The Americans surprised us by not keeping any of their training secrets from us, which means there must still be some decent people left in the world," said Soviet coach Sergei Vaitsekhovsky, whose star pupil was distance swimmer Vladimir Salnikov. "We're very sorry they aren't here."[6]

Regardless of the disappointment for the athletes, there still remained the prospect of picking a 1980 Olympic team, even if it was a hollow exercise. After long-shot legal challenges to the boycott failed, USA Swimming dubbed its outdoor national meet in Irvine, California, the Olympic Trials, recognizing the top three finishers in each event as Olympians for 1980, even if the event commenced two days after the races in Moscow concluded. Though the Olympics were no longer attached to success at the meet, the prestige of finishing among the top three from the United States in an Olympic year remained intact. Whatever the swimmers may have thought about the circumstances or the triple-digit heat of Irvine, the swims remained fast. Three world records were set there—Meagher and Craig Beardsley in the 200 fly and Bill Barrett in the 200 individual medley—as well as five American standards. Two of those American marks belonged to Caulkins. Such times were posted against a backdrop of conflicted emotions—anger, disillusionment, and even a bit of apathy. "I don't think I've been going as fast as I could because I don't think these are Olympic trials," said Bruner, who set a personal best in the 800 free to finish second to Brian Goodell, then topped Goodell in the 400 free. "The Olympics are almost over, and we didn't go. This is nothing more than a glorified national championship, and I've been having trouble motivating myself."[7] Without plane tickets to an Olympic Games awaiting top finishers, the rubric for event selection shifted. Steve Lundquist, for example, scratched his other two events after setting an American record in the 100 breast. Both Jeff Float (who finished third in the 400 IM and seventh in the 200 fly) and Nancy Hogshead (who was second in both the 200 fly and 400 IM) attempted that daring double with the finals on the same day, something they likely wouldn't have done at an Olympic Trials to increase the odds of qualifying for one. The events in Irvine resulted in a 45-strong team that was designated as 1980 American Olympians. Ten were holdovers from Montreal, eight of them medalists. Of the 45, 16 would continue on to the Los Angeles Games, 12 winning medals at the Eastern bloc–boycotted Games. (Sterkel also competed in the 1988 Games.) That left 19 swimmers, almost half of the squad, for whom the ill-fated 1980 Games was the only Olympic berth.

The boycott fueled the fire of hypothetical competition: How would the Americans have done against the assembled field in Moscow? With medals as the unquestioned measuring stick for the success or failure of an Olympic squad, how to gauge the relative strength of the 1980 team? For some, the question was moot, and somewhat ridiculous. "That means nothing," Gaines said of attempts to compare swims in Irvine to those from Moscow. "These have never been the Olympic Trials. It's like comparing diamonds with dirt. The level of excellence is reduced here. In the Olympics, you swim against people. My time in the 200 [free] would have won the silver medal in Moscow. I know that if I was there, I would have won the gold. I'm not bragging. I just know that."[8] Gaines wasn't alluding to the miniscule differences in speed dynamics from one pool to another; he knew that the head-to-head adrenaline rush, the exhilaration of the Olympic stage, the crescendo of intensity to one swim that represented the apex of a career—that was something that no trumped-up event title could duplicate.

Strictly looking at the times, there was little to suggest that the Americans wouldn't have retained their position as the world's preeminent swimming power on the men's side. The times in Irvine would've won medals in every Moscow final save for two, the 200 breast and 1,500 free, though each of those events comes with a caveat. The 200 breast final in Irvine proceeded without Lundquist, whose time in the 100 breast would've been good for gold in Moscow. Bruner's time in winning the 1,500 from the Austin Nationals (15:19.76) might not have challenged the momentous world record set by Salnikov (14:58.27) in Moscow. But given the chance to race, he could have conceivably snuck into the medal picture, which hovered in the 15:14 range.

Beyond that, though, the Americans figured to be in the thick of the medal pictures up and down the program. The times alone positioned the U.S. for 17 medals, seven of them gold. The Irvine times would've produced 1-2 finishes in the 100 free (Gaines and Chris Cavanaugh), 200 back (Steve Barnicoat and Peter Rocca), 100 breast (Lundquist and Barrett), and 100 fly (William Paulus and Matt Gribble). The 200 fly could've been a 1-2-3 finish, with Beardsley, Bruner and Bill Forrester each faster in Irvine than Moscow winner Sergey Fesenko. Gaines's time in the 200 free was two-tenths off Kopliakov's winning time in Moscow, a gap the Floridian would assuredly have closed given the winner-take-all stakes, while the top three finishers in Irvine were quicker than Moscow bronze medalist Graeme Brewer of Australia. Goodell and Bruner might have challenged Salnikov in the 400 free and certainly would've been in reach of a medal (though Canadian world-record holder Peter Szmidt was also missing in Moscow.) Schubert, despite friendly relationships with many Soviet coaches, was one of the most vocal in characterizing Salnikov's success in Moscow as at least partially borne out of the Americans' absence. "He has to be regarded as the best because he has the best times in the world," Schubert said. "If the United States was there, I don't think he would have accomplished what he did. I think a number of Americans could have gone as fast."[9] With three sub-57-second qualifiers, the Americans would've figured prominently in the 100 back medal discussion, while Jesse Vassallo's 400 IM time in Irvine was almost a second and a half faster than the Olympic record Aleksandr Sidorenko used to win in Moscow. In *Swimming World*'s end-of-year rankings, only four Olympic events featured a non-American swimmer with the fastest time in 1980— Szmidt in the 400 free, Salnikov in the 1,500, Sweden's Par Arvidsson in the 100 fly, and Soviet 200 breaststroker Robertas Zhulpa. The relays likely wouldn't have been much competition for the Americans either, with a composite of the top times in Irvine for the 400 medley and 800 free relays, even without the benefit of relay starts or the additive benefits of swimming for gold as a team, were well over a second clear of the golden times in Moscow. The medal hauls from Moscow could've been massive for some, like Gaines (as many as four) and Lundquist (three), totals that would've instantly ingratiated them as stars in the American sports mainstream and entered them in the pantheon of great American Olympic achievements.

The American women would've faced adversity in Moscow at the hands of the East Germans, who set six world records, including in both relays. Certain times might have been untouchable, like Rica Reinisch's backstroke double. But the American women would've fared much better than in Montreal, in line for 10 medals and several golds. Meagher's Irvine times, for instance, were faster than those turned in by Caren Metschuk and Ines Geissler in the 100 and 200 fly, respectively. Had Kim Linehan's Irvine times occurred in Moscow, she would've won gold in the 400 and 800 free, the former in a 1-2 finish, with Woodhead ahead of the golden time of Ines Diers. Behind Linehan in the 800 free, both Woodhead and Marybeth Linzmeier turned in times faster than that used by Diers to win silver in Moscow behind Australian Michelle Ford. Caulkins's time in the 100 breast in Irvine was within .29 seconds of Ute Geweniger's Moscow world record, a meeting that could've been one of the Games' best. Meagher's world records persevered in 1980, the 200 mark a monstrous four seconds faster than Geissler's Moscow time. In the 100 fly, the top three times of 1980 belonged to Americans, Meagher followed by Caulkins and Sterkel. Toppling the East

Germans in the relay would've been a tall task for the Americans, but they were certainly in prime position to take silver in each. The intellectual exercise of comparing times, though, is just that, a fact that provided little consolation to the athletes involved. "Beating a bunch of numbers means nothing," Woodhead said in Irvine. "Head-to-head competition is all that counts."[10]

The boycott's ripple effect impacted the decisions of swimmers for years to come. Many chose to soldier on, a path that was rarely easy. Gaines, for example, flirted with retirement several times in the early 1980s, disavowing the sport after several disappointing performances at major meets like the Trials for the 1983 Pan American Games and even the 1984 Olympic Trials. Through the years, the five-time NCAA champion at Auburn had developed a reputation as a perpetual comeback artist; his candor with the media made him a public face of the boycott, and his willingness to share his opinion in victory and defeat earned him a reputation as alternately brash and a crybaby. Meagher's decision to continue onward was taken a bit easier, as swimming was never central to her identity. The native of Louisville, Kentucky, who made Nationals as a 13-year-old, took to butterfly like she was genetically predisposed. As the 10th of 11 children, she wasn't one to make a big deal out of much, even world records. She was even oblivious to the fact that she set her first world record at the 1979 Pan Am Games until someone reminded her before the medal stand. Meagher even briefly contemplated retirement in 1979, satisfied in her early accomplishments. It wasn't until 1983 that she decided to fully commit to a run at the Los Angeles Games, training with Schubert in Mission Viejo. The 1984 Games were thought to be out of the reach of Caulkins, too far into the future for the girl heralded as a beacon of hope for American swimming at her startling emergence to the national scene in 1978. The desire to continue applied on both sides of the boycott, with the likes of Fesenko, who previously contemplated retirement after Moscow, instead continuing on in search of challenging his American counterparts.

The tough decisions to continue were by and large rewarded for the Americans in Los Angeles, a Games which the Soviets and East Germans boycotted. For the 16 members of the 1980 delegation who made the 1984 team, 12 earned medals. Meagher did the fly double and added gold in the medley relay. Gaines won the 100 free to go with a pair of relay golds, exorcising some demons. "I would have said before this that the only regret I had in swimming was not going to Moscow, if you can call that a regret," Gaines said in 1984. "But I can't say that now. Moscow is completely forgotten. This takes all the bad memories away."[11] Rick Carey swept the backstroke events to accompany medley relay gold, Lundquist won the 100 breast to complement his relay triumph, and Caulkins earned gold in both IMs. For many, the rewards justified the extra four years of striving. "The point I wanted to prove to myself was that I didn't stop after 1980, that I went ahead," said David Larson, who won gold in LA in the 800 free relay. "I didn't ever want to go through life thinking, 'Could I have made the Olympics?' or, 'Did I get scared and let someone else make the decision for me?' I made the decision. I stuck with it, and here I am now."[12] "This week I kept thinking about all the workouts, all the time, all the pain," said Hogshead, who at 22 grabbed gold in the 100 free, silver in the 200 IM, and a pair of relay golds. "I thought of the cold mornings. In winter our outdoor pool gets a layer of ice on the deck. I thought of all the times I slipped on that ice. I thought of everything I gave up, all the friends I couldn't socialize with, all the pain I was in during workouts. All of it."[13] Others, like Goodell, found peace along the way. After going nine-for-nine in NCAA titles over his first three seasons, a bout of the flu severely limited the UCLA senior in what should've been his capstone meet in 1980. By 1981, with the two golds from Montreal tucked away, Goodell called time on his career, citing a lack of competitive fire. "I feel good about quitting. I'm relieved," he said. "I've looked forward to this because I've been swimming for so long. I've been very successful, and if you're successful long enough you lose your drive. You get tired as you get older. I stopped setting high goals for myself."[14]

For every story of triumph, though, there's one of unrequited success. Many of the swimmers who caught lightning in a bottle in the summer of 1980 and were prevented from riding their success to Olympic medals were unable to duplicate it four years later. Take, for instance, breaststroker Glenn Mills, who made a massive jump from the cusp of junior Nationals in 1977 to sixth at senior Nationals in 1978. Dedicating himself to swimming after his brother died in a bout with cancer, Mills finished his high school career in the spring of 1980 with a national record in the 100 breast. His rapidly rising stock made Moscow seem like a probable stopover on his way from Ohio to the scholarship awaiting him at the University of Alabama. Though college swimming helped Mills persevere to 1984—with an NCAA title and a trip to the 1982 World Championships along the way—he finished third at the 1984 Trials, narrowly missing a trip to Los Angeles after the rules had been amended limiting each nation to two participants per event. Beardsley was denied an almost surefire medal in Moscow, leading to four more years of him training with the feeling that "I owed it to everyone else—my parents, coach. The last person I really felt I owed it to was myself."[15] That burnout, and a poorly timed illness, conspired against him at the 1984 Trials, with Beardsley shockingly slipping to third in the 200 fly.

The tragic motif of being at less than full strength in 1984 reared its ugly head for Sue Walsh, who approached the 1980 Games as the top 100 backstroker and second-fastest 200 backstroker in the world in 1979. But with a second chance at the Olympics and an easier path to the medal stand in Los Angeles without the Eastern European nations, Walsh couldn't get over the hump at Trials, finishing fifth in the 200 back and an agonizing third in the 100 back, .12 seconds behind Theresa Andrews. For Walsh, the loss delivered another dose of misery. "That probably hurt even more, because I thought I was at the end of what I felt like I could do as far as training," she said. "I know that was the last chance, and I was totally deflated."[16] Then there was the case of breaststroker John Moffet, immortalized in Bud Greenspan's documentary of the 1984 Games. The Stanford grad set a world record at the 1984 Trials in the 100 breast, but in the prelims in Los Angeles, he suffered a torn adductor muscle in his leg. In the final, Moffet somehow gutted out a fifth-place finish, .32 seconds out of the medals, as Lundquist coasted to the world record and gold. The injury was so bad that it caused a physically and emotionally "numb" Moffet to withdraw from the rest of his program, which included a good chance for a medal in the 200 breast and an almost assured gold for swimming the prelims of the medley relay.[17]

The boycott in 1980 was a great missed opportunity for American swimmers, collectively and individually. The final Games at which nations could enter three swimmers each, 1980 could've been the final hurrah for the great American swimming empire that dominated the 1960s and 1970s. Instead, all the American swimmers had to settle for recognition of their contributions to national security and the advancement of peace on earth, a quest for which they were at least awarded Congressional Medals of Honor. As a team, the 1980 Olympians owe their place in history to the gravity of their disappointment. However convincing the hypotheticals about their Moscow performance, they remain dishearteningly imaginary. "The sad part is that we'll never know how we would have done there," Gaines said.[18] For a generation of swimmers, "sad" seems an understatement.

Chapter Fifteen

1992 Unified Olympians

Before 1990, the term "unified team" was little more than a generic, slightly redundant term of encouragement bandied about by coaches down the years. Even after the 1992 Barcelona Olympics, the term rang hollow for plenty of participants from the remnants of the Soviet Union, all competing while tenuously united under the Olympic flag.

Despite this fragile bond, few nations shone brighter in the pool than the Unified Team. Led by stars like Alexander Popov and Yevgeny Sadovyi, a nation, or rather, a soon-to-be group of nations, in limbo managed to hold its own among the traditional powers, even amid a time of upheaval in the world order that had held sway for the better part of half a century.

The Unified Team's haul of medals—10 in total, including six gold, good for third and second, respectively, in the final medal table—didn't set any records or seriously threaten the Americans' long-established supremacy. But the unique circumstances endured by those athletes, representing a delicate and improbable alliance of states often in conflict and unsure of their futures, magnifies their accomplishments.

Before the 1992 Barcelona Games, few teams have traveled to an Olympic Games facing the type of adversity faced by the Unified Team. Eastern Europe was blighted by political and economic upheaval, precipitated by the long-foreseen dissolution of the Soviet Union in December 1991. The prevailing power structure of the previous half century—the push-and-pull of East versus West, with Warsaw Pact nations under the constant threat of conflict with NATO countries that defined the Cold War—had vanished. So, too, had the translation of those tensions onto the fields of athletic competition. No more was the Red Menace of the Soviet Union's athletic edifice the target for Western motivations. Athletic triumphs had long propped up the mythos of Soviet supremacy, even in the face of ballooning inflation, economic stagnation, and deteriorating living conditions for its citizens. (In the nine Summer Olympics from 1952 to 1988 in which they'd participated, the Soviets had finished first or second in the overall medal table each time.) As 1992 dawned, however, the new challenge for athletes and those around them who had long been sheltered by the Soviet command economy was adapting to the arrival of capitalism as the Eastern markets opened for the first time in decades, a transition for which the existing structures were wholly unprepared.

What filled the gap left by the Soviet Union in the athletic arena was the Unified Team. Modeled after the political and economic body that replaced the USSR, the Commonwealth of Independent States, the Unified Team was a stopgap measure put in place in early 1992 ahead of the Winter Olympics in Albertville, France. Athletes competed under the Olympic flag rather than their national banners, and the Olympic anthem was played when medals were won. Though many of the republics, loudest among them Georgia and Ukraine, clamored for the athletic independence that they would eventually enjoy—a fact that International Olympic Committee president Antonio Samaranch freely expressed in brokering the deal[1]—the finances and logistics were insufficient in such a narrow time window to propagate so many nascent delegations. Instead of trying to rapidly assemble, fund, and ratify individual national Olympic committees, the IOC opted to occupy the framework vacated by the Soviets, granting "provisional recognition" to the Unified Team and targeting admission of individual nations starting in 1993. The reasoning pertained to the best interests of the athletes. "This agreement means the athletes will not be punished," Samaranch argued. "The most important thing was to stick to the principle that the best athletes from all the 12 republics should participate in Barcelona."[2] In Albertville, six nations—Russia, Ukraine, Uzbekistan, Armenia, Belarus, and Kazakhstan—competed under the Unified label. Azerbaijan, Georgia, Kyrgyzstan, Moldova, Tajikistan, and Turkmenistan joined the summer contingent to bring the number to 12.

The reality of the Unified Team, though, was that the moniker rang profoundly hollow, especially in contrast to the strong feelings of nationalism over which it whitewashed. Decried as "a bad adman's catchword,"[3] the 12 former republics arrived in Barcelona "trembling between entropy and union . . . sharing one uniform but trailing a rabble of 12 flags."[4] At the first appearance of the term in Albertville, the Russian writer Andrei Petrov admitted that "somehow, the tongue just can't seem to turn to call the Olympians 'Unified Team of the C.I.S.' as the official protocol requires."[5] The hastily unified nature of the team made athletes cling to an empty, "soulless"[6] ideal that had no meaning, not unlike the red-flagged dictatorship that had crumbled months earlier. Recognition according to their flimsy coalition of nations came at the expense of the burgeoning and long-stifled sense of pride in athletes' newly independent republics. The loose confederation of nations was also tasked with reconciling deep nationalistic divides that were no longer subservient to a central force like the Soviet Union. There were severe disagreements in terms of athlete selection in sports like gymnastics, with certain republics feeling that other nations' candidates were shown undue favor or reproach. Smaller nations harbored profound suspicions about Russia, whose size and resources installed them as the primary power to emerge from the tatters of the Soviet Union. The fact that Russian athletes constituted roughly 90 percent of the Albertville delegation did little to quell other nations' reservations. Whatever the divisions, the athletic success of the Unified Team in the Winter Games wasn't much affected. The Unifieds picked up 9 gold and 23 total medals, second only to Germany on both counts.

In the transition from Albertville to Barcelona, myriad challenges presented themselves. One of the best-received modifications allowed individual gold medalists to hear their national anthems played and see their national flags flown rather than the Olympic versions. (The Olympic iterations were still used for teams, many of which were heterogeneous mixes of nationalities.) Ethnic conflict and other assorted strife localized to various regions precluded the Unified Team from utilizing some of the most vital, former Soviet training bases, like the high-altitude camp in Armenia that had long been a staple for many sports. [7]

But the biggest issue that arose ahead of Barcelona was monetary: how to scale up funding for a delegation of 512 athletes, nearly four times the number participating in Albertville. The financial needs reached dire proportions in May 1992, by which point the Unified Team had raised barely half of the $5.5 million required. Getting athletes and coaches to Barcelona necessitated intervention from foreign entities. The IOC's Olympic Solidarity program, aimed at developing nations, chipped in funds. [8] Sponsorship dollars were solicited from several companies, including the German apparel giant Adidas and a Yugoslav clothing company. The Turner Broadcasting Company invested a quarter of a million dollars, while the U.S. Congress mulled donating to the athletes. [9] On the eve of the Games, Russian alcohol makers Smirnoff stepped in with a seven-figure contribution, which put the team over the top. [10] As expected, relations grew increasingly fractious after the Games when the issue of divvying up the revenue from the Games was broached.

The irony of the Unified Team's struggles ahead of Barcelona was the prevailing hope for those Games as a rare realization of the Olympic ideal. No longer were powers of East and West waging a war of philosophies on the playing fields. The international community eased into Barcelona free from the threat of boycott for the first time since World War II. The Cold War, which had been the flashpoint for boycotts that stripped much of the spectacle from the 1980 Moscow and 1984 Los Angeles Games, had effectively ceased. These "de-ideologized" Games were also the stage for a passel of new members, some after long hiatuses.[11] A unified Germany attended for the first time since 1964. The Baltic republics of Latvia, Lithuania, and Estonia, which had splintered from the Soviet tree early in its felling, were participating as independent nations for the first time since the 1930s. Croatia, Slovenia, and Serbia and Montenegro were each making debuts as free nations, while the former Czechoslovakia was transitioning toward division, competing under the novel label of the "Czech and Slovak Federative Republic." Such emancipation occurred under the specter of the Catalan region's struggle for autonomy from Spain, but the joy of the Games was so profound that such an ironic juxtaposition was largely overlooked.

The impact of the splitting of Soviet talent was most profound in sports other than swimming. In track and field, weightlifting, and gymnastics, for example, the once mighty Soviet apparatus would see its medal hopefuls diffuse across reemphasized borders. There was no such fear for the Soviet swimming legacy since, well, it wasn't much to write home about. All the Olympic success rarely carried over into the pool for the Soviets, the obvious exception being the 1980 Moscow Games at which, absent the power of the Americans, the Soviets claimed 8 gold and 22 total medals, including 7 and 17, respectively, in the men's competition. Short of that, however, the tally was quite meager. At the other eight non-boycotted Olympics from 1952 to 1988, the Soviets garnered just 37 total medals, 24 from the men's team, an average of just over four and a half per Games. Only four of those medals were gold, and no Soviet male swimmer had won gold outside of the 1980 Games until Vladimir Salnikov (1,500 free) and Igor Polyansky (200 back) in the 1988 Games. In 1992, however, Popov and Sadovyi helped lead the Unified Team to 6 gold and 10 total medals, all of the golds and 90 percent of the total hardware earned on the men's side of the draw.

So drastic was the change in fortunes that the question was posed to Popov as to just what had altered in the brief evolution from the Soviet to CIS regimes. "Ah, there is no time to have a history lesson," Popov half joked. "To explain, I would have to start back in 1917."[12] In a sense, the sprinter's appraisal was spot on. While the vagaries of the Bolshevik Revolution didn't directly tie into Popov's training, the system it ushered in did. When those structures tumbled to the ground in the early 1990s, those best prepared to cope with the new era of capitalism thrived. And, somewhat improbably, one of the best-positioned groups to do that was the swimmers.

The nostalgia for the Soviet system in the early 1990s smacked of revisionist history. It's true that state support of athletics dried up quickly—in the words of Unified OC financial director Vladimir Koval, it "disappeared like a dream."[13] But for sports like swimming, that date didn't coincide with the fall of the Soviet Union. Unlike the common misconception in the West, state sponsorship began to recede in the 1980s, a process intensified by the era of Perestroika that dawned in 1986 when the Soviet government was rebuilt, diminishing its influence on markets. Among those entities that suddenly had to find new sources of revenue was Goskomsport, the State Committee for Sports. The method it chose involved opening up to the free market, shaking off the archaic practices of party cronyism to become appealing to foreign investors and sponsorship opportunities. The revocation of state control of athletics also developed a refreshing meritocracy. Under the state-orchestrated system that ruled until the early 1980s, top prospects were plucked from their youth coaches to work with a set pool of national team trainers, reducing the incentive for club coaches to develop talents. Within the new system, coaches had greater ownership over the success of their athletes, reaping the rewards financially and in terms of prestige. Such mobility encouraged innovation from all corners of Eastern swimming in a volume that hadn't been glimpsed in decades.

The rewards were also more tangible for the athletes. There were certainly financial benefits for Soviet athletes to succeed, but the national dictum was that athletes strove for excellence for the good of the Soviet Union and its communist ideals. The Order of Lenin didn't translate cleanly into dollar figures, especially in a sputtering economy governed by a corrupt system. With the Eastern markets opening to foreign investment and the anchor of Soviet tradition gone, athletes had a chance to grow their own brands and seek the highest bidders for their services and celebrity. Instead of the drab apartments and outdated Soviet cars the USSR once provided athletes, the stars of the Games could look outward to international endorsement deals and the possibility of prize money at World Cup meets to which they were once restricted from traveling. In Barcelona, there were more financial spoils to earn than the modest medal bonuses—$3,000 for gold, $2,000 for silver, and $1,000 for bronze—offered by the Unified Olympic Committee (and underwritten by Western donations, it should be noted). The Eastern European athlete finally had control over his fiscal destiny, and the promise of previously unattainable windfalls proved a compelling inducement. "In the past, under the Union, it was stressed that you're not winning for yourself, but proving that you represent the most progressive system in the world," Unified Olympic Committee head Vitaly Smirnov said in 1992. "Well, we were first. And it proved nothing, and it saved nothing."[14]

From those changes sprung swimmers like Sadovyi and Popov, nicknamed the "Perestroika twins."[15] Both lived in the town of Volgograd ahead of the Barcelona Games, and their paths to the pinnacle of swimming were defined by the newfound openness in Russia. Their rise to prominence in Barcelona was so sudden that neither had been selected for the Soviet delegation in January 1991 for the World Championships in Perth, Australia. It wouldn't be until August 1991 that Sadovyi and Popov both won their first major international medals, representing the Soviet Union at the European

Championships. Sadovyi was such a long shot to make noise in Barcelona that his bio wasn't even included in the broadcast manual prepared for announcers. They looked a bit of an odd couple: the 6-6 Popov who exuded a superstar quality even when that notion seemed foreign in his country for anyone not decked out in military regalia, and the boyish Sadovyi with this slight build and shaved head. Together, though, they blazed a new trail in Eastern European athletics.

Popov was discovered at age 16 by coach Gennadi Touretski, and three years later, they began a professional relationship that spanned more than a decade. Popov was a talented backstroker in his early days, ranking 15th in the world in the 100 back in 1990. It was under Touretski, though, that he blossomed as a sprint freestyler. In the first year working together, Touretski's approach cut two and a half seconds off Popov's best 100 free time. Such was the devotion to Touretski that when the coach changed his training base after Barcelona to the Australian Institute of Sport in Canberra, Popov followed. Popov's experience with Touretski was emblematic of many Eastern athletes at the time, who were sheltered from the hardships of the failing Soviet Union by "selfless coaches and generous domestic sponsors who stepped in to replace disappearing state financing."[16] Popov readily credited the "need to pay ourselves"[17] as a major motivating factor for his success. "I am a child of perestroika," Popov said before the 1992 Games, as he lived in a Volgograd dorm with neither phone nor car. "It gave me a chance to be my best."[18]

Sadovyi's history is an even more compelling advertisement for the freedom afforded those behind the Iron Curtain. The son of a black-market perfume dealer, Sadovyi didn't need much convincing as to the shortcomings of the Soviet system. His father's profession made Sadovyi the target of schoolyard bullying by the children of party hardliners. "They were communist youths who derided all businessmen," Sadovyi recalled. "But now, since perestroika, they admire everything about business—including my mother and me. It makes me laugh."[19] Sadovyi's rise was orchestrated by Viktor Avidenko, an innovative coach who epitomized the legions of trainers who had to fight for their financial and professional survival. Avidenko started a private club in Volgograd, where Sadovyi moved in 1989 to live in a small apartment with his mother and four others. Avidenko utilized unique methods in weight and dryland training, incorporating them into Sadovyi's heavy distance training and traditional emphasis on technique. Avidenko's day didn't end at the pool, though. Unlike his Soviet predecessors, he also had to be a financial steward for his club now that the payments from the state, which were regular if paltry, had been curtailed. He secured a sponsorship from a chicken-processing company as well as the city of Volgograd and forged partnerships with clubs across Europe, especially wealthy clubs in Italy and Monte Carlo, to send his athletes on training trips. Sadovyi blossomed, surprising many by winning the 400 free at the 1991 Euros and taking fourth in the 200 free. The difference was obvious. "Before, we had to win for the government, for politics, for communism," he said. "The freedom we now have can lead us to making very good money for ourselves. Now we can reap what we sow. Now, if I win, I become a famous person, I become a rich person. All athletes respond to this motivation."[20] What he and Avidenko sought was the utopia, as explained by the coach, of "life as it should be lived by an Olympic gold medalist."[21] That's not to say that patriotism was completely out the window for Unified athletes, shifting solely from collective good to self-interest as the Soviet loyalists believed. The context had just shifted. "We will make very good money, for sure," Sadovyi said. "But when I see Americans on the medal stand and they are weeping for their country, then I think that I also should let the world know that I am truly grateful to my country, to Russia, for allowing me the chance to be an Olympic champion."[22]

The performances of Popov, Sadovyi, and their countrymen in Barcelona typified a Games of heightened parity. Perhaps the most jarring disruption of the old guard was Popov in the sprints. In the 100 free, American Matt Biondi was the unquestioned king. The five-medal star of the 1988 Games, Biondi had lined up Barcelona as the third and final Olympics of his remarkable career. He entered the 100 free undefeated in major competitions since 1984, owner of the Olympic and world records, plus the eight fastest times in history. Perhaps with Popov in mind, Biondi took the Olympic final out faster than normal, covering the first 50 meters in 23.30 seconds, five-hundredths off world-record pace. Popov, meanwhile, was back in the pack, sixth at the turn in 24.03 but just .03 behind the first-50 split of the European record swim of 49.18 at the 1991 Euros. Seemingly unfazed by his competition or the Olympic pressure, Popov rallied to surge ahead, getting to the wall first in 49.02 seconds, a decisive win over Brazil's Gustavo Borges (49.43) and France's Stephan Caron (49.50). Biondi slipped to fifth in 49.53, two-hundredths behind American teammate Jon Olsen, marking the first non-boycotted Games since 1956 in which the Americans failed to medal in the signature freestyle event.

Popov's win in the 100 free dented the prevailing notion prior to the Games that the 50 free was almost certain to come down to a battle between Biondi and Tom Jager. Jager was one of the few to challenge Biondi's hold on the title of world's greatest freestyler for the previous decade, and the two had waged epic battles in the early days of the 50 as an Olympic event. So dominant was the duo that Biondi and Jager held 24 of the top 25 times ever. That mattered little to Popov, who crashed the two-man party by pulling the upset in 21.91 seconds, an Olympic record and the third-fastest time in history. Second was Biondi in 22.09, while Jager was never a factor for gold, taking bronze in 22.30. It wasn't just that the Russian interloper had stolen the show. He had done so with such dominance and elegance—Popov's long, languid technique required about 17 strokes per 50 meters, roughly half the cadence of Biondi and Jager—that the vanquished Americans couldn't help but be impressed. "I don't think this is a real big surprise when you look at how Popov has been swimming," Biondi said. "I don't think either Tom or I were looking past him. He deserved it. He's the Olympic champion."[23] "He also has a lot of courage," Jager said. "He stood up to Matt Biondi and Tom Jager and took us down. He's the first person to do that since, it seems, the event started. I take my hat off to him."[24]

Sadovyi's ascent was hardly unforeseen given how the stars aligned for the young Russian. Biondi finished second in the 200 free at the American Olympic Trials but opted out of the event. World-record holder Giorgio Lamberti failed to qualify for the event in Barcelona after suffering from the flu at his national Trials. Only Lamberti and 1988 silver medalist Anders Holmertz of Sweden had ever been under 1:47 in the event. Sadovyi, whose best time in 1992 was 1:48.75, was at best seen as a dark-horse medal contender, having finished 1991 ranked ninth worldwide. Sadovyi announced his credentials in prelims when he set an Olympic mark of 1:46.75, within .06 of Lamberti's world standard. He managed to duplicate that effort in the final, outkicking Holmertz over the final 50 meters to claim gold in 1:46.70, a scant hundredth of a second from Lamberti's record. Holmertz settled for silver again in 1:46.86, while Finland's Antti Kasvio snuck into bronze, the nation's first swimming medal. Two nights later, the 400 free final, although American-free, was poised to be "one of the great 400 free races in Olympic history."[25] Sadovyi, who like Popov was thoroughly unintimidated by his surroundings, carried a three-year unbeaten streak in the event, albeit against second-tier competition outside of the 1991 Euro crown. Though ranked just 12th in the world, he was buoyed by his 200 success. Seeking to overturn his gold-less fortunes, Holmertz was the early protagonist, leading the field for the first 300 meters of the final, mostly under the world-record pace of Australian Kieren Perkins from his nation's Trials. The Swede eventually faded, leaving Perkins and Sadovyi to go stroke for stroke in lanes four and five. With the world record long since having gone by the boards, Sadovyi outtouched Perkins, 3:45.00 to 3:45.16, for gold. The world record, a monstrous cut of 1.47 seconds off Perkins's standard, was also Sadovyi's.

Perhaps the truest measure of the Unified success came in the relays, where the men took gold in the 800 free to complement two silvers. The Sadovyi-fueled gold was notable as the first non-boycotted Games since 1956 in which the Americans didn't win the event. While Sadovyi got the glory as the anchor leg, turning a .08-second lead over the silver-winning Swedes to a triumph of over three and a half seconds, he wasn't even the fastest swimmer on his squad. That honor went to Vladimir Pyshnenko, who had finished fifth in the 200 free. After Dimitry Lepikov's slow start had the Unified Team mired in fifth, it was Pyshnenko who turned in a time of 1:46.58, the fourth-fastest split in history and second-fastest of the final (trailing only Holmertz's 1:46.16). The swim moved the Unified Team to second behind the Swedes. Veniamin Tayanovich vaulted them into the lead on the third leg, and Sadovyi put to bed any thoughts of a rally, allowing the Unified Team to clock in the first world record of the Barcelona competition in 7:11.95. The reputation of the Unified Team had grown so quickly that it left room for disappointment when they settled for silver in the 400 free relay. Without Popov, the prelim squad of Pavel Khnikin, Pyshnenko, Tayanovich, and Yuri Bashkatov came within a second of the world record. Popov did his part in finals, with a split of 47.83 that was the fourth-fastest in history. But Gennady Prigoda, the veteran holdover from Seoul, faltered on the second leg with a split of 50.05 that relegated the Unified Team to fourth—and out of the gold conversation after Biondi's 48.96—and left Popov with work to do to catch up. The finals squad was actually slower than prelims, leaving them .84 seconds behind the American team of Biondi, Jager, Olsen, and Joe Hudepohl. In the medley relay, the American dominance continued with a world record, but Popov's split of 47.91 pulled the Unified squad of Vladimir Selkov, Vasili Ivanov, and Khnikin up a place into silver.

Popov and Sadovyi were the headliners but hardly the only Unified success stories. Selkov took silver in the 200 back, falling four-tenths of a second behind home-country hero Martin Lopez-Zubero. Prigoda, despite his relay struggles, finaled in both the 50 and 100 free. Ivanov and Dmitry Volkov finished fifth and sixth, respectively, in the 100 breaststroke. Khnikin took fourth in the 100 fly, just four-tenths off the bronze-medal pace, while Denis Pankratov (200 fly), Bashkatov (100 free), and Serghei Marinius (400 individual medley) each made finals. Only two championship finals, the 200 IM and 200 breast, proceeded without a Unified swimmer. Of those key performers, only Bashkatov, Prigoda, and Volkov were holdovers from Seoul. The team also boasted notable diversity of nationalities. While the majority of swimmers claimed Russian heritage, Ukraine (Khnikin), Moldova (Bashkatov and Marinius), and Kazakhstan (breaststroker Aleksandr Savitsky) were also represented.

On the women's side, the struggle of the Unified athlete was exemplified by Yelena Rudkovskaya. The native of Gomel, Belarus, came from a republic particularly impacted by the Soviet collapse. She faced issues with transportation to and from meets and workouts and relied on her parents to bring food to her and fellow athletes during some of the darkest days of the transition. Making matters worse, her coach emigrated to Israel after the 1991 Euros, disrupting the 19-year-old's training. Those difficulties contributed to her lack of stamina in the 200 breast in Barcelona, where she faded to fourth.

Her speed, though, persevered through the training irregularities, allowing her to set a personal best of 1:08.75 in prelims that she improved to 1:08.00 in the finals of the 100 breast, thus allowing her to hold off American Anita Nall by .17 seconds for gold. Rudkovskaya's split on the medley relay was 1:07.44, within three-hundredths of the fastest in history, a big part of the bronze the Unified team claimed. Rudkovskaya's success underscored the conflict for Soviet athletes, the confluence of so much adversity and opportunity. "The situation has been difficult," she said. "Notwithstanding that, the team has done well. It's a contradiction. The financial problem has been difficult. It's just a case of getting to the pool and swimming. The trainer helps. Everyone helps as much as they can, friends and parents."[26]

For the chaos endured by the Unified Team preparing for Barcelona, the reward was significant. The swimmers finished second in the gold-medal rankings to the U.S., and third to the Americans and newly unified Germans in overall medals. The Unified Team topped the overall medal table with 112, 45 of them gold, via athletes of eight different republics. While the success of the joint venture was unquestioned, the logic behind it was less exemplary. For Samaranch and the IOC, it embodied a triumph of international cooperation and a shining example of the virtues of commercialism in sport. Many felt the Unified feats were as much a commentary on the "crumbling United States swimming dynasty" as anything else.[27] For Soviet loyalists clinging to the old Kremlin spin machine, the accomplishments of the Unified Team testified to Eastern supremacy, even if the Soviet veneer had been stripped. The state newspaper *Pravda*, for instance, rather romantically opined that athletes "turned their team into a commonwealth without borders and differences, and proved that the cause of the U.S.S.R. Combined Team lives on victoriously."[28] While that was true for certain individuals—Popov, for one, commented on the "double joy"[29] of seeing the Russian, not Soviet or Olympic, flag raised—it wasn't a pan-Soviet sentiment. More accurately, the prevailing feeling was distinctly bittersweet, taking into account the struggles the Unified Team overcame for what was by design a temporary existence. Among the most powerful emotions surrounding the Unified Team was the suddenness with which the alliance evaporated and the uncertainty that replaced it. The Barcelona Games closed on a Sunday; by the next day, athletes that had trained and competed side by side for months were suddenly no longer countrymen, the Unified Team persisting only in memory and in the record books. The prospect of success in the open market brought with it the possibility of failure. No longer was the Soviet command economy holding back the brightest stars, but it was also no longer a crutch to prop up the middling or risk averse. Even Popov and Touretski, the latter of whom returned to St. Petersburg after the Games to see his apartment occupied by squatters, found difficulties in their path.[30]

What the Unified Team represented in the grand scheme of history was a paradigm shift, the "last hollow victory of an intensive sports system and the totalitarian empire that spawned and funded such excellence."[31] Rather than a triumph for the old Soviet ways, though, the Unified team signaled a unique and novel narrative. American athletes at the time were struggling to support themselves beyond college age, many forced into early retirement by the financial requirements of full-time training. It took a generation of advocates in the late 1980s and early 1990s, foremost among them Biondi and Jager, to expand financial opportunities for athletes, from prize money at meets to endorsements and grants from bodies like the U.S. Olympic Committee and USA Swimming. What many American athletes sought, their Unified counterparts had already discovered by necessity. With the battle between Eastern and Western ideologies having clearly been won, it's ironic that this new athletic capitalism should spring from the East. "They were the most successful team in Barcelona because they took a very mature and professional approach," Biondi explained. "They were a unit. They earned money. They helped fund their coach and pay for travel expenses, and they got the training and competition you need to be successful at that level—all because they were forced out of what was comfortable and what they had known. They had to make do and strive and create something that had not been done before. I think what they found is the wave of the future. They were able to create the ultimate system."[32] No matter how briefly the organization existed, its ramifications have reverberated through the years.

Chapter Sixteen

2001 Australian World Championships

The hype seemed to have been building for years. For three consecutive summers, the showcase meet of international swimming was slated to take place in Australia, and after what seemed like decades of dormancy, the program finally appeared poised to capitalize on a golden chance to return to the summit of the world of swimming, a place many fans in the nation felt Australian swimming belonged.

One by one, though, the opportunities went by the wayside. Even as a generation of elite swimmers matured before the eyes of the nation's rabid fans, each showcase passed without the comprehensive success fans had hoped for. Whether one segment or specialty faltered, or a lack of depth was exposed, or a fast, hopeful start sputtered out, the light at the end of a long tunnel for Australian swimming seemed illusory, never getting any closer.

That changed in 2001. Whether or not the relief of distance from the pressure of home fans impacted them, the Australian swimming program ascended the medal table at the World Championships in Fukuoka, Japan, marking the first major meet since the Melbourne Olympics in 1956 that featured the Australians as the unquestioned power in swimming. With 13 gold medals, the Aussies bested their American counterparts for the first time in decades, shifting the balance of power and unburdening themselves from the hefty monkey of heightened expectations on their backs. The root of the revival was one of the most formidable squads of swimmers ever assembled.

Australia's wait for a return to swimming's summit seemed interminable. The last major meet the nation exerted its will upon was the 1956 Olympics in Melbourne, led by icons like Murray Rose and Dawn Fraser. Since that triumph, success was sporadic to say the least. Through the 1960s and 1970s, the Aussies maintained their footing as the second-choice swim power, though with increasing distance from the United States. When nations like

East Germany and the Soviet Union began devoting massive sums of resources to athletic endeavors, the medals they translated into seemed to come
directly from the share once owned by the Aussies. By the Montreal Games
in 1976, Stephen Holland's bronze medal in the 1,500 freestyle was the lone
piece of hardware gleaned by the Aussies. The numbers surged over the next
two boycott-blighted Games, aided by an expansion of the program and a
balancing of the women's program to mostly mirror the men's. But from the
five Olympiads from 1980 to 1996, the Australians won just seven swimming golds, still fewer than the eight captured at Melbourne's abbreviated
program. More paltry still was their return at the FINA World Championships, instituted in 1973 as a swimming Olympics between the Olympics.
The inaugural Worlds in Belgrade, Yugoslavia, earned the Australians just
one gold and five total medals, the lion's share of the spoils going to the
United States and the emergent East German women's program. Not until
1994 at the seventh Worlds did the Australians finish higher than third in the
medal table. They were limited to one medal in the 1982 competition in
Guayaquil, Ecuador, a silver in the 200 backstroke courtesy of Georgina
Parkes, and were shut out altogether at the 1986 iteration in Madrid. The
paucity of success was exacerbated by the watchful eyes of the Australian
public, a nation where the sport holds a revered place among a population
mostly settled near the ocean. Despite being one of the few countries capable
of fostering a vibrant spectator culture for swimming, the success to stir the
pot of fanaticism proved elusive.

The stagnation in medal production reflected the lack of new ideas entering the program. For years, the Australian swimming edifice went through
the same motions, relying on the same innovations that produced a passel of
elite swimmers in the 1950s to yield similar results decades later, even as the
rest of the world moved on to new—and unfortunately often illicit—methods. As noted by South African swimming coach, author, and historian Cecil
Colwin, the Amateur Swimming Union of Australia operated with little
change from 1908 through 1983. With the struggles of the late 1970s too
stark to ignore, the government moved to aid the swimming hierarchy, helping fund the Australian Institute of Sport (AIS) in Canberra, which would
become a haven for elite athletes and coaches and a nursery for advance-
ments in training, including the nation's first coherent and concentrated efforts at understanding and modifying the nutrition and health of athletes. The
financial outlay on the project exceeded $100 million, including accommo-
dations for athletes to live and train. There were certainly hurdles to overcome, and the rigidity of the entrenched system wasn't overturned overnight
with the erection of a building. The adjustment period was illustrated by the
shutout in Madrid, forcing a midstream rethink and a personnel houseclean-
ing. But the AIS era that dawned in the 1980s had far-reaching ramifications
over the methods used to develop swimmers. Even for those not directly

involved in the program, the system encouraged open sharing of ideas and methods between coaches and a centralized statement of mission and means of communication where the collective good of advancing Australian swimming reigned supreme. The institute provided not just the means to advance the careers of individuals but also a tool to meld swimmers into closer, more successful teams capable of representing the nation. In the words of Bill Sweetenham, Holland's coach and one of the foremost Australian coaches of the day, AIS existed "to supplement, complement and support existing programs and encourage Australian senior athletes to continue swimming while pursuing their long-term career goals."[1] It embodied a step toward cooperation and organization of which Australian swimming had long been in dire need.

The results in the 1990s had begun to turn a corner, and not a moment too soon. At the 1994 World Championships, Aussies returned with four golds and nine total medals, tied for second and fourth, respectively. The placement was buoyed by an uncharacteristically lackluster showing by the Americans in Rome, but adversely affected by the success of the Chinese thanks to rampant doping within its women's program. Two years later, the Aussies managed just two gold medals at the Atlanta Olympics. But their depth had swelled its overall medal haul to 12, a distant second to the Americans but the highest placement for the Aussies at a non-boycotted Games since 1972. The timing was just right for the nation as well, with the 2000 Olympics having been awarded in 1993 to Sydney. With the landmark millennium Games to be held Down Under, the pressure on each sports program was magnified. For the swim program, one requiring little extra attention heaped upon it and clearly tabbed as one of the showpieces of the Games, the clock to develop athletes was ticking.

Whether by fate or the delayed payoff of decades of hard work, the stars of the next generation finally began to emerge. By 1992, Kieren Perkins had proven worthy of the mantle of Australian distance swimming. The native of Brisbane claimed the world record in the 1,500 free at the Barcelona Olympics. His world record at Trials for that meet returned the world standard in Australia's signature event to the Land Down Under for the first time since Holland in 1976. Samantha Riley grew into a double Worlds champ in the breaststroke events in 1994, while Perkins's and Daniel Kowalski's four individual medals in Atlanta rewarded the resurgence of the distance program. The 1-2 performance of Susie O'Neill and Petria Thomas in the 200 butterfly in Atlanta was also a welcome breath of fresh air. But that was merely the tip of the iceberg.

In the Olympic cycle leading up to 2000, it seemed that the talent pipeline so long jammed up had burst open, revealing one world-class talent after another. The 1998 Worlds in Perth was the Michael Klim show, with the Polish-born 20-year-old earning four gold and seven total medals, including wins in the 200 free and 100 fly. O'Neill and Thomas continued to dominate the fly field. But the real revelations of the Games were a pair of teens. Perth spawned the legend of Ian Thorpe, the fresh-faced 15-year-old who won the 400 free to become the youngest male world champ in history. Already a font of mythology—from the chlorine allergy he conquered, to the 10 national age-group records he set in a single meet, to the size-17 feet and prodigious six-beat kick that epitomized swimming perfection—the youngest male ever to represent Australia at an international competition soon embarked on a record-setting stretch matched by few in history. The coincidence of his emergence at the time Australia was thrust into the international spotlight was almost divinely inspired. "That's right, a blessed miracle, a Lazarus risen from the grave," longtime Australian coach Forbes Carlile said of Thorpe in 2001. "He has so much going for him that it will be some time before a better swimmer than Thorpe appears—and there is none on the horizon now. . . . You can bet your farm on the Australian boy in Fukuoka and beyond."[2] He was joined by Grant Hackett, only 17 in Perth, who finished second to Thorpe in the 400 and won the 1,500 in one of the fastest times in history, staking claim to Perkins's throne as the world's foremost distance swimmer. With a growing stable of relay swimmers to complement the undeniable superstar talent, it appeared that Australia was ready for another golden age of swimming.

It would take some time, though, to put together the pieces to realize that goal. The Perth Worlds were premature for the kind of rousing dominance that the Australians hoped for. Thorpe wasn't yet ready for the burdensome workload he'd shoulder later in his career. Short of Klim's gold in the 100 fly and Geoff Huegill's bronze in that event, the success in 1998 was localized to freestyle. And while the Australian women medaled in all three relays (two bronzes and one silver), they mustered but one individual gold via O'Neill in the 200 fly from five medals. Results at the 1999 Pan Pacific Championships—a dress rehearsal for the Sydney Olympics in the same pool—held more promise. The Australians drew even with the Americans in gold medals with 13, 10 of which came from men, but still trailed significantly in overall medals, 35 to 22. Klim, Thorpe, and Hackett made sure the freestyle events were covered, and the Australian men saw a surge in depth up and down the board. They garnered four medals from backstroke, though none gold, while Matthew Dunn emerged as a prominent individual medleyist and Simon Cowley swept the breaststroke events. The women also improved in Sydney thanks to the likes of Sarah Ryan and Dyana Calub, though their progress still lagged the men's.

The hope was that the Sydney Olympics would be the stage where everything came together. The early returns were encouraging, with Thorpe winning the 400 free in a stunning world record of 3:40.59, then recovering to anchor the 400 free relay to gold in 3:13.67, another world mark, in a contentious and classic duel with the Americans on the opening night of competition. But that would account for 40 percent of the Australians' golds. Klim fell short of expectations, finishing fourth in the 100 free, an event he entered with the world record, to go with silver in the 100 fly. Hackett took most of the week to shrug off the effects of a viral infection, finishing well out of the medals in both the 200 and 400 frees before rallying to spoil Perkins's farewell swim in the 1,500 in a 1-2 finish. Thorpe was outdueled in the 200 free by Dutchman Pieter van den Hoogenband, who took his world record in the process. While Matt Welsh earned a pair of backstroke medals, the Aussies were shut out in breaststroke and the IMs. Huegill and Justin Norris picked up butterfly medals, though Huegill's was only a bronze despite turning in the second-fastest time in history in the semis. (It stood as a dubious homage to Klim, who entered the 1996 Olympics with the world record in the 200 free only to bow out in prelims.) The only other Australian male gold came in the 800 free relay, a decisive testament to the program's depth. The Aussie women also failed to match pre-meet hopes. Their only gold came via O'Neill, in her international swan song in the 200 free, though it was tempered by her and Thomas being upset in the 200 fly by American Misty Hyman. Besides the three medals from Thomas and O'Neill, the only other Australian woman to earn individual hardware was Leisel Jones, who took silver in the 100 breast. The Aussies managed two relay silvers but couldn't shatter the American stranglehold on relay gold.

The Australians came to the 2001 Worlds in Fukuoka, Japan, as a bundle of contradictions. Expectations were high, for certain—the retired Duncan Armstrong, 1988 gold medalist in the 200 free, described his anticipation for the team as "it's like Christmas and I'm 10 years old again."[3] The excitement was fueled by the equally swimming-obsessed culture in Japan, where Thorpe's stardom had reached a fever pitch. It wasn't all smiles though. Klim traveled to Japan having ruptured ligaments in his ankle and facing a race against the clock for fitness. Three weeks before the meet, Australian coach Don Talbot deemed Klim "a very long shot" to compete.[4] Hackett could relate to being hobbled at inopportune moments. He traveled to Japan seeking redemption for his shortcomings in Sydney, where he finished seventh and eighth in the 400 and 200 free, respectively, and was left off the finals squad of the 800 free relay that won gold, weakened by a battle with glandular fever caused by the Epstein-Barr virus. Success in Fukuoka would contribute toward putting those failures squarely in the past. "I know that sometimes you can have a great preparation and then fall flat," Hackett said. "I found that out at the Olympics. I've broken world records and come second in races before, too. But at the moment I'm trouble free."[5] Thorpe's gravest challenge lay in the daunting program he'd set for himself in an effort to match Klim's haul of seven medals in 1998, with the Thorpedo swimming the 100, 200, 400, and 800 frees to go with three relays. Not yet 19 years old,

Thorpe didn't shy away from the 3,700 meters of racing in Fukuoka. "It's a long program, but I want to swim the whole program and have something on each day," he reasoned. "And for me to really walk away satisfied it is going to take great performances in all of my events as opposed to just a few of them. I want to be consistent across the board and perform beyond my expectations in all of my races, which is something I've never done before."[6] Thorpe would be the bellwether for a team undergoing a generational shift. With Perkins and O'Neill having taken their professional bows, a new crop of swimmers—foremost among them Thomas, "after one of the longest apprenticeships in history"[7] that included eight years on the national team in O'Neill's shadow sans major individual gold—was tasked with advancing the program. They would take their lead from Thorpe. "While the hero-worshipping of Thorpe would be enough to tear apart other sporting teams with jealousy," wrote the Australian Associated Press's Janelle Miles, "the Australians plan to harness it to their advantage."[8]

The influence of Thorpe was evident from the get-go, much as it had been in Sydney. Despite Hackett setting the pace in the prelims of the 400 free, Thorpe, carrying the expectations of the world on his back, uncorked the speed in the final that no one dared match. Turning in a time over five seconds faster than his prelims effort, Thorpe got the better of his rival and friend in 3:40.17, bettering his world record from Sydney. It wasn't the usual race plan for Thorpe, who took a conservative approach by holding back in the early going and surging late. "Just as the most enthralling swimmer of our times had lulled his rivals into a false sense of security in the 400 meter freestyle," wrote *Swimming World*'s Craig Lord, "he tore the script to shreds, dug his head into the bow wave that rolls before him like a messenger from Neptune and sent fountains flying from his size-17 feet. The suddenness and indecent dimension of the gulf that developed between Thorpe [and his rivals] . . . was every bit as impressive as the time on the clock at the wall."[9] Hackett was also markedly faster than in prelims to capture silver comfortably in 3:42.51, over two and a half seconds ahead of Emiliano Brembilla of Italy. As in Sydney, Thorpe had enough left in the tank to power the 400 free relay to victory later that night. Klim, who had turned in a leadoff leg of 48.90 seconds in the heats, the fastest in the world that year, was slightly slower in finals. But the team of Ashley Callus, Todd Pearson, and Thorpe (47.87) picked up the slack to get to the wall first ahead of the Dutch and Americans in 3:14.10. Van den Hoogenband's anchor-leg split of 47.02 never challenged Thorpe for gold, but it represented the fastest split in history and powered the Dutch past American anchor Jason Lezak. The scoreboard originally showed the Americans in bronze, the first time in the 28-year history of the World Championships that an American squad had failed to win the event. But the Americans later revealed a roster snafu, with Nate Dusing swimming the final instead of Greg Busse, who was listed on the official sheet submitted to FINA. That transgression resulted in a disqualification, elevating Germany to the bronze.

Where the wave of momentum broke in Sydney, the Australians sustained it in Fukuoka, thanks to the long-awaited emergence of second-tier talents who helped stars like Hackett and Thorpe shoulder the burden of expectations. Enter Thomas, who completed her long-awaited ascent to the summit of the 200 fly, outdueling Germany's Annika Mehlhorn in an exciting race, Thomas getting to the wall in 2:06.73 to Mehlhorn's 2:06.97, a European record. "You have to wonder when you see 'two' next to your name so often," Thomas said. "I am ecstatic; I am almost lost for words."[10] The other Australian medal of Day 2 came from an unlikely source in Welsh. Though the backstroker had been trending upward—from sixth at the 1998 Worlds to silver at the 1999 Pan Pacs and Sydney Games—a shoulder injury suffered earlier in the year had disrupted his training. Welsh, though, put off surgery to compete in Fukuoka, where the door to gold was left wide open by the decision of Sydney double-gold winner Lenny Krayzelburg to compete in the Maccabiah Games. Gold didn't appear to be in the cards for Welsh in Fukuoka, though, after he posted the 10th-fastest time in prelims and then scraped into the next-to-last finals spot. But he found a bit of magic in the final, bringing the outside smoke to shock the field in 54.31 seconds, a wire-to-wire win and a decisive edge over Iceland's Orn Arnarson (54.75). "I knew I had it in me, it was just a matter of getting it right," Welsh said. "It's a dream come true, to finally win individual gold. Whether Lenny was here or not, I knew it would be a tough race. It took me seven years, it's been a lot of fun."[11] Supplementing the medal-mining effort was Jones, a grizzled veteran just a month shy of her 16th birthday, who took silver to China's Luo Xuejuan in the 100 breast. The gold tally at the end of two days was up to four for the Australians, already making it the second-most productive Worlds they'd ever participated in. But the medal avalanche had just begun.

While the supporting acts received strong reviews, Thorpe the headliner returned the following day, and there was no doubt that he and Hackett would put on a show in the 800 free. Despite Thorpe competing in the semifinals of the 200 free the same day and traipsing into what was supposed to be Hackett's specialty, Thorpe was clearly the aggressor in the final. The two Australians went stroke for stroke for 14 of the 16 lengths of the pool, separating themselves by a wide gulf from the rest of the field before Thorpe made his move, one that no one in the world could answer. "It may sound ludicrously bizarre to suggest that anyone could toy with a man of Hackett's supreme caliber," Lord wrote, "yet that is what the youngest world champion in history . . . did before he sprinted away from his teammate."[12] Thorpe's finishing kick got him to the wall in 7:39.16, the first man under 7:40 and a cut of 2.43 seconds off the world standard. Second was Hackett in 7:40.34, also better than the old world mark. Way back in third was Great Britain's

Graeme Smith, just shy of 12 seconds slower than Thorpe. Rarely was it so clear that Thorpe inhabited a class all by himself. Then again, with Thorpe, reminders of his quality were provided on an almost daily basis. The 200 free provided another opportunity, and as forecast, it became a pitched battle between him and van den Hoogenband at the intersection of their spheres of dominance. For 150 meters, a scant two-tenths of a second separated the combatants. Then Thorpe turned up his outboard motor of a kick to pull away from a tiring Hoogenband. The final verdict from the clock was 1:44.06 for Thorpe, over sixth-tenths faster than the world mark he had set four months prior and a remarkable improvement of 1.29 seconds over van den Hoogenband's time in Sydney. In Fukuoka, van den Hoogenband had plenty of time to contemplate that margin as he held on for silver, 1.75 seconds back, almost all the damage done over the last 50 furious meters. For Thorpe, it was four for four.

Thorpe had some time to ruminate on his assault on history for a couple of days while the Australians lamented a handful of medal near misses. On the fourth day of competition, the night of Thorpe's 200 free gold, medals were the exception more than the norm. Welsh rode his hot streak to bronze in the 50 back in a national record, but Jones fell short of a second medal in taking fourth in the 200 breast. The following night's additions to the medal tally were also clad in bronze, courtesy of Huegill (100 fly) and Norris (200 IM), though a hobbled Klim could only muster seventh in the 100 fly. (Huegill would later add gold in the 50 fly, including a world record in semifinals.) The toughest decision to stomach on Day 4, though, came courtesy of the women's 800 free relay. First to the wall was the Australian team, followed shortly thereafter by the Americans. But both were disqualified. The Australians got the boot for video evidence that showed Thomas leaping into the water to celebrate with her teammates before the final swimmer, Italian Luisa Stiani, had finished her race. The Americans, meanwhile, were sanctioned for a premature handoff between Julie Hardt and Cristina Teuscher detected by the touch pad. Despite protests filed by both sides and Talbot's rather vocal declaration of a "kangaroo court" on deck, gold went to the British team that had finished a distant third.[13]

Controversy continued on Day 6, this time affecting Thorpe. Easily the most challenging in his quest for a Spitzian seven gold medals, Thorpe faced a daunting task in interloping on the domain of the sprinters in the 100 free. The final was predictably chaotic, with Thorpe finishing near the front. The scoreboard showed Thorpe third, behind van den Hoogenband and Sweden's Lars Frolander. But the clear winner had been American Anthony Ervin, whose name lacked a number next to it. After some deliberation between the officials, the troublesome timing system was amended. First was Ervin in 48.33, an American record. Van den Hoogenband grabbed silver in 48.43, followed by Frolander in 48.79 and Thorpe, a hair outside of the medals in

48.81. Despite the result not meeting the lofty standards hefted upon Thorpe, the time was a personal best and the third-fastest in Australian history, which was plenty for Thorpe to celebrate. "I didn't expect to be able to get up there [in the finish]," Thorpe said. "I'm pretty ecstatic about my swim. I'm more than happy with the result because it's my first 100m at a big competition and I've been able to drop my time again." [14]

Even had he anything to lament, Thorpe had precious little time to, given a quick turnaround before he was pressed into relay duty. Though his best wasn't required, he provided it later anyway that night, drilling the anchor leg to the tune of a 1:44.14 split to lead the Australian team of Hackett, Klim, and Bill Kirby to a world record in 7:04.66, a win Klim dedicated to the women's team that had been DQed. The time was almost 2.4 seconds faster than the world mark that won gold in Sydney. Over six seconds back in the Aussies' wake was the Italian team, which earned silver in a European record 7:10.86; the margin to the bronze-winning Americans was a stunning 9.03 seconds. As if it was needed, Thorpe provided a "golden exclamation point" [15] the following night in the medley relay. Anchoring the team of Welsh, Regan Harrison, and Huegill, Thorpe inherited a deficit but surged to overtake Ervin on the anchor leg. The official results showed that Erving false-started, but that was academic to Thorpe, who booked his sixth gold of the week with a time of 3:35.35. In the process, he surpassed the total of five golds won by Jim Montgomery at the 1973 Worlds and the five-gold, one-silver haul of Tracy Caulkins in 1978 to become the most decorated swimmer in a single World Championships, capping a biblical feat. "And on the eighth day," wrote Lord, "Thorpe rested after helping the Green and Gold wrest the title of aquatic superpower from the hands of the United States for the first time since 1956." [16]

While Thorpe rested, the rest of the Australian contingent was busy minting gold medals at a record pace. The women did a fair share of that work. Despite lacking the men's star power, the Australians assembled a balanced team hearkening to the glory days of Fraser and Shane Gould. Giann Rooney, drawing inspiration from her disqualified relay teammates, pulled a minor upset in the 200 free, uncorking a time of 1:58.57 that bested a crowd that included Yang Yu of China, Camelia Potec of Romania, and 1996 Olympic gold medalist Claudia Poll of Costa Rica. It was a gutsy swim, with Rooney taking the lead just before the final wall, dropping back due to a sub-par turn and fighting back to get her hand on the wall first. Thomas added a second gold, getting the better of Poland's Otylia Jedrzejczak to win the 100 fly in 58.27 seconds. Her triumph made her just the third Australian woman to win multiple gold medals in the same Worlds, joining Tracey Wickham in 1978 and Riley in 1994. She added a third on the final day of competition when she joined Jones, Calub, and Ryan to outtouch the American medley relay team—despite Natalie Coughlin's American record in the 100 back—

by a margin of .31 ticks. The victory increased the tally of women's gold medals to four, the most decorated performance in the nation's history at Worlds. Beyond the medals, Ryan also ended a nagging drought of five years of major events without an Australian woman qualifying for a 100 free final. That confidence translated to the medley relay, where Ryan chased down American anchor Erin Phenix for gold, one of many inspired swims that seemed to rub off on teammates. "On paper I don't think we were even close to being favorites," Ryan said. "But we were inspired by what the men's medley relay did last night and I think it also lifted us that we were swimming the final race on the final night."[17] "We've always kept hearing that the women's team is the weaker team, that the men's team rules, the men's team this and the men's team that," Rooney said. "I think the girls are really starting to make a mark."[18]

Historic display of girl power aside, the final and perhaps most indelible performance of the meet belonged to Hackett on the final day. Swimming the race Australians most revered, the elegantly brutal 1,500, Hackett turned in arguably the swim of the meet—that question was beyond doubt in the mind of Perkins, working as a commentator[19]—to supplant Perkins once and for all as the preeminent distance swimmer of their generation. Swimming essentially by himself, Hackett set personal-best times at 400 and 800 meters (the latter the fourth-fastest in history). Though he admitted that he wasn't specifically gunning for Perkins's world record in Fukuoka, Hackett always recognized it as the one caveat to his otherwise sterling distance record. But that changed when Hackett stopped the clock in a peerless time of 14:34.56, a reduction of a "mind-boggling" 7.1 seconds over Perkins's record from seven years prior and a mark that would endure for the next decade.[20] "Seven seconds on the old record—I never expected that in a million years," Hackett said. "To get it by that much is such a big surprise. I wanted to dig really deep tonight. I wanted this record really badly. It's been a monkey on my back for so many years now. I kept my cool, stayed relaxed and went out there and put my heart and soul into that race."[21] At a time when only one other swimmer, the retired Perkins, had ever crossed the 14-minute, 50-second barrier, Hackett had hurtled under 14:35. Second in the event in Fukuoka was Smith—a staggering 24 seconds back.

Hackett's gold furnished an emphatic finale for an Australian team that reigned supreme. The final register featured only 19 total medals compared to the United States' 26, but 13 of the Aussies' trophies were golden to only 9 for Team USA. Though the Australians had won more total medals in Perth three years prior, they'd nearly doubled the gold output in Fukuoka. Not since Melbourne in 1956 had the Aussies ascended the top step of the gold-medal count. There was some brief blustering by the United States, in spite of their transitional roster befallen by all manner of relay calamities, claiming that it had retained the unofficial world title, but that was quickly shot down by the tenacious Australian supporters. Looking at FINA power points, which rate the top 10 swims in the world in each event, the Australians came ahead. A much simpler metric, though, was avowed by some. "I'm a purist—I operate on the gold standard," the pugnacious Talbot said. "I'll take golds any day."[22] For eight days in Japan, his swimmers certainly showed few qualms about taking golds.

Part III

Programs

Chapter Seventeen

1930s Japanese Men

The rich tapestry of swimming's history has been shaped by contributions the world over. Through the decades, particular styles or schools of thought have come to the fore, leaving indelible impacts on what is considered "elite" in a given era.

On both those counts, the performance of Japanese swimmers in the 1930s epitomized the way in which certain nations could rise to prominence. The Japanese swimmers didn't just utterly dominate the Olympic Games of 1932 and 1936, relegating the rest of the world to also-ran status. The true significance of those Japanese teams is the way in which they brought to bear a style so different, so revolutionary, that it was eventually seen as a technique all its own, distinct from what others in the world had developed. In time, the success on the Olympic stage made the Japanese way a model to be emulated if nations stood any chance at earning Olympic hardware. Not only were they able to sustain their status as the elite of the sport for an era, but it was also one of the most progressive ages in swimming, a time when records weren't just broken but demolished entirely, often by the Japanese.

Ultimately, the accomplishments of the Japanese were so outstanding as to constitute a golden age in swimming, one whose roots go back to centuries before the sport's modern era.

Long before the idea of sport had much meaning, swimming held an important place in the livelihoods of islanders throughout the Pacific Ocean and Polynesia. In that regard, Japan is not unique. Swimming plays a role in Japan's creation myth, something wholly expected for a nation comprised of over 6,000 islands. Swimming, as a military skill and as an art, constituted part of the code of the samurai, Japan's warrior class. In feudal Japan, swimming instruction in schools was mandated by imperial edict as early as the 15th century. Among the first organized swimming competitions held in the country was a three-day meet in 1810; though such events wouldn't become commonplace until two decades later, they were still a fixture in Japan long before they gained a foothold in Victorian England and Europe.[1] Japan's history in the water echoed that of many islands in the Pacific, where techniques and the development of strokes mirrored—or in some cases predated—the equivalent evolution in Western culture. By 1898, a Japan starting to look beyond its borders engaged in an international competition with British swimmers in Yokohama. Though they were absent from the Olympics until 1920 in Antwerp, the Japanese excelled in national meets, which began in 1915, and in regional competition. Once they got a taste of Olympic swimming, Japan was more active on the international scene, hosting swimming delegations from the United States in the late 1920s and traveling to meets in Hawaii and Australia in 1926. In 1927, Japan sent swimmers to the All-American Swimming Championship while also entertaining teams from France and Australia to ready for the 1928 Games in Amsterdam. That's where the program had its watershed moment: a gold medal in the 200 breaststroke by Yoshiyuki Tsuruta. The gold was one of three medals in Paris. Katsuo Takaishi, who had made a name for himself by downing the world records of Johnny Weissmuller after the 1924 Games, won bronze in the 100 free, and the 800 free relay anchored by Takaishi won silver.

The success in the 1920s was a strong foundation for the program. At a time when swimming remained little more than a gentleman's pursuit, in the process of growing its popularity in nations other than Australia and the United States and select pockets of Europe, the world scene was open for a new power to emerge. Despite that obvious opportunity, few could've imagined the explosion of talent the Japanese program would experience next. With the polarizing power of hindsight, the Olympic debut wasn't portrayed in the most flattering of lights. Instead, the *New York Times*' Arthur Daley in 1949 described the 1920 Japanese team as "easily the worst swimmers the world has ever seen. They swam a most unfashionable side stroke, such as your maiden aunt used to employ. Some of them were so dreadful that they would have seemed safer wearing water wings."[2] The biggest "moral victory"[3] from those Games was that no one drowned, quipped Daley. From humble beginnings, the Japanese medal haul multiplied to 23 combined in the 1932 and 1936 Games, 21 courtesy of male swimmers. At the 1932 Games, the Japanese won five of the six men's gold medals; they added three men's golds and four total golds in Berlin four years later. To put that in perspective, Japan won 23 medals for the entire rest of the 20th century (they participated in all but two Games, 1948, and 1980) and just four golds. The next gold medal for Japan didn't come until 1972. So drastic was the scope of Japanese domination that it turned the world of swimming on its axis, making Japan and the "Japanese crawl" the new gold standard.

The success in 1932 wasn't without warning, which included a victory over the United States in a dual meet in 1931. But the comprehensiveness of the haul was so sweeping as to shock the public and earn recognition as one of the highlights of the Olympics, held in Los Angeles amid the Great Depression and limited to about half the spectacle of 1928. Judging by the times, the Japanese had the potential to accumulate a historic medal collection in Los Angeles. The only question that remained was if they would rise to the occasion of the world's biggest stage. "I know of nothing so phenomenal in athletics as the rapid development of Japanese swimmers in the past eight years," wrote Yale coach Bob Kiphuth, then one of the biggest figures in American swimming, in the *New York Times* two weeks before the Games. "There is no question they have the stuff to beat any other Olympic outfit now, and it is only a question of whether they will come through under pressure."[4] The Japanese performance, in the words of noted swim historian Cecil Colwin, "marked the first occasion that a single country had put into effect a definite national play with the aim of achieving complete mastery."[5] Many of the questions centered on Japan's youth: 11 of the 17-strong contingent were teenagers, some as young as 14.

Nonetheless, the Japanese "quite stole the show" in the water.[6] From the first day of the Games, it was obvious that the pre-meet promise was on the road to realization. On that first day, Yasuji Miyazaki took down Weissmuller's Olympic record in the 100 free prelims before winning the final over countryman Tatsugo Kawaishi. Olympic records fell at will. Takashi Yokoyama set two in the opening rounds of the 400 free before faltering in the finals, opening the door to the only American male triumph of the program by Buster Crabbe. Hideko Maehata claimed an Olympic mark in the semis en route to silver in the women's 200 breaststroke. Reizo Koike, just 14 years old, shared the Olympic record in the semis of the 200 breast with Tsuruta before the latter, the elder statesman of the group, got the gold a spot ahead of his countryman in the final. The top four times in the event were all faster than the time Tsuruta had used to win gold four years earlier. The 100 backstroke was also a Japan 1-2-3 courtesy of Kusuo Kitamura (also 14), Toshio Irie, and Kentaro Kawatsu, unseating the Americans in an event they had owned dating back to 1912.

The Japanese reserved their biggest impact, though, for the distance freestyle events, due as much to their tremendous speed as their innovative technique. "After the showing of the Nipponese in the opening day of swimming competition," wrote the *Times'* Allison Danzig, "they are calling it the Japanese crawl now, instead of the Australian crawl."[7] The crowning achievement of this new crawl style was the 800 free relay. The world record entering the Games stood at 9 minutes, 17 seconds; the Olympic record was 9:36. The time posted by the Japanese in winning the final? A staggering 8:58.10, lopping 38 seconds from the top time of the previous Games and

almost 20 seconds from any other relay before it. The silver medalists from
the U.S. were also under the world record, but 12 seconds slower than the
Japanese. Bronze-winning Hungary was 33 seconds back. Perhaps most remarkable was that this wasn't the product of one virtuoso performance.
There was a remarkable consistency in the splits of all four participants:
Miyazaki (2 minutes, 14 seconds); Masanori Yusa (2:14); Hisakichi Toyoda
(2:12); and Yokoyama (2:17). At a time when the world record over 200
meters was 2:15, the Japanese contingent boasted a passel of challengers to
the world throne.

The 1,500 free also became an all-Japanese affair, the culmination of the
swimming competition after the Japanese had already wrapped up the unofficial team crown. The combatants were Kitamura and Shozo Makino. Kitamura set an Olympic record in the first semifinal heat, only to see it bettered
by Makino by 13 seconds in the second semi. The final was an exhilarating
race between the two Japanese swimmers, moving stroke for stroke through
most of the grueling race and "shoving off from the end walls as though
some invisible under-water thread held them tied together."[8] Kitamura got to
the wall first in 19 minutes, 12.4 seconds, chopping 39 seconds from the
Olympic record entering the Games and the second-fastest time in history.
(Retired Swedish ace Arne Borg had gone 19:07.2 at the 1927 European
Championships, but that was in a short-course pool and in an era where long-
course and short-course records weren't yet differentiated.) Makino was just
a beat behind, earning silver in 19:14.1. Way back in third was American Jim
Cristy, in 19:39.5. The fact that Kitamura, whose short stature was the complete antithesis of Weissmuller's ideal body for the sport, had achieved so
much was astounding. "The little five-footer from the Island of Kochi
traveled up and down the 50-meter pool like an automaton, never changing
his stroke until the last fifty meters when he closed with a spurt that a sprinter
would have envied," wrote Daley. "And as he pulled himself out of the pool
this infant phenomenon was not even breathing hard."[9] The final team score
for the meet had Japan victorious, 87–71, but the margin was only so slim
because it factored in the American control of the women's side—where
Helene Madison and Eleanor Holm contributed to the Americans winning
four of five golds—and diving.

The 1932 show of dominance was merely the beginning, with Japan
putting a redoubled emphasis on international swimming. In the summer of
1933, Makino made headlines when he took down the 400 and 800 free
world records owned by France's Jean Taris. He and Kitamura also took
turns with the 1,000-meter record, while Kitamura got within eight-tenths of
Borg's mark in the 1,500. The annual Japanese championship meets suddenly were newsworthy on the other side of the Pacific, and the Americans
regularly ventured to the Land of the Rising Sun for competitions. Among
the most high-profile was the 1935 Japanese–American meet in Tokyo,

which drew some 15,000 spectators, plus many others turned away at the door, to the Meiji Shrine Pool.

By 1936, there was no chance of the Japanese enjoying the element of surprise. About the only shock for spectators in Berlin was a fitting piece of symbolism: for financial reasons, the Americans had to recycle suits they had earlier worn for a Japanese–American meet, meaning that that Japanese flag was prominently displayed on them, providing a bit of confusion for those in attendance. The wardrobe snafu was at least indicative of the amiable relations between the swimming powers, with many of the Americans willing to adopt Japanese standards of formality and courtesy like bowing, while many in the Japanese contingent, including journalists and officials, were fluent in English. From the outset of the Games, it appeared that Olympic records were again on the endangered species list. The top eight swimmers in the 100 free were all under the Olympic record set by Miyazaki four years prior. In prelims, the record pinballed from American world-record holder Peter Fick to Japan's Masaharu Taguchi, a mark that was equaled in the semis by countryman Yusa. The final, though, held a surprise for the Japanese and Americans alike, with Ferenc Csik, regarded as "just another good swimmer" before the Games from the "humble" nation of Hungary, shocking the world by taking gold in 57.6 seconds.[10] Yusa won silver, Shigeo Arai touched out Taguchi for bronze, and Fick was well back in a disappointing sixth, though there were questions about the veracity of his time.

The Japanese freestyle depth was proven again in the semis of the 400 free, when Shumpei Uto, regarded as the third fastest of the Japanese corps, set an Olympic record of 4:45.5 that was faster than Crabbe's golden time from four years earlier. Uto held a lead of four yards entering the closing 50 meters of the final, but he was overtaken in a major upset by American Jack Medica, who bided his time and surged late to claim gold in an Olympic-record 4:44.5. Uto won silver, Makino bronze, and Hiroshi Negami, another of the stable of Japanese distance stars, was fifth. There would be no surprises in the 800 free relay, however. The Japanese team of Yusa, Shigeo Sugiura, Taguchi, and Arai not only set a world record in 8:51.5, almost seven seconds quicker than in Los Angeles, but they did so with the four fastest legs in the entire race. The fastest swimmer for the silver-winning Americans was Ralph Flanagan, who split a 2:15.4 for a team that finished 11.5 seconds behind the Japanese, whose slowest swimmer clocked in at 2:13 over 200 meters. When Arai coasted into the wall, Medica still had another 20 meters remaining, with silver well sewn up over the Csik-anchored Hungarian squad. In keeping with the theme of depth, the fastest split delivered by the Japanese was none other than the 2:11.9 turned in by Sugiura, ostensibly the squad's weak link. Wrote the *Times'* Albion Ross, "This shows just how far off the American calculations have been and just how much has been hidden behind the veil of secrecy surrounding the Japanese training."[11]

Breaststroke again was Japan's dominion, with Tetsuo Hamura winning gold, ahead of Germany's Erwin Sietas and Koike in bronze. On the women's side, Maehata, who had set the world record three years prior, rose a step on the podium to gold. The 100 back was a surprising triumph for the Americans, but not after a pitched battle with their Asian rivals. In the first heat, Adolph Kiefer and Masaji Kiyokawa went stroke for stroke, both under George Kojac's Olympic record from Amsterdam eight years earlier. Kiefer was quicker in the semis, though still two seconds from his world record. The final was a rare show of American resistance, with Kiefer setting an Olympic record of 1:05.9 ahead of countryman Al Vande Weghe and Kiyokawa a distant third. The Americans threatened to break the Japanese distance stranglehold when Medica and Noboru Terada tied in their preliminary heat of the 1,500 free. Terada was fastest in his semifinal, 5.8 seconds slower than the time Medica used to win the second heat. In the final, though, there was no question. Terada simply destroyed Medica, winning in 19:13.7 to Medica's time of 19:34.0. Uto took bronze, a half second behind the American. The final score for the competition put the Americans ahead on points, 83–77, mainly thanks to a 36–4 edge on the Japanese in diving. The final score for the male swimmers, though, was a 73–47 victory for Japan. "Four years ago at Los Angeles it might have been an accident," wrote Ross. "Now we know that the world's greatest swimming team is the Japanese."[12]

Theories explaining the Japanese ascendancy abounded, most falling back on convenient (and then, less frowned upon) cultural stereotypes. "There is something in the Japanese desire to succeed that cannot be calculated by experts or explained by coaches," wrote Ross in Berlin, labeling the medal total "a tribute to the iron resolve of the nation."[13] Such assertions underestimate the training methods and philosophy behind the nation's ability to churn out elite swimmer after elite swimmer, a depth that was truly unprecedented at the time. While there was the perception for some of "a veil of secrecy surrounding the Japanese training,"[14] it was quite the opposite, and the success was characterized by an unmatched openness to new ideas. The Japanese coaches didn't merely draw inspiration from Borg, Weissmuller, and Australian star Boy Charlton; they actively sought to assimilate facets of their training and technique into their own routines. A national psyche that emphasized organization and hard work, one where swimming was regarded as "virtually a martial art" and viewed as "a military science" by the revered samurai class for many centuries, certainly helped.[15] In some respects, the elite swimming ranks of Japan resembled military installations, with their rigid attention to detail, insistence on strict discipline, and "Spartan simplicity."[16] The increasing imperialism of the Japanese may have fed the nationalistic fervor, but swimmers like Kitamura admitted that those inklings were deemphasized in the context of international competition.[17] Even if that nationalism played a role, it didn't engender a sense of supremacy or isolationism, as the Japanese readily acknowledged the foreign influences fueling their success.

The performance of Tsuruta in 1928 was an eye-opener to the international potential contained within the Japanese ranks. It kicked off a spate of investment in the program, from new facilities to training for coaches. Overseeing that development was the Japanese National Swimming Organization, which formed a systematic plan, devised and maintained by the coaches, aimed at the identification of talent at an early age, and with an emphasis on stroke mechanics. (Under visionary coach Ikkaku Matsuzawa, Japan founded the Nippon Intercollegiate Swimming Association in 1921, which drastically impacted the quality of swimmers produced and was eons ahead of the governing bodies of many of the nations they competed against.) Whether they knew it or not, Japan had embarked on the first experiment in broad state-sponsorship of sports, a model that would become "the basic recipe for national success in international sport."[18] The Japanese proclivity to welcome ideas from abroad informed their motivation for inviting the world's best swimmers to visit the Land of the Rising Sun. For those no longer swimming, like Borg and Weissmuller, Japanese trainers sought out films to analyze the secrets behind their speed. Among the most important figures in Japan was none other than Kiphuth. Seen not as a rival but as a resource and beneficent mentor, Kiphuth was dubbed "the father of modern Japanese swimming" and was revered "like a national god in Japan" for his willingness to share the gospel of swimming with the nation's upstart program.[19] With scenes like the crowd of 100,000 people turning out at a train station in Osaka to greet Kiphuth and his team of Americans before a meet, it's no stretch to say that the Yale coach was more famous abroad than in his home country.

There was plenty of misinformation and legend about their methods—stories like Arai often using Fick's world records as intervals in practice or tales of world records falling with regularity in workouts. But the truth was that while the Japanese may have been portrayed as adopting draconian training methods in accordance with their perceived cultural norms, they were very much at the cutting edge of innovation. The Japanese of the late 1920s experimented with two-a-day workouts, stretching, and flexibility enhancement long before those concepts had infiltrated the mainstream consciousness. The tenets of distance training had yet to come into fashion, so the Japanese were well ahead of the curve, with swimmers logging four to five miles a day. Coaches like Matsuzawa were also at the vanguard of heralding the significance of dryland training.

At a time when the strokes were still differentiating and evolving—there were only three, with butterfly still seen as a variation of the breaststroke—

the Japanese school of thought left a significant imprint. The prevailing styles at the time were essentially categorized as Australian and American. The Australian crawl, which developed Down Under from indigenous influences and rose from the scissor-kicking sidestroke of antiquity, involved a longer stroke with a kick that was staggered and not in synch with the arm recovery. The American style, exemplified by the rangy Weissmuller, involved a strong arm recovery with the body sitting high in the water. Neither was ideal for the Japanese, who tended to be of shorter and squatter builds. So they modified the existing techniques to fit their strengths, optimizing such aspects as hip position and arm angles to form a marriage of the existing styles. The Japanese crawl, which Colwin described as "not fundamentally different"[20] from the American style from which it drew inspiration, put a greater emphasis on the leg strength Japan's swimmers readily possessed. Japanese coaches looked to the tinkering of American distance swimmer Charlie Daniels with different beat rhythms in kicking like the six-beat, which became the standard worldwide. The Japanese attempted to swim high in the water like Borg, a technique that many Westerners shied away from, thinking that their broader shoulders would create undue resistance. The legs of Japanese swimmers sat lower in the water, with a bent-knee kick like Weissmuller that relied on power from the hips transferred through naturally flexible ankles to maximize propulsion. With a generally smaller wingspan, the Japanese taught a shorter, quicker stroke that entered the water at a shallower angle relative to the shoulder. The more powerful kick allowed Japanese swimmers to power over the catch of water by the arms and allowed overlapping of the recovery with both arms in the water simultaneously. Where other nations were emphasizing the importance of upper-body strength and displacing as much water as possible, the Japanese wanted the hands to move through the water with as little resistance as possible, withdrawing the hand before it reached the hip. The important part of the stroke was a snap of the wrist on the finish as the relaxed hand prepared to exit the water. The kick varied, though the six-beat kick, either with or without a resting phase, was the preferred standard, as it was with earlier Australians and Americans. The Japanese were also the first to introduce the concept of shoulder roll, with the shoulders extending out to reach forward as the arms did. Where other swimmers would simply reach out, the Japanese were taught to make their shoulders "draw ellipses" up and down the pool.[21] That rolling and the balance between stroke length and tempo helped choreograph breathing and decreased resistance, which had previously slowed swimmers. The discovery of that happy median explains how the likes of Makino, at a mere 5-1 and 119 pounds in 1932, became so accomplished.

What served the Japanese best was identifying foreign influences and melding them into a coherent, distinctly Japanese style. Trying to emulate the likes of Borg and Weissmuller, with their obvious and unique physical gifts absent in the physiques of most Japanese, would've been sheer folly. As Matsuzawa observed in 1932, "for the Japanese swimmers to adopt the foreign racing style in its entirety was disadvantageous. In the crawl and back-strokes Japanese swimmers endeavored to aid the pull of the arms by the very strong beating of the legs. They have flexible ankles which gives them a lot of propulsion from their kicks without much effort."[22] The resistance to a dogmatic, one-size-fits-all solution was vital in producing so many renowned swimmers. "I do not know which form is best, but each swimmer should choose that which suits him," Makino said. "The most important and common point is that the swimmer has to push the water firmly away as soon as he puts his hands in, without resting."[23]

The 1930s were certainly the halcyon days for Japanese swimming, as extraneous factors intervened to derail their quest for sustained success. Despite being slated to host the 1940 Olympics in Tokyo, an honor trumpeted by many Japanese journalists and officials in Berlin in 1936, the imperial government reneged in 1938, focusing on military pursuits such as the Second Sino-Japanese War with China instead of a spectacle that reeked of the Westernism the nation was spurning. Even from the tatters of World War II—which suspended Olympic competition for 12 years and, for reasons financial and cultural, precluded Japan from participating in the Games' resumption in London in 1948—swimmers still prospered. Hironoshin Furuhashi, born in 1928, saw his career blighted by war, unable to perform on the Olympic stage until the 1952 Helsinki Games when his abilities were in decline. The 1967 inductee to the International Swimming Hall of Fame and eventual vice president of FINA, swimming's world governing body, still made an impact by setting 33 world records, some of which weren't recognized in the years when Japan was exiled from international sporting organizations. The "Flying Fish of Fujiyama" became a "symbol of the nation's collective psyche"[24] in the post-war era, his resilience in the face of long odds a galvanizing inspiration to many. While the assembly line of marvelous swimmers had stalled, Furuhashi typified Japan's ability to persevere.

The dying embers of the Japanese swimming empire burned bright one final time at the 1949 AAU National Championships in Los Angeles. Only once in the previous 22 years (via Japan's Tomikatsu Amano in 1938, no less) had the 1,500-meter free world record been bettered from Borg's legendary standard in 1927. In LA, the record was downed twice in a day. First, Japan's Shiro Hashizume lowered Amano's mark precipitously, from 18:58.8 to 18:35.7. Then along came Furuhashi, owner of the 400 and 800 records, who torched Hashizume's record with a 18:19.0. Within a day, the Japanese had lopped almost 40 seconds off the world mark, something the rest of the world had failed to do in over a decade. It was a fitting homage—and largely a farewell—to one of swimming's most magnificent eras.

Chapter Eighteen

1950s Australians

The history of modern swimming owes a large part of its development to the land of Australia. For a nation surrounded by water, swimming became as much a survival necessity as a natural pastime for generations.

Some of the most important contributors to the sport, both swimmers and thinkers, have had their inspiration originate in Australia. At various times in the sport's progression, the styles of Australia have held serve as the world's best. One such era was the 1950s. With the world moving past the scars of World War II, the resumption of the Olympic movement signaled a return to some semblance of normalcy. For Australia, it represented a chance to regain the past glory they enjoyed in the pools of Olympic competition, one of the most storied athletic triumphs in the nation's history. What they built in the 1950s was a comprehensive program that dominated the 1956 and 1960 Olympic competitions in a way few nations before or since have. So dominant was the style of the Australians that they ushered in a new era of swimming, one where nations the world over sought to emulate the Australian model in hopes of unseating them as the world's foremost power.

The history of competitive swimming dating back to the late 1800s is dotted with Australian innovators. One of the most significant names in the early advancement of modern strokes, specifically the crawl stroke that morphed into the modern freestyle, was the Cavill family. Transplanted Englishman Fred Cavill and his three sons, Syd, Arthur, and Dick, demonstrated and taught the new crawl all over the country in the final decades of the nineteenth century. Where techniques like the sidestroke or archaic trudgen stoke, using just one arm, predominated, the Cavills introduced a double-arm stroke that was the forerunner of modern freestyle. Australians were also among the first to eschew the scissor kick, where the legs moved across a horizontal plain, for the more tiring but propulsive vertical flutter kick. With the emphasis still mostly on the upper-body component, swimmers like Frank Beaurepaire and Boy Charlton collected Olympic medals from 1908 to 1928. The Australians allowed their swimming expertise to diffuse beyond their borders to influence other nations. An Australian, Willie Kendall, was the culprit in one of the most significant upsets in the early history of American collegiate swimming when his Harvard team handed powerhouse Yale its first loss in 13 years and 163 meets in 1937.[1] That exchange of information undermined Australia's monopoly on swimming power. The influence of world-record holders like Charlie Daniels and Duke Kahanamoku and the dominance of Johnny Weissmuller at the 1924 Games led to a renaissance for the Americans, followed by Japanese domination in the 1930s, each tweaking the styles of the Australians slightly with different kick choreographies and varied approaches to training certain parts of the body.

By the 1950s, with the 1956 Games on the horizon in Melbourne, the Aussies were on the precipice of a major breakthrough. That concerted effort yielded many of the nuances that have remained part of the swim culture to the modern day. Innovations like the use of a pace clock to govern interval training—adapted from the success of European runners like the first sub-four-minute miler Roger Bannister—originated at the North Sydney Olympic Pool in 1946. The notions of measuring heart rate to gauge training intensity, repeating efforts in sets, and warming up prior to practices all trace their roots to Australia, while the Aussies helped to popularize the calisthenics routines developed by Yale coach Bob Kiphuth. Even the tactic of shaving before meets, somewhat controversial in its origination, came from the Australian programs of the era. From this font of ideas sprung such notable coaches and innovators as Frank Cotton, Forbes Carlile, Harry Gallagher, Frank Guthrie, Sam Hereford, and Don Talbot, many of whom would impact the sport for decades.

Inevitably, this experimentation translated into new ways to cover distance in the pool, eventually giving rise to a unique style, a second version of the "Australian crawl" that had predominated in the years before and after World War I. The facets of the new technique weren't necessarily revolutionary, but the groundbreaking aspect was in the novel assemblage of elements that had been successful in other schools of thought across the world. Drawing from Weissmuller and his fellow Americans, the Australians sought to emphasize the upper body, though they sat lower in the water without the head and shoulders as high as the Americans to reduce drag. The arm recovery used was a bent-arm technique based on the American style. But the Aussies stopped short of the American pursuit of swimming on the surface of the water, attempting to hydroplane using the force of the leg drive, an endeavor the Aussies discovered to be counterproductive. From the Japanese, the Australians incorporated the notion of rolling the shoulders. But this was taken a step further by instructing a roll of the hips as well, entreating swimmers to extend fully onto their sides with every extension of the arms to harness the power of muscles in the torso. Unlike the Japanese, though, the leg motion of the Australians was secondary and attendant to the motion of the arms, highly variable depending on individual preference and primarily intended to facilitate the glide needed as a window for breathing.

The result over the next two Olympics left no doubt as to the Australians' place as the foremost swimming nation on earth. Of the 13 available golds in Melbourne, the Aussies claimed eight, including all seven of the freestyle events. They also beat the Americans to the summit of the medal table, collecting 14 to the United States' 11. The Americans regained their hold on the medal table in 1960, winning 9 golds and 15 total medals to the Australians' 5 and 13, but the Aussies still churned out a prominent constellation of stars for the meet.

There were plenty of reasons for the success of the Australians in 1956. The scheduling of the Games, which took place in November, contributed, with the events taking place well after the usual summer peak for the American training calendar. Part was the untapped reserves of talent in Australia. Despite claiming just two swimming golds in the last five Olympic Games combined, the Australians sat on a gold mine of swimming enthusiasm, a dormant hotbed that merely needed awakening. Long had Australia benefitted from the plentiful zeal for the sport; as evidence, tickets for the swimming competition in Melbourne were completely sold out a full year before the Swimming and Diving Stadium near the banks of the Yarra River was even completed. Interest in swimming and the desire to translate that into international success was omnipresent, even as the program ebbed. "Australians are not the sort of people who take everything except sofa and a floor lamp to the beach and then just sit," wrote Coles Phinizy and Fred Hubbard in *Sports Illustrated* prior to Melbourne. "Australians swim in the water. The big surf lines that roll past the headlands of the east Australian coast build the greatest reserve of raw talent in the world."[2]

The most significant reason for success in 1956, though, was the Australians finally identifying a style to call their own. Aided by increased investment, including state sponsorship in facilities, coaches, and athletes and the expansion of a club system that sought to rival its American counterpart, the uniquely Australian style was able to flourish. "Basically, I believe that the Australians trained harder and swam with better techniques than their rivals," Carlile explained. "They were the product of a swimming program well advanced for its time—but soon to be successfully copied in principle by the Americans and later by many Europeans. Australian coaches and officials encouraged boys and girls to train hard and to race from the early age of eight and even younger."[3] No longer were Australian coaches passing along, in Carlile's words, "bad imitations of Japanese techniques,"[4] a style tailored to and uniquely successful for the peculiarities of the Japanese swimmers and their training methodologies. The dependence on a unique—rather than a co-opted foreign—ideology aided the Aussies in innovating and personalizing mechanics to individual swimmers' strengths. The coaches implementing these new methods had also participated in their development, providing a sense of ownership and control. The best example is the degree to which kick contributed to freestyle speed. Sprinter John Devitt, for instance, derived the main thrust of his stroke from the arms rather than the legs. Murray Rose, one of the greatest distance swimmers in history, had a kick that was merely a trailing action of the legs, the main purpose of which was to maintain the body's optimally hydrodynamic position rather than provide propulsion. The strongest kick from the Australian swimmers of the day may have belonged to a woman, Lorraine Crapp. It didn't mean either approach was wrong, and the Australian coaches of the day had the freedom and foresight to teach many variants. The result of that willingness to compromise was a formidable team capable of dominating like few others. "Australia has not only built a brave, new swimming stadium," wrote *Sports Illustrated* before the Games, "but also a young, strong team such as the world has never seen."[5]

The freestyle dominance was obvious even before Melbourne and served as a rude awakening for the "smug, self-satisfied"[6] perception that the Americans would again reign in the pool. Despite the Australians collecting a solitary gold (John Davies in the 200 breaststroke in 1952) over the two post–World War II Games, the warning signs of an Aussie surge appeared long before festivities convened in Melbourne. Australian Rex Aubrey, who had finished sixth in the 100 free at the 1952 Games and set a world record in the 100-yard free while swimming for Kiphuth's Yale team in 1956, couldn't even make the Australian team at their Olympic Trials. Americans had also seen firsthand the ability of sprinter Jon Henricks, who toured the States in 1954, besting some of the top Americans in the 100 and 200 free, then duplicating the feat a year later in Hawaii. At the Australian Olympic Trials, Rose assumed the role as the prohibitive favorite in the distance events, setting the world record in the 800 free (then excluded from the Olympic slate) that was 6.4 seconds faster than the existing record of America's best distance threat, George Breen. When the *New York Times* prognosticated the results of the Olympic competition, they didn't just forecast eight golds for the host nation; they saw eight as the minimum, almost a foregone conclusion based on the times.[7] That rosy outlook went beyond the men's draw. Among the women, Crapp and Dawn Fraser were miles ahead of their American challengers. More central to the Australians, and historically significant, their times were remarkably faster than what earned gold in 1952. The best time posted by Crapp, for instance, in the 400 free prior to the Games was almost 25 seconds ahead of Valerie Gyenge's winning time four years prior. Henricks's best in the 100 free was an improvement of almost two seconds over Clark Scholes's pace in the 1952 final, a massive margin over such a short distance. As many of the stars from the 1952 Games—from established powers like Japan, the U.S., and war-torn Hungary, plus female swimmers from the Netherlands, which withdrew just prior to the Games—fought desperately to retain their past glory, Australia represented a new wave of challengers.

From the outset, the Australians fulfilled their promise in Melbourne. The 100 free became a two-man race between Henricks and Devitt. Absent a serious challenge from any of the three Americans in the final, the 21-year-old New South Wales native Henricks, whom some believed to be over the hill, got to the wall four-tenths of a second faster for a world record of 55.4 seconds. Aussie Gary Chapman filled in for bronze, holding off a trio of Americans who never posed a serious threat for gold. The 400 free was a romp for Rose, the vegetarian from Sydney who began swimming at age 3, competing at 7, and became one of the Games' biggest stars at 17. He pulled away from the field in the final, setting a world record of 4:27.3, over three seconds ahead of Japan's Tsuyoshi Yamanaka and five faster than Breen. It fueled the advanced billing of the 1,500 free as "the best single event of the 1956 Olympics and some of the greatest swimming in history."[8] They were the only two men in history to have broken 18 minutes, a feat Breen replicated in the preliminary heats, clocking in at 17 minutes, 52.9 seconds. Rose wasn't far behind, winning his heat in 18:04.1, Yamanaka in tow, to comfortably qualify for the finals. Some suspected the expenditure of energy was too much for Breen in the semis, and Rose preyed on that in the final. With the workhorse Breen content to set the pace, Rose sat back and bided his time. At the 900-meter mark, he surged to the lead and wouldn't be challenged by Breen again. Yamanaka made a late charge to overtake Breen and come within a second and a half of Rose, but the Aussie got to the wall first in 17:58.9. Watching Breen and Rose compete side by side brought into clear focus the differences in their programs. Rose, the rangy, elegant swimmer, needed an average of 30 strokes per 50-meter lap, compared to the 47 required by Breen, known as a "thrasher" in the water.[9] There was little doubt that the Australians would triumph in the only men's relay, the 800 free, despite qualifying only fifth fastest from prelims. The combination of Devitt, Henricks, Rose, and Kevin O'Halloran predictably proved too much for their opponents to resist, the Australians vanquishing the Americans by a shade under eight seconds in the final. The win vaulted Rose into the ranks of the old masters, the first male to win three golds in the same Games since Weissmuller in 1924. The fact that he did so with a style assimilating traditional tenets with new wrinkles made the accolade all the more impressive and apropos. "This boy gives the impression of sliding though the water as if propelled by an unseen jet," Kiphuth said, "but he uses the old Weissmuller-Borg system and there's plenty of locomotion there."[10]

The freestyle supremacy extended to the women's draw, where the Olympic record jockeyed between Crapp and Fraser in the 100 free. They were separated by one-tenth in the semifinals, two seconds faster than their nearest competition, and turned the finals into a two-horse race. Fraser got to the wall first in a world-record 1:02.0, four-tenths ahead of Crapp, with countrywoman Faith Leech slotting into bronze. Roles were reversed in the 400 free, with Crapp swimming away from Fraser and winning by almost eight seconds in an Olympic record. Fraser, Crapp, Leech, and Sandra Morgan set a world record in the 400 free relay, unsurprisingly trouncing the Americans by 2.1 seconds. On the men's side, the Australians also took first and second in the 100 backstroke, David Theile claiming a world record of 1:02.2, a second ahead of countryman John Monckton.

The success in Melbourne was the high-water mark for the Australians and a validation of the systems they had established. Set against the backdrop of the Soviet Union topping the overall medal table for the first time and the Japanese swimmers showing glimmers of resurgence from the program that dominated in the 1930s, the Australian revival was another cause for worry for the Americans. "It looks as if the United States will have to strap the water-wings a lot tighter if we are to return to the surface in 1960," wrote *New York Times* columnist Arthur Daley in December 1956.[11] What Daley and others sought to expose was an American pomposity in sports like swimming. The Australians devoted a half decade of training and improvement specifically to the Olympics. Among the Americans, the perception was that the existing systems, colleges, and clubs, could maintain a high baseline level of talent in the program that could be mobilized in short order for competitions like the Olympics. While the Americans were regrouping, the Australians rejoiced in the spotlight. The possibility of Rose attending college in the United States and his recruitment before settling on USC in 1958 made international news, as did Crapp's audience with Pope Pius XII in 1957.

By the 1960 Games in Rome, the Australian triumphs were less comprehensive but still significant. Devitt ascended the top step of the podium to gold in the 100 free, aided by Henricks's elimination in the semifinals. Devitt's gold wasn't without controversy, though, as he appeared to be beaten to the wall by American Lance Larson, who was crowded by photographers on deck afterward. Officially, they shared the Olympic record of 55.2 seconds, despite three backup watches on deck timing Larson at 55.0, 55.1, and 55.1 seconds, while Devitt's was unanimously determined to be 55.2. According to the flawed and head-scratching logic of officials, which somehow weathered protests by the Americans, Larson's time was adjusted a tenth of a second slower after the fact since the winner, ruled by finish judges on deck to be Devitt, had to have the fastest time. While the controversial decision didn't sit well with the Americans, Devitt was at least rewarded with individual gold to cap an accomplished career. Devitt's ascent through the ranks was emblematic of the inventiveness of Australian coaches of that day. In the search for warm water to practice in near his native Sydney, Devitt's coach Tom Penny commandeered a canal near Sydney Harbor that was warmed by runoff coolant water from the White Bay power station. The area of the bay under the boardwalk wasn't even a pool in any traditional sense, with swimmers in Devitt's group required to swim the perimeter of a 400-meter square, coping with the flow of current from variable directions depending on where in the circuit one was swimming. To cope with rapid and unpredictable changes in water temperature, Devitt often swam in shoes, while also doing timed intervals swimming against a particularly strong current in a 20-meter section of the pool.

Predictably enough, the other freestyle events in Rome were also captured by the Australian men. In a star-studded race that featured Rose, Yamanaka, Aussie wunderkind John Konrads, American-record holder Alan Somers, and European-record holder Ian Black of Great Britain, Rose retained his crown in the 400 free, with an Olympic-record time of 4:18.3. Despite being seen by some as "a has-been at [age] 21"[12] just like Henricks was four years prior, Rose took the lead for good at 250 meters and pulled away to create two body lengths of space between himself and Yamanaka, who edged Konrads for silver. Many of the same faces, including Breen, assembled for the 1,500 free, once again a centerpiece of the Games. Eventually, Konrads and Rose, the two Australian-cum-USC swimmers, separated themselves. Konrads pulled ahead late, winning in an Olympic record of 17:19.6 to Rose's 17:21.7, Breen sneaking into bronze-medal position. Theile repeated as the 100 back champ, challenged most closely by Monckton.

Fraser, who echoed the experience of Devitt by learning to swim in a tidal basin in the Parramatta River at age six but didn't compete until she was 16, claimed the 100 free gold, though she couldn't repeat her milestone sub-minute swim. Nonetheless, Fraser topped American opponent Chris von Saltza, slowed by a bad turn, by 1.6 seconds. The American got the better of her rival in the 400 free, though, winning decisively in an Olympic standard 4:50.6, with Fraser falling to fifth behind countrywoman Ilsa Konrads. Thanks largely to the influence of von Saltza, the Americans won both women's relays in world records, decisively over silver-winning Australian squads. In the freestyle relay, the margin of victory was sealed by 14-year-old Carolyn Wood, who overtook Crapp on the third leg after the Australians led off with Fraser and Ilsa Konrads in an effort to swim away early. The Australian men's relays stood no chance against the American teams, both anchored by Jeff Farrell, a long shot to be at the Games after requiring an appendectomy just after the Olympic Trials. He brought home a world-record-setting 800 free relay that was over three seconds faster than Japan and Australia, the latter team of Devitt, Rose, Konrads, and David Dickson relegated puzzlingly to bronze despite Rose challenging Mike Troy for the lead on the third leg. It appeared as though the era of rampant Australian dominance had come to an end.

In retrospect, the Australian domination of the 1950s represented the second of three golden ages for the nation's swim programs, the third coming near the dawn of the 21st century and fueled by the success of Ian Thorpe, Michael Klim, and Grant Hackett. Underpinning all three were certain hallmarks. Each had its epicenter in freestyle, over a variety of yardages, though the centerpiece was always the 1,500. In consecutive Games, John Konrads and Rose put their names next to Charlton as the touchstones of the Australian distance program. Fraser was the forerunner to a women's program that churned out champions through the 1960s and 1970s. But the system that was created by administrative openness and creativity among coaches through the 1950s was brought to its knees by the closed-mindedness of those same coaches. Success ebbed and flowed through the next few Games, including gold for Bob Windle in the 1,500 in 1964, double gold for Michael Wenden in 1968, and the emergence of Shane Gould for three golds and five total medals in 1972. But the program fell on hard times after that, bottoming out in 1976 when Stephen Holland's bronze in the 1,500 represented the only hardware for the Australians in Montreal.

Before his retirement, Rose experienced firsthand the kind of organizational ineptitude that informed the paucity of medal returns. He set world marks in the 400 and 800 frees in 1962, then proved he was again rounding into form in 1964 after an 18-month layoff from competition. Having stayed in the States after his studies at USC, Rose elected not to travel back to Australia for Trials, hoping his times from meets in the United States, like the world record of 17:01.8 he posted at Summer Nationals, and his undeniable reputation would be recognized instead. They weren't, and although Windle won gold in the 1,500 in Tokyo with countryman Allan Wood claiming third, Rose's presence could've been valuable, such as on the Australian 800 free relay that finished fourth. In decrying an act that was the "epitome of foolishness," Daley described the Australian swimming hierarchy as "consist[ing] in the main of stiff-necked blokes of uncompromising rigidity."[13] That stubbornness, so contrary to the values that propelled the Australians to the top of the international swimming heap, consigned the Australians to several decades of mediocrity, making the accomplishments of the 1950s seem like distant memories.

Chapter Nineteen

Indiana University Men

The career of James "Doc" Counsilman was so prolific in the scope of its accomplishment that it defies a simple summation. He was a coach, an author, and a supreme developer of talent. He was a researcher, an innovator, and a scientist with a never-ceasing creativity for investigation and experimentation. And he wasn't a bad swimmer, an NCAA champion in his youth and later the oldest man to swim the English Channel.

Any one of those line items would suffice for the headline on most people's curriculum vita. For Counsilman, even combined, they barely tell the whole story of a remarkable life that single-handedly changed just about every aspect of the sport, from how athletes physically move in the water to how their aquatic achievements are regarded.

For the bulk of his groundbreaking career, Counsilman called Bloomington, Indiana, home. Not only was it the launching point for his research and innovation, but the success of his Indiana University Hoosiers, both in collegiate and international competitions, served as one of the greatest canvases for his genius.

The difficulty of classifying the veneration showered upon Counsilman throughout his career is the contrasting nature of his approach. Counsilman could give any old-school taskmaster a run for his money in the intensity and frequency of his workouts. But his quick-witted, affable personality and the unquestionable results his methods brought to the swimmers who endured them meant that he was loved for his ability to wield the carrot and the stick. His innovation in training methods ran the gamut of extremes, Counsilman was surely the only man in history to invoke in equal parts both jelly beans and Bernoulli's principle to motivate and instruct his swimmers. But for all the science he uncovered about swimmers and what informed their speed— his 1968 book, *The Science of Swimming*, has been read the world over and stands as the seminal publication in swimming research—he was a proponent of a most unscientific and rather romantic notion, the idea of a swimmer needing to have a feel for the water. Cecil Colwin, a South African coach whose work as a swim historian earns him a place alongside Counsilman in the pantheon of pivotal swimming thinkers of the 20th century, best encapsulated the inherent contradictions of Counsilman. "It was not difficult to detect behind the notes a man of great creativity and originality whose mind was being directed to a methodical and unrelenting analysis of swimming techniques in a manner never before attempted," Colwin wrote in 1992. "However, when we met, my instant impression was of a practical pool-deck coach with a fine insight into human nature and a subtle way of handling his swimmers. . . . Above all else, he was a fine inspirational coach and as sensitive to the aspirations and emotions of his swimmers as a photographic plate to light."[1]

Swimming was a means of salvation for a young Counsilman, born in 1920 as a child of the Great Depression whose father left his family early in his upbringing. He and his brothers taught themselves to swim after a few drowning scares while his mother was off working long hours to support the family. A distinctly unmotivated student—at one point, he ranked 113th out of 116 students in his high school class—swimming was one of the few things that stirred a teenage Counsilman. His promise was recognized by Ernst Vornbrock, a YMCA coach in St. Louis who had a great impact on Counsilman's life, improving not just his swimming but his entire outlook on his potential in a very holistic way. Counsilman received a stroke of good luck with the AAU Nationals held in St. Louis after his senior year in high school, surmounting the financial limitations that would've precluded his participation were it anywhere else, and he impressed in the 200 breaststroke to earn a chance to swim at Ohio State University. He flourished there, setting several world records and winning an NCAA championship, before being drafted to World War II, where his education took on a more practical tenor as a decorated B24 pilot. In addition to piquing his interest in fluid dynamics, Counsilman was an adept pilot, flying 32 missions over the European theater and earning the Distinguished Flying Cross for crash landing a plane in Yugoslavia without loss of life after a mid-air mishap. After the war, he graduated from Ohio State with a degree in physical education, and he used coaching as a means of paying for his advanced degrees, including a master's at the University of Illinois and his Ph.D. in exercise physiology at the University of Iowa. One of his dissertation subjects there, as well as a pupil in the Hawkeye program for which Counsilman was an assistant, was Wally Ris, who won a gold medal in the 100 freestyle at the 1948 Olympic Games. Counsilman was hired by what was then Cortland State Teachers College in upstate New York as a teacher and head coach, where he discovered a tremendous athlete named George Breen. Relatively new to swimming, Breen was morphed by Counsilman's expert tutelage from an unpolished "water walloper" into a four-time Olympic medalist and one of the world's premier distance swimmers.[2]

In 1957, when Indiana swim coach Robert Royer stepped down, Counsilman was tabbed to take over the Hoosiers. He'd stay in that position through 1990, a span of 33 years and 23 Big Ten titles, starting from an era when Big Ten swimming began and ended with the University of Michigan. His coaching achievements—a 286-36-1 dual-meet record, six straight NCAA titles from 1968 to 1973, and a streak of 140 consecutive dual meets won over 13 years—are stunning. But it only tells part of the story. Counsilman's handiwork is most evident in the tremendous individual swimmers he mentored, 48 of whom went on to the Olympics, representing 10 nations and winning 46 medals, 26 gold. Counsilman-tutored swimmers set 52 world records and 154 American records. For a generation of American male swimmers in the late 1960s through the 1970s—a contingent that was arguably the most successful in the history of the world's most prosperous swim nation—the road to Olympic gold ran unwaveringly through Bloomington.

The cornerstone of Counsilman's approach was rooted in scientific inquiry and experimentation. Where other coaches were content to recycle tired aphorisms of conventional wisdom, Counsilman actively challenged the status quo and strove to view swimmers in novel ways, such as through the lens of his military training. Cementing his place as the "preeminent visionary in the history of swimming,"[3] Counsilman's work constituted the "first valuable contribution to the infant science of swimming biomechanics."[4] His academic work broke new ground interpreting and analyzing the movement of swimmers. His methodology entailed snapping underwater photographs of swimmers in complete darkness with tiny strobe lights attached to their feet or hands to trace their exact paths through the water at various intervals. That "trace-light" method eliminated anecdotes and guesswork from the appraisal of swimmers' movements and allowed Counsilman to correlate elite swimmers with the tendencies that made them so fast. His work debunked the long-held notion of swimmers pulling in straight-line paths under the body, introducing the concept of sculling, a pattern of short movements back and forth across the straight-line axis of movement. Counsilman was also the first, in a 1970 paper, to explain the role of lift in the water. Applying Bernoulli's principle, which held that the difference in pressure of a fluid on the upper and lower surfaces of an object creates lift or drag, Counsilman discovered that the need for lift—and the concomitant requirement to avoid the drag force of straight-line pulling—made sculling optimal for underwater motion. Among Counsilman's unique viewpoints was the emphasis on hand speed and acceleration in freestyle crawl as determining a swimmer's quickness, noting it to be exceptional in elite pupils like Mark Spitz and Jim Montgomery.

This insight necessarily led Counsilman to develop new training methods, but only part of Counsilman's training ethos can be traced to his scientific background. Counsilman's conception of power and hydrodynamics required a different kind of strength than what most programs furnished. Counsilman didn't support the blanket idea that raw strength equated to speed, instead believing that swimmers needed to develop the right kind of strength. Constantly and repetitively working the same muscle group wasn't efficacious; this was among the many reasons that Counsilman became one of the early proponents of interval training, changing the intensity and physical demands of a repetition to give it a different aerobic or muscular impact. He also popularized techniques like isotonic exercise and hypoxic conditioning, all in a quest to challenge the muscles at every turn. Partially because of the physiological needs of his athletes and partially due to the psychological imperative to keep their minds fresh and focused, Counsilman's practice sessions involved plenty of designed variation. That even led to the dreaded F-word from time to time: fun. There would be kickboard-throwing contests and "Jelly Bean Days," a wildly popular event that would elicit media coverage in Bloomington where swimmers would win jelly beans for accomplishing goal times in the pool in an exercise that was challenging both mentally and physically. He also utilized all manner of games and physical activities outside the pool that would exercise muscle groups other than those routinely taxed in the pool, creating a mental and physiological equilibrium. Such respites also provided swimmers a coping mechanism for the hours of tortuous punishment to which they would voluntarily submit at Counsilman's hand. Don't get the idea of Counsilman as lenient or relaxed; he authored for his elite swimmers a "regimen that would demoralize a monk."[5] So rigorous were his practice schedules that some of the almost two dozen swimmers who made Bloomington their training base before the 1960 Olympics would sleep in their swimsuits to get precious extra moments of rest before morning swims. It seemed the perfect attitude for a group that would spend mornings working out at a flooded quarry, the most reluctant participants of which would get a nudge from "Doc's automatic starter," a quick kick in the rear courtesy of Counsilman.[6] "He rarely yelled," recalled Dave Tanner, who swam at Indiana from 1968 to 1972 and served as Counsilman's assistant for two seasons. "In six years I saw him get mad three times."[7]

Counsilman's taskmaster identity wasn't self-serving or vindictive as others' could be. It always had a pragmatic purpose for the swimmer's betterment. He wasn't one to "sacrifice the rest of the team to develop the exceptional few."[8] His daunting workouts retained a sense of balance, provided by the classical music played on deck or the promise of his wife, Marge, making lasagna afterward. The equilibrium transferred to the pursuits of Counsilman's swimmers out of the water. Chet Jastremski, for instance, became a flight surgeon in the armed forces. The path of medicine was also followed by Gary Hall Sr., a prominent ophthalmologist, and Olympian Jack Horsley, while Indiana's well-known dental program helped lure Spitz to Bloomington before he launched himself into the realm of swimming superstardom. (As part of the recruitment process, Counsilman famously quipped, "I told him one of the happiest days in my life will be when I say, 'Dr. Spitz, take a look at my teeth.'"[9]) Distance specialist John Kinsella continued his studies at Harvard Business School, while Frank McKinney and Don McKenzie also embarked on notable business careers. And Counsilman practiced what he preached. When his doctor told him that he needed to get in shape, Counsilman set the goal of becoming the oldest man to swim the English Channel. After months of rigorous training in 1979, the once paunchy, out-of-shape 58-year-old endured more punishment than he'd ever meted out in a pool, making the crossing in 13 hours, 7 minutes, to become the oldest individual to tackle one of swimming's most daunting challenges.

Counsilman, though, was plagued with inherent and almost irreconcilable incongruities. Despite what seemed to be a natural aptitude for coaching and leading, Counsilman was regarded as a horrible pupil. The words of former Ohio State coach Mike Peppe in 1971 were less than flattering. "Counsilman was probably the most disloyal kid I ever had," Peppe told *Sports Illustrated*. "When he came back he had personal problems, was frustrated, kind of bitter. He couldn't understand why he wasn't any better. He was a big shot, though, with the kids on our team. They all liked his war stories, elected him captain. We couldn't handle him. He thought I was a lousy coach and he told the kids that. . . . Doc was belligerent, traitorous."[10] Counsilman the coach could inflict such physical suffering yet be revered as a father figure, thanks largely to his gregarious personality. "One way Counsilman gets his swimmers to both like and work for him is to keep their minds distracted with an endless outpouring of sly good humor," wrote *Sports Illustrated* in 1962. "This way Doc can put his boys through workouts for which a less high-spirited impresario would likely be thrown in jail."[11] Counsilman's practicality extended to his stroke tutoring, as well. Breen was the perfect example. For one of the foremost exponents of technique the sport has ever seen, the irony was that the pupil that put Counsilman on the map was an amateur technician—one who only started swimming competitively because Cortland didn't have a rowing team, his sport of choice at a younger age—with elite speed. Counsilman knew, though, that an overhaul of Breen's mechanics and the endless hours of frustration he'd undoubtedly be put through would do him no good. Instead, Counsilman sought to "nudge" swimmers toward slight refinements to maximize their innate abilities—in Breen's case, his tremendous athleticism and a drive that made him a phenomenal racer.[12] That tinkering required an open line of communication between swimmer and coach. As central to his tutelage as the motto of "hurt, pain, agony"[13] was the credo of "visualize, verbalize and feel," installing within swimmers' minds the ineffable concept of feel for the water to enable them to recognize, diagnose, and solve problems independently in training and races.[14] In many cases, such as with Spitz and Breen, that involved simply trusting what those swimmers brought to the pool and merely encouraging and inspiring that mentality to come to the fore. About the only swimmer on whom the lessons failed was Counsilman's son, Jim Jr., who had a couple of successful seasons on the national scene before studying abroad and losing interest in the sport.[15]

Counsilman's success stories are numerous. With Jastremski in the early 1960s, he helped revolutionize the discipline of breaststroke. He taught Jastremski, beautifully described by *Sports Illustrated* in 1964 as a "ferocious tugboat,"[16] to be more compact in his stroke. Eschewing the standard wide arm pull with a long, loping frog kick for a tighter arm recovery and a whip-like action in his kick generated below the knees, Jastremski ushered in a new stroke that was more violent, yet reduced the resistance in the water. It led to 12 world records, 21 American records, and 17 AAU national titles for Jastremski, even if it was so jarringly innovative that it got him disqualified from the 1956 Olympic Trials. Not bad for a swimmer who finaled at AAU Nationals at age 13 and was seen as a burnout before age 20. Jastremski, who should've been at the 1960 Olympics were it not for a mistake by the American coaches thinking they were limited to just two, not three, entrants in the event, had dim collegiate prospects. The speed of his youth had atrophied at a high school that lacked a program; when his coach at the Toledo YMCA left for Kenyon College, he more or less quit the sport. But Counsilman noticed the untapped potential still within Jastremski, who had been drawn to Indiana more for its academics. "I saw his fast movements and knew he fit our theory of what a breaststroke man should be," Counsilman said in 1962.[17] Combined with a seemingly endless tolerance for Counsilman's stroke fiddling, Jastremski won bronze in the 200 breast at the 1964 Tokyo Games as well as gold at the Pan Am Games the previous summer.

Counsilman's lack of one-size-fits-all solutions benefitted him time and again. He cajoled the talent out of Charlie Hickcox, making him the preeminent individual medleyist of his day, winning the 200 and 400 IMs at the 1968 Mexico City Games as well as taking silver in the 100 backstroke and gold on the medley relay. "He was good, but he was so raw," Counsilman said of Hickcox after he led the way for Indiana's long-awaited first NCAA title in 1968. "His turns were agonizing. I thought he'd kill himself going into the wall. But he worked, I'll tell you. After about two months, I guess he started believing in me."[18] Where quick patches did the trick for others, Counsilman's rehabilitation of Hickcox's breaststroke was more extensive, forcing him to swim with rather archaic-looking wooden leg braces designed to increase the flexibility of his Achilles tendon and remove rigidity from his stroke. The discomfort of such radical changes could've strained the relationship between coach and swimmer, but they persevered thanks to a dynamic where "the respect and affection Counsilman and Hickcox have for each other is usually disguised by a put-on enmity."[19] The 6-4, 175-pound Hickcox had a knack for playing the role of team clown, but when push came to shove at big meets like NCAAs, he was all business. With Mike Troy, the 1960 Olympic gold medalist in the 200 fly, Counsilman's task was to harness the untapped reserves of athleticism in a former frat boy who was built like a linebacker and whose frat house hosted the motley crew of aspirants to the Rome Olympics. Troy may not have been the most technically proficient swimmer, but Counsilman observed his "rare intuitive feel for the water; an instinctive reaction to push back when the pressure of water is felt on the hands,"[20] that he sought to foster and heighten.

For Counsilman's crowning achievement, most of the work was done outside the water. That of course was Spitz, the seven-time gold medalist at the 1972 Games. But the mustachioed Spitz who became an instant star after dominating Munich was a far cry from the confidence-shattered 18-year-old who arrived in Bloomington four years prior. Driven by his demanding father, Arnold, Spitz was positioned to be one of the stars of the 1968 Games in Mexico City. An exceptionally confident young man, Spitz had a habit of setting lofty goals and then achieving them. That goal-setting process was occasionally portrayed in the media as cocky, and his perceived hubris and naiveté made him a target for ridicule as one of the younger members on the 1968 squad. Combined with an illness that hampered his pre-Olympic training—in the eyes of other swimmers, his absence fed a superstar, too-good-for-practice persona that wasn't terribly deserved—Spitz's hopes for six golds in Mexico City fell flat. He took gold in the 400 and 800 freestyle relay but was outtouched in the 100 butterfly, his specialty, while settling for bronze in the 100 free and a massively disappointing eighth in the 200 fly. After the Games, he was looking as much for a refuge as an opportunity for redemption, and he found an eager partner in Counsilman, who'd made an impression on Spitz as an assistant on the 1968 Olympic team. Where Spitz was often left open to taunting at Santa Clara Swim Club under the aloof but accomplished George Haines—with whom he'd eventually experience an acrimonious split—he realized the need for a tight swimmer–coach relationship in college, and Counsilman fit the bill. Spitz begged out on an agreement to swim for Don Gambril at Long Beach State, citing a desire to pursue Indiana's renowned dentistry program, in the hopes that Counsilman would help him avoid a repeat of the Mexico City debacle. Counsilman's efforts weren't so centered on the pool, where Spitz's raw ability spoke for itself, but on deck and in the locker room.

Before Spitz's arrival in 1968, Counsilman exhorted his team to accept Spitz, warts and all. The adjustment period was brief and nearly seamless, and the rest was history. "Frankly, Doc really hasn't helped me that much with my strokes, but then I think when you become a champion you become a free thinker and you really don't need a coach in a sense," Spitz said in 1970. "What Doc has done for me is to make me more friendly. I think I've really grown up in that way. I wasn't friendly before because I was told I was dumb and stupid, so I began putting on, saying, 'Oh, look at me, I'm something.' I got tabbed as being young and cocky when I was 14 and beating guys 19, but I don't think it was hatred, just jealousy."[21] "I've always had a soft spot in my heart for Mark because he's gotten a raw deal," Counsilman said. "When he came to me his self-image was pretty low, and I felt he didn't have a true picture of himself. He felt very competent athletically, but he didn't think he was very smart because some people had told him he wasn't—and he didn't feel competent socially. Here, though, everybody likes him, and he's gained confidence intellectually and socially."[22]

While Counsilman was busy helping swimmers realize their Olympic dreams, they reciprocated in helping the Hoosiers finally earn an NCAA Championship that incomprehensively had eluded Counsilman for a decade. Indiana had announced its arrival on the national scene in the early 1960s, with Jastremski enrolling in 1961 and Hickcox in 1965. Their quest for a national title was suspended for three years as the school was placed on NCAA probation stemming from football-recruiting violations. But after that, the excuses fell squarely on the shoulders of Counsilman's swimmers. In their 1964 return to eligibility, they formed a 28-swimmer-strong contingent that was dubbed "the team nobody thought could be beaten."[23] Despite comprising just 13 swimmers, one of them triple-winning distance specialist Roy Saari, USC managed to upset the Hoosiers, who led after two days of the three-day meet. A year later, rule changes that scored the top 12 finishers in each event appeared tailor-made for the Hoosiers' depth. After letting an early lead slip away, the Hoosiers had a chance to win the meet on the culminating 400 free relay, but Saari prevented a reversal of fortune, distancing himself from Fred Schmidt to win the race and the meet, 285–278.5. In 1966, Indiana was again the heavy favorite and led USC 94–60 after one day, but Saari again wouldn't be denied, outracing Bill Utley in the 200 free and bringing home a victorious 400 free relay. The tendency of Indiana to come up small at NCAAs was epitomized in 1967 when Ken Webb, the 1966 champ in the 400 IM, barely made the consolation finals as Indiana dropped to third behind champions Stanford and USC.

By the 1968 meet at Dartmouth, everyone seemed to know the deal for Indiana. "Indiana would come on with a team that was unbeatable," *Sports Illustrated*'s Tom C. Brody wrote. "And Indiana would lose—to Stanford, to Yale, to Southern California, to Vassar, if it came to that. One way or another, the Hoosiers would find a way to blow it."[24] The 1968 NCAAs, though, were different. The reason was Hickcox, who set two American records in the 200 IM and also swept the 100 and 200 backstrokes. What occurred at Dartmouth was a team effort that exceeded the sum of its parts, the precise quality that had so long evaded them. Hickcox's performances "aroused the entire Indiana team. Swimmers who thought they were only good found they were much better than good and suddenly great hunks of time were falling off old standards and unknown Hoosiers were winning or finishing right up there with the most glamorous names in swimdom."[25] The additive effect of Hickcox's performance was evidenced by swimmers like Bryan Bateman, a middle-of-the-road sprinter and relay depth swimmer who, in the fervor of NCAAs, went from barely making finals in the 50 free to second, giving odds-on favorite Zac Zorn of UCLA a challenge for gold. Swims like that put Indiana in commanding position after the first night, allowing them to hold on for a 93-point win over rivals USC.

Counsilman was able to sell that beneficial team atmosphere to swimmers like Spitz, who received an honorific luncheon thrown by Hickcox upon his arrival. Such an ambience fed the cycle of success. More of the nation's best swimmers bought in, and the cohesion of the team improved with each triumph, which led to more swimmers and more victories. By 1969, with the home-pool advantage, the Hoosiers were just about unstoppable. One fan likened the Hoosiers' depth to "having an atomic bomb while everyone else just has a water gun."[26] The 1969 iteration had the veteran expertise of Hickcox, who was ill and botched two of his turns in being upset in the 100 back but rallied to close his collegiate career with a win in the 200 back. The NCAA rule change permitting freshmen to compete seemed a direct nod to Spitz, who won the 100 fly and the 200 and 500 frees. McKenzie won the 100 breast, part of a 1-2-4 finish for Indiana that included Counsilman Jr., while Indiana's divers, led by double-winner Jim Henry, took first, second, and third in the one-meter springboard and the top two places in the three-meter. USC ended up scoring 71 points on the first day, more than it had in winning the title three years prior. But it was easily eclipsed by the meet-record total of 427 that Indiana would compile over the three days, 121 points clear of the Trojans. Counsilman reaped the benefits of the culture he had forged, one bringing the best out of Spitz, whom Counsilman was content to label "the greatest natural swimmer I've ever seen."[27] Under Counsilman's wing, Spitz had shed the reputation as an entitled brat. "He fights for the team as much as he does for himself now," said Counsilman, "and the kids all like him. He's actually learned to smile and laugh."[28]

The team's ability to overshadow the individuals comprising it became obvious the following year. Spitz stumbled to third in the 200 free, despite holding the world record in the event, on Night 2, giving USC the chance to briefly surge ahead. But two straight wins by freshmen—Hall in the 400 IM and Larry Barbiere in the 100 back—counterpunched for Indiana. The depth was demonstrated as the Hoosiers won just five individual golds and had only one double winner (Henry in diving), yet still booked the second-largest margin of victory in NCAA history. Spitz, who was second in the 50 in his first major competition in that event, rallied to win the 100 fly on the final night, just another cog in the machine. By 1971, the Hoosiers had reached the pinnacle, the apotheosis of a college swimming team. The names—Spitz, Hall, Kinsella, and Mike Stamm—defined a generation of swimming, yet somehow they all jammed into the same few lanes at practice every day. So comprehensive was the anticipated domination that USC coach Peter Daland had already prepared alternative goals, knowing full well that victory was out of the question.[29] Hall, the introspective intellectual who was the glue of the team, won three events. Kinsella, who had won the AAU's James E. Sullivan Award as the nation's top amateur athlete, won the 500 and 1,650 frees, cutting 10 seconds off the American record in the latter. Spitz did his customary fly double. In all, Indiana won eight golds and set four American records and seven NCAA marks. Their first event, the 200 IM won by Hall, involved six swimmers in the top nine places, a total of 53 points. That was a decent first-day total for a team eyeing a national title, all in one event. The final margin, 351–260 over USC, was deceptively narrow because of Kinsella causing a winning relay to be disqualified by jumping into the water to celebrate before the other teams had finished.

The Indiana juggernaut had a chance to crumble in 1972, with an Olympics looming large on the horizon. Somehow, USC's divide-and-conquer strategy, using a variety of fresh bodies for the relays, nearly worked. It managed, rather improbably, to upset an 800 free relay that included Kinsella, Hall, and Spitz, but the top-end depth of the Hoosiers proved too much. Kinsella, Hall, and Spitz each won two events to help the Hoosiers cling to a 19-point win. Spitz became one of only three men in history to win the same event four straight years when he repeated as 100 fly champ, with teammates Barbiere and Pat O'Connor third and fourth to ease ahead of USC for good. The tenuousness of the win in 1972 caused many to cast aspersions that the fall of the Indiana empire was imminent in 1973, especially sans Spitz. But with six Olympians in the fold—even if Hall and Kinsella struggled after Munich—it would have to wait a year. The introduction of adversity for the first time in the better part of a decade brought the best from the Hoosiers. "It's a team that's real 'tight,'" freestyler Gary Connelly said. "Everyone wants the other guy to swim well. I'd be tempted to say that that kind of feeling is stronger with us than anyone else, and it's stronger now than it's ever been."[30] Spitz's absence on deck was as profound as the void he left in the lineup, a testament to the degree to which he'd been shaped by and helped to shape Counsilman's culture. "We could always count on Mark for a laugh," Kinsella said. "He'd say something irrelevant at our team meetings, and everyone would crack up. This year we're too serious. We're not laughing enough."[31] In any event, Kinsella did his distance double for a third straight year, Hall won the 200 fly comfortably to go with two silvers, Fred

Tyler delivered by finaling in the 200 IM and 500 free minutes apart, and Stamm swept backstroke to give the Hoosiers a 358–294 win over host Tennessee, clinched by the 800 free relay anchored by Hall that broke a puzzling 12-relay winless streak at NCAAs.

By the early 1970s, the cracks had appeared in Indiana's monopoly. By increasing the popularity and visibility of NCAA swimming, they incentivized colleges to enter the fray, creating competitors for talent. As the dual-meet win streak crept into the triple digits, Counsilman's team became targets: swimmers wanted to take down the establishment, not join it. Talent had diffused to such far-off places as Washington and Tennessee, no longer aggregating among the five or six schools that to that point had controlled the vast majority of NCAA titles contested over four decades. The strength of the team remained in Kinsella's senior year of 1974. But amid the "lynch-mob atmosphere"[32] in Long Beach, an upset of Kinsella in the 500 free by USC freshman John Naber and disqualification for the 400 medley relay cost the Hoosiers dearly in a 339–338 loss to the Trojans that curtailed the streak at six years. The magic wasn't there the next year at Cleveland State either, with the likes of Tyler and Montgomery underachieving as the Trojans triumphed again.

It would be some time before Indiana's influence on the national swimming scene completely waned. Counsilman, who would coach two of the most successful Olympic squads ever in 1968 and 1976, certainly remained a pivotal figure. The true measure of Counsilman's success at Indiana, though, wasn't in team titles or gold medals or even world records. It lay in creating a program that unfailingly extracted the most out of swimmers, in just about every conceivable context. "Doc taught us all one thing," Spitz said in 2004 upon Counsilman's passing after a long battle with Parkinson's disease. "We were special, whether we were Olympians or not."[33] "Special" barely begins to describe the coach and what he built.

Chapter Twenty

Mission Viejo Nadadores

By the 1970s, California still represented to many a land of untapped potential and opportunity. Few mined those rich veins of possibility with as much success as Mark Schubert.

Just as developers and entrepreneurs flocked en masse to the untamed rolling landscape of the Golden State, Schubert envisioned a blank slate for his coaching ambitions. As a determined 23-year-old, Schubert became the figurehead of the Mission Viejo Nadadores, a full-service swim club that was equal parts amenity and advertisement for an impeccable planned community rising up in Orange County.

In just over a decade, Mission Viejo resculpted the landscape of American club swimming, ushering in a level of excellence few clubs had ever dreamed of. In just over a decade at the helm, Schubert had not only guided his club to a record haul of national titles, but he also furnished a generation of America's most prominent talents, the club's national-team group reading like a who's who of Olympians. In the process, the indomitable Schubert solidified himself as one of the nation's foremost coaches, embarking on a path that took him to some of the nation's top clubs and universities, as well as a stint as USA Swimming's national director after inclusion on numerous Olympic team staffs.

It all began with a quintessential opportunity . . . and a stroke of genius on the part of Schubert. First, there was the man himself. A middle-of-the-road swimmer often hampered by injuries and his short stature, Schubert was once cut from his high school team at Firestone High School in Akron, Ohio, but used a work ethic that was second to none to improve and earn a swimming scholarship to the University of Kentucky. There, his career was curtailed by a broken leg as a freshman from which he never really recovered. Instead, he channeled his passion and laser-like focus to coaching, starting with a country-club team while he was in high school and moving on to a girls' club team in college that operated out of a three-lane, 15-yard pool in Versailles, Kentucky. By his junior year at Kentucky, he was made an assistant coach on the squad as a way to keep his scholarship, and with Schubert's aid, the Wildcats placed a program-best nine swimmers in the NCAA Championships in what would've been Schubert's senior season. He parlayed that success into a coach/teacher position at Cuyahoga Falls High School, a rival of his alma mater. But Schubert's unfailing intensity there proved to be too much for people to stomach. As he pushed the Cuyahoga Falls department of parks and recreation to fund an Olympic-size pool for the community and his program, Schubert was harshly rebuked by what turned into a prophetic admonition. "You know, Mark, someday you're going to be a great coach," a municipal official told him, "but it's never going to be in Cuyahoga Falls."[1]

Secure in both of those assertions, Schubert set out on his own, traveling in the fall of 1972 to interview for a number of jobs, eventually settling on the Mission Viejo aquatics director gig. The club was co-sponsored by Mission Viejo Company, the urban development firm that had planned the community for 43,000 people, a number that has since climbed to over 90,000, and essentially carved it out of former cattle ranching land in the Orange County hills in the 1960s. The company envisioned the sporting club, formed in 1968 with a mere 27 members, as a state-of-the-art recreation facility, mainly for tennis and swimming, for prospective residents, the kind of community hub that would help build a sense of identity—and desirability of plots of land—in an area that was nearly deemed uninhabitable less than two decades prior. That imperative was a swim coach's dream, with all the facilities Schubert wanted, including an Olympic-sized pool, auxiliary pools to train multiple group simultaneously, weight rooms, and ample seating to host meets like Nationals in the near future, not to mention year-round outdoor training in the utopian weather of Southern California. The success of the firm eventually led it to be acquired by tobacco giant Philip Morris, and Mission Viejo remains a model for planned communities in the United States.

With that corporate might behind the nascent club Schubert was taking over, the young coach struck a deal that seemed innocuous at the time for a club that had barely gained a foothold in the local, much less national, scene: any expenses for Mission Viejo swimmers going to Nationals, in terms of travel and lodging, would be covered by Mission Viejo Company. To the corporate side of the bargaining table, it may have seemed like foolish optimism in 1972 from a team that was less than half a decade old and had only recently raised its competitive level enough to entreat other local clubs to schedule dual meets. But a decade and hundreds of trips all over the country later, it proved a valuable coup and one of the myriad bargaining chips for Schubert as he sought to attract the world's best swimmers to California. The deal was also an early demonstration of the business acumen that landed the club a long-term and extremely beneficial sponsorship by swimsuit and apparel company Speedo.

The coaching track record Schubert would compile from Mission Viejo onward makes it plausible that he could've succeeded in any era of swimming. But it's undeniable that certain factors aligned to work in his favor at the time. The writing had long been on the wall for American swimming's dominance. Yes, the United States was still the world's top swim nation, but the gap was closing rapidly and the crowd of claimants to the throne was becoming ever more voluminous and diverse. Any clinging to consolations from yesteryear was jolted away at the 1973 World Championships in Belgrade, Yugoslavia. There, the team of bulky East Germans who had never before been an international factor dominated the world, achieving a near clean sweep of the women's events and cutting the American women's gold-medal haul from eight at the previous summer's Olympics to a mere three. Things had to change, and the innovation offered by Schubert's approach to a more comprehensive, sometimes harsh regimen was permitted to flourish. Schubert sought to distance himself—and by extension, the tenor of American age-group swimming—from the dainty, country-club model that had long held serve. With nations like East Germany and the Soviet Union implementing vast, state-sponsored systems of development, the responsibility of keeping up with improvements in techniques and times fell to the capitalistic and dendritic network of American clubs. In an era before the passage of Title IX when equity in collegiate athletic opportunities was still a decade or more away, that directive fell squarely on the shoulders of the clubs. The Southern California market also opened up in 1973 when Flip Darr folded the highly successful Huntington Beach Aquatics program, leaving star swimmers like Bruce Furniss and Shirley Babashoff without a club. Schubert's ability to incorporate those swimmers to his swelling ranks and pilot them to success helped popularize his early efforts, adding cachet and plenty of hardware to the Mission Viejo name.

The glaring needs Schubert's club had stepped in to fill allowed the young, hotheaded coach greater latitude in setting rules and scripting workouts that were among the most rigorous in the world. For 11 or more months out of the year, his elite training group's workouts were held six days a week at the pool and weight room. The typical workday involved up to six hours split across two sessions. Distances covered would range from 18,000 to 20,000 yards a day, a massive amount at a time when mega-distance training was just coming into vogue. Sometimes swimmers would get an easy morning—just an eight-mile race across Lake Mission Viejo, which could be as intense as just about any meet short of the Olympic finals. The growing popularity of these workouts—or at least the results they produced—in elite swimming circles led Schubert to form what he called the "Animal Lane," reserved for the swimmers willing to put themselves through the longest sets, hardest yards, and most punishment. From that lane that bore the brunt of Schubert's most severe regimens sprung swimmers like Babashoff, Mike O'Brien, and Brian Goodell, among the world's best distance swimmers for the better part of a decade.

While the emphasis on seemingly endless, mind-numbing yardage seemed like a swimming Spanish Inquisition, Schubert's methods weren't nearly as draconian as the punishment they meted out seemed to indicate. Not only was he near the vanguard of implementing heavy distance training, he was one of the first to jump on the need for weight training, especially for female swimmers, in the early 1970s. (He also immediately recognized the advantage of the light, skintight racing suits worn by the East Germans at the 1973 Worlds and arranged for his club to be amply equipped with what would become known as "Belgrad" suits.) With conclusive proof of the systemic scourge of East German doping still a quarter century away, all the American swimmers could legally do was try to replicate the outward symptoms they could observe. Without stooping to illegal means, that meant trying to mimic East German methods like weight training and emphasis on diet and nutrition. Without pharmacological enhancements, the Americans would never match the physiological stress the East Germans endured in training. But at a time when sleek and wiry builds were seen as ideal in the West, the East Germans proved that brawny swimmers could succeed as much if not more, issuing a wake-up call to conventional wisdom. Schubert's training, in and out of the pool, wasn't a unidirectional process. What Schubert said on deck was gospel, for sure, but the coach was always inquisitive when it came to the impact of his training methods. He mandated daily blood tests for his swimmers—at a considerable cost of $4 per swimmer per day—to test the level of lactic acid and other muscular stress indicators in his swimmers to fine-tune what worked and to what degree.

The training methods, though, only illuminate part of the Mission Viejo mythos. As a new club, Schubert took a Machiavellian approach to creating what he called "traditions" for the club that were really loosely disguised commandments to swim by, all splashed with the blue and gold colors bombarding the eye from every angle at the club's facilities to reinforce loyalty as if to a royal crest. The Lombardiesque sign on his door—"Mission Viejo isn't everything; it's the only thing"—was emblematic of the prevailing ideology he exhorted from others.[2] Such edicts mandated punctuality for all workouts, enforced by Schubert locking the gates, as much to keep the tardy out as the on-time in. Practices, of course, were not optional, even if participation on the team was. Schubert was offering a total package: all of his rules, or none of them. Parents, an unwelcomed source of distraction from the task at hand, were strictly forbidden from deck during practice. Swimmers were to maintain logbooks of their workouts and time progressions.

Every yard of practice, from starts to turns to the smallest eccentricity of stroke technique, was to be attended to with the same precision and diligence as a race in front of the eyes of the world. Arguably more stress inducing and punitive was the constant oversight of Schubert, who had no qualms about patrolling the deck with a whistle and his megaphone of a voice to correct the slightest imperfection. Weaknesses were to be attacked and remedied rather than avoided or ignored. This level of discipline was instilled from the 11- and 12-year-old groups up, Schubert reasoning that the future stars of his program should get acquainted with the high standards at an early age. "The stars have to toe the line and set an example for the younger kids," explained Schubert in 1978. "The younger kids have to toe the line because they're the future stars."[3] On and on, the self-perpetuating cycle spun. What Schubert always believed set his program apart wasn't the technical dogma of his coaching or administrative philosophy—which were exemplary if not necessarily unique—but the degree to which he followed through on every aspect of its application. Schubert's ideals were espoused by a handful of other coaches at the time, but none to the fanatical degree that characterized Schubert's at-all-costs "willingness to do what is necessary" to ensure success.[4] That entailed invoking the carrot and the stick. Those who sowed the most effort and belief in Schubert's program reaped the rewards of the international accomplishment to which it often correlated. Using the financial might of the club, Schubert regularly arranged for his top swimmers to go on training trips, such as several jaunts behind the Iron Curtain to meet Soviet swimmers and coaches in Moscow and Leningrad in the mid-1970s that were granted what would've been considered high levels of access for national teams, much less a club.

The arrival of the whirlwind that was Schubert caused plenty of upheaval. His proclamation banning parents from deck didn't sit well with several families, who withdrew their kids from the program rather than subject them to the stern routines of the haughty owner of the Mission Viejo–blue Porsche with vanity plates who was still a decade their junior. There were some who questioned his methods, his distance philosophy, and his emphasis on weightlifting. Anecdotes aplenty told of swimmers who floundered under the stringent demands of Schubert, in what to some constituted "aquatic strip mining," but flourished when given greater freedom elsewhere.[5] (A prime example was Tony Corbisiero, an accomplished distance swimmer at Columbia University who found his confidence shattered by just a few workouts in the Animal Lane in 1978.) The stories of swimmers succeeding after they left Schubert for more relaxed atmospheres—like Tracey Wickham in her native Australia, Sippy Woodhead on the club scene, or Furniss in his collegiate setting—undersells the importance of the aerobic and competitive base installed by Schubert's workouts. And Schubert wasn't one to shy away from controversy. His brusque nature was piqued repeatedly in the late 1970s by all manner of institutions. He was irked by the stringent limits on the time high school coaches in California were permitted to work with their pupils, precipitating his resignation from Mission Viejo High School. He drew the ire of the NCAA when the governing body barred four swimmers, under penalty of ineligibility, from taking part in a training trip to the Soviet Union in 1977. And the conflicting objectives and persistent, petty squabbles of organizations like the NCAA and AAU that hindered the efforts of club coaches to develop world-class swimmers was often an issue that found its way into his crosshairs.

But Schubert didn't sweat those setbacks. Nor did they dent his status as the club's no-nonsense supremo, since Mission Viejo Company—not the membership fees of parents—paid his salary, liberating him from the specter of what he saw as detrimental parental meddling. From just over 100 swimmers, the roster quickly ballooned to over 200 before maxing out at around 550 by late 1970s. That's not to mention a loyal group of part-time members, visiting delegations from overseas, and college swimmers who would either return from their schools to train under Schubert during breaks or local collegians who would supplement their scholastic training at Mission Viejo. For every parent who shied away from the obligations Schubert placed on their kids, there was a family like the Babashoffs. In Schubert's hands, Shirley accumulated five medals—one gold and four silvers behind doped-up East Germans—at the 1976 Games, while younger brother Jack added silver in the 100 free in Montreal. After the double whammy of disappointment in Belgrade and Darr closing up shop, Schubert's consistent approach and unfailing devotion to her improvement was precisely what Shirley Babashoff needed. They would often come to loggerheads over the particulars of Babashoff's training over the years—a standoff between the unflinching stubbornness of Babashoff and the eruptive anger of Schubert—but the mutual benefit, and respect, was undeniable. "Babashoff is the hardest-working, most talented swimmer I have ever coached," Schubert said just before the 1976 Games in which Shirley was positioned to be the American darling.[6]

Almost four years into his grand experiment, Schubert had cultivated a group possessing the mature understanding he required from his swimmers: It was going to be difficult, as all things worth attaining are, but that effort will translate directly into rewards. "When Mark came here nobody in the club liked him," said Goodell, who had a long history with the club that led him to the 1976 Games while still in high school. "He was always yelling. But he kind of grows on you. Besides, he got the best out of us. Mark runs the toughest program in the country and sometimes I ask myself if it's worth it. But I like to win and that's what it takes."[7] "Swimming in Mission Viejo is like taking medicine," said Australian Mark Tonelli, who also swam for renowned American coach Don Gambril at the University of Alabama and won gold at the 1980 Games. "You may not like it, but it's good for you."[8]

The mentality Schubert sought in his swimmers was epitomized by the "tenacious as a bull terrier" mind-set of Tiff Cohen.[9] One of the most promising distance swimmers of the early 1980s, Cohen wasn't much in terms of physicality, standing a slight 5-foot-9 and 137 pounds in 1984 (still an improvement from the 5-foot-4, 97-pounder that burst on the scene at age 13 in 1980). Under Schubert, Cohen extracted every iota of achievement from her potential, claiming double gold in the 400 and 800 frees at the 1984 Olympics. "I remember one time this year she was having kind of a mediocre set," Schubert said of Cohen in 1984. "We got down to the last swim, and I said, 'Gee, I wonder what [East German distance specialist] Astrid Strauss is going for in a 200 freestyle right now'—and suddenly she was spectacular. Little comments like that have a big effect on Tiffany."[10] Schubert always seemed able to push those buttons, but he needed the kind of talent that could respond to that type of prodding.

Perhaps the greatest display of the Nadadores' organizational might came at meets like Nationals, where Schubert and his army of coaches and support staff scripted the week down to the millisecond. Where other swimmers scrambled for whatever food was convenient—or, in the case of the starving artists of the swimming world, the post-grad swimmers on tight budgets, affordable—Mission Viejo swimmers had their nutritionist-planned meals catered. The team would monopolize hotel floors and ballrooms for dining areas, or take over kitchens to churn out the high-calorie fuel that kept swimmers going. When it came time to swim, Mission Viejo arranged customized transport systems to ensure that swimmers got to and from the pool for races and practices on precise schedules. (As the Nadadores ranks bulged to include college swimmers and international stars, the transportation network extended to facilitate the team's convergence on a meet from disparate home bases.) All these operations were carried out by Mission Viejo chaperones clad in the club's colors, all perfectly coordinated by day—blue on Day 1, gold on Day 2, etc.—per Schubert's orders. Curfews, with bed checks, were enforced, while Schubert even went as far as to have hotels remove the mouthpieces of phones from the rooms of swimmers particularly prone to gabbing during hours reserved for rest. Each of the peculiarities may have come off as arrogant, earning the Nadadores a derisive reputation as the "best team money can buy," drawing the same vitriol as the New York Yankees.[11] But each decision was rooted in sound logic. High-carbohydrate, low-fat food the night before races ensured adequate energy in the pool. Bed checks guaranteed sufficient rest and recovery to help swimmers perform optimally. Massage tables weren't a sign of decadence, but an avenue to loosen muscles and rid them of strength-sapping lactic acid. The swim caps mandated by Schubert were meant to showcase the Nadadores brand, but with an added scientific component: white caps absorbed less heat under the high sun at outdoor meets, lessening the risk of exhaustion or overheating, especially pertinent for distance events. Schubert had the luxury of entering meets secure in the knowledge that his team had out-trained everyone in the nation; the elaborate logistical choreography was designed to free them of the accessory pressures of a meet, removing the obstacles to letting the training shine through in competition. "When I was a high school coach in Ohio, all I heard from swimmers was excuses why they couldn't do better," Schubert said at the 1982 USS Short-Course Championships, where his Nadadores nearly tripled the point total of runner-up, Florida Aquatic Swim Team. "I wanted a program that was top notch, where there'd be no excuses."[12]

The results eventually swung the overwhelming support of the community in Schubert's favor. Six of the swimmers on the 1976 American Olympic team called Mission Viejo their training home. On the team front, Mission Viejo made its first major impact at the 1973 Nationals in Louisville. In all, nine swimmers made Nationals that year, including Terry Stoddard, a former football player who had committed himself to swimming full time under Schubert at Cuyahoga Falls and had ventured west to continue under Schubert's tutelage. Among the nine was Peggy Tosdal, whom Schubert had coaxed out of retirement. After never finishing higher than fifth in her signature 100 fly, Schubert catapulted her to second at Nationals, earning a spot on the inaugural Worlds team. It was a seminal moment for the club. "This lit a fire throughout the club," Schubert said in retrospect in 1975. "It was possible and it wasn't some crazy person standing up there telling them they could go to the Nationals and score points. If this hadn't happened, I might still be coaching six-and-unders."[13] The Babashoffs joined several months later, and the Nadadores, with a contingent that had swelled to 22 qualifiers, finished second in the women's competition of the 1974 Short-Course AAU Nationals, trailing only Santa Clara Swim Club. (The victorious 800 free relay team of Valerie Lee, Babashoff, Tosdal, and Kelly Hamill did grace the cover of *Swimming World* magazine after the meet, with Babashoff having won the Kiphuth Award for individual high-point scorer.) They rectified their runner-up finish over the long-course format in the scorching heat of Concord, California, in late August. Though Santa Clara defended its overall title, the Nadadores claimed the women's crown, thanks in large part to Babashoff, that "lithe, golden tousled mermaid"[14] capturing world records in the 200 and 400 frees. The cover-girl relay from Dallas repeated as the 400 and 800 free relay champs, and Babashoff, Lee, and Tosdal earned spots on the American delegation that locked horns with the East Germans in a dual meet later that month. At age 25, despite his youthful exuberance causing him to often be mistaken for some of his swimmers, Schubert had "the most powerful swimming team in America."[15] "I remember being soaked wet after being thrown into the pool, and [longtime Santa Clara and eventual UCLA and Stanford coach] George Haines coming up and shaking my hand," Schubert recalled in 1985. "That was a thrill."[16]

Success quickly snowballed for Schubert, with the club's reputation doing the lion's share of the recruiting. (Epitomizing the hubris for which he was occasionally ridiculed, Schubert in 1978 likened swimmers coming to Mission Viejo as being "propelled by the same impulse that sends aspiring actors to New York and true believers to Lourdes."[17]) Over the next 11 years, Schubert's club would win 44 national titles, split across the men's, women's, and overall competitions at winter and summer Nationals. In home water in 1985, the Nadadores won their 44th national title, achieving Schubert's long-held goal of surmounting Santa Clara as the most prolific in American history.

Perhaps more than the Mission Viejo Company ever imagined, families began flocking to the community not for the scenery or amenities but specifically to have their children train with the Nadadores. Diver Jennifer Chandler relocated from Bloomington, Indiana. The five brothers in the Vassallo family, led by world-record holding medleyist Jesse, traveled from Puerto Rico. Mission Viejo highlighted the lure of California, then the unquestioned leader among the states in churning out talent like UCLA star Robin Leamy and diver Greg Louganis, both Nadadores. O'Brien, a native of Skokie, Illinois, whose family settled in Costa Mesa, showed early talent but got sloppy as a teen with Darr, who'd moved on to Irvine Novaquatics. When a severe ankle injury on the basketball court refocused his attention back on swimming, he signaled his devotion by matriculating to Mission Viejo. Ricardo Prado wrote to Schubert at age 13, hoping for guidance and a challenge he couldn't get in his native Brazil. After a two-year wait to physically prepare for the rigors of Schubert's program and the difficulty of living in a foreign country, the native of São Paolo joined in 1980. By 1982, he was the world champion in the 400 IM, then won silver at the 1984 Olympics. When Dara Torres's talent in the early 1980s made her one of the hottest commodities on the sprinting block, she came to Schubert to "get more guts," and enough stamina to get to the Olympics in the 100 free in an era when the 50, her specialty, was not yet part of the Olympic program.[18] When Mary T. Meagher, long regarded as the world's foremost butterflier but denied the chance to prove it in the 1980 Olympics thanks to the American boycott of the Moscow Games, sought to reboot her career for another Olympic run, she turned to Schubert. Together with the likes of Amy White and Rich Saeger, Mission Viejo sent six American Olympians to the 1984 Los Angeles Games, a group that returned a crop of 13 medals, 10 gold.

The Nadadores were left open for the criticism that they weren't really a team in their heyday. By the mid-1980s, it was true that they came to meets with quite a few swimmers training elsewhere who, while claiming Mission Viejo as an important influence, weren't in the pool in Mission Viejo with any regularity. The joke was that national meets featured a multitude of "getting to know you" conversations to form the united front that would

challenge for titles.[19] But the club still retained a core membership, swimmers like Goodell and Taylor Howe who rose from the age-group to national-team setups. One of the lasting images of the 1984 wins at Nationals came
via Channon Hermstad, a plucky and determined swimmer not blessed with
the physical gifts of many of her teammates but who worked just as hard in
practice and had risen through the ranks. With an Olympic year at hand, it
was almost a foregone conclusion that the 400 IM, Hermstad's favored event,
would be won by Tracy Caulkins, a swimmer who like Meagher had long
dominated her discipline and was trying to extend her career to obtain the
Olympic moment the boycott denied her. But Caulkins scratched the event
after a fast qualifying time, leaving the door open. Improbably—and with the
cheers of her team, few louder than Schubert—Hermstad won the title, inspired by, and in turn inspiring, her teammates.

Schubert's teams didn't just pile up national titles at an unprecedented
rate during his tenure from 1972 to 1985. They had a way of changing the
paradigms of competitive swimming. Vassallo, for instance, was among the
first backstrokers to swim primarily underwater using the dolphin kick that,
while breaking the mind-numbing monotony of one Schubert set, he found to
be superior to the above-water stroke. That technique would later lead to a
revolution in the stroke, rewriting the record book before being outlawed by
harsh rebuke from swimming's governing body. Decades before Torres's
three-silver-medal take at age 41 at the Beijing Olympics redefined what is
too old for an athlete, she introduced a much more subtle nuance to the sport:
a track start with one foot back, rather than both curled over the front edge, to
capitalize on the leverage of the slanted block. Goodell, O'Brien, and Babashoff were among the innovators of the idea of negative-splitting, swimming the second half of an event as fast as or faster than the front, which
intuitively should be faster given the advantage of the start. Schubert's utilization of certain psychological techniques, like visualization and the instilla-
tion of positive image of the self, characterized the broadly termed field of
sports psychology still in its infancy. For all his bluster and perceived pomposity, Schubert developed a remarkable ability to adapt his ideologies, both
to individuals and the circumstances. Perhaps the most telling example is
Schubert's mellowing in his latter days with Mission Viejo. No longer needing to vehemently prove his legitimacy, he transformed from authoritarian to
cajoler to cheerleader. It proved a vital skill when he transitioned to the
college ranks, with Schubert needing to develop significant tolerance for the
distractions presented by academic schedules and other inconveniences he
had to accommodate.

Mission Viejo also drastically impacted the landscape of American swimming. Seeing the connection between investment and success, the Nadadores
model was emulated elsewhere, most notably by the John E. DuPont investment in Team Foxcatcher outside of Philadelphia. Even Schubert couldn't

replicate what Mission Viejo had done. Once he'd supplanted Santa Clara in national titles, Schubert began looking for a new challenge. That led him to the Mission Bay Makos, a swim club in a planned community in Boca Raton, Florida, that did little to disguise the overt homage to the Nadadores. As part of a $200 million community, Schubert was paid handsomely to preside over a swim team that would include state-of-the-art facilities surpassing even what Mission Viejo offered. Despite the complex not yet being complete, Schubert—with longtime assistant Larry Leibowitz doing the advance scouting while Schubert tied up loose ends in California—increased enrollment at the Makos from zero swimmers in June 1985 to 70-some in the fall, to national champions in 1986. While Mission Viejo teetered on the brink of open parent-sparked rebellion against Stoddard, another of Schubert's longtime lieutenants who was installed at the helm of the Nadadores, Schubert led the Makos to nine national titles in four years. But the success was short-lived. Citing pressures from the financial side of the business, which were exacerbated by a lull in the real-estate market that stunted the growth of Mission Bay in the late 1980s, Schubert left for the college pools in 1989, the club collapsing behind him. It was a far cry from his tone at the new beginning four years prior. "Quite frankly, I have all the confidence in the world that this will be a better position than Mission Viejo," Schubert said upon assuming his position in 1985. "I think we'll have superior facilities and superior support as far as working with medical support like physiologists and psychologists, that sort of thing. I felt for the 13 years I was at Mission Viejo that it was the best position in swimming, but I think this will develop into an even better position."[20] Schubert found out the hard way that topping Mission Viejo, then and now, is an almost impossible proposition.

Chapter Twenty-One

Stanford University Women

In the swimming oasis of California, Stanford University has always held an important place. For decades, in both the men's and women's collegiate ranks, the Cardinal has been an important facet of the swimming landscape, occasionally dominant and always relevant. Few collegiate programs can rival the pantheon of stars tracing their roots through Palo Alto.

Across both genders, Stanford has accounted for 16 team national championships through the end of 2013, split evenly at eight and eight. That total is the second most among schools, trailing only the University of Texas. At the heart of many of the Stanford titles—and many of the Texas titles, for that matter—is arguably the most successful collegiate coach in history, Richard Quick.

The numbers of titles, wins, and Olympians tell a great deal about what the late Quick was able to accomplish on the pool deck. But perhaps the most important aspect of his coaching tenure was what the swimmers he mentored did after they left the Cardinal. Quick didn't just run off a streak of six national titles in 10 years at Stanford. He didn't just, dating back to his time with Texas, pilot teams to top-three finishes at the NCAA Championships in 22 consecutive seasons. He isn't just the most decorated college coach in history with 13 national titles. The swimmers Quick coached at Stanford included a legion of stars that, at a time in the late 1980s and early 1990s when swimming was venturing into the mainstream popularity of American sports, helped put women's swimming back on the map. Household names that transcended the popularity of their sport, stars like Summer Sanders, Janet Evans, and Jenny Thompson, all have Quick and Stanford to thank for a large part of their successes.

The marriage of Quick and Stanford in 1988 brought the best out in both. Stanford had had a respectable history of success in the pool, spawning such

Olympians as Linda Jezek, Susan Rapp, Kim Peyton, Chris von Saltza, and Sharon Stouder. The Cardinal won the 1983 NCAA Championship under former Santa Clara Swim Club coach George Haines—a man and club that loomed large in the pre-Quick history of the program—and won the 1980 AIAW Championship, a precursor to the NCAA's assumption of dominion over women's collegiate sports, with Claudia Kolb Thomas at the helm. From 1948 to 1984, the women of Stanford accounted for 18 Olympic medals, six individual, with the only two individual golds coming via von Saltza and Stouder. At the 1992 Barcelona Games alone, four years into Quick's tenure, the Stanford contingent managed 11 medals, seven individual and two golds.

Quick, an assistant coach on that team after serving as the head man in 1988, also had his fair share of success before arriving in Palo Alto. He had established himself as an up-and-coming star in the coaching ranks, moving from his alma mater, Southern Methodist University, to the Iowa State men's program to the helm of both men's and women's swimming at Auburn in 1978. At Auburn, his star pupil was Rowdy Gaines, whom Quick coached through the 1980 Olympic boycott and whose comeback he handled, even while relocating again, up until the 1984 Games in Los Angeles. After four years at Auburn, Quick returned to the Lone Star state to head up the University of Texas women's program, where he enjoyed monstrous success. From 1983 to 1988—led by the likes of Carrie Steinseifer, Tiff Cohen, Betsy Mitchell, and Jill Sterkel—Quick won five straight women's national championships, establishing the Longhorns as the first dynasty of an NCAA women's swimming competition still in its infancy. His accomplishments earned him a spot on the 1984 Olympic staff and the honor of coaching the delegation sent to Seoul in 1988. Quick's decision to head to Stanford surprised many. Even more shocking was the fact that he managed a national title, his sixth straight, in his first season with a 1989 Stanford team that he had virtually no hand in shaping and that Quick predicted to be the third-best squad at NCAAs that year.[1]

Much of the growth of Stanford's program is down to the vigor of Quick's tutelage. The native of Akron, Ohio, swam for Highland Park High School outside of Dallas, Texas, and matriculated to SMU, where he earned his bachelor's and master's degrees. Where some coaches achieved their success by relentlessly innovating, the story of Quick's success was more personal. Quick didn't have some magical method whereby his swimmers could zoom to international prominence without hard work. But Quick made that workload easier with his innate powers of motivation. From the time he began coaching at little Dad's Club in Houston, Texas, Quick developed a reputation as a master motivator, one who could encourage good swimmers to become great and great swimmers to become internationally renowned. Quick had a knack for knowing what swimmers needed, physically and

mentally, to achieve their goals, and fostered the type of individual account-
ability that drove swimmers to push their limits.

That ability to extract the best from swimmers up and down the team's
depth chart is what most contributed to his collection of national championships. "He made you believe you could do anything," said Jennifer Webb,
who swam for Quick at Dad's and SMU. "That's part of his legacy."[2] "Richard's biggest strength is his enthusiasm and his intensity," said Misty Hyman, one of Quick's Olympic success stories at Stanford. "The way that
Richard inspires our team is that he believes that anything was possible if we
work hard and believe in ourselves."[3] Much of Quick's ability to relate to
swimmers was his unflinching desire to give everything of himself to their
efforts, devoting his life to coaching until his mid-60s when in 2008 he was
diagnosed with a brain tumor that would end his life just months later. If his
team needed a break from monotonous lap swimming, Quick would design
some other strenuous activity like water polo, then help even out the teams
by jumping in the water and playing if that's what was needed. At some of
his earlier gigs, like Dad's, Quick was the low-cost option to deputize as the
bus driver. No one ever beat Quick to practice, and his energy on deck and
enthusiasm for his profession were unmatched. Though his outbursts of intensity and constant patrolling of the deck could be jarring, those displays of
passion and dedication were prominent facets of an approach that many
remembered with the most fondness and appreciation. "He instilled a competitive spirit in my body," former Dad's swimmer Brent Barker recalled
after Quick's passing in 2009. "He'd drive the bus to meets, and if we didn't
do well, there wouldn't be a word said on the bus. When we got home, he'd
stand on the bottom steps, and you had to make eye contact with him as you
were getting off. He had some great swimmers, but he was equally excited by
the guy that had to give it everything just to, say, qualify for consolation
finals. Richard loved the underdog."[4] The admiration still flowed despite
Quick having put swimmers through their paces to a legendary degree for
decades. At the center of it was faith that emphasizing the collective good
would necessarily lead to individual success. "He made everyone believe that
if they were working for the greater good of the team, it would bring out the
best in each individual," said Lea Maurer (nee Loveless), who eventually
succeeded Quick in coaching Stanford. "He was right."[5] His ability to meld a
group of individuals into a successful team is one of the central themes of his
NCAA success.

Discussing Quick's motivational tactics in isolation doesn't give him
enough credit for his ability to innovate in the pool. Being able to mentally
nurse swimmers through workouts would've only been beneficial had those
practices contained enough substance to test swimmers' mettle. While Quick
was certainly an innovator, he also approached the process with a certain
amount of humility. "I don't think there's a coach worth a damn, when the

athletes they're in charge of don't perform well, who doesn't ask himself, 'What could I have done better to give the athletes every opportunity to perform better?'" Quick told *Swimming World* magazine in 1986.[6] That openness to change prevented Quick from getting stuck ideologically. Quick was willing to listen to the many technological fads passing through the industry but reticent to jump too quickly on any. He yielded to scientific research on certain aspects, such as the massive towing device he had installed the early 1990s. Derived from a device used by champion sprinter Alexander Popov, the network of pulleys was designed to pull a swimmer at high speeds, allowing them to more easily detect and iron out stroke inefficiencies.[7] Quick also utilized beeper sets, programming a tiny, digital metronome that attached to the caps of swimmers, particularly distance freestylers, to help them monitor and internalize their stroke cadences. The device is emblematic of Quick's approach: advanced, but eminently customizable. Quick always had an open-door policy with his swimmers, inviting suggestions for workouts and allowing a give-and-take that was unusual among his generally dictatorial colleagues. (Those lessons were instilled early thanks to Gaines, and such adaptability aided his coping with the vacillations in Gaines's commitment to the 1984 Games.) That two-way communication is what convinced Thompson to move cross-country and shift her training in an Olympic year in 1992, and what informed the trust cultivated between Quick and Loveless that transformed her from a partial scholarship recipient to a 19-time All-America. While Quick wasn't above having his swimmers stretch their muscles by pushing his car out of the parking lot when it wouldn't start—though his swimmers often wondered if it was purely for the workout value—he was also fanatical in helping his swimmers regulate their nutrition. During his preparation of Thompson and Dara Torres for the 2000 Olympics, Quick employed numerous nutritionists and other (rather exotic) biological specialists to help them properly fuel their bodies and eliminate any substances unconducive to optimal performance.

For all the credentials Quick brought to California, the adjustment to the Cardinal in the fall of 1988 featured a fair bit of uneasiness. "It was interesting at first. It was difficult," middle-distance freestyler Aimee Berzins said. "It was hard to succumb to his authority. It took a few weeks before we began to respect him and for him to respect us."[8] There was angst from the Cardinal in acclimating to methods like weight training that they'd never before been exposed to, while intensity and yardage, particularly for the sprinters, was ramped up. Some were also concerned that Quick's stay in Palo Alto would be brief, as the men's job at his alma mater, SMU, soon became available. It didn't take long, though, for Quick the master motivator to work his magic. "Richard's pep talks were the greatest," Berzins said. "He was like a salesman and talked in his Southern lingo. He'd say, 'Ladies, this is what we're going to do.' He'd rattle off a set that's impossible to do. He'd be all serious. You didn't ever know if he was upset. He'd always approach it matter-of-fact but in a very gentlemanly manner. Everyone got a kick out of it."[9]

At least the expectations were reasonable for the Cardinal. Quick reckoned them to be the nation's third-best team, behind Florida and his former club, Texas. The coach wasn't about to lump more pressure on them either; being a group he had no hand in recruiting, there wasn't as much pressure on him to get results with his inherited group. The Stanford roster boasted just one Olympian in sprinter Jenna Johnson, who was five years removed from the Los Angeles Games and hadn't even finaled at the previous summer's Olympic Trials. On paper, Quick scored the Cardinal 100 points behind Florida, a margin that sent them to Indianapolis harboring only long-shot dreams of a title. But as was often the case, Quick made the stars align. They scored an impressive 610.5 points, easily outpacing Texas (547) and Florida (536), albeit by "winning ugly."[10] The Cardinal won only two events—Michelle Griglione in the 400 IM and Johnson in the 100 fly—tied for the lowest total for a championship team in NCAA history. But the depth of the Cardinal was Quick's coaching trump card. All but two of his swimmers scored that weekend, and seven of them finaled in all three of their individual events. A Stanford swimmer found her way into every final save for one. They didn't win a relay, but finished second twice and third once. And despite the lack of victories, the Cardinal still accounted for three of the meet's top six individual scorers: Griglione in second with 52 points, Jenna Johnson fourth with 50, and Jill Johnson sixth with 48.5. While the depth of Stanford's roster stepped up, other teams' second-tier swimmers faltered. Texas sprinter Leigh Ann Fetter was outstanding again, earning a hug from her former coach Quick after each win, but the Longhorns couldn't get consistent points from other sources. Florida's three-time champ from 1988, Tami Bruce, was slowed by injury, dampening the efforts of teammates Julie Gorman and Lorraine Perkins. That opened the door for Stanford, and Quick made sure every single member of his team had a hand in pushing their way through. Despite a landslide victory, Quick showed his rational side in evaluating the triumph. "The best team doesn't always win," Quick said. "Of the six championships I've won, I think three were won with inferior talent."[11]

With his foot in the door—and his hand on a championship trophy—Quick set to building an empire in Palo Alto. That quest included landing a trio of recruiting classes unmatched in the nation. The headliner in the fall of 1989 needed little introduction. Evans, a native of Placentia, California, stormed into Stanford off a dominant golden treble in the 1988 Seoul Games, winning the 400 and 800 frees and 400 IM. Amid a lull in American women's swimming, the slight 17-year-old was the only female wearer of the Stars and Stripes to return from Seoul with gold. The following fall brought Sanders, already tabbed as a rising star by her performances in the junior ranks, the versatile Janel Jorgensen and backstroker extraordinaire Loveless, whose preferred move to Florida broke down when Coach Randy Reese left. The following fall's arrivals featured Thompson, one of the most successful female swimmers in NCAA history.

Amazingly, Stanford was blanked on titles in Evans's two years there, though not for lack of effort by the eight-time All-America. With Quick headed to familiar, if suddenly hostile, territory, for the 1990 NCAA Championships in Austin nursing a personal streak of six straight titles, the pressure was on. But Quick made sure most of that onus fell on his shoulders rather than his swimmers, minimizing the devastation of a narrow loss to Texas, 632–622.5. "There's no pressure except the pressure of wanting the team to win and do their best times," Quick said afterward, always looking on the bright side. "I'm an emotional guy and wanted to win in the worst way. If we had to lose this meet, I'd want to lose it to Texas, though. I coached the seniors and juniors and recruited the sophomores. I feel close to them."[12] Evans did her part, and historically so. She didn't just win the 500 and 1,650 frees and 400 IM, but she set American records in the former two and settled for an NCAA record in the third. Her 500 free swim downed the oldest existing American short-course standard, dating back to Tracy Caulkins in 1979. (She also trounced Cohen's NCAA record from 1985.) Evans's 400 IM swim toppled Caulkins's NCAA mark from 1984, while her 1,650 swim chopped a whopping 11.72 seconds off the NCAA record set by Bruce two years prior and earned her recognition as the meet's most outstanding swimmer. Jorgensen started her career with a trifecta of wins, taking the 200 IM and 100 and 200 fly, while Jill Johnson and Lori Heisick went 1-2 in the 200 breaststroke. The 1990 meet also featured a pair of relay wins in the 800 free and 400 medley relay, both featuring Jorgensen. Despite having the meet's top two scorers and increasing their event win total from two to nine, Stanford could only muster the silver medal in the team competition.

The same script played out the following year. Stanford didn't lose the title, scoring 653 points, their third-highest ever in an NCAA meet. The Longhorns simply wrestled it away from them, tallying an astounding 746 points, a stunning 85 points more than any team before them. The final member of the Big Three, Florida, was a distant third with 353 points. The team competition became a two-team slugfest by Day 3, but where Stanford tried to win with haymakers from its stars, Texas got a steady, consistent supply of jabs from up and down the roster to beat the Cardinal into submission. Stanford scored an early upset when its 800 free relay team of Jorgensen, Karen Kraemer, Eva Mortensen, and Evans topped Texas despite the Longhorns placing three swimmers in the final of the 200 free. Evans repeated as champion in the 500 and 1,650, albeit in slower times than the previous year in what Quick called "an off meet."[13] Evans settled for second in the 400 IM to Sanders, who was six seconds faster to claim Evans's NCAA record. The freshman sensation also grabbed the 200 IM title, dumping Caulkins's seven-year-old record a spot ahead of Jorgensen, and 200 fly in an NCAA record. Stanford again boasted the top two scorers, this time Sanders and Evans, and three of the top six. But it was no match for the depth of Texas. Using Quick's recipe from two years ago, Texas coach Mark Schubert managed to find enough talented swimmers with potential like Dorsey Tierney and Katy Arris and supplemented them with veteran transfers like Beth Barr and Erika Hansen to get the job done.

Shortly after the meet, things completely changed for Stanford. Evans, along with 1992 Olympic hopeful butterflier Mel Stewart at the University of Tennessee, announced their intentions to leave school to intensify preparations for the Barcelona Games. The pressure on Evans was obvious to Quick during the meet, and the combination of stagnating times and the limits set by the NCAA on supervised workouts to just 20 hours a week—about half of what Evans estimated was necessary—precipitated the decision. Ironically enough, Evans bolted to Schubert's club program at Texas, where she continued to take classes, and followed Schubert to the University of Southern California after Barcelona.

Enter Thompson, who had a large hand in turning around the fortunes of Stanford and would become to Quick in the 1990s the kind of star pupil that Gaines was in the early 1980s. The native of Dover, New Hampshire, would win 9 individual and 10 relay titles over four NCAA Championships, 26 times designated an All-America over distances ranging from 50 to 200 yards, in free, fly, and the IM. Her NCAAs career didn't start in the most auspicious of ways, false-starting to disqualify her team in the 200 free relay. Those lost points, though, didn't preclude a win, only preventing a historic margin of victory. Stanford still racked up 735.5 points, the second most in history, to top Texas's 651. The Cardinal set nine American records and 10 NCAA marks. Sanders took two national records in the 200 and 400 IM and an NCAA mark in the 200 fly. Thompson won the 50 free, set an American record in the 100 free, and finished second to Florida's Nicole Haislett in the 200 free. As a team, the Cardinal weathered an early salvo by Texas, with the Longhorns winning the 200 free relay and taking the top four places in the 500 free, led by Hansen. But the Cardinal rallied, taking a massive 70 points in the 200 IM thanks to Sanders, Jorgensen (third), Mary Ellen Blanchard (fourth), Loveless (sixth), and the top three spots in the consolation final. From there, the points flowed liberally. Loveless set an American record in the 100 back off the front of the American-record-setting 400 medley relay squad of Heisick, Sanders, and Jorgensen. With Thompson subbing in for Jorgensen, the Cardinal claimed another national mark in the 200 medley relay. Sanders swept the 400 IM, downing Caulkins's 11-year-old American record, and 200 fly to earn her second straight Most Outstanding Swimmer Award. Thompson set an American record in the 100 free. Jorgensen was second in the 100 fly, Loveless won the 100 back, and Stanford took the 400 and 800 free relays to make it 12 wins in 21 events, including four of five relays. Eileen Richetelli, winner of the three-meter and platform competitions, became the school's first-ever diving champ en route to earning the outstanding diving award and becoming the meet's third-highest scorer, behind Sanders and Thompson.

The difference this time around was twofold. First, there was Quick, who scaled back his role with the national team to redouble efforts in helping the Cardinal shake an uncharacteristic losing streak. "Richard rededicated himself to making the team the best," Sanders said. "He gave some amazing pep talks. His leadership pulled us together."[14] "Last year the team and Richard seemed in a lull," Jorgensen echoed. "The spark was back this season. It was a nice feeling to walk on the pool deck at six in the morning and see Richard with a smile."[15] The other factor was the introduction of Thompson. She not only replaced Evans's contributions in individual terms but also provided the versatility to bolster the team's relay depth in a way Evans couldn't, a harbinger of Thompson's future as one of the world's most decorated relay swimmers. "I believe it was the team chemistry," Quick diagnosed. "The swimmers were unselfish and happy working together. The addition of Jenny Thompson solidified a lot of areas. It was awesome to have someone like her at the end of relays."[16]

The 1992 meet would prove to be the last collegiate one for Sanders. The first American woman since Shirley Babashoff in 1976 to qualify for four individual events in the same Olympics, Sanders left Barcelona with four medals, two of them gold, and chose to cash in her celebrity by turning pro. That was but a minor loss for the Cardinal, who wouldn't lose an NCAA title for the duration of Thompson's college stay. They romped past Florida, 649.5–421, in the 1993 meet. Texas, in its first year under Sterkel after Schubert's departure, was never a factor. Stanford won 13 of the 21 events, tying the 1982 and 1988 Florida title teams for the most in history. In the afterglow of the Olympics, only one record was set in the meet, but that didn't preclude a fast meet. Loveless recorded the second-fastest times in history en route to wins in the 100 and 200 back, while Thompson repeated as champion in the 50 and 100 free. Haislett narrowly denied Thompson in the 200 free, while the Gator also beat Jorgensen to Sanders's vacated crown in the 200 IM. Jorgensen returned to the title board, winning the 100 and 200 fly for her first titles since her freshman year. Lisa Jacob, winner of the 500 free, helped Thompson, Jorgensen, and Jane Skillman earn Stanford's fourth straight title in the 800 free relay, while the team of Loveless, Heisick, Jorgensen, and Jacob clinched the school's fourth consecutive 400 medley relay victory, all four starting Heisick in breaststroke. The 1993 team added wins in the 200 free and 200 medley relays, each anchored by Thompson. With Richetelli again dominant on the boards, the win was a collective triumph that even surprised Quick. "I thought we could win that many events, but I did not think we'd win by that many points," he said. "I think this year more than any other the swimmers and divers transcended their individual needs for the team. Last year some team members made the Olympics and some didn't. There could have been a big letdown. But we had an excellent team effort all year long."[17]

The following year, Stanford typified the saying "a team above all . . . above all a team" that Quick had long trumpeted.[18] Stanford's persistence on top was more impressive given the upheaval around them, led by Amy Van Dyken. The swimmer from Colorado State, hardly a traditional power, won most outstanding swimming honors by setting an NCAA record in the 50 free and finishing second to Thompson in the 100 free and 100 fly. When it came to relays, 62 races at the NCAA Championships had elapsed through the years, each and every title going to one of the Big Three—Stanford (24), Florida (19), and Texas (19). That changed when Auburn won the 200 medley relay, and the revolution was reasserted when USC took the 800 free relay title. The newfound parity limited Stanford's to 512 points, the first time a Quick-coached team failed to top the 600-point mark since 1983. The Cardinal became the first team to win a title with fewer than 600 points, comfortably outgaining Texas (421). Much of the credit went to Thompson, who added a second-place finish to Van Dyken in the 50. Loveless won the 100 back and was second to Kristine Quance (200 IM) and Whitney Hedgepeth (200 back). The difference, though, was Texas transfer Jessica Tong. Facing the loss of major points with Richetelli's absence due to injury, Tong was a major coup, stepping up to score 40 individual points.

What should have been easy in 1995 in Austin turned into an unexpected struggle for a fourth straight title. The combination of Stanford returning 14 of its 16 scorers (though not Loveless), the promise of Richetelli's return and the struggles of Texas and Florida should've made it easy. Throw in the defections of Van Dyken and Florida's Janie Wagstaff to concentrate on the 1996 Olympics, and the Cardinal should have romped. Instead, they barely survived the challenge of top-three newcomer Michigan, 497.5–478.5, in the first breaking of the Big Three embargo and the fourth straight year Stanford's margin of victory narrowed. Michigan, which joined SMU and Georgia as first-time relay winners, got all of its points from the swimming portion where it outscored Stanford by 35 points, but Richetelli and Megan Gardner made the difference from the diving well. Thompson took her career total of NCAA titles to nine, eschewing the 50 free to beat short-course world-record holder Allison Wagner and Quance in the 200 IM. She defended her 100 fly title while winning a fourth straight title in her specialty 100 free, etching her name alongside Fetter (50 free), Haislett (200 free), and Mary T. Meagher (200 fly) as the only four-time NCAA champs in the same event. Her nine titles moved her into second all-time behind Caulkins, who won 12 in three seasons in Florida, back when swimmers could compete in five individual events. Thompson also anchored the 400 free relay which officially sealed the win. The Cardinal, holding an 11-point lead, had qualified fifth for finals with Michigan first, enough of a swing that had the seeds held, the team title would've gone to Ann Arbor. But anchoring the team of Becky Bicknell, Claudia Franco, and Tong, Thompson powered the Cardinal to victory.

With Thompson gone in 1996, surely Quick's empire was in danger. But with Tong back and Franco taking over Thompson's role as 100 free national champ and de facto relay anchor, the Cardinal coasted to a 478–397 win over SMU. When things looked more assured in 1997—with Quick returning 10 All-Americans though publicly expressing doubt about his team—was when Stanford finally proved fallible, thanks to an upset by Schubert's USC team led by Quance and Lindsay Benko. The lull was temporary, though, as the infusion of talent in the form of two-time *Swimming World* high school swimmer of the year Hyman and sprinter Catherine Fox led Stanford back to the summit in 1998.

Quick's talent of filling the trophy case is unrivaled in college swimming history. But the assembly line of swimmers who fulfilled their potential outside the college arena is even more impressive. Quick's Stanford swimmers brought home 11 medals, 6 gold, from the 1992 Games. In 1996, a team coached by Quick, Evans, Fox, Jacob, and Thompson, combined for seven gold medals, all in relays. One of the highlights of the 2000 Games was Hyman winning the 200 fly. Torres, thanks to Quick's training, won three individual bronze medals, the honor in the 100 free shared with rival Thompson, who anchored the Americans to gold in three relays.

In all, Quick produced Olympians from seven countries in his stint with Stanford, which lasted until 2005. He was able to attract talented individuals like Sanders, Thompson, and Blanchard, all of whom had made big impacts on the national age-group record board, to Palo Alto and made sure they left better swimmers than they arrived. In the lead-up to the 1992 Olympics, lanes in the Stanford pool became prime California real estate, attracting all manner of Olympic hopefuls. In addition to those in the college ranks like Loveless, Thompson, Sanders, and Jeff Rouse, an accomplished backstroker for Skip Kenney's men's team, the likes of Pablo Morales and Angie Wester-Krieg, veteran swimmers in their late 20s hoping for one last throw of the dice, dialed up Quick for the unique atmosphere he created. "What surprised me about Richard and the group was that when I was tired from work, I wouldn't go in saying, 'I'm going to train great today,'" said Wester-Krieg, then a 27-year-old accountant training just to chase a dream. "But by the end of practice, I did. It's something about the way he presents it. He truly believes what he's saying and he truly believes in the athletes, and that makes you believe in yourself."[19] The willingness of swimmers to put their careers in Quick's hands paid dividends time and again, for swimmer and coach. "I think the critical aspect of training is mental. You can't doubt," Loveless said. "You can't get to the taper and say, 'Maybe we should have done more or rested less or rested more.' We put it all on Richard's shoulders. At the same time we're responsible. When he says 'Go!' you go."[20] Few programs have ever "gone" as far or as fast as the ones Quick piloted.

Chapter Twenty-Two

University of Texas Men

Not many people may have known of the University of Texas's swimming prowess in the late 1990s and early 2000 by name. Given the lukewarm attention often paid to collegiate swimming, it's likely that few knew about the three national titles posted by the Longhorns or the slew of records that went to the burnt orange-clad swimmers.

But even casual fans of the Olympics were familiar with the products of Eddie Reese's dynamic program in Austin. Fans may not have known the particulars of Texas's impact on the international scene—the combined 51 Olympic medals, 28 of them gold, won by American men from 1996 to 2012, or the fact that every world record in the 400 medley relay for over a decade has featured not one, but at least two Longhorns. But the factory of talent overseen by Reese churned out household name after household name to fuel America's swimming dominance.

Other college programs have had more success, over dual meets and NCAAs, than the Longhorns of that era. But few produced so many enduring talents whose excellence translated so prolifically onto the international scene, defining a generation of American swimming.

The source of Texas's success, whether he would admit it or not, is ultimately the atmosphere created by the eminently deferential Reese. An accomplished swimmer at the University of Florida in the early 1960s, Reese was an assistant at his alma mater before taking the reins at Auburn and morphing the Tigers from a national non-factor to second in the NCAAs in 1978. He parlayed that into the Texas job in 1978, a position he hasn't relinquished in three and a half decades. Along the way, he's won 10 national championships, earned induction into the International Swimming Hall of Fame, and taken part on the American Olympic staffs for each edition from 1988 through 2012, serving as the men's head coach in 1992, 2004, and

2008. His impact in Austin was almost immediate, winning his first national title in 1981 with an overachieving group composed mostly of transfers like Scott Spann Sr., Phil Nenon, and Kris Kirchner, that he had cajoled to join him in Austin. Two years prior, in Reese's first NCAA meet with Texas, the Longhorns were a distant 21st. From 1988 to 1991, Texas reeled off four straight national titles led by the likes of Olympians Doug Gjertson and Shaun Jordan. And Reese captured title No. 6 in 1996 with a balanced squad that became the first team since 1983 to win an NCAA championship without claiming an individual event. That basis of strong team swimming set the stage for a run of three straight NCAA titles from 2000 to 2002 when the foundation of relay depth was augmented by several superstar performers.

That type of team success owed a great debt to Reese, a man capable of developing swimmers in just about any discipline and who founded one of the great reservoirs of stroke talent in the nation. Reese's method was delightfully simple, yet understatedly inventive. Swimmers lauded Reese's ability to never give them the same workout twice, tailoring practices for a wide range of specialties. "I try to make it very simple," Reese said in his typically low-key nature after the 1996 NCAA title. "Come to the meet and swim very, very fast. Number one, it's fun. It's fun to swim fast. That's our goal, and swimming fast takes care of points."[1] Accolades were never the main objective for Reese, a man who has a habit of using his National Coach of the Year trophies as office doorstops and admitted that after a quarter century on the job, he still gets nervous making recruiting calls. "It's not the culture. It's not the water," Reese defers. "It's the people in the water."[2] At the risk of contradicting someone as accomplished as Reese, there's no denying that the coach plays a large part in not just accumulating such talented people in the same body of water, but helping those people extract the most from their innate abilities. Reese governs by the principle that "the leader should always bear the pain and not give it,"[3] a sentiment expressed by bestselling motivational author Max De Pree.

His modesty undersells Reese's role as the master tinkerer. He has always absorbed new techniques and technologies like a sponge, drawing upon a massive database of drills, sets and ideas to keep tedious workouts fresh and constantly challenge swimmers. The customization in his regimens helps keep his swimmers mentally fresh and engaged, a factor that no doubt has contributed to many of his Longhorn Aquatic club swimmers excelling internationally well into their late 20s or 30s. He adds to that an emphasis on the mental aspect of swimming and racing. His implementation of sports psychology, with former Texas women's coach Dr. Keith Bell, upon his arrival in Austin was one of the contributing factors to the monumental turnaround that led to the 1981 title.[4] "Eddie is like the world's best auto mechanic who can look under the hood and know exactly what's wrong," said Brendan Hansen, Reese's world-record breaststroke pupil.[5] The technical aspect is but part of the equation. "Eddie stays on the cutting edge of training and technique," longtime U.S. national team coach Mark Schubert said in 2007. "But what sets him apart is his personality. He's impossible not to like. When he brings you in and tells you something, you can't help but believe him because of the way he cares about people."[6] However fatherly and compassionate his public persona, Reese the master motivator is anything but all smiles. Often, Reese is the one stirring competition among his stable of thoroughbreds, keeping the level of motivation as high as he envisioned in assembling such talents. "He's certainly the calming influence most of the time, but he can actually be the instigator of some disagreements," Neil Walker said of his former coach. "He's so competitive. He wants to bring out the best in all of us. That's a great feature of him as a coach and as a person. It's like he's almost in the water with us when we're swimming. His emotions come out, too."[7] Those competing forces of his personality constituted a balancing act for Reese: there is fine line between healthy and unhealthy competition in practice, and Reese always seemed to guide his Longhorns to the right side of the line, to the betterment of the program. "Sometimes I'll get to the wall first in a set. Well, that's like getting to the wall first in a race," Walker said. "It's like you've really accomplished something because you're swimming with the best in the world. If you can hang with these guys, you can hang with anybody."[8]

No matter how he did it, Reese's skill in attracting talent from every corner of the nation, from Maine to California and Wisconsin to Pennsylvania, is undeniable. And by 2000, that collection was championship worthy. The constellation of stars on that team was truly remarkable. The groundwork for NCAA championships was laid some years earlier with the likes of Walker, regarded by the younger crop as a "godfather" figure. He served as a forerunner to the swimmer-of-the-year candidates that would follow and remained a constant presence after his graduation in 1997 by training with Longhorn Aquatic for a 10-year stint with the national team. Adding to the embarrassment of riches for the two-time defending champs in the fall of 2000 was Hansen, who would go eight-for-eight in his college career in breaststroke events and become the first American since the 1970s to simultaneously hold the world records in the 100 and 200 breast. Also part of that class was Ian Crocker, a laidback native of Maine who became one of the world's foremost butterfliers. For two years, their careers overlapped that of Aaron Peirsol, one of a handful of teenage American male Olympians in Sydney in 2000 who would dominate backstroke for the next decade. Behind them were swimmers that could be stars anywhere else: The versatile Nate Dusing, who accumulated points all over the board at NCAAs, and tremendous relay competitors like Scott Goldblatt, Tommy Hannan, and Jamie Rauch.

They all arrived in the Lone Star State with such diverse backgrounds. Hansen, the native of Havertown, Pennsylvania, was one of the most accomplished high school breaststrokers the nation had ever seen. He arrived in Austin in 2000 just weeks after the disappointment of finishing third in the Olympic Trials in both breaststroke events, using that shortcoming as fuel to his competitive fire for the next four years. Reese was a frequent confidant and mentor, helping Hansen cope with and recover from his falling short of expectations at both the 2004 and 2008 Olympics. Crocker, meanwhile, experienced a dip in results after making it to Sydney, taking time to acclimate to the strength-training regimen of Reese. Peirsol was a hot commodity before his junior year of high school—as evidenced by a wiry, 15-year-old Peirsol gracing the February 1999 cover of *Swimming World* magazine—the beach-bum California kid winning silver in the 2000 back in Sydney. Their personalities split along fascinating lines. The intense Hansen found a kindred spirit in Walker, both outdoorsmen. Peirsol and Crocker turned up the intensity only in the pool, able to power it down as soon as their hands touched the wall. Thanks in large part to Reese's tutelage, such diverse personalities managed to not just co-exist but prosper. "We all have our own kind of lives outside of the pool," Crocker said. "We all spend a lot of time in the pool, and we've also got our own balance outside of the pool. I'd say we're all relatively close. We share common goals, and that brings people together."[9] Part of the reason was their discreet specialties. Hansen would supplement his breaststroke prowess—he famously never lost a breaststroke race at the collegiate level—with the occasional individual medley. Peirsol dabbled in some middle-distance freestyle, while Crocker was a pure sprinter, in free or fly. The lack of overlap rarely brought them into direct competition, helping maintain the peace. When they did race, it was usually spectacles like Peirsol challenging Hansen to a breaststroke race, provided Hansen was wearing shorts and a shirt in the pool. (For the record, Hansen won.[10]) "We all swim different races, and I know that helps probably our relations with each other. We're rooting for each other," Peirsol said. "I want to see Ian and Brendan win their races. I know they deserve them. They work just as hard or harder than anybody in that pool."[11]

Such mutual respect paid dividends when they shed their burnt orange and donned the Stars and Stripes. From 2000 through the end of 2013, the Americans set six long-course world records in medley relay, a standard the American program monopolized sans interruption since 1971. All six featured multiple Texas and Longhorn Aquatic members. Peirsol led off four of them, from the 2002 Pan Pacific Championships to the 2009 Worlds; in all four, he handed off to Hansen. Crocker was part of three of them, including the 2000 Olympic race which was anchored by Gary Hall Jr., who cut his eligibility at Texas short in 1994 after helping the Longhorns break the American record in the 400 free relay. When the 2004 NCAA Championships were held in a short-course meters pool—in an effort to prepare for the looming Athens Games—and recognized world records could be set, the Texas team of Peirsol, Hansen, Crocker, and Garrett Weber-Gale did just that in the 400 medley relay with a time of 3:25.38. It held from March to October, when an American team that featured Peirsol, Hansen, Crocker, and Jason Lezak nipped it by .29 seconds at the World Short-Course Championships. The relay component carried over to other disciplines, as Weber-Gale took part in the American foursome that won the 400 free relay at the 2008 Beijing Games powered by Lezak's furious final leg, while Texas alum Ricky Berens was on the world-record squads that won gold in the 800 free relay at the 2008 Olympics and 2009 World Championships, the latter alongside former college teammate David Walters. Under the bright lights of the world stage, the presence of a familiar face on deck was a reassuring boost. "It was pretty great, because when you got up for a relay, whether you were at NCAAs or at World Championships or the Olympics, it was the same guys, so it was really a special environment to have that much talent in the water," Crocker said in 2007. "It also makes for a great training environment at Texas, because we've got the best of all the strokes there to teach the younger guys and help them out."[12]

The individual accomplishments were just as impressive for Reese's men. Peirsol counts five gold medals and two silver over three Games to his résumé. From August 2004 to the end of 2013, Peirsol has held the world record in the 100 backstroke for all but a one-week, fastsuit-fueled interlude by Spain's Aschwin Wildeboer in the summer of 2009. He was the first 100 backstroker under the 53- and 52-second marks. Across the 100 and 200 back, Peirsol set 13 world records in his career. Though individual Olympic gold eluded him, Hansen set five world records in the two breaststroke distances and was three times a member of America's gold-winning medley relay, including in 2012 after a stirring comeback from the disappointing finish to the 2008 that led him to call time on his career. Crocker spent the better part of a decade as the main combatant with Michael Phelps for the crown of world's fastest butterflier and three times established the world record in the 100 fly, a mark he clung to from 2005 to 2009 during the pinnacle of Phelps's career. "We more or less, in the last six years, have grown up together, have gone through college together, know the ins and outs of each other extremely well," Peirsol said in 2008 as he and Crocker were preparing for their third Olympics together. "We've all helped each other, not just physically, but letting each other know we belong here and that is half the battle. It really is."[13] With the notable exception of Phelps, who turned pro after the 2004 Games and trained with the University of Michigan's Club Wolverine after foregoing college eligibility, the trajectory of almost a decade of American swimming was primarily shaped by Reese's Texas contingent, training in what Hansen called an "oasis" of swimming.[14]

"We just push each other so well," Peirsol said. "I've learned more the past two years than I've learned my entire career. Just from the guys I swim with."[15]

The dividends for that chemistry in the NCAA ranks were obvious, manifesting themselves in three straight titles from 2000 to 2002. The seeds were sown two years prior in 1998, Walker's senior year. That season, he won the 100 back and finished second in the 100 free and fourth in the 50. More importantly, the Longhorns finished in the top five in all five relays, including a win in the 800 free relay with the team of Bryan Jones, Goldblatt, Dusing, and Rauch. The anchor Rauch made the difference, helping Texas overturn USC's third-leg lead and hold off the charge of Arizona by under a quarter second. With all four of those swimmers underclassmen, the hope for the future was obvious. Texas finished third that year, a placement matched in 1999, although somewhat disappointingly given their advanced billing, with Walker representing the only serious contributor to be replaced from the previous season. Dusing finished second in the 200 IM and third in the 100 fly, and Joe Montague was third in the 200 IM and fourth in the 400 IM. The 800 free relay—with Jon Younghouse leading off instead of Jones—was again victorious, but the margin in the team competition to defending champion Stanford and Auburn was simply a bridge too far. To be NCAA champs, the Longhorns had to shore up a few key weaknesses. Their breaststrokers didn't make either of the A finals in 1999 and accounted for just six points in 1998, also hampering their medley relay prospects. That deficiency made Hansen a major recruiting priority for the fall of 2000. And where the divers of Stanford and Auburn didn't register a point in 1998, Texas scored a major coup by reeling in accomplished California high school diver Troy Dumais, and later getting his younger brother, Justin, to transfer from USC.

The stars took time to align, but when they did in 2000, the squad was unstoppable. A veteran-laden squad in 2000—12 of the 18 taking part at NCAAs had swum in the meet before—accumulated 538 points at the University of Minnesota, easily outdistancing themselves from Auburn (385). For many of the returnees, the result banished years of frustration. Rarely did they trail in the meet, and the Longhorns were represented by at least one swimmer in each championship final over the meet's last two and a half days. With the meet held in a 25-meter format, Texas's swimmers prospered. They swept both medley relays in U.S. Open record time, with the 400 squad of Hannan, senior Russell Chozick, Dusing, and Jones giving the Longhorns the lead after the first day of the meet. The victory for the 200 squad of Matt Ulrickson, Chozick, Dusing, and Jones earned the added bonus of Ulrickson setting a U.S. Open record in the 50 back off the front. Dusing was second in the 200 IM and 100 fly, Rauch was third in the 200 free, and the same 800 free relay squad as the year prior (Younghouse, Dusing, Goldblatt, and Rauch) made it three straight years claiming that event for the Longhorns, again in a U.S. Open record that was a whopping 4.3 seconds ahead of second-place Arizona State. Coupled with Troy Dumais's stellar performance in the diving well, winning the one- and three-meter springboard events and taking second in the platform, there was no way the Longhorns would be caught. While no one individual lit up the scoreboard as Walker did two years prior (their leading individual scorer was Dusing with 43 points, eighth best at the meet), Reese's men placed four scorers in the top 20. Afterward, Reese characteristically downplayed his role, focusing on keeping his team mentally fresh and distracted from what some dubbed a piling up of failures over the previous years. "Our philosophy has just been to keep it fun, to keep smiling and keep laughing," Reese said. "The last two years, we worked too hard coming into the meet, and now I'm getting them the right amount of rest. We knew if things went our way, we could do a lot."[16]

Adding Crocker and Hansen the following year, the odds of the Longhorns relinquishing their crown was quite slim, seeing as how they got 387 points from underclassmen the previous year, enough to win the championship without the seniors. The result in 2001 was a stampede victory, Texas scoring the second-most points in NCAA history with 597.5, easily outpacing runner-up Stanford (457.5). Dusing concluded his career splendidly, winning the 200 IM with an NCAA record of 1:42.85, upending Greg Burgess's eight-year-old mark. He also won the 200 back and finished second to Crocker in the 100 fly, finishing with 57 individual points. The medley relays were again victorious, with the 400 squad of Dusing, Hansen, Hannan, and Crocker setting American, U.S. Open, and NCAA records, including downing a six-year-old NCAA mark. The 200 squad of Ulrickson, Hansen, Dusing, and Leffie Crawford was forced to settle for just an American record. Hansen, also winner of the 100 breast, made quick work of one of the most hallowed records on the books, Mike Barrowman's 11-year-old NCAA record in the 200 breast, outracing Auburn's Dave Denniston to the honor. And the meet concluded with the Longhorns winning the 400 free relay, the foursome of Dusing, Crocker, Hannan, and Rauch topping California, led by Anthony Ervin's dizzying anchor-leg split of 41.80 seconds, by a comfortable 2.32 seconds.

The departure of Dusing and Rauch threw open the doors to the 2002 meet, ushering in an era of parity that hadn't been seen in years. No matter how lopsided the win in 2001 had been, Reese didn't see his team as the favorites the following year, a sentiment echoed by the national coaches poll placing the Longhorns third behind Stanford and Auburn. The consensus was that Stanford, led by Markus Rogan, Randall Bal, and Peter Marshall, was the favorite to regain the title; Michigan coach Jon Urbanchek even went so far as to call the Cardinal "too solid not to win."[17] From a swimming perspective, the prognostication was accurate. But the meet was the "NCAA Swimming and Diving Championships," and therein lay Stanford's downfall.

Where the Cardinal were shut out in diving, Texas used the Dumais brothers (Troy was first in both springboards and fifth in platform, while Justin was second in platform to go with fourth and seventh in the springboards) to score 113 points and score an overall upset of Stanford, 512–501. The victory was in doubt going into the concluding event, the 400 free relay; with the Longhorns leading by 13 points, Stanford could've stolen a win in the team standing with a win in the relay and Texas dropping to sixth or worse. It looked plausible after three legs, with Bal and Marshall keeping Stanford neck and neck with Cal's Duje Draganja and Ervin and Texas slipping to seventh. But as Andrew Schnell failed to reel in Cal anchor Matthias Ohlin, Crocker moved the Longhorns up to third, solidifying a win. Crocker had earlier set an NCAA record in the 100 fly as the Longhorn's stroke depth finally surpassed its freestyle prowess. Where Texas's best finish in a freestyle event was Chris Kemp's fourth in the 500, they tallied significant points in breaststroke with Hansen, setting NCAA and American records in the 200. Hannan made championship final appearances in the 100 back and 200 IM, as did Montague in the 400 IM, while Crocker's win in the 100 fly complemented Daniel DiToro finishing eighth and Ranier Kendrick taking third in the 200 fly. Somewhat surprisingly, the Longhorns didn't win a relay, though they finished no worse than fifth. Their medley relays squads twice finished second, a combined .45 seconds behind Stanford. The consolation prize, though, was becoming the first school since the Stanford teams of the early 1990s to win three straight titles.

The 2002 meet proved to be the untimely end of the Texas dynasty, despite them hosting NCAAs in 2003. The struggles to cope with the loss of the Dumais brothers' massive point accumulations was evident in dual-meet losses to Michigan and Auburn, but even that didn't presage the domination of Auburn in Austin, topping the Longhorns by a 609.5–413 margin, the most points ever collected in an NCAA Championships. Texas notched its wins, led by arguably the swim of the meet from freshman Peirsol, who got the better of Rogan and Marshall in the 200 back in an American record of 1:39.16, the first time to fracture the 1:40 barrier. Hansen also recorded his third straight breaststroke double, and the Longhorns managed to win three of five relays, including NCAA and American records in the 200 (Peirsol, Hansen, DiToro, and Crocker) and 400 medley (Peirsol, Hansen, Crocker, and Kemp). Where they stumbled, though, was in freestyle, where Kemp (seventh in the 100, second in the 200, sixth in the 500) was the only A finalist. Peirsol was second in the 100 back and Kendrick third in 200 IM, but that was far outstripped by the depth of the Tigers. The story was similar the following year, with Texas slipping to third behind Auburn and Stanford. The Longhorns' individual performances, including a prominent contribution to the bucket load of world records displaced, were among the highlights. Hansen joined backstroker John Naber (1974–77) and butterflier Pablo Morales (1984–87) as the only stroke quadruple-double winners in a career. Crocker set a world record in the 100 fly at 49.07 seconds, his fourth straight title in that event, as well as a world record in the 100 free at 46.25 while settling for second in the 50. Peirsol set a world record in the 200 back (1:50.64) after being relegated to third in the 100 back behind Marshall's world record. Kendrick, who won the consolation final of the 100 fly, took the championship in the 200 fly. Despite finishing second to Auburn (led by Frenchman Frederick Bousquet), the 200 medley relay team of Peirsol, Hansen, Crocker, and Weber-Gale set an American mark, while that same foursome set a world record in a sweeping victory in the 400 medley relay. The lack of freestyle depth, though, was illustrated by the Longhorns lacking a free relay finish better than fourth, the 400 free squad unable to make the final altogether.

The 2004 meet and subsequent Olympics spelled an end to the halcyon days for Texas. With Crocker and Hansen out of eligibility and Peirsol turning pro after winning three golds at the Athens Games, it would take several years for Reese to assemble a championship-caliber group again. That time finally came in 2010, led by IMer Austin Surhoff and tremendous freestyle depth with Walters, Berens, and Jimmy Feigen. Though each of those guys went onto individual, international success, Reese's 10th banner didn't usher in the same kind of era of dominance. Then again, few performances at the collegiate level ever have.

Chapter Twenty-Three

North Baltimore Aquatic Club

When Michael Phelps's first assault on the Olympic record books began in 2004, there were four letters that seemed to be on the minds of everyone in swimming. Not "g-o-l-d," but rather NBAC, the club that had propelled Phelps toward superstardom, and vice versa.

Phelps wasn't the first star forged in the foundry of the North Baltimore Aquatic Club, but the two will forever be linked as responsible for the rise of the other to the forefront of the American sports consciousness. What Phelps and his coach, Bob Bowman, did to elevate swimming from a quadrennial oddity for mainstream America to a sport worthy of constant interest and significant spectator appeal is due in large part to the background, in and out of the pool, instilled in Phelps on the north side of Baltimore. In turn, NBAC has enjoyed an elevated profile as one of America's and the world's foremost swim clubs, a haven for elite swimmers of both genders hoping to attain even a modicum of the success the club helped Phelps achieve.

But NBAC didn't open its doors just for Phelps, and even after his temporary retirement following the 2012 Olympic Games, it has continued to be a hot spot for swimmers from all over the world. In the process, NBAC has become a model for the development of elite swimmers as well as sustaining its enduringly successful age-group system, a cornerstone of the American swimming pyramid.

To equate NBAC's consistent success through the decades with one man isn't entirely accurate, and pegging Phelps as the lightning rod for NBAC's achievements would certainly be incorrect. Instead, the font from which NBAC's prosperous philosophy flows is founder, coach, and owner Murray Stephens. The daily toil of the swimmer held a powerful symbolism to Stephens, a largely self-taught former swimmer and a graduate of Loyola College who sought to get into coaching after graduation. When his former club

239

team lacked room on their staff, he and a partner started the North Baltimore Aquatic Club out of Loyola High School in 1967, where Stephens also taught and coached. Inspired by what Lefty Driesell was doing to advance the University of Maryland basketball program at the time, Stephens drew upon the model used by George Haines at Santa Clara Swim Club, then one of the nation's best. From nothing, in the face of doubters who thought Stephens couldn't even carve out a niche for his club on the local scene, he transformed the club into an internationally renowned destination for Olympic hopefuls. In 1987, Stephens purchased the dilapidated Meadowbrook Aquatic Center in North Baltimore, and he turned his diligent attention toward renovating the building and installing an indoor 50-meter pool, making it one of the premier training facilities on the East Coast.

The accomplishments since have been remarkable. It took a while for NBAC to make an impact on the national level, but by 1984, NBAC had produced its first Olympians in Theresa Andrews and Patrick Kennedy. Andrews returned from the Los Angeles Games with gold in the 100 backstroke and the medley relay. Being shut out from the 1998 Games was a temporary setback for Stephens and his team, but they entered the 1990s ready to be major players. Among the headliners at the 1992 Olympics in Barcelona was Anita Nall, a quirky 15-year-old breaststroker. The native of Harrisburg, Pennsylvania, who moved to the Baltimore area to train with Stephens, Nall burst onto the scene as a 14-year-old at the 1991 Spring Nationals in Federal Way, Washington, where she won the 200 breast in the second-fastest time in history, earning the meet's award for most outstanding performance. Her finals time of 2:27.08 was 2.5 seconds faster than the American record held by Amy Shaw. It was a credit as much to the growth spurt she'd had, shooting up four inches from the height with which she claimed seventh in the 200 breast the previous year, as to her coaching. Nall emerged as one of the stories of the Olympic Trials in 1992 when she twice set the world record in the 200 on the same day in Indianapolis, her finals time of 2:25.35 a cut of 1.36 seconds from the previous world record of East Germany's Silke Horner in 1988. The tree-hugging, fanatical recycler and devotee of water beds also won the 100 breast at Trials and parlayed that into three medals—gold in the medley relay, silver in the 100, and bronze in the 200—in Barcelona, all before her junior season in high school.

Nall helped set off a string of Olympic products. In 1996, Beth Botsford, who credited her training with NBAC coach Tom Himes as vital in her taking the next step athletically, and York, Pennsylvania, native Whitney Metzler represented NBAC in Atlanta, where Stephens served as an assistant for Team USA. By 2000, Phelps was ready to assume his place in swimming history, becoming the youngest male American Olympic swimmer in 68 years by qualifying for the 200 fly in Sydney. Phelps would participate in the next four Games, joined by the likes of Katie Hoff and Allison Schmitt.

That's in addition to a bevy of productive college and age-group swimmers churned throughout the years by NBAC.

It's no wonder then that both Jon Urbanchek,[1] the longtime University of Michigan coach alongside whom Bowman coached at Club Wolverine from 2004 to 2008, and Mark Schubert,[2] the 44-time national champion with Mission Viejo Nadadores, have called NBAC the best program in America. Most of the plaudits stem from Stephens's approach. In many ways, he's an old-school taskmaster, but with a new-school twist. He was never above the excitability and hollering of the archetypal coach, a bit gruff and rough around the edges, but he also wasn't timid about innovating and defying convention. Stephens and Stephens alone determined what meets his team would prepare for and which they would train through, an autonomy furnished by his owning the club, freeing him from being subservient to a board of directors or beholden to parental influence. Stephens wasn't necessarily set in his ways, always keeping an open mind and exhibiting a willingness to evolve his training philosophy based on new research. But he wasn't one to jump at each passing fad, preferring to remain loyal to the old masters, like groundbreaking swim researcher, writer, and coach Doc Counsilman. Where he was most adept, though, was in tailoring—or in some cases, completely disregarding—his personal beliefs for the betterment of each individual. The goals would always be similar and very lofty, and the values underpinning their achievement would never waver, but that didn't mean each athlete had to take the same road to get there. And the most remarkable part was that this guiding mythos held serve from the novice seven- and eight-year-olds on up to the college-ready prospects and later elite, post-graduate groups. Nall is a perfect example of Stephens's creativity and lack of philosophical rigidity. Before her record-breaking performance at Trials in 1992, Nall was training seven days a week, but the time commitment was a relatively limited 20 hours a week over eight practice sessions, including no weight training and limited dryland work with techniques like aerobics. Given the inborn competitiveness Nall possessed—Stephens said that, "competitively, she's probably 25"[3] —Stephens just had to put her in a position to do what she does best: swim faster than the person next to her.

The most important facet that set NBAC apart might have been the integration of the mental component of training. Paul Yetter, who served as a coach at NBAC for almost a decade and was recognized as USA Swimming's Developmental Coach of the Year in 2007, found Stephens's biggest strength to be his ability to get swimmers to believe in themselves and their process.[4] When so many other coaches seemed to drill swimmers beyond the point of coherent thought, Stephens did the opposite. "He's a visionary, ahead of his time," Andrews said in 2008. "The best way to describe it is, he develops with athletes a way to think through a situation. He doesn't teach you just to swim fast; he teaches you how to think."[5] The approach entailed placing the onus for swimmers to succeed on their shoulders. Yards and sets were never to be swum for Stephens's benefit but for swimmers to make progress in realizing the ambitions they set for themselves, clearly and realistically articulated with the help of Stephens and his staff. Where other coaches could be timid about raising expectations of swimmers—and, as is usually the bigger nuisance, of parents—Stephens never shied away, citing it as the best method to raise the bar of performance. A decision like the one in 2007 to distribute swim caps with "NBAC" on one side and "Beijing '08" with the Chinese characters for excellence on the other was seen by some as lumping unnecessary and detrimental pressure on swimmers. That's not how Stephens viewed it. "Too many places are afraid to raise anyone's expectation levels," Stephens said. "I think every person had a vision in their heart of being in the Olympics. To get there, you have to evaluate, refine, and record how you want to make yourself better every day."[6] Stephens's model exuded a degree of universality. "I think if you took Murray, put him in Billings, Montana, and gave him 10 years," said Kevin Botsford, Beth's father, "he'd give you a few Olympians."[7] Where other clubs became cults of personality, though, NBAC was clearly never to be about Murray Stephens. "[Murray has] taken his ego, he's put it aside, he's let other people do the deal so that the team could continue to grow," Yetter said, likening Stephens's relationship to his assistants as "more like a supportive colleague than a commander."[8] Without that aspect of Stephens's personality, the greatest windfall the club has ever seen might have never reached its full potential.

When Bowman was hired in 1996 by North Baltimore, two years after Stephens's brainchild club summited the mountain by winning its first national title, Stephens recognized promise within Bowman in which the younger coach had yet to fully believe. The meticulous Bowman instead had realized that his future likely lay somewhere not near a pool. Bowman seemed to be a ball of contradictions in his largely undistinguished swimming career, not least among them the fact that he was smart enough to realize it. A child psychology major with a minor in musical composition and a love of classical music, Bowman wasn't exactly the typical athlete. He had some success in the pool at Florida State where he was named a team captain, but his physical ability never matched his mental acuity, disenchanting him from competition. He bounced around the country at various swim jobs in Cincinnati, Ohio; Las Vegas; and Napa Valley, California (where he worked under Tracy Caulkins's former coach, Paul Bergen, and coached 1996 Olympian Eric Wunderlich). By the time NBAC and Stephens came knocking, Bowman was severely frustrated by his inability to make headway into the coaching world despite seven gigs in five states over almost a decade. An escape plan had presented itself, though, as Bowman had agreed in principle to take a position with Auburn's swim program under David Marsh, giving him a way to defray the costs of further schooling to transition out of swimming and into a more cerebral pursuit. When Stephens discovered Bowman's strategy to flee coaching, he offered to more than triple Bowman's salary to have him come to Baltimore and forestall his disappearance from the sport, a move that almost two decades later still looks like a steal. What Bowman couldn't shake, through all those relocations and fizzled expectations, was the fascination with swimmers moving fast in the water, an obsession he traces back to seeing Caulkins swim when he was young near his home in Clover, South Carolina, a spectacle akin to "hearing an orchestra the first time."[9] The musical metaphor is one Bowman would rely on often in his coaching, a fitting allegory to his exacting personality with its desire to orchestrate from behind the scenes rather than shine as the primary performer.

NBAC energized Bowman, but the job wasn't complete until Bowman encountered a gangly, troublemaking 11-year-old. The Phelps-Bowman creation myth is the stuff of legends. As the story—told and retold in inch after column inch and in television studio specials the world over—goes, Bowman busted up a customary session of locker-room horseplay involving Phelps and a group of his overactive partners in crime. The reaction after what would become their first of many arguments was unanimous: Phelps was counting his blessings he'd never have to work with Bowman, then coaching an older group, while Bowman breathed a sigh of relief that he'd ride off into the academia sunset before being subjected to the torture of coaching Phelps. Soon after, Bowman took over a 13- and 14-year-old training group that included Phelps, for whom swimming at Meadowbrook was merely a way to expend his boundless energy. Phelps started swimming as a convenience for his mother, keeping him corralled in the same location as older sisters Whitney and Hilary, the former an Olympic hopeful in 1996, and as a non-pharmaceutical remedy for his attention deficit hyperactivity disorder. Despite himself, and with little knowledge of his own ability, it became clear that Phelps could become something special. Bowman foresaw taming the wild horse within Phelps, helping him realize enough of his potential to be neatly shipped down the line of coaches as a passable prospect. That feat was to be Bowman's "farewell gift to swimming."[10] Instead, what ensued was a two-decades-long relationship that redefined the sport.

Bowman's foresight in handling Phelps was evident in 1997 when he met with his parents, Debbie and Michael Sr., to outline the possible trajectories for the then 12-year-old swimmer, measuring the optimal distance in each step, from junior, then senior, national cuts, titles, and Olympic chances. For a family that had just gone through that choreography with Whitney in the previous Olympic cycle and had seen how a debilitating back injury rent asunder their best-laid plans, it may have seemed sudden, but it would go on to benefit Phelps through four Olympic Games. From his debut in the 2000 Sydney Games, where he took fifth in his only event, the 200 fly, at age 15, through 22 medals, 18 of them gold, at the next three Olympics, Bowman and Phelps were together every step of the way. Through some out-of-the-pool indiscretions, Bowman's move to the University of Michigan and Club Wolverine from 2004 to 2008, and the lull in desire by Phelps after his unprecedented eight gold medals in 2008, the two were together. A large part of that time was spent at NBAC.

The relationship between Bowman and Phelps evolved through the years to more closely resemble one of "collaborators and partners [more] than coach and swimmer."[11] At the beginning, much of that was down to the willingness of Bowman, following in the mold of Stephens, to relent to Phelps's peculiarities. When Phelps was in eighth grade, for instance, and contended that Bowman's two-a-day workouts were "ruining his life,"[12] Bowman knew to reduce the workload until Phelps was better able to mentally endure it. There were some unflinching cornerstones of Bowman's approach, though, that the coach simply would not compromise on, such as a rigid attention to detail and the insistence that every lap, every repetition, be done with the utmost attention to detail. That's why, when Phelps began swimming for Bowman, the coach threw him out of practice every day for a week straight until Phelps reversed his adamant stance about changing his freestyle technique from a two-beat kick to the more physically demanding yet propulsive six-beat kick. As Phelps progressed and the miles suffered under Bowman's whip translated into age-group records and emergence on the national stage, Bowman's task shifted from being less of a motivator—there he relied on a self-motivation that was one of Phelps's most exemplary qualities—and more of a challenger to Phelps, physically and mentally. (When Phelps's desire waned after the 2008 Games, Bowman again put on the hat of motivator, a pursuit aided by the presence of elite swimmers like American Olympian Schmitt at NBAC, to constantly challenge and stoke Phelps's competitive fires.) The unseen force propelling both of them forward was Stephens, whose influence was beneficial precisely because of its discretion. Where many coaches would've adhered to the group system—with different coaches for different ages and a set progression as swimmers aged—that he'd invested plenty to establish, Stephens deferred to Bowman as Phelps's personal tutor, sensing something special in both athlete and coach. The temptation for many club directors would've been to direct the training of a prized pupil like Phelps personally, stepping into the spotlight that would eventually belong to the swimmer. Stephens lacked that compulsion.

The relationship that developed between Bowman and Phelps was as much father and son as coach and swimmer, a fact admitted by Phelps's mom, Debbie, who was as omnipresent poolside during Phelps's career as Bowman. From time to time, Phelps's accomplishments in the water resembled a precisely executed symphony by Bach, Phelps the virtuoso performer and Bowman the fastidious, exacting conductor. But there was plenty of dissonance along the way, what has been described as "mutual tantrums," some quite explosive. [13] The consensus from the swimming community is that Michael Phelps wouldn't have been Michael Phelps without Bob Bowman. So lofty were the heights to which Phelps ultimately ascended that it's hard to imagine anyone getting there alone. "You hear people say anybody could have coached Michael Phelps. That's [not so]," said Urbanchek, as qualified a voice as any on matters of coaching who often played referee between the two in Ann Arbor. "I'm the first person to say that I feel I know how to coach champions, but only Bob could have done what Bob did with Michael." [14] You won't get an argument from Phelps. "There's zero chance anyone else could have taken me where Bob did," he said after Beijing. "Zero. I've thought about it so many times. I've thought about so many other coaches. Bob just knew me the best, had me figured out. I owe him so much." [15]

Bowman is the first to admit that mentoring someone with the talent, drive, and range of Phelps is like letting a kid loose in a candy store. [16] But forging a relationship that allowed Phelps to flourish as he did required work. Since Phelps's entire career was masterminded by Bowman, there's no comparison to what Phelps alone could do. But the distance between Phelps and the rest of humanity in a swimming pool, in terms of accomplishment and longevity, indicate that he was more than just another phenom. "I would say the reason we have [worked] so well together is that we are both absolutely honest with each other all the time," Bowman said. "We know exactly where each other stands at all times. That can mean some fireworks sometimes, because neither one of us likes to back down on anything. But I think that's the deal. We don't really play any games. We just keep it simple." [17] The assessment of Bowman's strengths as a coach sounds much like the descriptions of Stephens a generation of swimmers earlier. "One of the reasons why Bob is such a good coach is that he honestly cares about a swimmer's success, as evident by his actions," said Jamie Barone, who swam under Bowman at NBAC and Club Wolverine. "I can't remember a day where I got to the pool for morning practice and he wasn't in the parking lot, and I don't remember a day where he left the pool before me. He was 100 percent dedicated to his athletes. He also has the ability to cater his approach to each swimmer." [18]

Tagging Phelps as the only success story of either Bowman or NBAC is shortsighted. For proof, look no further than the tongue-in-cheek profile of Bowman that ran in *The Australian* prior to Beijing that labeled him "a Machiavelli in sneakers, who has done more to bring about the downfall of the Australian swimming team in the past seven years than anyone else. As the Olympics approach, Bowman should be declared public enemy No. 1 on this side of the Pacific." [19] Joking aside, three of the seven medalists in the

800 free relay in Beijing, including two of the four finalists, were Bowman pupils. He helped reignite the career of Eric Vendt in his late 20s at Club Wolverine, while also leading Peter Vanderkaay to bronze, behind Phelps of course, in the 200 free in Beijing. With the help of Phelps, Bowman's influence wrested control of the 800 free relay away from the Australians, who had temporarily assumed control of the race on the world stage. Bowman drew upon the lessons of the golden generation of Australian freestylers like Grant Hackett and Ian Thorpe to use on his swimmers—both as teaching aides and as motivational carrots—and worked training trips to the Land Down Under into Phelps's schedule.

NBAC boasted a deep roster of swimmers, many of whom emerged in time for the London Games. Schmitt, who swam for Bowman at Club Wolverine and withdrew from school for her senior year at the University of Georgia to prepare for London at NBAC, made the jump from relay medalist and ninth in the 200 free in Beijing to five medals in London. There, she won the 200 free, took silver in the 400, and earned gold in the 800 free and 400 medley relays. "I know [Bowman] knows how to get me to the places I need to [go]," Schmitt said in 2013. "I fully trust whatever he does."[20] Some of the first age-group records set by Elizabeth Pelton were with NBAC under Yetter before she followed Yetter to T2 Aquatics in Florida. NBAC has proven adept at churning out young talent, including some of the top college recruits in the country in recent years, including Austin Surhoff, Connor Kalisz, Annie Zhu, Cierra Runge, and Gillian Ryan.

Then there's the inevitable parallel between Phelps and Hoff. Hoff burst onto the scene as a 15-year-old at the 2004 Olympic Trials but fell short of the lofty expectations placed on her in Athens, finishing 7th in the 200 IM and 17th in the 400 IM. In addition to the overlapping specialties and the congruence in the ages of their Olympic debuts, Hoff was poised to compete in five individual events at the 2008 Games, earning her the label as "the female Michael Phelps." (In fairness, they weren't the training partners the media often portrayed them as, with Phelps and Bowman working at the Meadowbrook campus and Hoff training with Yetter at NBAC's location in Harford County, some 30 miles away.) Despite triumphs in the intervening years, including three golds at each of the 2005 and 2007 World Championships, Hoff's 2008 Games fell flat. Instead of the six golds many projected her to contend for, she returned with silver and two bronzes. Seeing her world record in the 400 IM taken by Stephanie Rice, leaving Hoff with bronze, and having Great Britain's Rebecca Adlington overtake her in the final meters of the 400 free on back-to-back days to open her Beijing Games had an understandably deflating effect. When Hoff's American record in the 200 free was good for just fourth place, the same place she earned in the 200 IM, .34 seconds behind countrywoman Natalie Coughlin for bronze, her psyche was devastated enough to limit her to a sluggish 11th place in the 800 free and a disappointing climax to the Games. Hoff transitioned to Bowman's training group afterward in an effort to rebound, creating what was instantly recognized as a bit of an "odd couple."[21] But the inability of Hoff to deal with Bowman's workouts led to a spiral of reduced confidence that bottomed out when she failed to qualify for the 2009 World Championships, precipitating a move to Fullerton, California, to work with Sean Hutchinson's Fullerton Aquatic Sports Team (FAST).

Hoff's struggles with Bowman were undoubtedly an outlier. In the era of Phelps's short-lived retirement after the London Games, Bowman has branched out to a variety of endeavors. A noted gourmet attracted to the rigorous demands and exacting standards of the kitchen, Bowman has also ventured into the world of racehorses, co-owning several with Phelps. In the pool, Bowman's job offers have included international consulting, trying to apply the NBAC method to national federations like Great Britain—after their disastrous showing of three medals, none gold, in London—and Turkey. In the post-Phelps era, NBAC has attracted a new crop of international swimmers, with Bowman returning to coaching as well as succeeding Stephens as the CEO of NBAC, with a co-owner by the last name of Phelps.

Among those flocking to the north side of Baltimore are some familiar American faces, like Schmitt, London relay gold medalist Conor Dwyer, and Tom Luchsinger. But even in the second year of the Olympic cycle, international stars like France's Yannick Agnel, a three-time medalist in London including gold in the 200 free, and Denmark's Lotte Friis have shifted their training bases to Baltimore. The lure for most athletes, including families who uproot their lives from all over the East Coast to have their teens train at NBAC, is "more metaphysical than physical."[22] Swimmers looking for the slightest of edges, the difference between gold and silver, have the confidence to seek them out at NBAC. "It is the best sporting group I've ever been in," Friis said. "It is very special, and it is very stimulating. This means that I get a whole new perspective on many things by being in so high-profiled a group. I see how others tackle things, and we do a lot to help each other to be better in the water where the other swimmers can see things that the coach cannot because he is on deck."[23] Agnel, whose emergence at age 20 in London led to obvious comparisons to countrymen like Alain Bernard and Laure Manaudou who were unable to parlay early triumphs into a sustained presence on the international medal stand, sought out Bowman for a new approach to training, and not just for what NBAC delivered in the water. "I want to find with Bob Bowman what was lacking in Nice: warmth, sharing, sincerity," said Agnel, who as a 12-year-old swimmer derived inspiration from Phelps's performance at the 2004 Athens Games. "That, [longtime coach] Fabrice [Pellerin] has always wanted to avoid. He always wanted to put distance between himself and his swimmers. It is a choice that I respect and that works; I'm a double Olympic champion and I owe him."[24] Bowman also has the chance to build on the foundation he helped establish with swimmers like Kalisz, who joined the Schmitt-Phelps elite group in 2010 at age 16 and earned the silver medal in the 400 IM at the 2013 Worlds. "Bob's helped lay the groundwork for all the great swimmers here," Kalisz said. "And so he helped change my mindset to where I wanted to go farther than being just a college swimmer. Swimming with Michael definitely helped, too."[25]

The elite-training branch of NBAC is just one facet of its achievement, though. After the 2008 Olympics, NBAC was designated as a USOC national training center, one of only three at the time (along with Marsh's Mecklenburg Aquatic in Charlotte, North Carolina, and Hutchinson's FAST), receiving a $100,000 grant. The inclusive nature of the club has always been one of the hallmarks, from Stephens's first days, born out of the outsider mentality that Stephens developed in the aftermath of his attempts to gain a foothold in the Baltimore swim scene being rebuffed. One of the most remarkable aspects of the club is that the elite-training group, on any given day, could be doing some of the most intense workouts ever concocted a couple of lanes over from a group of elementary school students. The unassuming environs of Meadowbrook, one that belies the success fostered within, aid the perception of a "homey" atmosphere.[26] " Hoff may be a superstar," wrote one profile of the club in 2008, "but at Meadowbrook, she is just another pair of arms and legs, wheeling up and down the pool."[27] The inclusiveness has a strategic purpose, bringing talent into the door that can be coached up by the NBAC staff. "Any child in Maryland can come in those doors right there and know they will go as far as their talent can carry them," Bowman said.[28]

Phelps retains an active role, even as his status as a retired swimmer proved tenuous with his comeback in early 2014. The stated goal, constructed alongside Bowman, when Phelps began his career was to change the nation's perception of the sport. NBAC has become part of the arsenal with which Phelps can accomplish that. While Phelps was still competing, Stephens described him in 2008 as "a resource to help the club he's part of himself develop and to help swimming develop,"[29] one that exceeds simple name recognition. After London, Phelps's co-ownership role has helped Bowman expand the scope and comprehensiveness of the program up and down the age-group scale. Phelps's public profile has made NBAC synonymous with his success, in the pool and in ventures such as the Michael Phelps Swim School, an initiative to introduce children to swimming that has 15 locations in four states as of the end of 2013. His efforts are just the latest example of NBAC's ability to breed more success, a cycle that has entrenched the club atop the world of swimming for the foreseeable future.

Chapter Twenty-Four

U.S. Men's Backstroke

Jeff Rouse and Tyler Clary were born almost 19 years apart. They never attended the same national team camps, never swam in the same senior national meets, and never even occupied the same era of state-of-the-art swimsuits. Their heydays were separated by almost as long as their births.

But there's a common bond that unites Rouse, Clary, and a number of backstrokers in between them: for five straight Olympic Games, American men have had a stranglehold on backstroke gold medals, claiming all 10 on offer. Half of those races have seen 1-2 sweeps, and six have featured a pair of medaling Americans.

The swimmers who've compiled that streak—from Lenny Krayzelburg to Aaron Peirsol, from Ryan Lochte to Matt Grevers—have included some of the best exponents of the stroke ever to don a cap and goggles. They've come from a variety of backgrounds, from different clubs and colleges and coaches. But one feature unites them. Through the years, the backstroke dominance by the Americans has spurred all of them on to loftier heights, pushing them to be constantly better. A team by association, the American backstrokers have forged a dynasty few swim nations can claim.

As is often the case, the American backstroke success sprung from disappointment. From the politically charged atmosphere of the 1980s, currents of innovation ran through backstroke. In the pools at Harvard University, David Berkoff began experimenting with the streamlined underwater dolphin kick, the propulsion of which was unlike anything a surface backstroker could duplicate. The tinkering led him to the "Berkoff blastoff," with the swimmer traveling as many as 35 or 40 meters of each lap underwater with a technique that, while faster, was an affront to many traditionalists. (It also was less effective over 200 meters, given the crippling effects of oxygen debt.) The results were difficult to argue. As the world crept toward the Seoul Olympics in 1988, Berkoff set a pair of world records in the 100 back at Olympic Trials, then lowered his world standard by four-tenths of a second in the preliminaries in Seoul. But in the final, he was beaten at his own game by Japanese swimmer Daichi Suzuki, .13 seconds ahead of Berkoff, forcing the Philadelphia native to settle for silver.

So jarring was the effect of Berkoff's strategy that it drove FINA, swimming's world governing body, to outlaw the technique and require swimmers to surface after no more than 10 (later amended to 15) meters off each wall, including the start. With the backstroke realm resetting itself, Berkoff was one of many forced to adapt, retiring briefly before earning a trip to the 1992 Barcelona Games. But by then, he was no longer the favorite thanks to Jeff Rouse, who became the first swimmer under 55 seconds without the benefit of the exaggerated underwater kick at the 1990 U.S. Nationals. Rouse, who hadn't been as dependent as Berkoff on his underwaters but still spent an average of 20 to 25 meters per long-course lap underwater, set a world record (53.93) at the 1991 Pan Pacific Championships in the 100 off the front of the medley relay after winning the individual event. That title, plus gold at the 1991 World Championships, installed Rouse as the favorite in Barcelona. For the second straight Games, though, an American world-record holder in the 100 back left without gold, Rouse getting upset by .06 seconds by Canadian Mark Tewskbury. The win for Tewksbury, a Calgary native who played second fiddle to Rouse's world record at the 1991 Pan Pacs in Edmonton, came as a surprise, given that his personal best in the 100 back before the Games stood at 55.19. Given the atmosphere of the Barcelona Games, though, where eight world-record holders left Spain without gold medals in their events, Tewksbury's surprise fit right in. Berkoff slotted into bronze. Rouse, who had missed making the American team in the 200 back by four-tenths of a second at Trials, earned a modicum of revenge in the medley relay, where he again set a world record, this one in 53.86, .13 faster than Tewskbury's gold-winning time. But even relay gold and a world record with the team of Nelson Diebel, Pablo Morales, and Jon Olsen was only so much consolation.

If anyone was to break what increasingly seemed like a curse around the program, it would have to be Rouse, the laser-focused native of Fredericksburg, Virginia, who had been setting national age-group records since age 12. He was first and foremost a 100-meter specialist. But he also epitomized the challenge facing the American backstroke program as the 1996 Atlanta Olympics loomed. Amazingly, Rouse had finished the calendar year ranked first in the world in the 100 eight consecutive years from 1989 to 1996, a streak that only East Germany's Roland Matthes and Hungary's Krisztina Egerszegi matched. What those swimmers possessed in spades that Rouse lacked, though, was individual Olympic gold. Despite entering Atlanta holding the world record uninterrupted for five years, owning four straight Pan

Pacific titles in the 100 and posting 8 of the top 10 times in history, Rouse was nagged by a reputation of not winning the big one. Fairly or not, the swimming calendar boils down to one or two meets every four years for most spectators, and in those, Rouse had only the 1991 World title to show. He was upset at the 1994 Worlds by Martin Lopez-Zubero, the home-nation hero of the Barcelona Games for his 200 back win. All that most people remembered Rouse for was his loss in Barcelona.

That defeat shaped the growth of Rouse's career. On the deck at the Piscines Bernat Picornell, Rouse made a vow that the next four years would be devoted to winning Olympic gold in Atlanta. He scrutinized every aspect of his technique and honed his mental approach by trying to apply the relaxation that he credited with his tendency to set world records in relays. Rouse faced resistance qualifying to Atlanta, bested by Tripp Schwenk in the Trials by .19 seconds. But Rouse managed to touch ahead of former Stanford teammate Brian Retterer to earn the second berth. In Atlanta, he took much of the drama out of the race early. Rouse was the fastest in prelims by six-tenths at 54.20. The second-fastest qualifying time was turned in by Cuban Nessier Bent, who admitted before the Games a goal of merely breaking 56 seconds, while Schwenk qualified fifth. In the final, Bent slipped on the start, not that Rouse needed the opening. The American was first to the 50 wall and couldn't be stopped on the way home, clocking in at 54.10 seconds. Though not a world record, he bested the field by .88 seconds in a decisive statement that Rouse's name belonged in the pantheon of backstroke greats. One of his first acts upon winning informed the burden he'd been carrying the last four years. On deck in Atlanta, Rouse sought out Tewksbury. "I thanked him for beating me in '92," Rouse said. "I wouldn't be here if it wasn't for '92. I learned a lot about life and myself after that loss. That experience made me what I am today."[1] Second behind Rouse wasn't Bent, who slid into bronze, but his countryman Rodolfo Falcon, taking home the first—and through the 2012 Games, the only—Cuban swimming medals.

Though Schwenk tumbled to fifth in the 100, the 200 back, his stronger event, remained. But once again, the University of Tennessee grad would be relegated in favor of a tale of redemption. Brad Bridgewater had found the pressure of the 1992 Olympic Trials paralyzing. A high riser with a shot at qualification in the 200, the University of Texas swimmer finished a disappointing seventh, over three seconds slower than Royce Sharp's winning time. The four years between Barcelona and Atlanta entailed a great deal of change. After a two-year hiatus from college, Bridgewater relocated from Austin to the University of Southern Carolina, where he hoped the distance-based program of Mark Schubert would aid his 200 quest. Motivating Bridewater, Schwenk, and the rest of the world was the presence in the 200 of a swimmer arguably more favored than Rouse: Russia's Vladimir Selkov, the reigning world and European champ and a silver medalist in 1992. The ranks got increasingly crowded as 1996 neared. Lopez-Zubero, who had retired to a comfortable living as a sporting hero, returned. Italian Emanuele Merisi joined select company under 1:58 at the Italian Trials. And Schwenk and Bridgewater went 1-2 at Trials, each clocking in at under two minutes. When Selkov faltered in his prelim heat in Atlanta, slipping to ninth overall to miss the final by 12-hundredths of a second, the door was blown wide open. The American duo seized the opportunity. Bridgewater, who qualified first from prelims, was second to the 100-meter wall in the final behind Schwenk. But Bridgewater pulled away on the third 50, reaching the final wall first in 1:58.54, just ahead of Schwenk (1:58.99), who barely outtouched Merisi for silver. Just like that, the Americans were on top of the backstroke world again.

The hard work and determination of swimmers like Schwenk, Rouse, and Bridgewater laid the foundation. But the backstroke program's true blossoming was yet to come, as the nation was blessed with a glut of transcendent talents. The first in that lineage was attracted to the United States by more than just the promise of a swimming education. Lenny Krayzelburg's parents had a comfortable enough middle-class lifestyle in Odessa, Ukraine, in the late 1980s. But even before the imminent collapse of the Soviet Union reached its tipping point, Oleg and Yelena Krayzelburg knew their children would face limited opportunities. Lenny had already begun to show promise in the pool, but the specter of military conscription for a nation perpetually on the brink of war and the institutional limits on advancement for a child of Jewish heritage forecast a dim future. The answer was to uproot their lives and head for the hopefulness of the United States. Even in the promised land, the adjustment for 13-year-old Lenny was occasionally uncomfortable. His English proficiency lacking, he often felt isolated among his peers in Los Angeles. About the only place Krayzelburg was a natural fit was the pool, where his physique made him preordained to win backstroke races. Opportunities to impress, though, were limited, with Krayzelburg bouncing around clubs whose facilities were a far cry from the pristine, state-sponsored ones of the Soviet Union and attending a high school that lacked a swim team. Where he found peace was at the Westside Jewish Community Center, where Krayzelburg swam and worked as a lifeguard. The lack of consistent, organized competition made coach Stu Blumkin wary when the lanky teen appeared in his office at Santa Monica College hoping to walk onto the swim team, willing to endure a morale-testing, 50-minute bus ride daily. By the end of his first season with the Corsairs, culminating in a national junior college record in the 200 back, all doubts were silenced. The confident Krayzelburg never harbored uncertainty about his abilities; Blumkin and others soon followed suit. "At the track, if you watch a horse walk, you won't see anything special. But the minute you see him gallop, you know," Blumkin said. "Like the jockeys always say, 'the horse has his mind on business.' That's Lenny."[2]

Krayzelburg's career took off once Blumkin put him in contact with USC coach Schubert. Krayzelburg, who became a naturalized citizen in 1995, wound up fifth in the 200 back at the 1996 Olympic Trials. His coming-out party on the national scene was the 1997 Nationals, where he posted the fifth-fastest time in history in the 200 back. The time of 1:58.04 lowered his personal best by over a second and stood a half second faster than Bridgewater's gold-winning time in Atlanta. At the same meet, he also bested Texas standout Neil Walker in the 100. Krayzelburg gave a large part of the credit for his improvement not just to Schubert's tutelage but to the influence of Trojan Swim club teammate Bridgewater, his training partner for five years, without whom Krayzelburg believed he wouldn't have made such large strides. "Day-in, day-out, twice a day . . . we're just going at it," Krayzelburg said. "It's amazing, and it's fortunate for me. He's definitely helped me out."[3] What Krayzelburg best retained from his days behind the Iron Curtain was an austere Soviet work ethic. Though his time in the United States gave him a nuanced sense of dual nationalism with his former Ukraine, the dedication instilled at a state-run swim school that included 12 hours of studying and practicing from the age of six endured. "I picked up a lot of good growing up in the Soviet system, training so hard and intense at a young age," he said. "When I got older, I realized they wanted us to train so hard, and to commit to something and to dedicate our whole lives to it, because that's what it took. There were no shortcuts if you want to accomplish something."[4]

By the 2000 Olympic Trials, Krayzelburg should have been the unquestioned favorite, especially after his double gold at the 1999 Pan Pacs in Sydney, setting world records in the 100 (53.60) and 200 (1:55.87). That triumph made him the first American to simultaneously hold both marks since Rick Carey in 1983. The well of talent also sprung a challenger for Krayzelburg's throne in prodigy Aaron Peirsol. With a Southern California beach bum demeanor, Peirsol began setting national age-group records at age 10. By the 1998 senior Nationals, Peirsol was fourth in the 200 at 14, a level of youth usually reserved for female swim wunderkinds. His growth silenced skeptics who believed a swimmer peaking so early couldn't sustain his dominance. With Peirsol, though, the success of his youth wasn't due to early physical development or maturity; he was just naturally predisposed to swim backstroke quickly. His Irvine Novaquatics coach Dave Salo called him a "once in a lifetime swimmer,"[5] a moniker he'd live up to time and again. In the run-up to the 2000 Olympic Trials, Peirsol and Krayzelburg's collisions became a flashpoint for the rivalry between the Novaquatics and Schubert's Trojan Swim Club, not that either of the swimmers noticed much. The aspect of Peirsol's personality that most struck Krayzelburg was his laidback demeanor, particularly poignant for backstroke, where too much tension or effort can be counterproductive. Peirsol even beat Krayzelburg in the summer of 2000 when the 17-year-old prevailed in the 200 at the Janet Evans Invitational. Peirsol's attitude toward the looming Trials epitomized the surfer's optimism and immunity from pressure. "I've thought about it a lot. I realize that I'm young, and if I don't make the team, it won't be the end of the world," he said. "I mean, I'll be 21 when the next Olympics come. I'm working my butt off to make the 2000 Games. But if I don't, so be it."[6]

Where the 2000 Olympic Trials in Indianapolis were viewed by Peirsol as the beginning of his Olympic story, Krayzelburg saw it as the culmination of three years in the international spotlight. He wasted little time showcasing his authority over the field, buzzing within seven-hundredths of his world record in prelims, without a fastsuit or cap. In the final, he covered the first 50 three-tenths under world-record pace, but he faded over the back half, still winning by over a second in 53.84, just .24 off the world mark. Second was Walker, while Peirsol, despite the second-fastest final 50 in the field, finished fourth. Despite his brush with a world record, Peirsol's takeaway from Krayzelburg's early swims was that "King Lenny" didn't look "unbeatable."[7] For any other pair, such a verbal salvo would up the ante. But in the burgeoning backstroke rivalry, there was no vitriol, just a healthy appreciation of the effect each had on the other. "For the last two years I've been swimming by myself," Krayzelburg said. "If someone is with you, you have to use a lot more strategy in your race. It's going to be better for me."[8] Krayzelburg was less appreciative of Peirsol setting the pace in the prelims of the 200 at 1:57.93. But Krayzelburg responded with a 1:57.32 in finals—still well off his world mark and also trailing Peirsol's 1:57.03 from Nationals, the fastest in the world in 2000 prior to Sydney—to top Peirsol (1:57.98). Among those missing out was Bridgewater, who finished sixth in the 200 to go with seventh in the 100.

About the only misstep Krayzelburg made in Sydney was having the misfortune of swimming around the same time as one Ian Thorpe, the Aussie headliner of the Games. With the 100 back final coming after an epic 200 freestyle final, a rare reminder of Thorpe's mortality in which Dutchman Pieter van den Hoogenband bested him, the rabid Sydney fans were recovering emotionally when Krayzelburg's turn in the limelight arrived. At any other Games, the renewal of hostilities between Krayzelburg and Australian Matt Welsh, whom the American bested at the Sydney Pan Pacs, would've monopolized headlines. In the blinding glow of "Thorpemania," the Welsh-Krayzelburg duel was relegated to an afterthought. But Krayzelburg, who fought the nerves of the day, drew inspiration from the upset by van den Hoogenband. Krayzelburg and Welsh were 1-2 in prelims and semis, the only two under 55 seconds each time. In the final, they distanced themselves from the pack early and were separated by less than a tenth at the midway point. But Krayzelburg found more in his legs on the way home, outsplitting Welsh by a quarter second over the final 50 and touching in an Olympic record of 53.72 to top Welsh (54.07). Walker slotted home sixth. For his new country—and the special place in his heart for his old—an elated Krayzelburg had summited his "Everest."[9]

In the 200, Peirsol showed a veteran's poise in setting the second-fastest times of the first two rounds, prompting him to reiterate his belief that "Lenny can be beaten."[10] Krayzelburg's swims, though, dispelled that myth. He set Olympic records in prelims and semis, the latter at 1:57.27, over a second quicker than Peirsol. The final was all Lenny. Once again drawing inspiration from his peers—this time, Misty Hyman's stunning upset of home-nation darling Susie O'Neill in the women's 200 butterfly—he led at each wall, working the third 50 to balloon his lead to a second over Peirsol with 50 meters to go. Though he admitted "overswimming" his race so much that he lost feeling in his arms over the last lap and needed a five-minute rest to recover from the intense pain, Krayzelburg had enough left to touch for gold in 1:56.76, comfortably holding off Peirsol (1:57.35) and Welsh (1:57.59).[11] Krayzelburg had enough strength left to climb into the stands, though, and celebrate with his parents, ascribing a huge part of the credit for his win to their sacrifice and support. His effort put him alongside Carey (1984), John Naber (1976), and Matthes (1968, 1972) as achievers of the backstroke double. Even though he was a step lower, Peirsol came out feeling like a winner as well. "I got the silver, but I still get to stand up there for the U.S. national anthem," he said.[12] Krayzelburg (and for his prelims participation, Walker) earned gold in the medley relay, the U.S. setting a world record. Krayzelburg staked the squad of Ed Moses, Ian Crocker, and Gary Hall Jr. to a healthy lead, and the Americans coasted by over a second.

Though Krayzelburg was seven years Peirsol's senior and stated no intention to leave the international picture, the Sydney Games represented a changing of the guard. Over the next four years, Peirsol ascended the throne as the world's best, through the completion of his high school career and two years at Texas. He set his first long-course world record in the 200 at the 2002 Spring Nationals, dashing .72 off Krayzelburg's 1999 mark. It was becoming clear that for Peirsol, it was "my time."[13] The realization of that swim as a seminal moment wasn't unique to Peirsol. "He grabs my head—my head—and starts shaking it! He's all smiles and I'm dog-tired from coming in second," recalled two-time Olympian and Texas teammate Josh Davis. "I thought: the crown is exchanged. Aaron is now the King of the Backstroke."[14]

While Peirsol sized up crowns and scepters, Krayzelburg was struggling through a long-brewing physical ordeal. He'd had a history of injuries, like a back issue that flared up in late 1998, probably stemming from the overuse of 12-hour workouts from childhood onward. Shortly after Sydney, Krayzelburg tore a shoulder muscle that required surgery, then a cleanup procedure that still didn't fully eradicate the problem. All that surgery and rehab precluded Krayzelburg from taking part in any major international meets between Sydney and Athens. The lead-up to the 2004 Olympic Trials was a time of physical torment for Krayzelburg, who had to swim through constant pain. It became apparent that part of the solution for Krayzelburg was a change of scenery in 2003, away from the distance-based toil of Schubert. The answer was the sprint-specific program espoused by Salo, one that had proven effective with Peirsol and that Krayzelburg found "rejuvenating."[15] Peirsol's studies in Austin meant the friendly rivals were rarely in direct opposition, and the arrangement was mutually beneficial. "Lenny was always a huge influence on me," Peirsol said in 2004. "He's kind of shown me the ropes."[16]

As if the collision of present and future in the offing for the 2004 Trials wasn't dramatic enough, the concoction got a dose of the past when Rouse threw his hat in the ring for another Olympic go at 34. Already inducted to the International Swimming Hall of Fame, Rouse's bid to be the oldest male American to ever qualify for the Olympics was spurred by a lack of competitiveness in his non-swimming life and a desire to again strive for the structured, "specific goals" once a fixture of his swimming life.[17] Once he regained some of his world-class form, he naturally wondered how far he could take it, all the while thoroughly enjoying a journey that took him back to his old college stomping grounds. "I could swim badly and the comeback journey would still be worth it," Rouse said. "I don't need a gold medal. I already have that. I just needed the swimming goals again. That's the thing I'm really going to miss."[18] With the Trials field loaded with three of the greatest backstrokers ever, the stakes were amazingly high. "Honestly, the guy who gets third in that one probably deserves to go to the Olympics," an undaunted Peirsol opined in 2002 about the 100. "It's kind of awesome that we'll have almost like three generations in the race."[19]

Whoever else was present, Peirsol's talent was irrepressible in Long Beach. The 21-year-old swam away with the 100 in 53.64 seconds. The second-place battle was decided by just four-hundredths of a second, and the result had Peirsol doubling up on the celebration. "I turned around and looked at who got first, and it was me, which was pretty sweet," Peirsol said. "I couldn't see who had finished second and while I was waiting to hear, I heard Lenny yelling. I cracked up because I was so elated for him."[20] Using his veteran guile, the sentimental favorite rocketed through the final 50 to finish in 54.06, a hair faster than the Stanford duo of Peter Marshall (54.10) and Randall Bal (54.20), with Rouse sixth. For the "nothing-to-lose" Krayzelburg, his main goal of the Olympic cycle had been realized.[21] Krayzelburg and Rouse skipped the 200, but a more tantalizing matchup loomed between Sydney roommates Peirsol and Michael Phelps. While Peirsol was winning silver in 2000, Phelps took fifth in the 200 fly as the youngest American male Olympian in 68 years. With a slew of world records since Sydney, Phelps positioned himself to challenge Mark Spitz's record seven gold medals in Athens. One of the biggest choices came between the 200 individual medley and 200 back, the finals of which were held on the same night, about a half hour apart. At the Trials test run, Phelps coasted to a win in the IM over Ryan Lochte by over two seconds, then set his sights on Peirsol. With Phelps's push, Peirsol sent a warning shot that the 200 IM was the Baltimore native's better bet, Peirsol setting a world record of 1:54.74 in finals. Over a second back was Phelps in 1:55.86, a medal-worthy time, though unlikely to challenge Peirsol's supremacy. Phelps decided against the 200 back in Athens, largely in deference to Peirsol, elevating Auburn's Bryce Hunt, who was almost four seconds slower than Peirsol, to the second qualifying spot.

With Phelps eschewing the 200 back in Athens, there was little chance of anyone usurping Peirsol's dominance. The 100 back was again overshadowed by the 200 free, dubbed the "Race of the Century," with Thorpe avenging his loss to van den Hoogenband and Phelps earning bronze. The 100 back shaped up as a hectic final, with the top six qualifiers clustered within three-tenths of a second. Peirsol put his stamp on the final, though, winning in 54.06. The big race was for the secondary medals, with Austrian Markus Rogan (54.35), Japan's Tomomi Morita (54.36), and Krayzelburg (54.38) hitting almost simultaneously and leaving the American an eyelash away from a medal.

Peirsol made up for the lack of intrigue in his first triumph with a tidal wave of controversy in the 200. The American did his part in the water, blitzing the field with an Olympic record of 1:54.95 that was fastest by 2.4 seconds. But there was a delay posting results, and when the board in Athens finally lit up, it revealed that Peirsol had been disqualified. Controversy was no stranger to the American delegation in Athens. Peirsol had been one of the most vocal critics of Japanese breaststroker Kosuke Kitajima, whom replays showed to have clearly used an illegal dolphin kick during his win in the 100 breast at the expense of Peirsol's Texas teammate Brendan Hansen. In what felt like retribution, Peirsol's disqualification cited a violation on his final turn, elevating Rogan to gold and producing tense moments on deck for Peirsol, his family, and the American team. After some deliberation—and before a formal protest could be lodged by the Americans—the DQ was overturned and Peirsol was awarded his gold. Protests by the Austrian federation on Rogan's behalf and the Great Britain federation for displaced bronze medalist James Goddard were rejected, with FINA finding the incident report to be "inadequate" and "not in the working language of FINA" (i.e., English or French), essentially a blank report that was erroneously signed off on.[22] A relieved Peirsol, grateful at the "grace" of his rivals, was rightly granted gold.[23] "I feel like the second-best backstroke swimmer in the world; the best is Peirsol," Rogan admitted. "I never felt like an Olympic champion. I never accepted it in my heart."[24] Peirsol added a world-record icing on the cake to start the medley relay (53.45) and earn a third gold.

With Beijing next on the Olympic itinerary, the faces again changed. Rouse (again) and Krayzelburg called it quits, but the pool of talent hardly thinned. With Peirsol transitioning from chasing to defending the throne, he had plenty of challengers. The 50-meter world record was held by Bal, a consummate sprinter. Though Phelps concentrated his efforts elsewhere despite times consistently faster than everyone not named Peirsol, the 200 back—and the 200 IM/200 back challenge—became a prime objective of Lochte. The two-time NCAA swimmer of the year at the University of Florida who took silver behind Phelps in the IM plus relay gold in Athens had parlayed his short-course prowess to become a major player on the long-course scene, garnering the dubious distinction as the best swimmer the mainstream has never heard of. The crowd of competitors Peirsol stepped over on his way to greatness was a source of great pride. "I think that keeps me humble and motivates me," Peirsol said. "Sometimes, making our team is the hard part. It keeps you honest and working hard. I can't expect to automatically make our team."[25]

Peirsol was less tickled, though, when Lochte swiped his crown at the 2007 Worlds in Melbourne, scoring an upset in the 200 back and taking Peirsol's world standard in 1:54.32. Peirsol, who had earlier bested Lochte in the 100 back in Melbourne as the first man ever under 53 seconds (52.98), cramped up on the final 50 of the 200 despite being under world-record pace early, allowing Lochte to make up ground over the final 50 meters. Lochte's surge marked Peirsol's first major loss since before the Sydney Olympics. The pair authored an epic chapter in their duel at the 2008 Olympic Trials, where Peirsol tied Locthe's world mark in the 200 to edge him by .02 seconds. Earlier at Trials, Peirsol had trimmed his world record in the 100 back to 52.89, topping Matt Grevers and Lochte. With swimmers like Peirsol, Phelps, and Lochte all occupying the same era, the collection of so many once-in-a-generation talents could have generated myriad questions of "what if." Instead, each swimmer's humility and mutual respect was spun into a healthy motivating factor. "Because my events have guys like Michael and Aaron, I have to think it's going to take a world record to win," Lochte said. "But I'm a guy who loves to race against anyone. I like to be challenged. I've never been someone who backs down from anything."[26]

The Beijing Games featured one certainty and one surprise for Peirsol. In the 100, Peirsol looked to be in trouble when he qualified just fifth from semifinals to occupy an unfamiliar Lane 2 in the final. He turned second in the final, though, then roared through the final 50 and stuck the finish to shatter his world record in 52.54. Second, in 53.11 seconds, was Grevers, his massive 6-foot-8 frame beating a crowd to the wall. "Matt and I sharing the podium together, I don't think it could have gotten any better," Peirsol said.[27] The 200 featured another 1-2, though not the one Peirsol envisioned. Lochte and Peirsol were dead even at the last wall of the final, a quarter second behind the early pacesetter, Russia's Arkady Vyatchanin. Lochte's final-wall surge once again proved too strong, and he clocked in a world record of 1:53.94, .39 ticks ahead of Peirsol. Just 27 minutes before Lochte rallied for bronze in the 200 IM behind Phelps, the backstroke torch was passed once again. "I gave it my all and I had nothing left," the always gracious Peirsol said. "I'm very proud of what I've done. Ryan swam well. He earned it."[28]

The 2008 Games proved to be Peirsol's final Olympiad, though he didn't draw the curtain on his career in Beijing, even after he and Grevers added medley relay gold to their cache of hardware. Before calling it quits in early 2011 after nearly a decade in the spotlight, Peirsol reclaimed his 200 back world record at the 2009 Nationals, a stunning drop to 1:53.08. At the fast-suit-aided 2009 World Championships, Peirsol bypassed 1:52 altogether in a staggering 1:51.92, with Lochte in bronze. That time was a response to Peirsol's failure to make the 100 back final in Rome, languishing in ninth in semis despite entering as the world-record holder, a mark he regained at Nationals after a one-week stay in the hands of Spain's Aschwin Wildeboer. The final major international meet of his career occurred on home soil at the 2010 Pan Pacs in Irvine, where he won the 100—after Lochte (second in prelims) scratched the event, a gesture for which Peirsol expressed his thanks[29] —and saw Lochte and Tyler Clary go 1-2 in the 200.

In the vacuum created by Peirsol's retirement, the backstroke field was suddenly more open than it had been in a decade. For some, it was a just reward for patience under the reign of Peirsol. Grevers is the best example of a swimmer whose international prospects were dimmed by Peirsol. A native of Chicago and graduate of Northwestern, Grevers had to wonder if his time would ever come. At the 2004 Olympic Trials, Grevers finished seventh in the 100 back with a time that would've finished seventh in Athens. Because his parents were Dutch, the door was open for him to swim for the Nether-lands, an increasingly enticing proposition given how van den Hoogenband had increased the prestige of the program. But Grevers's only move was to Arizona to train with Tucson Aquatics, accepting the challenge of earning a spot on the American team. "I sometimes like easy routes. But this is one challenge that I did want to undertake," he said. "I wanted it to mean some-thing if I swam in the Olympics. I didn't want to just get handed a spot. A lot of people I've known will just try to represent a country they're barely related to. I don't think that's the true spirit of what the Olympics are all about."[30] The biggest change Grevers made was adding the 100 free to his repertoire to pursue one of six Olympic berths on offer for the 400 free relay. He qualified fifth for Beijing, and as an added bonus, Grevers turned in a personal best in the 100 back—an event he only entered at the behest of coach Frank Busch as a warm-up for the 100 free—to edge Lochte for second and a spot in Beijing. Grevers left China with two relay golds as well as individual silver and was poised for a bigger haul in London four years later.

It was there that another long-overshadowed swimmer, Nick Thoman, shone. The Cincinnati native who bounced around clubs for years long sought a foothold in the elite backstroking scene. After finishing fifth in the 200 and sixth in the 100 at the 2008 Olympic Trials, the 22-year-old graduate of the University of Arizona was ready to call time on his career and move on with his life. Only one thing stopped him: a free plane ticket to the U.S. Open in Minneapolis in late July. "I was giving fairly considerable thought to not coming back," Thoman said. "I was offered a free ticket out there, so I said, 'Why the hell not?'"[31] Thoman's second chance at swimming life spurred a hot streak, one that began with a U.S. Open record of 52.92 seconds, just three-hundredths off Peirsol's world record. Thoman set a short-course world mark in the 100 back at the 2009 Duel in the Pool and missed a trip to the Rome Worlds by one-hundredth behind Peirsol and Grevers. Not a bad résumé for the nation's fourth-best backstroker. With Peirsol gone and Lochte lukewarm on the 100, the door to London was wide open. At Trials, Lochte's prelims time was almost a second slower than Grevers's, leading him to scratch from semis. Grevers was clearly the class of the final by winning in 52.08, and Thoman (52.86) outtouched David Plummer (52.98) to earn a trip to the Games. In London, Grevers set the pace at every turn of the event with Thoman floating in the middle of the pack. But in the final, both raised their games. Grevers was the unquestioned winner in 52.16 seconds, an Olympic record. Thoman beat a pack of swimmers to the wall for silver, clocking in at 52.92. "I must be selfish because it took me a good 10 seconds to realize he got second," the gregarious Grevers said. "That's something I should do right away. But when I noticed, that moment became much more special. To know that we can go 1-2 in that event, again really shows the USA's dominance in backstroke right now when we're able to step up."[32] "When I looked up at the scoreboard and saw Matthew next to me in first place, I was so happy I got to share this moment with a teammate," Thoman added. "We are all members of team USA. They're great teammates and we all help push each other. They're great guys and this result is down to everyone."[33]

Sans Peirsol, the 200 back remained Lochte's domain. But the second spot remained up for grabs. Into that void stepped Clary, who also inherited Lochte's mantle as the best swimmer no one had heard of before London. The development of the outdoorsy native of Southern California and former University of Michigan swimmer had long been stunted by the unrelenting dominance of Phelps and Lochte in the IMs, an event where Clary would've been an international contender for medals were he to survive domestic Trials. Clary, who left Michigan in 2010 to follow coach Jon Urbanchek back west to Fullerton Aquatic Swim Team, had a brash fearlessness that spurred him to challenge Phelps and Lochte in events like the 200 free, 200 fly, and 200 back. While Phelps enjoyed time away from the sport, Clary swooped for silvers in the 400 IM at the 2009 and 2011 Worlds. His hubris led to an overextension of his program at the 2012 Trials, qualifying for London in only the 200 fly and 200 back. In the latter, he was clearly worthy of joining Lochte, touching a half second behind him at Trials and over two seconds faster than Thoman. After dealing with the disappointment of fading to fifth in the 200 fly in London, Clary uncorked a 200 back eerily reminiscent of Lochte's unseating the established favorite Peirsol four years earlier. Clary, who had qualified with the fastest time, seven-tenths ahead of Lochte, pulled what was considered a massive upset in the final, delivering a long-awaited breakthrough in 1:53.41, an Olympic record. Lochte, who appeared to be in control of the race for the first 150 meters, was beaten at his own game in the last 50 with Clary motoring off a strong underwater to overtake Lochte, who faltered to bronze in 1:53.94 behind Japan's Ryosuke Irie (1:53.78). For Clary, who staunchly resisted the temptation of others to pity him for the era of swimming that fate dropped him into, the win was a just reward for his stick-to-itiveness. "That's just something that always kept me clawing for more," he said. "It's tough to swallow sometimes, but it makes moments like these that much more sweet."[34]

Lochte's bronze may not have been exemplary compared to his high individual standards, but it represented the ninth medal in the 200 back for the Americans over five Games. Combined with the triumph in the 100 back, the Americans claimed 16 of 20 possible backstroke medals over five Games. Add to that gold in each medley relay—10 medals, for the participants in prelims and finals—and you have 26 medals split among the back-stroking corps. Since Krayzelburg in 1999, the world record in the 200 back has stayed the exclusive property of Americans through the end of 2013. In the 100, save for Wildeboer's one-week interlude in 2009, an American has held the world record uninterrupted since Berkoff reclaimed it on August 12, 1988—seven months before Clary was born. What makes the group as special as anything is the stunning lack of animosity. Whether it was Peirsol giving private lessons to Grevers at the pre-Beijing camp or the training partnership between Krayzelburg and Bridgewater, the program's secret to sustaining success lies in the collective elimination of rivalry and hostility between swimmers. The biggest thrill for swimmers is always to win a gold; but for the American backstrokers over the last two decades that have time and again authored 1-2 finishes on the world's biggest stage, the delight at seeing a teammate there is a close second.

Notes

INTRODUCTION

1. Michael Phelps and Brian Cazeneuve, *Beneath the Surface* (Champaign, IL: Sports Publishing, 2008), 209.

1. 1976 U.S. WOMEN'S 400 FREESTYLE

1. Sarah Pileggi, "Up from Plop, Plop," *Sports Illustrated*, June 21, 1976, accessed November 18, 2012, http://sportsillustrated.cnn.com/vault/article/magazine/MAG1091228/index.htm.

2. Jerry Kirshenbaum, "Good Times Roll for Shirley," *Sports Illustrated*, April 12, 1976, accessed November 18, 2012, http://sportsillustrated.cnn.com/vault/article/magazine/MAG1090951/index.htm.

3. Associated Press, "For the Women, It'll Be a Struggle," *Eugene Register-Guard*, July 8, 1976, accessed August 6, 2013, http://news.google.com/newspapers?id=xatVAAAAIBAJ&sjid=3uADAAAAIBAJ&pg=5123,1885289&dq=babashoff+petra+thumer&hl=en.

4. Richard Panek, "State-Sponsored Drug Use Has Tarnished the Olympic Games," in *Drugs and Sports*, edited by William Dudley (San Diego: Greenhaven Press, 2001), 26.

5. Brent Rutemiller, "Shirley Babashoff Breaks 30-Year Silence on East Germany's Systematic Doping of Olympians," *Swimming World*, January 11, 2007, accessed November 8, 2012, http://www.swimmingworldmagazine.com/lane9/news/13191.asp.

6. Dave Anderson, "Out of the Pool Every Four Years," *New York Times*, July 24, 1976, 17.

7. Steven Ungerleider, *Faust's Gold: Inside the East German Doping Machine* (New York: St. Martin's, 2001), 1.

8. Associated Press, "Shirley Smug on Medal Goal," *Spokane Daily Chronicle*, July 15, 1976, 18.

9. Jerry Kirshenbaum, "Theirs Was a Midas Stroke," *Sports Illustrated*, August 2, 1976, accessed November 18, 2012, http://sportsillustrated.cnn.com/vault/article/magazine/MAG1091375/1/index.htm.

10. Neil Amdur, "Olympic Women: The Sniping between American, East German Women More than Just Rivalry," *Star-News*, August 1, 1976, accessed January 6, 2013, http://news.

google.com/newspapers?id=E7UsAAAAIBAJ&sjid=GRMEAAAAIBAJ&pg=4508,189573&dq=usa+east+german+rivalry&hl=en.

11. Amdur, "Olympic Women."

12. Jerry Kirshenbaum, "They're Pooling Their Talent," *Sports Illustrated*, July 10, 1978, accessed November 18, 2013, http://sportsillustrated.cnn.com/vault/article/magazine/MAG1093851/3/index.htm.

13. Panek, "State-Sponsored Drug Use Has Tarnished the Olympic Games," 27.

14. Rutemiller, "Shirley Babashoff Breaks 30-Year Silence."

15. Christine Brennan, "Babashoff Had Mettle to Speak Out about Steroids," *USA Today*, July 15, 2004, accessed November 8, 2012, http://usatoday30.usatoday.com/sports/columnist/brennan/2004-07-15-brennan_x.htm.

16. Kenny Moore, "Babashoff and Ender," *Sports Illustrated*, July 13, 1992, accessed November 18, 2012, http://sportsillustrated.cnn.com/vault/article/magazine/MAG1003984/index.htm.

17. Associated Press, "Shirley Smug on Medal Goal," 18.

18. Panek, "State-Sponsored Drug Use Has Tarnished the Olympic Games," 27.

19. Phillip Whitten, "The 10 Greatest Relay Races of All Time!" *Swimming World*, April 2005, 8.

20. Phillip Whitten, "The 10 Greatest Olympic Upsets of All Time!" *Swimming World*, June 2005, 10.

21. Bob Ingram, "Women's Events." *Swimming World*, September 1976, 45.

22. Neil Amdur, "Top Feats by Montgomery, Strachan," *New York Times*, July 26, 1976, 15.

23. Ingram, "Women's Events," 45.

24. Ingram, "Women's Events," 45.

25. Ingram, "Women's Events," 45.

2. 1984 U.S. MEN'S 800 FREESTYLE

1. Daniel F. Chambliss, *Champions: The Making of Olympic Swimmers* (New York: Morrow, 1988), 167.

2. Craig Neff, "The Albatross Will Fly," *Sports Illustrated*, July 18, 1984, accessed August 27, 2013, http://sportsillustrated.cnn.com/vault/article/magazine/MAG1122295/index.htm.

3. "Michael Gross Superstar," *Swimming World*, February 1984, 55.

4. Neff, "The Albatross Will Fly."

5. Craig Neff, "Four Finals, Two Records and Five Gold Medalists," *Sports Illustrated*, August 6, 1984, accessed August 27, 2013, http://sportsillustrated.cnn.com/vault/article/magazine/MAG1122381/2/index.htm.

6. Neff, "Four Finals, Two Records and Five Gold Medalists."

7. Neff, "Four Finals, Two Records and Five Gold Medalists."

8. Craig Neff, "The U.S. Will Rule the Pool," *Sports Illustrated*, July 18, 1984, accessed August 27, 2013, http://sportsillustrated.cnn.com/vault/article/magazine/MAG1122296/2/index.htm.

9. Frank Litsky, "U.S. Swimmers Win Two More Golds," *New York Times*, July 31, 1984, A1.

10. Craig Neff, "The U.S. Is Back . . . and How!" *Sports Illustrated*, August 13, 1984, accessed August 27, 2013, http://sportsillustrated.cnn.com/vault/article/magazine/MAG1122401/1/index.htm.

11. Neff, "The U.S. Is Back . . . and How!"

12. Mike Penner, "Snapshots from the Games," *Los Angeles Times*, July 25, 2004, accessed August 26, 2013, http://articles.latimes.com/2004/jul/25/sports/sp-olysnapshots25.

13. Litsky, "U.S. Swimmers Win Two More Golds," A1.

14. International Olympic Committee, "16 Days of Glory—Albatross," 1985, video clip, accessed August 27, 2013, http://www.youtube.com/watch?v=NeBKZhUhy9s.

15. Neff, "The U.S. Is Back . . . and How!"

16. Tom McMillan, "Gross Busters: U.S. Swimmers Finally Beat West German," *Pittsburgh Post-Gazette*, August 1, 1984, 18.

17. Jim Lassiter, "Splish-Splash America Drenched by Fabulous Gold-Medal Fact," *The Oklahoman*, August 1, 1984, accessed August 26, 2013, http://newsok.com/splish-splash-america-drenched-by-fabulous-gold-medal-fact/article/2076606.

18. "Looking Ahead: Gross Surprises U.S. and Himself," *New York Times*, August 1, 1984, B9.

19. Chris Georges, "Men's 800 Free Relay," *Swimming World*, September 1984, 43.

20. Georges, "Men's 800 Free Relay," 43.

3. 2000 AUSTRALIAN MEN'S FREESTYLE

1. Ron Carter, "Sweetenham Sour," *The Age*, July 22, 1976, accessed August 6, 2013, http://news.google.com/newspapers?nid=1300&dat=19760722&id=-_FUAAAAIBAJ&sjid=Q5IDAAAAIBAJ&pg=5523,5253887.

2. Craig Lord, "King Kong," *Swimming World*, June 1999, 33.

3. Chloe Saltau, "Veteran Fydler Won't Play Second Fiddle," *Sydney Morning Herald*, May 17, 2000, accessed November 15, 2013, Newspaper Source Plus.

4. Saltau, "Veteran Fydler Won't Play Second Fiddle."

5. Jere Longman, "Sydney 2000: Swimming; Australia Aglow as Young Star Gets Two Golds," *New York Times*, September 17, 2000, accessed August 9, 2013, http://www.nytimes.com/2000/09/17/sports/sydney-2000-swimming-australia-aglow-as-young-star-gets-two-golds.html.

6. Michael Cowley, "Can the King Make a Nation Cry?" *Sydney Morning Herald*, September 16, 2000, accessed August 13, 2013, Newspaper Source Plus.

7. Chloe Saltau, "When the Edge Is in the Sledge," *The Sunday Age*, September 10, 2000, accessed August 13, 2013, Newspaper Source Plus.

8. Brian Cazenueve, "G' Day: Will Ian Thorpe and the Rest of the Aussies Rule the Pool?," *Sports Illustrated*, September 11, 2000, accessed November 21, 2012, http://sportsillustrated.cnn.com/vault/article/magazine/MAG1020313/2/index.htm.

9. John Lingard, "Hear the Message, Says Relay Team's Overnight Hero," *Sydney Morning Herald*, September 18, 2000, accessed November 15, 2013, Newspaper Source Plus.

10. Leigh Montville, "Fast Lanes," *Sports Illustrated*, September 25, 2000, accessed November 21, 2012, http://sportsillustrated.cnn.com/vault/article/magazine/MAG1020434/index.htm.

11. Caroline Wilson, "The Dream Machine," *The Sunday Age*, September 17, 2000, accessed November 15, 2013, Newspaper Source Plus.

12. Brian Cazeneuve, "Everybody Loves Ian," *Sports Illustrated*, September 17, 2000, accessed September 21, 2013, http://sportsillustrated.cnn.com/olympics/2000/swimming/news/2000/09/16/cazeneuve_olympics.

13. Cazeneuve, "Everybody Loves Ian."

14. Wilson, "The Dream Machine."

15. Montville, "Fast Lanes."

16. Greg Growden, "Joy, Joy, Joy to Australian, and Hollowness for the Winners in the Grandstand," *Sydney Morning Herald*, September 20, 2000, accessed November 15, 2013, Newspaper Source Plus.

17. Phillip Whitten and Michael Collins, "Party Smashers," *Swimming World*, October 2000, 27–28.

18. Michael Cowley, "Relay Kings Refuse to Be Outshone," *Sydney Morning Herald*, September 20, 2000, accessed November 15, 2013, Newspaper Source Plus.

19. Growden, "Joy, Joy, Joy to Australian."

20. Cowley, "Relay Kings Refuse to Be Outshone."

21. Growden, "Joy, Joy, Joy to Australian."

22. John Huxley, "Race that Stops a Nation," *Sydney Morning Herald*, September 22, 2000, accessed August 13, 2013, Newspaper Source Plus.

23. Whitten and Collins, "Party Smashers," 28.

24. Cowley, "Relay Kings Refuse to Be Outshone."

4. 2000 U.S. WOMEN'S MEDLEY

1. Phillip Whitten, "China's Short March to Swimming Dominance: Hard Work or Drugs?" *Swimming World*, January 1994, 35.

2. Phillip Whitten, "The China Drug Controversy: What Is to Be Done?" *Swimming World*, February 1994, 29.

3. Craig Lord, "Chinese Takeout," *Swimming World*, November 1994, 60.

4. Lord, "Chinese Takeout," 60.

5. Lord, "Chinese Takeout," 60.

6. Whitten, "China's Short March to Swimming Dominance," 39.

7. Whitten, "China's Short March to Swimming Dominance," 39.

8. Whitten, "China's Short March to Swimming Dominance," 35.

9. Lord, "Chinese Takeout," 60.

10. Elliott Almond, "Chinese Woman Tests Positive, May Face Ban: Swimming: World 400-Meter Champion Found to Have Used Muscle-Building Hormone Testosterone," *Los Angeles Times*, November 17, 1994, accessed December 3, 2013, http://articles.latimes.com/1994-11-17/sports/sp-63897_1_world-champion.

11. Whitten, "China's Short March to Swimming Dominance," 35–36.

12. Jack McCallum, "Unflagging," *Sports Illustrated*, August 14, 2000, accessed August 6, 2013, http://sportsillustrated.cnn.com/vault/article/magazine/MAG1019901/index.htm.

13. Merrell Noden, "Jenny Thompson," *Sports Illustrated*, March 28, 1994, accessed August 6, 2013, http://sportsillustrated.cnn.com/vault/article/magazine/MAG1004999.

14. Jere Longman, "Swimming; U.S. Ban of Chinese Swimmers Criticized," *New York Times*, February 15, 1995, accessed August 6, 2013, http://www.nytimes.com/1995/02/15/sports/swimming-us-ban-of-chinese-swimmers-criticized.html.

15. Richard Panek, "State-Sponsored Drug Use Has Tarnished the Olympic Games," in *Drugs and Sports*, edited by William Dudley (San Diego: Greenhaven Press, 2001), 33.

16. Mike Penner, "Latest Drug Scandal Has China Critics Seeing Red," *Los Angeles Times*, January 18, 1998, accessed December 3, 2013, http://articles.latimes.com/1998/jan/18/sports/sp-9735.

17. Sharon Robb, "Regret Lingers over Pan Pacific Ban of China," *Sun-Sentinel*, August 9, 1995, accessed August 6, 2013, http://articles.sun-sentinel.com/1995-08-09/sports/9508090116_1_fina-systematic-drug-drug-testing.

18. Leigh Montville, "Wet and Wild," *Sports Illustrated*, January 19, 1998, accessed August 6, 2013, http://sportsillustrated.cnn.com/vault/article/magazine/MAG1142789.

19. Montville, "Wet and Wild."

20. Penner, "Latest Drug Scandal Has China Critics Seeing Red."

21. Montville, "Wet and Wild."

22. Philip Hersh, "For Want of a Dish of Ice Cream, a Silver Medal was Lost," *Chicago Tribune*, October 2, 1994, accessed August 9, 2013, http://articles.chicagotribune.com/1994-10-02/sports/9410020366_1_backstroke-dennis-pursley-swimming.

23. Dara Torres and Elizabeth Weil, *Age Is Just a Number: Achieve Your Dream at Any Stage in Your Life* (New York: Broadway Books, 2009), 58.

24. Filip Bondy, "Bronze Tie Won't Dampen Swim Rivalry: Thompson, Torres Make Waves in Pool and Out," *New York Daily News*, September 22, 2000, accessed August 6, 2013, http://www.nydailynews.com/archives/sports/bronze-tie-won-dampen-swim-rivalry-thompson-torres-waves-pool-article-1.886548.

25. Lisa Dillman, "Quann Adds Brash Stroke," *Los Angeles Times*, August 13, 2000, accessed August 9, 2013, http://articles.latimes.com/2000/aug/13/sports/sp-3706.

26. Lisa Olson, "Two for the Show: Dara Torres, 33, and Jenny Thompson, 27, Already Have Made Splashes with Their Comebacks, but Now It's Time for the Prime-Time Performances," *New York Daily News*, September 10, 2000, accessed August 9, 2013, http://www.nydailynews.com/archives/nydn-features/show-dara-torres-33-jenny-thompson-27-made-splashes-comebacks-time-prime-time-performances-article-1.877391.

27. Phillip Whitten and Michael Collins, "Party Smashers," *Swimming World*, October 2000, 21.

28. Elliott Almond, "U.S. Women and Men Smash World Records in 400-Meter Medley Relay," *San Jose Mercury News*, September 23, 2000, accessed August 9, 2013, Newspaper Source Plus.

29. Almond, "U.S. Women and Men Smash World Records in 400-Meter Medley Relay."

30. Bondy, "Bronze Tie Won't Dampen Swim Rivalry."

31. Almond, "U.S. Women and Men Smash World Records in 400-Meter Medley Relay."

5. 2004 U.S. MEN'S MEDLEY

1. Lynn Zinser, "Olympics: Swimming; South Africa's Relay Upset Leaves U.S., Phelps 3rd," *New York Times*, August 16, 2004, accessed August 9, 2013, http://www.nytimes.com/2004/08/16/sports/olympics-swimming-south-africa-s-relay-upset-leaves-us-and-phelps-3rd.html.

2. Zinser, "Olympics."

3. Associated Press, "Americans Fail to Reach 100 Free Final," ESPN, August 17, 2004, accessed August 24, 2013, http://sports.espn.go.com/oly/summer04/swimming/news/story?id=1860931.

4. Associated Press, "Americans Fail to Reach 100 Free Final."

5. John Lohn, "Hansen's Silver: Dolphin-Kick Controversy Dogs Gold Winner," *Delaware County Daily Times*, August 16, 2004, accessed August 24, 2013, http://www.delcotimes.com/articles/2004/08/16/sports/12702778.txt.

6. Lohn, "Hansen's Silver."

7. Lohn, "Hansen's Silver."

8. Associated Press, "Peirsol Gets Gold after All," ESPN, August 19, 2004, accessed August 20, 2013, http://sports.espn.go.com/oly/summer04/swimming/news/story?id=1862948.

9. Associated Press, "Peirsol's Disqualification Overturned, Wins Gold," *Sports Illustrated*, August 19, 2004, accessed August 20, 2013, http://sportsillustrated.cnn.com/2004/olympics/2004/swimming/08/19/peirsol.disqualified.ap.

10. Christopher Clarey, "Summer 2004 Games—Swimming: 200 Backstroke; Flip-Flop Leaves Peirsol with the Gold," *New York Times*, August 20, 2004, accessed August 20, 2013, http://www.nytimes.com/2004/08/20/sports/summer-2004-games-swimming-200-backstroke-flip-flop-leaves-peirsol-with-the-gold.html.

11. Clarey, "Summer 2004 Games."

12. Associated Press, "Peirsol Gets Gold after All."

13. Barry Svrluga, "Peirsol, Beard: Worth Their Wait in Gold," *Washington Post*, August 20, 2004, accessed August 20, 2013, http://www.washingtonpost.com/wp-dyn/articles/A15563-2004Aug19.html.

14. Clarey, "Summer 2004 Games."

15. Michael Phelps and Brian Cazeneuve, *Beneath the Surface* (Champaign, IL: Sports Publishing, 2008), 217–18.

16. Kelli Anderson, "Break out the Bubbly," *Sports Illustrated*, August 30, 2004, accessed November 14, 2012, http://sportsillustrated.cnn.com/vault/article/magazine/MAG1105891/index.htm.

17. Michael Phelps and Alan Abrahamson, *No Limits: The Will to Succeed* (New York: Free Press, 2008), 196.

18. Phelps and Cazeneuve, *Beneath the Surface*, 218.

19. Anderson, "Break out the Bubbly."

20. Phelps and Abrahamson, *No Limits*, 196.

21. Lynn Zinser, "U.S. Men Smash Record to Take the Final Gold," *New York Times*, August 22, 2004, SP8.

22. Zinser, "U.S. Men Smash Record to Take the Final Gold," SP8.

23. Zinser, "U.S. Men Smash Record to Take the Final Gold," SP8.

24. Zinser, "U.S. Men Smash Record to Take the Final Gold," SP8.

6. 2004 SOUTH AFRICAN MEN'S 400 FREESTYLE

1. Greg Hansen, "Under Busch, UA Swimming Made Waves," *Arizona Daily Star*, August 15, 2011, accessed August 13, 2013, http://azstarnet.com/sports/college/wildcats/under-busch-ua-swimming-made-waves/article_51eec756-fd47-54ee-8c8b-0d3dd41e902c.html.

2. Steve Rivera, "Tucson Connection," *Tucson Citizen*, August 5, 2004, accessed August 13, 2013, http://tucsoncitizen.com/morgue2/2004/08/05/51120-tucson-connection.

3. Lynn Zinser, "After Shaky Start, Hall Is Pleased with Finish," *New York Times*, July 12, 2004, D1.

4. "American Swimmer's Bid for 8 Golds Sinks in Relay," *Winnipeg Free Press*, August 16, 2004, Newspaper Source Plus.

5. Kelli Anderson, "Break out the Bubbly," *Sports Illustrated*, August 30, 2004, accessed August 13, 2012, http://sportsillustrated.cnn.com/vault/article/magazine/MAG1105891/index.htm.

6. Lynn Zinser, "With the Cameras Rolling, Phelps Is Set for His First Four Minutes of Fame," *New York Times*, August 14, 2004, D4.

7. Lynn Zinser, "Olympics: Swimming; South Africa's Relay Upset Leaves U.S., Phelps 3rd," *New York Times*, August 16, 2004, accessed August 9, 2013, http://www.nytimes.com/2004/08/16/sports/olympics-swimming-south-africa-s-relay-upset-leaves-us-and-phelps-3rd.html.

8. Norm Frauenheim, "Hometown Heroes," *Arizona Republic*, August 19, 2004, accessed August 13, 2013, http://tucsoncitizen.com/morgue2/2004/08/19/52997-hometown-heroes.

9. Frauenheim, "Hometown Heroes."

10. Rebecca Williams, "You Ain't Seen Neethling Yet," *Herald Sun*, March 6, 2006, Newspaper Source Plus.

11. Zinser, "Olympics."

7. 2008 U.S. MEN'S 400 FREESTYLE

1. Christine Brennan, "Phelps Always a Team Player," *USA Today*, August 12, 2008, Newspaper Source Plus.

2. Francois Thomazeau, "I'm Favorite and We'll Smash U.S.: Bernard," Reuters, August 7, 2008, accessed November 6, 2013, http://www.reuters.com/article/2008/08/07/us-olympics-swimming-bernard-idUSSP28868620080807.

3. Michael Phelps and Alan Abrahamson, *No Limits: The Will to Succeed* (New York: Free Press, 2008), 60–61.

4. Pat Forde, "Handicapping Phelps' Run at Olympic Glory," ESPN, August 17, 2008, accessed November 6, 2013, http://sports.espn.go.com/oly/summer08/columns/story?columnist=forde_pat&id=3524709.

5. Phelps and Abrahamson, *No Limits*, 92.

6. Karen Crouse, "A Swim for the Ages by a Team's Oldest Racer," *New York Times*, August 12, 2008, D1.

7. Henry Araton, "Looking All Too Human in Superhuman Quest," *New York Times*, August 16, 2008, D1.

8. Karen Crouse, "Teammate Puts on a Show to Keep Phelps Pursuit Alive," *New York Times*, August 11, 2008, D1.

9. Phelps and Abrahamson, *No Limits*, 92.

10. NBC Sports, "Men's 4 × 100 Freestyle Relay 2008 Olympics (Full Race)," 2008, video clip, accessed December 15, 2013, YouTube, http://www.youtube.com/watch?v=sVZrne7X5ww.

11. Phelps and Abrahamson, *No Limits*, 61.

12. Phelps and Abrahamson, *No Limits*, 1.

13. Susan Casey, "Gold Mind," *Sports Illustrated*, August 18, 2008, accessed August 13, 2013, http://sportsillustrated.cnn.com/vault/article/magazine/MAG1143980/index.htm.

14. Phelps and Abrahamson, *No Limits*, 2–3.

15. Crouse, "A Swim for the Ages by a Team's Oldest Racer," D1.

16. Crouse, "A Swim for the Ages by a Team's Oldest Racer," D1.

17. George Vecsey, "A Medal Chase Ignored by Phelps, Watched Closely by Everyone Else," *New York Times*, August 11, 2008, D7.

18. Araton, "Looking All Too Human in Superhuman Quest," D1.

19. Araton, "Looking All Too Human in Superhuman Quest," D1.

20. Kristen Heiss, "Life after the Olympics with Garret Weber-Gale," *Swimming World*, November 27, 2008, accessed August 24, 2013, http://www.swimmingworldmagazine.com/lane9/news/19693.asp.

21. John Lohn, "Olympics, Swimming: Flash United States Crushes World Record in 400 Free Relay, Eamon Sullivan Claims 100 Free Global Standard," *Swimming World*, August 10, 2008, accessed August 23, 2013, http://www.swimmingworldmagazine.com/lane9/news/18757.asp.

22. Phelps and Abrahamson, *No Limits*, 93.

8. 2012 FRENCH MEN'S 400 FREESTYLE

1. Dhananjay Khadilkar, "The Towering Face of French Swimming," *New York Times*, August 21, 2013, accessed August 24, 2013, http://www.nytimes.com/2013/08/22/sports/olympics/-Yannick-Agnel-is-leading-a-renaissance-in-French-swimming.html.

2. Derek Parr, "Hard Work Drives Frenchman Bernard to World Records," Reuters, March 22, 2008, accessed August 24, 2013, http://uk.reuters.com/article/2008/03/22/uk-swimming-europe-bernard-idUKL2265840220080322.

3. Francois Thomazeau, "I'm Favorite and We'll Smash U.S.: Bernard," Reuters, August 7, 2008, accessed November 6, 2013, http://www.reuters.com/article/2008/08/07/us-olympics-swimming-bernard-idUSSP28868620080807.

4. Associated Press, "What a Race! U.S. Wins Swim Relay by a Finger," ConnectTriStates.com, August 12, 2008, accessed August 24, 2013, http://www.connecttristates.com/sports/sports_story.aspx?id=173516#.UhlpLj_OD-A.

5. Joe Posnanski, "France's Bernard Finds Salvation in 100-Meter Freestyle," *Kansas City Star*, August 13, 2008, accessed August 24, 2013, http://www.mcclatchydc.com/2008/08/13/48112/frances-bernard-finds-salvation.html#.UhlpMT_OD-A.

6. Karen Crouse, "A Victory Can't Erase a Defeat in Beijing," *New York Times*, May 19, 2009, B13.

7. Crouse, "A Victory Can't Erase a Defeat in Beijing," B13.

8. Crouse, "A Victory Can't Erase a Defeat in Beijing," B13.

9. John Lohn, "U.S. 400 Freestyle Relay Could Be in Big Trouble," *Swimming World*, June 28, 2012, accessed August 24, 2013, http://www.swimmingworldmagazine.com/lane9/news/USA/31030.asp.

10. Kevin Armstrong, "France's Yannick Agnel Catches Ryan Lochte in Final Leg of 4 × 100-Meter Freestyle Relay as U.S. Finishes Second," *New York Daily News*, July 29, 2012, accessed November 8, 2013, http://www.nydailynews.com/sports/olympics-2012/frances-

yannick-agnel-catches-ryan-lochte-final-leg-4x100-meter-freestyle-relay-u-s-finishes-article-1. 1124447.

11. John Lohn, "France Gets Revenge," *Swimming World*, July 29, 2012, accessed August 24, 2013, http://www.swimmingworldmagazine.com/lane9/news/USA/31448.asp.

12. Armstrong, "France's Yannick Agnel Catches Ryan Lochte."

13. Armstrong, "France's Yannick Agnel Catches Ryan Lochte."

14. Tim Layden, "Phelps, U.S. Fail to Recreate Beijing Magic, Drop Silver in 400 Relay," *Sports Illustrated*, July 29, 2012, accessed November 8, 2013, http://sportsillustrated.cnn.com/2012/olympics/2012/writers/tim_layden/07/29/france-us-400-relay-olympics/index.html.

15. Layden, "Phelps, U.S. Fail to Recreate Beijing Magic."

16. Karen Crouse, "This Time, It's the U.S. Overtaken for the Gold," *New York Times*, July 29, 2012, accessed November 8, 2013, http://www.nytimes.com/2012/07/30/sports/olympics/phelps-lochte-and-the-us-fall-to-french-in-the-400-relay.html?_r=0.

17. Agence France-Presse, "Olympic Swimming: France Engineers Epic Upset over Phelps, Lochte-Led USA," *InterAksyon*, July 30, 2012, accessed November 5, 2013, http://www.interaksyon.com/interaktv/olympic-swimming-france-engineers-epic-upset-over-phelps-lochte-led-usa.

18. Lohn, "France Gets Revenge."

9. 1924 U.S. OLYMPIANS

1. "U.S. Girl Swimmers Gain Olympic Final," *New York Times*, July 15, 1924, 20.

2. "U.S. Swimmers Win 2 Olympic Finals," *New York Times*, July 18, 1924, 8.

3. "U.S. Team Clinches Olympic Swim Title," *New York Times*, July 19, 1924, 5.

4. "U.S. Takes 6 Finals; Wins Olympic Swim," *New York Times*, July 21, 1924, 6.

5. "U.S. Takes 6 Finals; Wins Olympic Swim," 6.

6. "U.S. Takes 6 Finals; Wins Olympic Swim," 6.

7. Paul Gallico, *The Golden People* (Garden City: Doubleday, 1964), 224.

8. Arlene Mueller, "Johnny Weissmuller Made Olympian Efforts to Conceal His Birthplace," *Sports Illustrated*, August 6, 1984, accessed October 13, 2013, http://sportsillustrated.cnn.com/vault/article/magazine/MAG1122383/index.htm.

9. "Comment on Current Events in Sports," *New York Times*, April 3, 1922, 18.

10. "Comment on Current Events in Sports," *New York Times*, June 11, 1923, 11.

11. Cecil M. Colwin, *Swimming Dynamics: Winning Techniques and Strategies* (Chicago: Masters Press, 1999), 119.

12. Jim Gullo, "The Beloved Duke of Waikiki," *Sports Illustrated*, September 17, 1990, accessed October 11, 2013, http://sportsillustrated.cnn.com/vault/article/magazine/MAG1136450/index.htm.

13. Gullo, "The Beloved Duke of Waikiki."

14. Gullo, "The Beloved Duke of Waikiki."

15. Gullo, "The Beloved Duke of Waikiki."

16. "'Weissmuller Is Greatest Swimmer,' Says Kahanamoku," *New York Times*, July 15, 1922, 10.

17. Glenn Stout, *Young Woman and the Sea: How Trudy Ederle Conquered the English Channel and Inspired the World* (New York: Houghton Mifflin Harcourt, 2009), 45.

18. Colwin, *Swimming Dynamics*, 119.

19. Stout, *Young Woman and the Sea*, 110.

20. Stout, *Young Woman and the Sea*, 162.

21. Richard Severo, "Gertrude Ederle, the First Woman to Swim across the English Channel, Dies at 98," *New York Times*, December 1, 2003, accessed October 11, 2013, http://www.nytimes.com/2003/12/01/sports/gertrude-ederle-the-first-woman-to-swim-across-the-english-channel-dies-at-98.html?pagewanted=all&src=pm.

22. Michael K. Bohn, *Heroes & Ballyhoo: How the Golden Age of the 1920s Transformed American Sports* (Washington, DC: Potomac Books, 2009), 110.

10. 1950S HUNGARIAN WOMEN'S OLYMPIANS

1. "Alfred Hajos," Olympic.org, accessed October 10, 2013, http://www.olympic.org/alfred-hajos.

2. Bill Mallon and Jeroen Heijmans, *Historical Dictionary of the Olympic Movement* (Lanham, MD: Scarecrow, 2011), 152.

3. Camillo Cametti, "A 113 Year Long Success Story," Federation Internationale de Natation, 2011, accessed September 17, 2013, http://www.fina.org/H2O/index.php?option=com_content&view=article&id=1144:a-113-year-long-success-story-&catid=225:highlight&Itemid=179.

4. "Name Change Helps Katalin, Helsinki 1952," MSN Sport, February 7, 2012, accessed September 19, 2013, http://sport.uk.msn.com/olympics-2012/news/articles.aspx?cp-documentid=250442230.

5. "Eva Szekely, Swimming," *Haaretz*, July 12, 2005, accessed September 20, 2013, http://www.haaretz.com/news/eva-szekely-swimming-1.163648.

6. Joe O'Connor, "Valerie Gyenge," *National Post*, December 2, 2006, accessed September 19, 2013, http://www.hungarianpresence.ca/sports/valerie-gyenge.cfm.

7. O'Connor, "Valerie Gyenge."

8. Jennifer Quinn, "Of Love and Water," *Toronto Star*, February 12, 2005, E1.

9. Marton Dunai, "Feature—Olympics—Water Polo's Gyarmati Recalls Last London Games," Reuters, March 12, 2012, accessed September 20, 2012, http://www.reuters.com/article/2012/03/12/olympics-waterpolo-idUSL5E8EC1KJ20120312.

10. Dunai, "Feature—Olympics—Water Polo's Gyarmati Recalls Last London Games."

11. Quinn, "Of Love and Water," E1.

12. Bryan Dawson, "Hungarian Olympic Triumph," American Hungarian Foundation, accessed September 19, 2013, http://www.americanhungarianfederation.org/FamousHungarians/olympic_1952.htm.

13. Alexander Wolff, "The Revolution Games," *Sports Illustrated*, June 18, 2012, accessed September 27, 2013, http://sportsillustrated.cnn.com/2012/magazine/06/13/hungarians/index.html.

14. Simon Burnton, "50 Stunning Olympic Moments No. 7: Hungary v Soviet Union: Blood in the Water," *The Guardian*, December 28, 2011, accessed September 10, 2013, http://www.theguardian.com/sport/blog/2011/dec/28/olympic-hungary-soviet-union-blood-water.

15. O'Connor, "Valerie Gyenge."

16. Dawson, "Hungarian Olympic Triumph."

17. Wolff, "The Revolution Games."

18. Lesley Ciarula Taylor, "Olympian Defected for Love, Thrills . . . and a Free Ticket from the Star," *Toronto Star*, June 1, 2009, accessed September 20, 2013, http://www.thestar.com/news/gta/2009/06/01/olympian_defected_for_love_thrills_and_a_free_ticket_from_the_star.html.

19. Sterling Slappey, "Many Hungarian Stars Won't Be Going Home," *Windsor Daily Star*, December 3, 1956, 23.

20. Dunai, "Feature—Olympics—Water Polo's Gyarmati Recalls Last London Games."

11. 1968 U.S. OLYMPIANS

1. Arthur Daley, "Sports of the Times: The Golden Boy," *New York Times*, October 11, 1968, S8.

2. Frank Litsky, "U.S. Expected to Win the Most Medals (112) and the Most Gold Medals (43)," *New York Times*, October 6, 1968, S7.

3. Bob Ottum, "Fresh, Fair and Golden," *Sports Illustrated*, November 4, 1968, accessed October 14, 2013, http://sportsillustrated.cnn.com/vault/article/magazine/MAG1081761/index.htm.

4. Bill Becker, "U.S. Olympic Swim Girls Hailed," *New York Times*, August 30, 1968, 41.

5. Becker, "U.S. Olympic Swim Girls Hailed," 41.

6. Emerson Chapin, "Coach Hails U.S. Swim Team, Rates It Unmatchable in Future," *New York Times*, October 19, 1964, 41.

7. Sherm Chavoor and Bill Davidson, *The 50-Meter Jungle: How Olympic Gold Medal Swimmers Are Made* (New York: Coward, McCann and Geoghegan, 1973), 57.

8. Neil Amdur, "Olympic Swimmers Thrive on Training Grind and Keep Their Whimsy," *New York Times*, September 29, 1968, S4.

9. Richard J. Foster, *Mark Spitz: The Extraordinary Life of an Olympic Champion* (Santa Monica: Santa Monica Press, 2008), 51.

10. Chavoor and Davidson, *The 50-Meter Jungle*, 76.

11. Ottum, "Fresh, Fair and Golden."

12. Ottum, "Fresh, Fair and Golden."

13. Foster, *Mark Spitz*, 60.

14. Foster, *Mark Spitz*, 63.

15. "Victories and Trauma at Mexico 68," *Swimming World*, October 1968, 7.

16. "Victories and Trauma at Mexico 68," 9.

17. "Victories and Trauma at Mexico 68," 13.

18. "Victories and Trauma at Mexico 68," 14.

19. Frank Fitzpatrick, "Carl J. Robie III, 66, Olympic Swimming Champion," *Philadelphia Inquirer*, February 12, 2011, Newspaper Source Plus.

20. Fitzpatrick, "Carl J. Robie III."

21. "Victories and Trauma at Mexico 68," 18.

22. "Victories and Trauma at Mexico 68," 15.

23. Neil Amdur, "U.S. Wins 3 Swimming and 2 Boxing Gold Medals," *New York Times*, October 27, 1968, S1.

24. Joseph M. Sheehan, "U.S. Swimmers Shatter World Marks in Taking Men's and Women's Relays," *New York Times*, October 18, 1968, 55.

25. Neil Amdur, "Kaye Hall Brakes World Swim Mark as U.S. Captures 6 More Gold," *New York Times*, October 24, 1968, 61.

26. "Victories and Trauma at Mexico 68," 15.

27. "Pokey Watson, Claudia Kolb Gain 2 More Swimming Gold Medals for U.S.," *New York Times*, October 26, 1968, 44.

28. Steve Cady, "Cheers for an American Monopoly," *New York Times*, October 25, 1968, 54.

29. Amdur, "U.S. Wins 3 Swimming and 2 Boxing Gold Medals," S1.

30. Ottum, "Fresh, Fair and Golden."

12. 1973 EAST GERMAN WOMEN'S WORLD CHAMPIONSHIPS

1. Bob Ingram and Nick Thierry, "Women's Events," *Swimming World*, October 1973, 14.

2. Ingram and Thierry, "Women's Events," 16.

3. Ingram and Thierry, "Women's Events," 16.

4. Ingram and Thierry, "Women's Events," 18.

5. Al Schoenfield, "A New Era in Swimming," *Swimming World*, October 1973, 8.

6. Ingram and Thierry, "Women's Events," 18.

7. Schoenfield, "A New Era in Swimming," 3.

8. Bernard Kirsch, "On Surface, U.S. Swim Domination Has Gone Down," *New York Times*, September 2, 1973, 156.

9. Jule Campbell, "Light, Tight and Right for Racing," *Sports Illustrated*, August 12, 1974, accessed November 17, 2012, http://sportsillustrated.cnn.com/vault/article/magazine/MAG1088870/index.htm.

10. Campbell, "Light, Tight and Right for Racing."

11. Donna De Varona, "East Germany's Secret: Almost Everyone Can Get in the Swim," *New York Times*, September 1, 1974, 2S.

12. De Varona, "East Germany's Secret," 2S.

13. Bernard Kirsch, "E. Germans and U.S. Set Swim Pace," *New York Times*, September 6, 1973, 45.

14. Jean Pierre LaCour, "Why Are the East Germans So Good?," *Swimming World*, October 1972, 33.

15. Schoenfield, "A New Era in Swimming," 4.

16. LaCour, "Why Are the East Germans So Good?," 33.

17. De Varona, "East Germany's Secret," 2S.

18. Kenny Moore, "Babashoff and Ender," *Sports Illustrated*, July 13, 1992, accessed November 18, 2012, http://sportsillustrated.cnn.com/vault/article/magazine/MAG1003984/index.htm.

13. 1976 U.S. MEN'S OLYMPIANS

1. Mark Merfeld, "U.S. Olympic Trials: Records . . . and Tears Fall on Road to Montreal," *Swimming World*, July 1976, #.

2. Jerry Kirshenbaum, "Theirs Was a Midas Stroke," *Sports Illustrated*, August 2, 1976, accessed October 2, 2013, http://sportsillustrated.cnn.com/vault/article/magazine/MAG1091375/index.htm.

3. Mark Merfeld, "Men's Events," *Swimming World*, September 1976, 49.

4. Kirshenbaum, "Theirs Was a Midas Stroke."

5. Merfeld, "Men's Events," 65.

6. Merfeld, "Men's Events," 49.

7. Merfeld, "Men's Events," 66.

8. Frank Litsky, "U.S. Men Smash 3 World Swim Marks and Capture 2 Gold Medals in Olympics," *New York Times*, July 20, 1976, 25.

9. Merfeld, "Men's Events," 58.

10. Merfeld, "Men's Events," 59.

11. Merfeld, "Men's Events," 53.

12. Merfeld, "Men's Events," 56.

13. Merfeld, "Men's Events," 51.

14. Merfeld, "Men's Events," 52.

15. Merfeld, "Men's Events," 49.

16. Brendan Gallagher, "Inspired Wilkie Left the World in His Wake Thirty Years On, Britain's Montreal Hero Recalls His Glorious Olympic Triumph with Brendan Gallagher," *Daily Telegraph*, July 24, 2006, 20.

17. Gallagher, "Inspired Wilkie Left the World in His Wake Thirty Years On," 20.

18. Jim Scott, "Hero Wilkie Dived in at the Sleep End; Sports Person Millennium," *The Sun*, November 30, 1999, 46.

19. Merfeld, "Men's Events," 50.

20. Merfeld, "Men's Events," 69.

21. Merfeld, "Men's Events," 71.

22. Al Schoenfield, "Looking Ahead to Russia," *Swimming World*, September 1976, 5.

23. Merfeld, "Men's Events," 49.

14. 1980 U.S. OLYMPIANS

1. Richard Espy, *The Politics of the Olympic Games* (Berkeley: University of California Press, 1981), 190.

2. Espy, *The Politics of the Olympic Games*, 194.

3. Jimmy Carter, "Remarks to Representatives of U.S. Teams to the 1980 Summer Olympics" (speech, March 21, 1980), American Presidency Project, http://www.presidency.ucsb.edu/ws/?pid=33171.

4. Chris Georges, "Flying in the Face of a Boycott," *Swimming World*, May 1980, 16.

5. Georges, "Flying in the Face of a Boycott," 16.

6. Craig R. Whitney, "3rd Gold for Salnikov; Soviet Team Upset," *New York Times*, July 25, 1980, A1.

7. Frank Litsky, "Bruner Finally Gets a Swim Title in 400," *New York Times*, August 1, 1980, A15.

8. Frank Litsky, "U.S. Swimmers Agree: Olympic Trials Not Real Thing," *New York Times*, August 4, 1980, C5.

9. Frank Litsky, "Salnikov's Supremacy Questioned," *New York Times*, July 25, 1980, A16.

10. Litsky, "U.S. Swimmers Agree," C5.

11. Craig Neff, "The U.S. Is Back . . . and How!" *Sports Illustrated*, August 13, 1984, accessed November 26, 2012, http://sportsillustrated.cnn.com/vault/article/magazine/MAG1122401/index.htm.

12. Chris Georges, "Delayed Dreams," *Swimming World*, September 1984, 23.

13. Neff, "The U.S. Is Back . . . and How!"

14. Frank Litsky, "Goodell Is Happy to Retire," *New York Times*, April 20, 1981, C9.

15. Tom Caraccioli and Jerry Caraccioli, *Boycott: Stolen Dreams of the 1980 Moscow Olympic Games* (New York: New Chapter Press, 2008), 71.

16. Caraccioli and Caraccioli, *Boycott*, 78.

17. Mark Muckenfuss, "All That Glitters Isn't Gold," *Swimming World*, September 1984, 28.

18. Frank Litsky, "World Record Set in 200-Meter Butterfly," *New York Times*, July 31, 1980, D17.

15. 1992 UNIFIED OLYMPIANS

1. Associated Press, "12 Former Soviet Republics to Have Unified Team Again," *Los Angeles Times*, March 10, 1992, accessed October 22, 2013, http://articles.latimes.com/1992-03-10/sports/sp-3510_1_unified-team.

2. Associated Press, "12 Former Soviet Republics to Have Unified Team Again."

3. Steven Erlanger, "Olympics; Unified Team Faces Splintered Future," *New York Times*, July 19, 1992, accessed September 25, 2013, http://www.nytimes.com/1992/07/19/sports/olympics-unified-team-faces-splintered-future.html?pagewanted=all&src=pm.

4. Gary Smith, "Let the Games Begin," *Sports Illustrated*, August 3, 1992, accessed September 25, 2013, http://sportsillustrated.cnn.com/vault/article/magazine/MAG1004055/index.htm.

5. Serge Schmemann, "A Unified Feeling of Ambivalence: Russians Ponder Olympic Success," *New York Times*, February 25, 1992, B12.

6. Schmemann, "A Unified Feeling of Ambivalence," B12.

7. Schmemann, "A Unified Feeling of Ambivalence," B12.

8. Michael Janofsky, "For Russians, the Quest for Money Comes before the Quest for Gold," *New York Times*, May 6, 1992, B24.

9. Janofsky, "For Russians, the Quest for Money Comes before the Quest for Gold," B24.

10. Gerald Eskenazi, "As the Flame Flickers, a Sense That Sport Will Never Be the Same," *New York Times*, August 7, 1992, B9.

11. Schmemann, "A Unified Feeling of Ambivalence," B12.

12. Leigh Montville, "World Beaters," *Sports Illustrated*, August 10, 1992, accessed September 25, 2013, http://sportsillustrated.cnn.com/vault/article/magazine/MAG1004076/index.htm.

13. Erlanger, "Olympics; Unified Team Faces Splintered Future."

14. Erlanger, "Olympics; Unified Team Faces Splintered Future."

15. William Oscar Johnson and Jeff Lilley, "Swimmers for Sale," *Sports Illustrated*, August 10, 1992, accessed September 25, 2013, http://sportsillustrated.cnn.com/vault/article/magazine/MAG1004082/index.htm.

16. Johnson and Lilley, "Swimmers for Sale."

17. Russ Ewald, "The Russian Capitalists," *Swimming World*, March 1994, 38.

18. Johnson and Lilley, "Swimmers for Sale."

19. Johnson and Lilley, "Swimmers for Sale."

20. Johnson and Lilley, "Swimmers for Sale."

21. Johnson and Lilley, "Swimmers for Sale."

22. Johnson and Lilley, "Swimmers for Sale."

23. Sharon Robb, "U.S. Duo Upended in 50 Free," *Fort Lauderdale Sun-Sentinel*, July 31, 1992, accessed September 26, 2013, http://articles.orlandosentinel.com/1992-07-31/sports/9207310656_1_matt-biondi-tom-jager-alexander-popov.

24. Bob Ingram, "Party in the Pool," *Swimming World*, September 1992, 38.

25. Ingram, "Party in the Pool," 41.

26. Ingram, "Party in the Pool," 71.

27. Filip Bondy, "Barcelona: Swimming; American Male Swimmers Come Back in Waves," *New York Times*, July 30, 1992, accessed October 22, 2013, http://www.nytimes.com/1992/07/30/sports/barcelona-swimming-american-male-swimmers-come-back-in-waves.html.

28. Steven Erlanger, "Break Up the Unifieds? It's Now History," *New York Times*, August 12, 1992, B13.

29. Filip Bondy, "A Good Day for the U.S., but It's Popov at Head of the Fleet," *New York Times*, July 31, 1992, A1.

30. Christopher Clarey, "A Dolphin Swimming with the Sharks," *New York Times*, July 14, 1996, SO5.

31. Erlanger, "Break Up the Unifieds?"

32. Ewald, "The Russian Capitalists," 38.

16. 2001 AUSTRALIAN WORLD CHAMPIONSHIPS

1. Cecil M. Colwin, *Swimming into the 21st Century* (Champaign, IL: Human Kinetics, 1992), 194.

2. Bill Bell, "International Review: Thorpe May Be the Best Ever," *Swimming World*, April 8, 2001, accessed December 31, 2012, http://www.swimmingworldmagazine.com/lane9/news/2410.asp.

3. Duncan Armstrong, "Cheering on Thorpedo Will Be a Major Blast," *Sun-Herald*, July 22, 2001, Newspaper Source Plus.

4. Wayne Smith, "No Swim for Klim—Champ out of World Titles," *Sunday Telegraph*, July 8, 2001, Newspaper Source Plus.

5. Chloe Saltau, "Healthy Hackett Ready for Next Step," *The Age*, July 16, 2001, Newspaper Source Plus.

6. Michael Cowley, "Thorpe's Poised to Conquer the World," *Sun-Herald*, July 22, 2001, Newspaper Source Plus.

7. Nicole Jeffrey, "Finally, Petria Top of the World," *The Australian*, July 24, 2001, Newspaper Source Plus.

8. Janelle Miles, "Swim: Australians Catch Thorpemania Wave," AAP Australian Sports News Wire, July 20, 2001, Newspaper Source Plus.

9. Craig Lord, "Thorpe Sets WR, Wins Two Gold on First Day of Competition at World Champs," *Swimming World*, July 22, 2001, accessed October 10, 2013, http://www.swimmingworldmagazine.com/lane9/news/2724.asp.

10. Jeffrey, "Finally, Petria Top of the World."

11. Chloe Saltau, "Matt's Joy at Getting Monkey Off His Back," *Sydney Morning Herald*, July 24, 2001, Newspaper Source Plus.

12. Craig Lord, "Fukuoka Feast," *Swimming World*, September 2001, 19.

13. Dennis Passa, "Australian Swim Team Disqualified," Associated Press, July 25, 2001, Newspaper Source Plus.

14. Michael Cowley, "Ervin Wins as Science Loses Touch," *Sydney Morning Herald*, July 28, 2001, Newspaper Source Plus.

15. Wayne Smith, "Fantastic Four Grabs Record," *Herald Sun*, July 28, 2001, Newspaper Source Plus.

16. Lord, "Fukuoka Feast," 18.

17. Wayne Smith, "Greatest; Hackett Smashes 1500m Record as Aussies Top World," *Herald Sun*, July 30, 2001, Newspaper Source Plus.

18. "Women's Swim Team Not Good as Gould," *Illawarra Mercury*, July 30, 2001, Newspaper Source Plus.

19. Smith, "Greatest."

20. Smith, "Greatest."

21. Smith, "Greatest."

22. "American Swimmers Still Claim Mantle," *The Mercury*, August 1, 2001, Newspaper Source Plus.

17. 1930S JAPANESE MEN

1. Cecil M. Colwin, *Swimming into the 21st Century* (Champaign, IL: Human Kinetics, 1992), 185.

2. Arthur J. Daley, "Sports of the Times: Back with a Splash," *New York Times*, August 17, 1949, 31.

3. Daley, "Sports of the Times: Back with a Splash," 31.

4. Bob Kiphuth, "Japanese Swimmers Regarded as Real Threat to American Olympic Hopes by U.S. Coach," *New York Times*, July 27, 1932, 14.

5. Cecil M. Colwin, *Swimming Dynamics: Winning Techniques and Strategies* (Chicago: Masters Press, 1999), 201.

6. "Japan's Swimmer Shone in Olympics," *New York Times*, December 25, 1932, S3.

7. Allison Danzig, "Japan's Natators Impress Observers," *New York Times*, August 8, 1932, 19.

8. Arthur J. Daley, "Japan's Swimmers Annex Team Crown," *New York Times*, August 14, 1932, S1.

9. Daley, "Japan's Swimmers Annex Team Crown," S1.

10. Albion Ross, "Upset Triumph in Olympic 100-Meter Swim Final Scored by Csik of Hungary," *New York Times*, August 10, 1936, 13.

11. Albion Ross, "U.S. Divers Sweep First Three Places as Japanese Clip World Relay Mark," *New York Times*, August 12, 1936, 22.

12. Albion Ross, "Japanese Men Second," *New York Times*, August 13, 1936, S1.

13. Ross, "U.S. Divers Sweep First Three Places," 22.

14. Ross, "U.S. Divers Sweep First Three Places," 22.

15. William Oscar Johnson, "A Star Was Born," *Sports Illustrated*, July 18, 1984, accessed October 11, 2013, http://sportsillustrated.cnn.com/vault/article/magazine/MAG1122298/2/index.htm.

16. Daley, "Sports of the Times: Back with a Splash," 31.

17. Johnson, "A Star Was Born."

18. Colwin, *Swimming Dynamics*, 203.

19. Colwin, *Swimming Dynamics*, 291.

20. Colwin, *Swimming Dynamics*, 201.

21. Forbes Carlile, "A History of Crawl Stroke Techniques to the 1960s: An Australian Perspective: Section IV," *Swimming Science Bulletin*, accessed August 27, 2013, http://coachsci.sdsu.edu/swim/bullets/carlhis4.htm.

22. Carlile, "A History of Crawl Stroke Techniques to the 1960s."

23. Carlile, "A History of Crawl Stroke Techniques to the 1960s."

24. Ed Odeven, "Swim Legend Furuhashi Inspired Japan at Tough Time," *Japan Times*, August 9, 2009, accessed August 29, 2013, http://www.japantimes.co.jp/sports/2009/08/09/general/swim-legend-furuhashi-inspired-japan-at-tough-time/#.UiAQ0j_OD-A.

18. 1950S AUSTRALIANS

1. Charles F. Pollak, "Sports of the Crimson," *Harvard Crimson*, January 17, 1939, accessed November 22, 2013, http://www.thecrimson.com/article/1939/1/17/sports-of-the-crimson-pharvards-swimming.

2. Coles Phinizy and Fred Hubbard, "The Host Is Best," *Sports Illustrated*, November 19, 1956, accessed October 22, 2013, http://sportsillustrated.cnn.com/vault/article/magazine/MAG1128519.

3. Forbes Carlile, "The Australian Revival: Section VI," *Swimming Science Bulletin*, accessed August 27, 2013, http://coachsci.sdsu.edu/swim/bullets/carlhis6.htm.

4. Carlile, "The Australian Revival."

5. Phinizy and Hubbard, "The Host Is Best."

6. Arthur Daley, "Sports of the Times: A Big Splash," *New York Times*, December 11, 1956, 64.

7. Robert Alden, "Aussies Expect to Do Swimmingly in Games," *New York Times*, November 6, 1956, 51.

8. Robert Alden, "Breen and Rose Ready for Swim," *New York Times*, December 7, 1956, 44.

9. Phinizy and Hubbard, "The Host Is Best."

10. "Aussie Swim Ace Hopes to Attend U.S. College," *New York Times*, February 17, 1957, S4.

11. Daley, "Sports of the Times: A Big Splash," 64.

12. "Rose Keeps Title in 400 Free-Style," *New York Times*, September 1, 1960, 19.

13. Arthur Daley, "Sports of the Times: The Strange Case of Murray Rose," *New York Times*, August 5, 1964, 30.

19. INDIANA UNIVERSITY MEN

1. Cecil M. Colwin, *Swimming into the 21st Century* (Champaign, IL: Human Kinetics, 1992), xv.

2. "When Doc Talks, Swimmers Gain," *New York Times*, April 26, 1964, S4.

3. Cecil M. Colwin, *Swimming Dynamics: Winning Techniques and Strategies* (Chicago: Masters Press, 1999), 265.

4. Colwin, *Swimming into the 21st Century*, 24.

5. Ray Cave, "Swim! Swim Till It Hurts," *Sports Illustrated*, August 1, 1960, accessed September 27, 2013, http://sportsillustrated.cnn.com/vault/article/magazine/MAG1071615/index.htm.

6. Cave, "Swim! Swim Till It Hurts."

7. Kelli Anderson, "Stroke of Genius," *Sports Illustrated*, April 26, 2004, accessed September 27, 2013, http://sportsillustrated.cnn.com/vault/article/magazine/MAG1031851/index.htm.

8. Colwin, *Swimming Dynamics*, 271.

9. William F. Reed, "They Sent the Boys to Do a Man's Work," *Sports Illustrated*, April 7, 1969, accessed September 29, 2013, http://sportsillustrated.cnn.com/vault/article/magazine/MAG1082265/index.htm.

10. William F. Reed, "It's the Hoosier Title Wave," *Sports Illustrated*, March 22, 1971, accessed September 29, 2013, http://sportsillustrated.cnn.com/vault/article/magazine/MAG1135536/index.htm.

11. Arlie W. Schardt, "Jamboree by Jastremski," *Sports Illustrated*, January 29, 1962, accessed September 27, 2013, http://sportsillustrated.cnn.com/vault/article/magazine/MAG1073477/index.htm.

12. Colwin, *Swimming Dynamics*, 271.

13. Ray Kennedy, "Go for the Gold, Doc," *Sports Illustrated*, September 24, 1979, accessed September 27, 2013, http://sportsillustrated.cnn.com/vault/article/magazine/MAG1095399/index.htm.

14. Colwin, *Swimming Dynamics*, 200.

15. Reed, "It's the Hoosier Title Wave."

16. Camille Bersamin, "Chet Jastremski, Breaststroker," *Sports Illustrated*, April 2, 2001, accessed September 27, 2013, http://sportsillustrated.cnn.com/vault/article/magazine/MAG1022173/index.htm.

17. Schardt, "Jamboree by Jastremski."

18. Tom C. Brody, "Indiana Wins the Big One Big," *Sports Illustrated*, April 8, 1968, accessed September 27, 2013, http://sportsillustrated.cnn.com/vault/article/magazine/MAG1081028/index.htm.

19. William F. Reed, "Q. What Makes Charlie Swim? A. Jelly Beans," *Sports Illustrated*, March 24, 1969, accessed September 27, 2013, http://sportsillustrated.cnn.com/vault/article/magazine/MAG1082215/index.htm.

20. Cave, "Swim! Swim Till It Hurts."

21. William F. Reed, "Swimming Isn't Everything, Winning Is," *Sports Illustrated*, March 9, 1970, accessed September 29, 2013, http://sportsillustrated.cnn.com/vault/article/magazine/MAG1083400/index.htm.

22. Reed, "Swimming Isn't Everything, Winning Is."

23. "They Brought It Home," *Swimming World*, April 1964, 6.

24. Tom C. Brody, "Indiana Wins the Big One Big," *Sports Illustrated*, April 8, 1968, accessed September 27, 2013, http://sportsillustrated.cnn.com/vault/article/magazine/MAG1081028/index.htm.

25. Brody, "Indiana Wins the Big One Big."

26. Reed, "They Sent the Boys to Do a Man's Work."

27. Reed, "They Sent the Boys to Do a Man's Work."

28. Reed, "They Sent the Boys to Do a Man's Work."

29. Reed, "It's the Hoosier Title Wave."

30. Bob Hammel, "Six Straight for Indiana," *Swimming World*, March 1973, 15.

31. Jerry Kirshenbaum, "Big Orange Country Sees Red," *Sports Illustrated*, April 2, 1973, accessed September 30, 2013, http://sportsillustrated.cnn.com/vault/article/magazine/MAG1087199/index.htm.

32. Jerry Kirshenbaum, "Yes, We Are Believers," *Sports Illustrated*, April 7, 1975, accessed September 30, 2013, http://sportsillustrated.cnn.com/vault/article/magazine/MAG1089707/2/index.htm.

33. Anderson, "Stroke of Genius."

20. MISSION VIEJO NADADORES

1. Daniel Chambliss, *Champions: The Making of Olympic Swimmers* (New York: Morrow, 1988), 21.

2. Chambliss, *Champions*, 47.

3. Jerry Kirshenbaum, "They're Pooling Their Talent," *Sports Illustrated*, July 10, 1978, accessed September 30, 2013, http://sportsillustrated.cnn.com/vault/article/magazine/MAG1093851/index.htm.

4. Chambliss, *Champions*, 32.

5. Kirshenbaum, "They're Pooling Their Talent."

6. Sarah Pileggi, "Up from Plop, Plop," *Sports Illustrated*, June 21, 1976, accessed September 30, 2013, http://sportsillustrated.cnn.com/vault/article/magazine/MAG1091228/index.htm.

7. Kirshenbaum, "They're Pooling Their Talent."

8. Kirshenbaum, "They're Pooling Their Talent."

9. Craig Neff, "A Pinch of T.L.C. for L.A.," *Sports Illustrated*, May 28, 1984, accessed September 30, 2013, http://sportsillustrated.cnn.com/vault/article/magazine/MAG1122123/index.htm.

10. Neff, "A Pinch of T.L.C. for L.A."

11. Chambliss, *Champions*, 39.

12. Chuck Mulling, "The Swimmers on Mission of Greatness," *Gainesville Sun*, April 11, 1982, 4D.

13. Bob Goff, "Mission Viejo Nadadores Swim Team: A Success Story," *Swimming World*, January 1975, 6.

14. Al Schoenfield, "Nationals: Shaw, Babashoff Lead Record Parade," *Swimming World*, September 1974, 33.

15. Chambliss, *Champions*, 30.

16. Bob Ingram and Russ Ewald, "Mission Accomplished," *Swimming World*, September 1985, 26.

17. Kirshenbaum, "They're Pooling Their Talent."

18. Chambliss, *Champions*, 69.

19. Chambliss, *Champions*, 133.

20. Tracy Dodds, "Schubert Is Selling Top Swimmers and Others on Boca Raton Facility," *Los Angeles Times*, October 1, 1985, accessed December 3, 2013, http://articles.latimes.com/1985-10-01/sports/sp-19317_1_mission-bay.

21. STANFORD UNIVERSITY WOMEN

1. J. E. Vader, "Once More, with Feeling," *Sports Illustrated*, March 27, 1989, accessed December 11, 2013, http://sportsillustrated.cnn.com/vault/article/magazine/MAG1126665/index.htm.

2. Richard Justice, "Quick Left Lasting Impression In and Out of Pool," *Houston Chronicle*, June 14, 2009, Newspaper Source Plus.

3. Rick Eymer, "Richard Quick: 'He Believes Anything Is Possible,'" *Palo Alto Online*, January 6, 2009, accessed November 4, 2013, http://www.paloaltoonline.com/news/2009/01/06/richard-quick-he-believes-anything-is-possible.

4. Justice, "Quick Left Lasting Impression In and Out of Pool."

5. Rusty Simmons, "Only Now Has Coach Quick Left the Pool," *San Francisco Chronicle*, June 12, 2009, accessed November 3, 2013, http://www.sfgate.com/sports/article/Only-now-has-coach-Quick-left-the-pool-3295478.php.

6. Frank Litsky, "Richard Quick, Swim Coach, Dies at 66," *New York Times*, June 12, 2009, B15.

7. Christopher Kelly, "Stanford Towing," *Swimming World*, April 1993, 41.
8. Russ Ewald, "Stanford Learns Quick," *Swimming World*, May 1989, 33.
9. Ewald, "Stanford Learns Quick," 33.
10. Vader, "Once More, with Feeling."
11. Vader, "Once More, with Feeling."
12. Russ Ewald, "An Orange St. Pats," *Swimming World*, May 1990, 32.
13. Russ Ewald, "A Texas Stampede," *Swimming World*, May 1991, 34.
14. Russ Ewald, "A Cardinal Meet," *Swimming World*, May 1992, 29.
15. Ewald, "A Cardinal Meet," 29.
16. Ewald, "A Cardinal Meet," 30.
17. Russ Ewald, "A Quick Victory," *Swimming World*, May 1993, 34.
18. Russ Ewald, "A Team Above All," *Swimming World*, May 1994, 46.
19. Theresa Munoz, "Cardinal and Gold? Stanford Has a Rich Selection of Olympic Swimmers with Six Taking Different Stories to Barcelona," *Los Angeles Times*, July 7, 1992, accessed December 11, 2013, http://articles.latimes.com/1992-07-07/sports/sp-1652_1_olympic-team.
20. Munoz, "Cardinal and Gold?"

22. UNIVERSITY OF TEXAS MEN

1. Bob Ingram, "Focus and Finish," *Swimming World*, May 1996, 28.
2. Lisa Dillman, "Peirsol Is a 'Horn of Plenty,'" *Los Angeles Times*, August 5, 2004, accessed October 30, 2013, http://articles.latimes.com/2004/aug/05/sports/sp-olyswim5.
3. Chip Brown, "Reese Is Why Texas Rules the Pool: Horns' Swim Coach Turns Olympic Dreams Gold," *Dallas Morning News*, March 16, 2007, Newspaper Source Plus.
4. Bill Bell, "Mind Games," *Swimming World*, March 2002, 39.
5. Brown, "Reese Is Why Texas Rules the Pool."
6. Brown, "Reese Is Why Texas Rules the Pool."
7. Associated Press, "Special Group of Swimmers in the Lone Star State," *NBC Olympics*, July 3, 2008, accessed October 30, 2013, http://www.2008.nbcolympics.com/swimming/news/newsid=128539.html.
8. Associated Press, "Special Group of Swimmers in the Lone Star State."
9. Phillip Baston, "Texas Trio Takes World by Storm," *Columbia Tribune*, February 18, 2007, accessed October 20, 2013, http://archive.columbiatribune.com/2007/Feb/20070218Spor003.asp.
10. Dillman, "Peirsol Is a 'Horn of Plenty.'"
11. Baston, "Texas Trio Takes World by Storm."
12. Baston, "Texas Trio Takes World by Storm."
13. Jennifer Floyd Engel, "Ian Crocker, College Buddies Back for More Olympic Gold," *Fort Worth Star-Telegram*, August 3, 2008, accessed October 30, 2013, http://www.sunjournal.com/node/416528.
14. Associated Press, "Special Group of Swimmers in the Lone Star State."
15. Dillman, "Peirsol Is a 'Horn of Plenty.'"
16. Kari Lydersen, "Texas Turnaround," *Swimming World*, May 2000, 22.
17. Bill Bell, "Mind Games," *Swimming World*, March 2002, 20.

23. NORTH BALTIMORE AQUATIC CLUB

1. Katharine Dunn, "Different Strokes," *Baltimore Magazine*, August 2008, accessed October 16, 2013, http://www.baltimoremagazine.net/this-month/2008/08/different-strokes.

2. Childs Walker and Candus Thomson, "Where Only Swimmers' Best Will Do," *Baltimore Sun*, August 14, 2008, accessed October 16, 2013, http://www.baltimoresun.com/sports/bal-te.sp.nbac14aug14,0,6046658,full.story.

3. Frank Litsky, "Day of Records for 15-Year-Old," *New York Times*, August 1, 1984, B5.

4. Dunn, "Different Strokes."

5. Walker and Thomson, "Where Only Swimmers' Best Will Do."

6. Frank Fitzpatrick, "Maverick Coach Has Made Waves in Swimming World," *Philadelphia Inquirer*, August 14, 2007, Newspaper Source Plus.

7. Walker and Thomson, "Where Only Swimmers' Best Will Do."

8. Dunn, "Different Strokes."

9. Karen Crouse, "Swimming: The Maestro behind Phelps's Rhythm in the Water," *New York Times*, July 31, 2007, D6.

10. Amy Shipley, "Bowman, Phelps Have Golden Partnership," *Washington Post*, January 23, 2009, Newspaper Source Plus.

11. Jean Marbella, "Bob Bowman Has Proven to Be More than Michael Phelps' Coach," *Baltimore Sun*, July 25, 2012, accessed October 16, 2013, http://www.baltimoresun.com/sports/olympics/bs-sp-olympics-bowman-20120725,0,3573665,full.story.

12. Tim Layden, "Hold Your Breath," *Sports Illustrated*, August 2, 2004, accessed October 17, 2013, http://sportsillustrated.cnn.com/vault/article/magazine/MAG1032577/index.htm.

13. Shipley, "Bowman, Phelps Have Golden Partnership."

14. Childs Walker and Chris Korman, "Bob Bowman Returns to Coaching after Post-Olympic Odyssey," *Baltimore Sun*, June 29, 2013, accessed October 16, 2013, http://www.baltimoresun.com/sports/olympics/bs-sp-bowman-year-after-20130629,0,5743217,full.story.

15. Walker and Korman, "Bob Bowman Returns to Coaching after Post-Olympic Odyssey."

16. Michael Cowley, "Life in the Fast Lane a Breeze," *Sydney Morning Herald*, November 26, 2003, Newspaper Source Plus.

17. Paul Newberry, "Phelps & Bowman: A Partnership Like No Other," Associated Press, August 4, 2012, Newspaper Source Plus.

18. John Lohn, "The Genius behind the Masterpiece," *Swimming World*, January 2009, 20.

19. Nicole Jeffrey, "U.S. Team's Mastermind Plotting Our Fall—Olympics," *The Australian*, July 19, 2008, Newspaper Source Plus.

20. Joe Paisley, "Regardless of Results, This Promises to Be a Big Summer for Swimmer Allison Schmitt," *The Gazette*, June 25, 2013, Newspaper Source Plus.

21. Kevin Van Valkenburg, "Demanding Bowman Puts Hoff through Paces," *Baltimore Sun*, May 6, 2009, accessed October 15, 2013, http://www.baltimoresun.com/sports/olympics/bal-sp.hoff06may06,0,2823978.story.

22. Amy Shipley, "NBAC Keep Drawing Elite Pool of Athletes," *Washington Post*, June 22, 2009, Newspaper Source Plus.

23. Rokur Jakupsstovu, "Lotte Friis Gives Candid Interview to Danish Newspaper BT about Move to NBAC," *Swimming World*, October 13, 2013, accessed October 17, 2013, http://www.swimmingworldmagazine.com/lane9/news/world/36250.asp.

24. Braden Keith, "It's Official: Agnel Explains Decision to Swim with Bob Bowman in Press Conference," *SwimSwam*, May 21, 2013, accessed October 16, 2013, http://swimswam.com/its-official-agnel-explains-decision-to-swim-with-bob-bowman-in-press-conference.

25. Jordan Littman, "Lessons Learned from Phelps Help Swimmer Kalisz Gain Elite Status," *Baltimore Sun*, June 24, 2013, accessed October 14, 2013, http://www.baltimoresun.com/sports/bs-sp-swimming-chase-kalisz-0625-20130624,0,5375023.story.

26. Walker and Korman, "Bob Bowman Returns to Coaching after Post-Olympic Odyssey."

27. Dunn, "Different Strokes."

28. Walker and Korman, "Bob Bowman Returns to Coaching after Post-Olympic Odyssey."

29. Anne Riley, "North Baltimore Aquatic Club Riding Wave of Phelps, Hoff," *Daily Record*, August 12, 2008, Newspaper Source Plus.

24. U.S. MEN'S BACKSTROKE

1. Jere Longman, "Rouse Exorcises the Ghosts of Barcelona," *New York Times*, July 24, 1996, B7.

2. Jere Longman, "Multiple Gold Prospect Who Was Born to Swim," *New York Times*, June 18, 2000. SP7.

3. Bob Ingram, "Strength in Numbers," *Swimming World*, September 1997, 43.

4. Longman, "Multiple Gold Prospect Who Was Born to Swim."

5. Erik Hamilton, "A Solid Gold Hit," *Swimming World*, February 1999, 27.

6. Hamilton, "A Solid Gold Hit," 30.

7. Beth Harris, "Peirsol: Krayzelburg is Beatable," *Associated Press*, August 13, 2000, Newspaper Source Plus.

8. Harris, "Peirsol."

9. Jere Longman, "Swimming: Thorpe Comes Up a Big Hand Short to a Flying Dutchman," *New York Times*, September 19, 2000, S1.

10. Michael Cowley, "We're Not Krayzy, Says Teammate, Lenny Can Be Beaten," *Sydney Morning Herald*, September 21, 2000, Newspaper Source Plus.

11. Richard Sandomir, "Krayzelburg Powers to Second Gold Medal," *New York Times*, September 22, 2000, S2.

12. Philip Whitten and Michael Collins, "Sydney 2000: Party Smashers," *Swimming World*, October 2000, 31.

13. Judy Jacob, "A Changing of the Guard," *Swimming World*, May 2002, 32.

14. John Maher, "Former Horns Standout Peirsol Retires from Swimming," *Austin American Statesman*, February 3, 2011, accessed December 20, 2013, http://www.statesman.com/news/sports/college/former-horns-standout-piersol-retires-from-swimmin/nRXHy.

15. Vicki Michaelis, "Sydney Champ Tries Turning Back Time," *USA Today*, July 9, 2002, Newspaper Source Plus.

16. Beth Harris, "Krayzelburg Earns Return Trip to Olympics," *Associated Press*, July 10, 2004, Newspaper Source Plus.

17. Eli Saslow, "Rouse's Watershed Moment," *Washington Post*, July 7, 2004, Newspaper Source Plus.

18. Saslow, "Rouse's Watershed Moment."

19. Michaelis, "Sydney Champ Tries Turning Back Time."

20. Lynn Zinser, "Krayzelburg Finds the Will and a Way to Qualify," *New York Times*, July 10, 2004, D1.

21. Zinser, "Krayzelburg Finds the Will and a Way to Qualify," D1.

22. Christopher Clarey, "Flip-Flop Leaves Peirsol with the Gold," *New York Times*, August 20, 2004, D1.

23. Clarey, "Flip-Flop Leaves Peirsol with the Gold," D1.

24. Clarey, "Flip-Flop Leaves Peirsol with the Gold," D1.

25. John Lohn, "Still Going Strong," *Swimming World*, April 2010, 9.

26. John Lohn, "Ryan Lochte: Ready for the Challenge," *Swimming World*, August 2007, 19.

27. Christopher Clarey, "Coughlin and Peirsol Repeat Their Sweep of 100 Backstrokes," *New York Times*, August 12, 2008, D7.

28. "Lochte Edges U.S. Teammate Peirsol, Sets World Mark," ESPN, August 15, 2008, accessed December 20, 2013, http://sports.espn.go.com/oly/summer08/swimming/news/story?id=3536048.

29. Wayne Drehs, "Aaron Peirsol Makes Most of Second Chance," ESPN, August 18, 2010, accessed December 20, 2013, http://espn.go.com/blog/olympics/post/_/id/55/pan-pacific-swimming-championships-peirsol-makes-most-of-100-backstroke.

30. Karen Crouse, "Changing His Luck, Keeping the Flag: Wooed by the Netherlands, Grevers Stayed for the Challenge," *New York Times*, July 13, 2008, 215.

31. Bryce Miller, "Former Arizona Swimmer Nick Thoman Continues His 'Great Ride' at the Olympics," *USA Today*, July 30, 2012, accessed December 20, 2013, http://www.azcentral.

com/sports/articles/2012/07/30/20120730former-arizona-swimmer-nick-thoman-continues-his-great-ride-olympics.html.

32. Associated Press, "Matt Grevers Set Olympic Record," ESPN, July 30, 2012, accessed December 20, 2013, http://espn.go.com/olympics/summer/2012/swimming/story/_/id/8215200/2012-london-olympics-matt-grevers-sets-olympic-record-100-meter-backstroke.

33. "2012 London Olympics: Matt Grevers Sets Olympic Record in 100 Back Win; Nick Thoman Gives U.S. 1-2 Finish," *Swimming World*, July 30, 2012, accessed December 20, 2013, http://www.swimmingworldmagazine.com/lane9/news/World/31465.asp.

34. Bonnie D. Ford, "Tyler Clary Finally Breaks Through," ESPN, August 3, 2012, accessed December 20, 2013, http://espn.go.com/olympics/summer/2012/swimming/story/_/id/8228298/2012-olympics-tyler-clary-breaks-big-stage.

Index

About the Author

Matthew De George is a reporter and the assistant sports editor for the *Delaware County Daily Times* in suburban Philadelphia. A former swimmer of no distinction, *Pooling Talent* is Matthew's second book on the sport of swimming.

CPSIA information can be obtained at www.ICGtesting.com
Printed in the USA
BVOW07*1530270614

357461BV00001B/1/P